MUSICAL FORCES

Foreword by
ROBERT S. HATTEN

MUSICAL MEANING & INTERPRETATION

Robert S. Hatten, editor

INDIANA UNIVERSITY PRESS

Bloomington & Indianapolis

Motion,
Metaphor, and
Meaning in Music

MUSICAL FORCES

STEVE LARSON

This book is a publication of

INDIANA UNIVERSITY PRESS
601 North Morton Street
Bloomington, IN 47404–3797 USA

iupress.indiana.edu

Telephone orders 800–842–6796
Fax orders 812–855–7931

♾ The paper used in this publication meets
the minimum requirements of the American National Standard for Information
Sciences – Permanence of Paper for Printed
Library Materials, ANSI Z39.48–1992.

*Manufactured in the
United States of America*

*Library of Congress
Cataloging-in-Publication Data*

Larson, Steve, [date]
    Musical forces : motion, metaphor,
and meaning in music / Steve Larson ;
foreword by Robert S. Hatten.
        p. cm. – (Musical meaning and
interpretation)
        Includes bibliographical references
and index.
        ISBN 978-0-253-35682-6 (cloth :
alk. paper) – ISBN 978-0-253-00549-6
(e-book) 1. Music – Physiological aspects. 2. Music – Physiological effect.
3. Music – Psychological aspects.
I. Title.
        ML3820.L36 2012
        781'.1 – dc23
                                2011024022

1 2 3 4 5   17 16 15 14 13 12

IN MEMORY OF ROBERT TROTTER

CONTENTS

FOREWORD

ROBERT S. HATTEN, SERIES EDITOR

Musical Forces is the culmination of over 25 years of speculation, research, and empirical inquiry into the ways we experience motion, and hence meaning, in music. Inspired by the work of Rudolf Arnheim on visual perception and Douglas Hofstadter on analogy, Steve Larson develops a theory of musical forces that affect our perception of both melody and rhythm, by analogy to our embodied (and cultural) understanding of physical forces.

Written for a wide audience, the book reflects Steve's engagement with several often-overlapping scholarly and pedagogical communities. Cognitive scientists will find extensive empirical testing of Steve's hypotheses concerning our metaphorical understanding of musical forces in terms of our experiencing of corresponding physical forces, along with a generous sampling of basic musical examples. Students will find a careful sequencing of concepts and applications, with frequent summaries and cross-referencing, and a helpful glossary. Experienced musicians will find more sophisticated music examples demonstrating Steve's sensitivity to tonal musical styles, ranging from classical to jazz. Speculative music theorists will appreciate Steve's careful balancing of musical intuitions and hard science, and his encyclopedic knowledge of the relevant scientific, music theoretical, and music historical literature on movement, metaphor, and meaning. And future researchers will find a suggestive list of recommendations for further exploration within the paradigm Steve has so artfully constructed.

In the fall of 2010 Steve learned he had a brain tumor, and although he had completed the entire manuscript, he did not live to see this book appear. I am thus especially grateful to music editor Jane Behnken, her able assistant Sarah Wyatt Swanson, June Silay, and the production staff at Indiana University Press for their diligent work preparing the manuscript for publication. Jodi Jolley compiled the index. As series editor, I responded to the copyeditor's queries after consulting on the phone with Steve as much as was then possible, and in late summer I gave the entire manuscript a close proofreading in his stead. Not only were Steve's ideas fully formed, he also expressed them with his inimitable voice, wit, and charm—all of which you will find preserved here.

Those of us who were privileged to have known Steve will remember his courage and serenity throughout his last months. He was a dear friend and colleague to many, and we will miss him terribly. This book may serve as a fitting memorial to his visionary ideas, his love of music, and his passion for sharing both.

PREFACE

This book describes a theory of "musical forces" and some of the evidence for that theory. Thus it is aimed primarily at professional music theorists. I hope, however, that it may interest other types of readers as well – including cognitive scientists (especially those with interests in psychology and expectation, the phenomenology and aesthetics of music, computer science and artificial intelligence, and cognitive linguistics), musicians from other sub-disciplines of music (especially history, ethnomusicology, music education, jazz, and popular music), and general readers with an interest in music.

Because it is written for such different audiences, members of each will inevitably find some portions too difficult or maybe even painfully simple. I hope the overview in chapter 1 will help readers find those portions of greatest interest (and to identify passages they may wish to skip). I have also included a glossary at the end of the book, partly as a way to summarize and review its basic concepts but also to help those readers who find its terms unfamiliar (or who find that my use of those terms differs from what they are used to or would have expected).

The theory of musical forces concerns the experience of certain listeners: those listeners of tonal music who have internalized the regularities of "common-practice tonal music" to a degree that allows them to experience the expectations generated by that music (the music of Bach to Brahms and much jazz and popular music). When this book talks about "we" or "us," it is talking about members of that musical culture.

This book assumes that its readers are familiar with musical notation and have some grasp of the fundamentals of harmony. (Readers who have not learned harmony by taking piano lessons or an undergraduate course on this topic may wish to consult a book on music fundamentals such as Victor Zuckerkandl's *Sense of Music* [1959].) While I hope that this volume will be of interest to professional music theorists, much of what I say does not require a prior understanding of the technical vocabulary of advanced music theory.

ACKNOWLEDGMENTS

First things first: thank you, Sonja Rasmussen, for your love and support – I have incorporated a number of your valuable substantive suggestions, and your encouragement has really helped me to put this all into a final form.

My interests in motion, metaphor, and meaning go back to my years as a student at the University of Oregon, where my 1981 master's thesis, written under the supervision of Robert Trotter and Peter Bergquist, explored the role of metaphor in musical meaning by offering my own metaphorical descriptions of pieces by the group Oregon and then asking how music analysis could illuminate the types of motion described.

At the same time Marion Guck was doing her seminal work on metaphor at the University of Michigan. And when, just a few years later, I encountered her work – and her encouragement to pursue my own – I decided to dig deeper into the topic. Marion's work continues to be an inspiration and model for my own.

This book began to take shape more than twenty-five years ago, as a term paper for a course at the University of Michigan. That course, called "Psychology of Comparative Arts," was taught by Rudolf Arnheim. During his office hours we had many conversations about how his ideas on Gestalt psychology and the perception of art might be applied to music. My correspondence and conversations with him after completing that course continued to inspire my work. In fact, this book may be regarded as an elaboration of his 1986 article "Perceptual Dynamics in Musical Expression."

At the same time I had the great fortune to work as Graduate Research Assistant to Robert Hatten, exploring issues of music and meaning in twentieth-century opera. He and many of my other teachers (especially Richmond Browne, Robert Hurwitz, and William Rothstein) may notice ideas they shared with me long ago. I hope they will forgive my inability at this point to say where some of those ideas came from.

Although there are very few specific citations of the work of Alexandra Pierce, her approach to musical meaning through movement has long been an inspiration to my thinking in and thinking about music.

The Center for Research on Concepts and Cognition (CRCC) at Indiana University, under the direction of Douglas Hofstadter, supported research that started turning ideas about musical forces into conference presentations, published articles, and computer models. (I was a Visiting Faculty Research Associate at the Center from 1992 to 1993 and again from 2002 to 2003.) My colleagues at CRCC (especially Doug Hofstadter, Gary McGraw, and James Marshall) offered thoughtful ideas on music and considerable help with computer programming. Doug read several chapters of this book and offered many helpful suggestions. He has also provided support in myriad other ways.

I am deeply grateful to Hallgjerd Aksnes, who invited me to serve as Visiting Faculty Research Associate for her project "Music, Motion, and Emotion: Theoretical and Psychological Implications of Musical Embodiment" at the Institutt for Musikkvitenskap of the University of Oslo in 2010. That appointment provided time and support for the final stages of the book and gave me the pleasure of working with her and members of her research project (Anita Høyvik, Ingvild Amundsen, Mari Haugen, and Ragnhild Solberg), whose feedback enriched this book and helped shape a planned sequel (on musical forces and music analysis).

I have had numerous opportunities to share these ideas with students in the courses I have taught. These ideas have shaped, and have been shaped by, my teaching of courses on musicianship skills and music analysis (in fact, I first came up with the patterns described in chapter 6 while teaching aural skills in the late seventies). Temple University provided a large number of such courses. But some of the most fruitful of these courses were taught at the University of Oregon. One course, a seminar titled "Music and Meaning," which I team-taught with my colleague Mark Johnson, led to our article, "Something in the Way She Moves – Metaphors of Musical Motion" (Johnson and Larson 2003), which appears here as chapter 3 (and as a chapter in Johnson 2007). Part of that article also appears in chapter 2 (in a section on conceptual metaphor theory). Thank you, Mark, for allowing me to include our article in this book. Mark and I are indebted to Arnie Cox for his help with that article; we also learned a great deal about the metaphorical understanding of musical experience by working with him on his doctoral dissertation. We also thank our colleague Scott Pratt for his helpful comments on an earlier draft of that article. Mark also read several chapters of this book and offered suggestions that improved them all. Students in another seminar taught at the University of Oregon in 2004, called "Musical Forces," read a nearly complete draft of this book. The students in that course (Darin Hoskisson, Kalin Kirilov, Kaori Noland, Jennifer Russell, Keith Salley, LeeAnn Sterling, and Jamie Webster) all provided thoughtful feedback.

Another colleague at the University of Oregon, Leigh VanHandel, coauthored an article with me called "Measuring Musical Forces," parts of which appear throughout this book. Her skills as experimental psychologist, computer programmer, and writer were very helpful indeed. Thanks Leigh!

Thanks also to Fred Lerdahl, who heard one of my first public presentations of these ideas in 1993 and has offered suggestions and encouragement on this work in various stages since then. At that same 1993 presentation, Carol Krumhansl and Jamshed Bharucha noted the similarity between my computer's algorithm for the interaction of musical forces and the general formula for multiple regression, and encouraged me to learn about this method of statistical analysis.

A grant from the University of Oregon provided time in the summer of 1999 to help finish computer models and articles based on them. Robin High and Joe St. Sauver of Statistical Consulting at the University of Oregon helped with the statistical analyses.

Bill Lake supplied me with a copy of his dissertation and offered help and advice. Erick Carballo helped translate Lake's transcriptions of his participant responses from musical notation into integers that the computer could read.

My computer models were written in MacScheme. Scheme is a dialect of LISP invented by Guy L. Steele Jr. and Gerald Jay Sussman. Scheme for the Macintosh was developed at the Massachusetts Institute of Technology (© 1984). MacScheme was published by Lightship Software, Inc. (© 1992).

Thanks also to David Butler, Richard Cohn, Anne Danielsen, Steven Demorest, Gina Fatone, Cynthia Folio, Thomas Goolsby, Robert Hatten, Robert Hurwitz, Bunny Laden, Patrick McCreless, Anne Dhu McLucas, John Rahn, Sonja Rasmussen, Lee Rothfarb, William Rothstein, Caitlin Snyder, Steven Strunk, and Keith Waters for reading chapter drafts (or drafts of articles that became chapters in this book).

I also appreciate the encouragement that so many friends and colleagues have provided for this project. To give just one example, when I mentioned that I suspected there might be some relationship between the pattern map of Example 6.9 and the motives that make up hidden repetitions, Janet Schmalfeldt suggested I write the journal article (Larson 1997–98a) that became the starting point for some of the repertoire-based types of evidence presented in part 2.

Because parts of this book were originally published as free-standing articles or book chapters, I also extend my thanks to the patient and helpful suggestions of several editors – Thomas Demske and Ramon Satyendra (*Journal of Music Theory*), Mary Wennerstrom (*Journal of Music Theory Pedagogy*), Raymond Gibbs (*Metaphor and Symbol*), Anthony Gritten and Elaine King (*Music and Gesture*), Lola Cuddy and Mari Riess Jones (*Music Perception*), and Taylor Greer (*Theory and Practice*) – as well as other, anonymous readers for those journals and books.

The book publication process gave me encouragement and helpful suggestions from a number of readers (most of them anonymous). Of these readers, the comments of David Temperley were particularly valuable. I also thank the staff at Indiana University Press, including copyeditor Rita Bernhard.

Finally, I thank my parents, not only for their love and support in other ways but also for providing, in their cottage on the Oregon beach, many opportunities to write and think in an inspiring and idyllic location.

MUSICAL FORCES

1

Introduction

Sometimes we ask "How does that melody *go?*" At times we might say that a melody "*moves* by *steps* and *leaps.*" Or we might talk about melodies "*ascending* and *descending.*" In fact, it is hard to think of words for describing physical motion that have not been applied to musical motion. So this book's first question might be, "Why do we talk about music as if it actually *moved?*"

Sometimes music can make us laugh, cry, or want to dance. At times it might induce us to see or remember colorful shapes and images, to recall painful or pleasant episodes, or to experience all kinds of different feelings. In fact, music and emotion have long been described as intimately linked. So this book's second question (to rephrase our first question only slightly and to shift from motion to emotion) might be, "Why does music actually *move us?*"

This book gives partial answers to both questions by showing some ways in which physical motion influences our experience of classically tonal music (music of the Bach-to-Brahms era as well as much jazz and popular music) and contributes to its meaning. (As noted in the preface, the theory of musical forces concerns the experience of certain listeners: those listeners of tonal music who have internalized the regularities of "common-practice tonal music" to a degree that allows them to experience the expectations generated by that music. When this book talks about "we" or "us," it is talking about members of that musical culture.)

The central argument of this book is that our experience of physical motion shapes our experience of musical motion in specific and quantifiable ways – so that we not only *speak* about music as if it were shaped by musical analogs of physical gravity, magnetism, and inertia, but we also actually *experience* it in terms of "musical forces." Part 1 (chapters 2–7) describes this theory of musical forces, and part 2 (chapters 8–13) summarizes the substantial (and growing) body of evidence that supports it.

Of course, writers have long discussed music in terms of the metaphors of motion and forces.[1] But the theory of musical forces presented in this book takes five further steps. Although none of these is entirely unprecedented, their combination is novel. First, the book identifies and rigorously defines three melodic forces ("melodic gravity" is the tendency of notes above a reference platform to descend; "melodic magnetism" is the tendency of unstable notes to move to the closest stable pitch, a tendency that grows stronger as the goal pitch is closer; and "musical inertia" is the tendency of pitches or durations, or both, to continue in the pattern perceived) and two rhythmic forces ("rhythmic gravity" and "metric magnetism"; these are discussed in chapter 6, where the rhythmic aspects of musical inertia are also explored in greater depth).[2] Second, the book embraces the metaphorical status of those musical forces as central to, explanatory for, and constitutive of both our discourse about music and our experience of music. In other words, although these forces may feel to us as though they are inherent in the sounds themselves, they are actually a creation of our minds, where they are attributed (consciously or unconsciously) to the music – shaping our thinking *about* music and our thinking *in* music – so that they become a part of what may be called "musical meaning." Third, the book explicitly grounds the operation of those musical forces in the theories of Heinrich Schenker. Fourth, it shows that the musical forces provide necessary and sufficient conditions for giving a detailed and quantifiable account of a variety of musical behaviors (for example, the regularities in the distributions of musical patterns in compositions and improvisations, and the responses of participants in psychological experiments). Fifth, it finds converging evidence for the cognitive reality of musical forces from a variety of practical and experimental sources.

In order to clarify the claims of this book, it may also be helpful to say what I am *not* arguing. I do not claim that the account given here completely explains the roles of musical forces in our experience of music. I do not claim that musical forces completely explain musical experience. I do not claim that every melodic motion results from giving in to musical forces. I do not claim that musical forces have the same universality or "natural" status that physical forces do. I do not claim that such forces are an important part of every culture's music. I do not claim that gravity, magnetism, and inertia are the only forces that shape melodic expectations. I do not claim that musical forces and musical motion are the only metaphors that inform music discourse and musical experience. And I do not claim that the ideas of pattern, analogy, and metaphor offered in this book give a complete account of human meaning-making.

A THEORY OF EXPRESSIVE MEANING

I suspect, however, that readers will want to think about how the idea of musical forces might contribute to a larger theory of expressive meaning – one that explains more thoroughly how and why music moves us the way it does. Therefore, in this introduction, I sketch the larger theory of expressive meaning in music that guides my thinking about musical forces. I do this in order to lay my cards on the table, as well as to contextualize the arguments of this book. But I do not claim that mine is the only possible theory of meaning that would encompass the idea of musical forces.[3] I do not suggest that this book provides a complete description of that theory of expressive meaning. Nor do I believe that this book provides a complete defense of the value or the truth of that larger theory. Although the claims of this book may be seen as supporting that larger theory, they should be understood as claims about musical forces rather than claims about such a larger theory of expressive meaning in music. In other words, although this book makes claims about musical forces that could be understood as part of a larger theory of expressive meaning in music, I am not going to defend that larger theory – but I do want readers to see how the idea of musical forces might fit into such a larger theory. The theory of expressive meaning in music toward which my earlier writings point makes the following claim:

> It is useful to regard part of what we call "expressive meaning" in music as an emergent property of metaphorical "musical forces."

The remainder of this chapter clarifies what I mean by that statement – elaborating on the terms "expressive meaning," "emergent property," and "metaphor" – and it offers an overview of how some of these
ideas inform the remainder of the book. Along the way it will be useful
to respond to some of the objections that have been raised to this theory
of expressive meaning.

Much has been written about emotion and meaning in music. In
a book with that title, Leonard Meyer (1956) wrote that music excites
emotions when it departs from what we expect. Others (e.g., Coker 1972;
Cooke 1959; Davies 1994; Ferguson 1960; Kivy 1989; and Robinson 1997)
have written about whether music can express emotions (or anything, for
that matter), about whether music can "express" or simply be "expressive
of" emotions, and about how musical meaning (if it exists) might differ
from other types of meaning.

The theory of expressive meaning simply assumes that music has
"expressive meaning" – that quality we experience in music that allows
it to suggest (for example) feelings, actions, or motion. This quality may
not translate well into words, nor relate clearly to the emotions felt by the
creators (the composers, performers, and improvisers) of the music, but
it seems to be one reason why we derive so much pleasure from listening
to music. In other words, I use this term in the same way that Robert Hatten (1994, 2004) does and in the same way that Rudolf Arnheim (1974)
uses the term "expression."

Like Meyer, I also find an intimate connection between meaning and
expectation. My theory further argues, however, that expressive meaning in music arises from the *specific* ways in which music moves when it
denies – or confirms – our expectations. And I argue that we understand
those specific ways of moving, in part, by using our knowledge of analogous physical motions – and the forces that shape those physical motions.

To illustrate some of the ways in which music can move us, and to
help clarify the theory of expressive meaning in music, Examples 1.1
and 1.2 offer two types of musical examples. Example 1.1 gives the music
for "Dido's Lament" from Purcell's *Dido and Aeneas* – an example of a
"lamento bass." Example 1.2 (p. 16) gives a few excerpts that include what
I call the "hallelujah figure").

EXAMPLE 1.1. "Dido's Lament" from Purcell's *Dido and Aeneas*.

TWO LAMENTO BASSES

In "Dido's Lament," Dido sings of how she would like to be remembered, just before she takes her own life. The music seems to capture the meaning of its text very well. It is based on a repeated bass line, the so-called lamento bass, which descends chromatically from tonic to dominant, in a minor key, and in a slow triple meter. A similar repeated bass line occurs in the "Crucifixus" from Bach's B-minor Mass – which tells of Christ's death. The lamento bass has a long history of association with texts expressing sadness and death (Williams 1997).

Why have these (and other) lamento basses appealed to their composers as an excellent way to set such texts? One answer to this question might be caricatured as "rote learning of conventions." According to this argument, we first hear "Dido's Lament," then notice that the words are sad, and finally come to associate that sadness with that piece and its bass line. Later, when we hear another lamento bass, we think something like "Oh, this sounds like 'Dido's Lament' . . . so it must be sad, too." Although I do not deny that learning such associations is possible, I am convinced that this view of musical meaning leaves out something important.

CONVENTION AND CULTURE

One problem with assuming that all musical meaning relies solely on "rote learning of conventions" is that it seems to assume that the musical material is entirely arbitrary – that it is purely conventional. However, if the musical material were really arbitrary, then any association between material and meaning would be possible.

One reaction to this argument concerning associations between material and meaning is to believe that "musical association is cultur-ally determined – symbolic – and that is why just any association is not possible."[4] This reaction is emblematic of a line of thinking that is coun-terproductive to the project of this book, so I examine it here at some length.

Note, first of all, that such a reaction makes an important point: cul-ture does play a central role in helping to shape the associations we make between material and meaning. In fact, although the specifics of their claims have proven controversial (or at least thought, by some, in need of qualification), ethnomusicologists have noted relationships between culture, meaning, and musical material that seem to go beyond "rote learning of conventions." Judith Becker (1981) has shown interesting connections between Javanese conceptions of time and the organization of their gamelan music. Steven Feld (1981, 1988) has discussed relations between the music of the Kaluli people and their stories about native soundscapes, as well as their habits of conversation. Alan Lomax ([1968] 2000) has suggested that, in folk songs from all around the world, cor-relations between attitudes about sex or authority seem to be reflected in aspects of a culture's music (such as its vocal tension or textural orga-nization). If these authors are right (and even if their claims need qualification), then culture does play an important role in shaping musical material and meaning.

At first glance, this reaction ("association is culturally determined – symbolic – and that is why just any association is not possible") also seems to agree with at least part of the idea I am arguing for here: that it is not possible to make just any association between musical material and musical meaning. Nevertheless, this reaction implies that culture is the *sole determinant* of such associations ("association is culturally *determined* – symbolic – and *that is why* just any association is not possible"), and it describes those associations as "symbolic," a term from semiotics implying that the association is arbitrary (more about this term in a moment).

THE SINGLE-MECHANISM FALLACY

Let us begin with three responses to the idea that associations between musical material and musical meaning could be determined solely by "culture." These three responses concern single-mechanism explanations, the complexity of culture, and the logic of this reaction.

First, I am skeptical that anything as complicated as associations between musical material and musical meaning could be determined solely by any single mechanism – even one as complex as culture. Nevertheless, it is an interesting aspect of our minds (which seem to have a drive toward simple explanations) that they tend to seek causality in terms of a single mechanism. This idea (that our minds prefer to attribute meanings to single mechanisms even though mechanisms, including mental processes, tend to be multiple) is a recurrent theme in this book. For example, chapter 11 ("Evidence from Music-Theoretical Misunderstandings") will re-examine single-mechanism explanations by noting that some prior writings about musical forces make an understandable but mistaken assumption: that only one force (whether physical or musical) operates at a time.

Second (or perhaps this just puts the same argument in a different way), if we understand "culture" in such a way that it is reasonable to regard it as the sole determinant of such associations, then culture must itself be a very complicated entity; that is, in this view, culture must surely include things like embodiment, body image, and body schema – factors that, as this book argues, reflect nonarbitrary relations between material and meaning.

Third, the logic of the reaction ("and that is why") is not sound. Even if culture were the sole determinant of associations between musical material and musical meaning, it does not automatically follow that culture would *therefore* forge such associations arbitrarily. The reaction seems to suggest that if culture were the sole determinant of such associations, then the nature of the material would necessarily be irrelevant – that the nature of the material would not help determine such associations. The reaction implies that for any association that one culture might make between material and meaning, another culture could make apparently opposite associations – and that nothing about the musical material itself would make this improbable.

LEARNING, STATISTICS, AND INTERNAL REPRESENTATION

The reaction we are discussing raises an important practical question: "If associations are arbitrary, then how do we learn them?" In other words, if we assume that the association of the lamento bass with sadness (especially the sadness of death) is solely "culturally determined – symbolic," then we might next ask, "How did that association come about, both for individual listeners and for our musical culture as a whole?"

The belief that members of a culture can learn anything simply through repeated exposure is widespread. In an important and recent book, David Huron (2006) notes that "auditory learning is dominated by statistical exposure" (72) and that "listeners appear to be sensitive to the frequencies of occurrence of different auditory events" (73). Huron's work provides ample evidence that musical expectations are shaped by, and tend to reflect, the frequencies with which musical events occur.

Once again, if one were prone to what I am calling "the single-mechanism fallacy," one might assume that we expect what we expect *solely* because it happens more often – and then dismiss any investigation into what those expectations *mean*. I do not level this criticism at Huron's work. I just caution that the combination of statistical learning and the single-mechanism fallacy might discourage the kind of thinking essential to the goals of this book.

Huron's work with Paul von Hippel on "post-skip reversal" nicely illustrates the point I want to make here. Von Hippel and Huron (2000) studied a sample of traditional European folk songs, Chinese folk songs, South African folk songs, and Native American songs. They found that the majority of larger intervals were followed by a change in directions (what they called a "post-skip reversal").

The results seem consistent with the age-old compositional advice that leaps (especially large leaps) should be followed by steps in the opposite direction. Their further analysis showed, however, that the results could best be explained *not* in terms of post-skip reversal but rather as regression to the mean. In other words, statistically, large upward leaps that took melodies to the upper part of a melodic range tended to descend because they were thus in the upper part of the melodic range; large upward leaps from low pitches that took melodies into the middle part of a melodic range do not show a consistent tendency to be followed by reversals in direction.

But the punch line is that von Hippel's subsequent experimental studies showed that (despite the statistical facts) the *expectations* of trained listeners are better explained in terms of a preference for post-skip reversal (rather than an expectation for regression to the mean). In other words, experienced listeners seem to have learned the wrong lesson from their statistical learning. My point here is not to argue with the notion that we are sensitive to frequencies of occurrence of musical events (there is plenty of evidence that we are). Rather, I suggest that meaning and expectation involve more than memorizing the frequency with which events have occurred (and while Huron is interested in what we expect and how we came to expect it, this book asks about the relationship between those expectations and our sense of meaning). As Huron notes, "how minds represent music has repercussions for what listeners remember, what listeners judge to be similar, and other musically important functions" (2006, 73).

Let us return, then, to the question of how we learn to associate the lamento bass with sadness – and the role of mental representation and meaning in that learning. Each lamento bass is at least a little bit different from other lamento basses, and each may be embedded in a different musical context. If presented with fifty-seven different passages containing lamento basses, do listeners have to learn – separately – that each one implies an affect of sadness? How do they learn that association without using the words "lamento bass" and "sadness," and without someone else pointing out how each new passage shares those features (including its slow tempo, its descending contour, its triple meter, its chromatic motion, the tonic and dominant end points it connects) that we think of as making up a lamento bass – especially when each new passage will likely contain features not necessarily contained in the other passages, some of which may be thought of as essential to a lamento bass, some of which may be thought of as specific to the passage but not essential to describing it as a lamento bass, and some of which may also appear in passages having a contradictory affect? If presented with a fifty-eighth passage of music that also has a (different) lamento bass, how would the listener know that it also was a passage of music implying a sad affect?

Eventually the listener would have to develop the concept of a lamento bass as an abstract concept having a set of potentially shared features (some of which may not be present in every example). Without the ability to create such abstract categories, listeners would not recognize the fifty-ninth passage of music with those same features as a "lamento bass," and would thus (according to the quoted reaction) be unable to attribute the associated affect to it.

Notice that the problem does not go away if we simply move to a "lower level." One might claim that listeners are not primarily learning to associate the lamento bass with sadness but that they are learning to associate sadness with the lower-level features that make up the lamento bass (such as slow tempo, descending contour, chromatic motion). This relocates the problem but does not solve it. We would still need to explain how listeners recognize those lower-level features as categories (with their own still-lower-level features).

Furthermore, a single musical culture's associations between material and affect seem to form rich and nuanced webs of meaning. Members of any one musical culture share numerous such associations. We know enough about cognition to see that it is much easier for a group of people to learn the same or similar associations if they are nonarbitrary. Given the large number of associations built up by a single musical culture, it seems highly improbable that all those associations could be arbitrary.

The point I am getting at here is that we have (or develop) the ability to create such abstract categories. That ability is necessary in order to forge the associations that the quoted reaction attributes solely to the black box of "culture." Listeners within a culture cannot learn to associate a specific affect with a specific musical relationship in any deep or consistent way until they can recognize that specific musical relationship as a representative of an abstract category – a category with its own feature set and internal logic. That internal logic is essential.

That logic is a product of the mind, but (as noted above) the mind prefers simplicity. It is hard to learn categories if they are arbitrary; our minds will have an easier time of that when the material "affords" easy opportunities for such "logic." Chapter 2 will say more about the relationship between meaning, simplicity, pattern, and memory. Let us return now to the quoted reaction by considering its use of the term "symbolic."

ICON, INDEX, AND SYMBOL

Semiotics is the science of how meanings (such as facts, relationships, or feelings) become associated with material (such as pictures, sounds, or gestures – all called "signs"). The recent popularity of semiotics in music theory might suggest that there are many who believe that associations between material and meaning are completely arbitrary – after all, many semioticians, such as Ferdinand de Saussure ([1916] 1966), begin with the assumption that signs bear only a conventional (that is, purely arbitrary) relation to their meanings. The semiotician Charles Sanders Peirce ([1931] 1960), however, has suggested a more nuanced view of signs, distinguishing between "icon," "index," and "symbol."

An icon is a sign whose meaning we recognize because of a static likeness between aspects of the icon and what it signifies. As Robert Port (2000) notes, "The little square with a *picture of a printer* on your computer screen is an icon for the *print function*. (Whereas a little box that has the word 'PRINT' is *not* an icon since it has no physical resemblance to printing or the printer.)"⁵ Port also gives the example of the no-smoking icon that has a picture of a circled diagonal bar across a drawing of a smoking cigarette. He notes that this icon develops the meaning "no smoking" for people with "appropriate cultural experience." Notice that this view of association between meaning and material grants a role to culture while recognizing that the association may be nonarbitrary. This example highlights something else. Obviously the drawing of the smoking cigarette bears a nonarbitrary relationship to the act of smoking. It is less obvious that the circled diagonal line means "no"; hence the observation that the association requires "appropriate cultural experience." But the circled diagonal line is nevertheless nonarbitrary; its bar "bars" the activity like any other barrier, and its placement "on top of" the smoking cigarette (rather than beside or behind it) helps make the function of this barrier (as prohibition) clear. Just because cultural experience is required to learn an association, that does not mean that the association is therefore arbitrary. Furthermore, some things that might at first appear arbitrary are nonetheless nonarbitrary.

An index is a sign whose meaning we recognize because of a dynamic likeness between the behaviors of the index and what it signifies. In other words, whereas an icon depicts the appearance of something it represents, an index points to a correlation involving change over time. Port notes that "dark *clouds* in the west are an index of impending *rain* (at least in Indiana)." The Dow-Jones Index is a number whose size correlates with the performance of certain stocks. The correlation between dark clouds and rain is not perfect, and the relationship between the Dow-Jones number going up and the aggregate price of stocks going up is abstract (and some other indexes are even more abstract), but they are not arbitrary. Some correlations seem more arbitrary than others, but the more arbitrary they seem, the harder they are to learn.

A symbol is a sign whose meaning is purely conventional and therefore presumably completely arbitrary – that is, neither icon nor index. The Nazi swastika and the Nike "swoosh" trademark are both symbols. Words are symbols. The quoted reaction's use of the word "symbolic" ("association is culturally determined – *symbolic* – and that is why just any association is not possible") thus seems to imply that associations between material and meaning are completely arbitrary.

If musical signs include iconic and indexical associations, then not all associations between material and meaning are arbitrary. Furthermore, those who study signs recognize that the dividing lines between icon, index, and symbol are not sharp. For example, words are symbols, but onomatopoetic words (like "squish," "zip," or "hiccup") are also iconic, and words that imply a pointing gesture (like "here," "there," "you," "he," "this," "that," etc.) are said to be indexical. The concluding sentence of Port's Web page suggests that even symbols (because of their rich webs of associations with other signs, and because of the ways in which they are learned) ultimately find correlations with environmental properties:

> A **symbol** is an arbitrary pattern (usually a sound pattern in a language) that gets its meaning **primarily from its mental association with other symbols** and only **secondarily from its correlation with environmentally relevant properties. (emphasis in original)**

Music theorist Robert Hatten (1994) has applied ideas from semiotics to the question of how expressive meanings become associated with musical material. He asks,

> how can we explain the way expressive meanings are tied to structures such that his [Nelson Goodman's] metaphorical exemplification can be musically motivated, and that it will support consistent interpretations by listeners? . . . The answer, I believe, is correlation. Oppositions in sound structure correlate with (cultural) oppositions in expressive structures by means of the more sophisticated iconism hinted at earlier. (166–167)

In fact, Hatten's applications of semiotics to music lead him to question the notion of a completely arbitrary symbol:

> Saussure considered the sign to be arbitrary, but it is safer to assume that other motivations (iconic, indexical) involved in the origins of that convention have simply been lost. (294)

Notice that the correlations to which Hatten refers are between music and cultural oppositions – acceptance of the central role of culture in mapping meaning onto musical material does not require viewing that mapping as arbitrary.[6] A closer reading of the work of other music theorists who draw on semiotics, such as Naomi Cumming (2000), shows that they also find important relationships between musical material and expressive meaning that depend, at least in part, on the nature of the musical material.

Let us return to the examples (of the role of culture in creating associations between meaning and material) with which we began: Becker, Feld, and Lomax. Becker (1981) suggests interesting connections between the Javanese calendar (with its complex of cycles) and the organization of gamelan music (with its complex of cycles). I believe she is able to describe these mappings because there are nonarbitrary relations between those cycles. Feld (1981, 1988) relates specific aspects of Kaluli music to specific aspects of Kaluli culture. I believe he is able to describe these mappings because there are nonarbitrary relations between Kaluli discourse and Kaluli musical texture, and because the Kaluli purposely fashion their music to imitate what they find compelling about the motion of waterfalls. Lomax ([1968] 2000) suggests correlations across folk-song cultures between attitudes about vocal tension and degrees of sexual permissiveness, and he suggests that cultures with certain types of social hierarchies tend more often to use musical-textural hierarchies that he describes as analogous. Though one may debate the degree to which these generalizations apply to all members of the culture they are applied to, if these relationships exist (as these scholars suggest), then they must rely on some systematic or logical relationship between culture and musical material. My point here is not to agree (or disagree) with Becker, Feld, and Lomax but rather to suggest that, if culture shapes musical material and meaning, then that shaping may (at least in some cases) rely on systematic and logical relationships between culture, material, and meaning.

I have taken so much time with this reaction ("association is culturally determined – *symbolic* – and that is why just any association is not possible") not only because I believe it is misleading but also because it seems to me that it tends to discourage the sort of deeper analysis central to this book. We should not underestimate the role of culture. But understanding how culture and other factors shape the association between musical material and human meanings requires deeper analysis. I am not claiming that associations between musical meaning and musical material are never (or never become functionally) symbolic or conventional. I just want to make it clear that this book is based on the reasonable assumption that at least some such associations are nonarbitrary ("motivated," as Hatten says).

THE "HALLELEJAH FIGURE"

Deryck Cooke's (1959) *Language of Music* does an excellent job of contradicting the idea that musical material is completely arbitrary. Cooke argues that music is a language, that certain tonal successions may be regarded as "terms" in that language, and that each of these terms has a different expressive meaning (meanings that are further differentiated by the specific musical contexts in which those terms appear). Exploring the "common-practice tonal tradition" (the same "language" with which my book is concerned), Cooke finds many such terms, like the melodic succession he calls "ascending 5–1–(2)–3 major" (which, for example, sets the title of the popular song "You Are My Sunshine"). For each of the terms he identifies, he offers a large number of melodies based on that term and shows that they can be understood as expressing related meanings – either because they all have similar texts or because their location within a dramatic work makes it clear that they are associated with the expression of ideas similar to the texts of the texted examples. For each term, he discusses how aspects of its structure may be related to the shared meaning of the texts with which it is associated. Cooke's views have been criticized by some. It may be that a more nuanced theory is possible (it seems to me, however, that some of Cooke's critics have jousted at a straw man by ignoring all the important qualifications he offers concerning his theories). But one does not have to buy all that Cooke writes on the subject to agree with his basic point that musical material contributes to musical meaning (he also notes that other factors – such as rhythm, articulation, dynamics, orchestration, texture, and other contextual features – also contribute). No musically sensitive person who reads Cooke's book thoughtfully can come away without some skepticism about the idea that musical meaning is completely arbitrary.

Consider the excerpts given in Example 1.2. Each involves an alternation between the fifth and sixth scale degrees in major in a moderately fast duple meter, and many include a prominent leap to or from the first

EXAMPLE 1.2. Examples of the "hallelujah figure."

scale degree right before or after that alternation. Because Example 1.2a (from the "Hallelujah Chorus" of Handel's *Messiah*) and Example 1.2b (from Handel's "Saul") both set the text "Hallelujah!" I will call this family of figures the "hallelujah figure." Cooke's Examples 29, 61, and 64 (which he uses to illustrate the use of the sixth scale degree in major, and to represent two different "terms" that Cooke defines as "(5)–6–5 major" and "1–(2)–(3)–(4)–5–6–5 major") give another four dozen such examples of this same figure, each of which bears a text or comes from a context that clearly suggests an outgoing expression of happiness, innocence, thanks, comfort, and/or joy. Although Cooke notes important differences between the examples he offers, they all have an affect that differs from that of the lamento-bass examples.

The hallelujah figure differs from the lamento bass in several ways. While the lamento bass descends, the hallelujah figure moves up and down. While the lamento bass moves by step, the hallelujah figure includes a leap. While the lamento bass is chromatic, the hallelujah figure is diatonic. While the lamento bass is in minor, the hallelujah figure is in major. While the lamento bass moves slowly, the hallelujah figure moves more rapidly. And while the lamento bass is in triple meter, the hallelujah figure is in duple meter.

If musical material were really arbitrary, then we could have learned to associate the hallelujah figure with the sadness of death. This seems improbable to me, and I hope that these examples underscore that point.

I shall return to these examples – and several others – throughout this book. And I shall offer some explanation of why I feel that the nature of musical materials is not completely arbitrary, why I feel that the lamento bass expresses the sadness of death better than the hallelujah figure does, and what all this has to do with musical forces.

THE ATOMIST FALLACY

One of my points here is to question the assumptions we make at the outset of our inquiry. The assumption that musical "signs" are purely arbitrary or simply conventional is one such assumption. The assumptions that our expectations are shaped solely by statistical frequency or that any one effect can have only one cause (the single-mechanism fallacy) are other such assumptions. Yet another such assumption (the atomist fallacy) is a certain sort of pseudo-scientific approach to music that says "we can't assume anything" and proceeds to assume that only the most atomistic elements count. Authors who take this approach apparently do not see that (a) assuming that "only the most atomist elements count" is itself a HUGE assumption, and (b) this assumption flies in the face of the evidence of science and common sense.

Eugene Narmour's implication-realization model of melodic expectation may seem like an example of such an approach – his 1990 book begins by arguing that we should ignore relationships between nonadjacent notes (relationships that are commonly asserted to be important in Schenkerian analyses) when constructing a theory of melodic expectation – but when his 1996 article begins by presenting a Schenkerian analysis and continues by basing the application of his theory on relationships between nonadjacent notes depicted in his Schenkerian analysis, it seems clear that any complete account of melodic expectations must grant an important place to such relationships.

Arnheim (1966) nicely disposes of the atomist fallacy with examples from visual perception which show that we often recognize global shapes and overall structures before we understand the details they contain – and that our grasp of overall structure is one of the factors that shapes the way we understand the details.

EMERGENT PROPERTIES

I have described expressive meaning as an "emergent property." An emergent property is a global phenomenon that results from the interactions of more local phenomena – in which it appears that the whole is unexpectedly greater than the sum of its parts. Two classic examples of emergent properties are the flocking behavior of birds and the chemical properties of molecules.

Birds fly in flocks. The flock may make a V shape. Or it may form a cloud that can switch direction or move as a whole in a way that makes us think of the flock as an "it" instead of "them." But individual birds do not know about such formations – they don't think, "Hey, let's make a V in the sky" or "Now the whole flock should make a sudden turn together." The global behavior of flocks "emerges" from the ways in which individual birds make more local responses to factors such as wind, threats, and other birds.

Likewise, individual atoms combine to make larger units called molecules. For example, sodium and chlorine atoms combine to form molecules of table salt. Table salt can make food taste much better. And (even if some people sometimes consume too much) it is an important part of our diet. But sodium and chlorine, when they are not combined, are both deadly poisons. The global properties of table salt "emerge" from the interaction of its constituent atoms.

HIERARCHIES AND LEVELS OF EXPLANATION

The idea of emergence entails the notion of "levels." We may distinguish between the level of the bird and the level of the flock. We may distinguish between the level of the atom and the level of the molecule. We may characterize lower levels as local and higher levels as global. Such levels create hierarchies.

The idea of emergence is also related to the notion of "levels of explanation." The phenomena that scientists try to explain are usually hierarchical. For example, they might study molecules (which are made of atoms, which include protons, which are made of even smaller subatomic particles). Or they might study the human body (which includes organs, which are made up of cells, which are made up of parts like nuclei and organelles, which are made of even smaller things – including molecules).

Partly because of the nature of emergent properties, we are interested in explanations that typically deal with a limited number of levels. We do not always require that the apparently lowest level in any explanation be explained. For example, an explanation of the behavior of groups of people might rely on some assumptions about how individuals behave – without explaining why individuals behave that way. Nor do we require that all possible higher levels be explored. For example, an explanation of how certain hormones in our bodies might affect our attention or other aspects of our behavior is not deemed incomplete when it fails to go on to account for how those effects might alter behavior of a group that contained someone affected by that hormone.

In the same way, the theory of musical forces assumes (without proof or explanation) the lower-level processes on which it depends. For example, the theory does not explain how listeners attribute a single pitch to a complicated collection of frequencies or how they learn about the physical forces it claims they map onto musical experience.

Nor does the theory explain all higher-level phenomena. For example, this book speaks of our "embodied understanding" of physical and musical forces (that is, what we "know" in our bodies about the effects of those forces on the motions we experience) without attempting a complete explanation of all the different ways in which this and other embodied knowledge contribute to our musical experience. Writers such as Elisabeth Le Guin (2006) and Alexandra Pierce (1989) have explored questions such as "How will the performer's body configure itself in order to play music?" and "How may we read these configurations for meaning?" Although a detailed consideration of the role of physical and musical forces in what LeGuin calls "carnal musicology" might be productive, it is beyond the scope of this book.

Similarly, this book describes the experience of what it calls "experienced listeners of tonal music" (and refers to the same group as "we") without really explaining what determines membership in that category. As fascinating as some questions are – such as "Who are these 'experienced listeners' of tonal music?"; "How are such musical communities created?"; "Why and how do our listening experiences with tonal music create the sense that we share some 'musical language'?"; and "How clearly defined are the boundaries of a category like 'experienced listener of tonal music'?" – they are beyond the scope of this book.

Notice, by the way, that to say that a thing has an "emergent property" is not so much an observation about a property literally possessed by that thing as it is an observation about how our minds work. If our minds understood immediately – that is, if we could feel in our bodies, without having to think it out – how the (poisonous) individual properties of sodium and chorine combine to create the (life-sustaining) emergent properties of salt, then we would not regard those properties as emergent.

The larger theory of expressive meaning that lies behind the claims of this book is built on the idea that higher-level musical meanings can emerge in part from patterns of lower-level interactions of musical materials and musical forces in the same way that global "flocking" behavior emerges from the more local interactions of individual birds. This book focuses primarily on explaining the theory of musical forces and describing some of the converging evidence for that theory. Nevertheless, I hope that it will provide a useful basis, and some evidence, for that larger theory.

The theory of musical forces concerns our *experience* of music. Thus we will need tools to describe how some aspects of musical experience arise. Those tools include the following concepts: pattern, meaning, analogy, metaphor, and hierarchical levels. Chapter 2 examines each of these concepts in greater detail, but a brief discussion of them now will provide an overview of the whole book.

Analogies and Metaphor Theory

The idea we have just discussed (that the emergence of musical meaning is like the flocking of birds) is a metaphor. By "metaphor" I mean that conceptual process described by George Lakoff and Mark Johnson (1980, 1999) in which we understand one kind of thing (from a "target domain") in terms of some other kind of thing (the "source domain"). Metaphors are thus "cross-domain mappings." In the metaphor of meanings emerging the way flocks do, we conceptualize musical meaning (the target domain) in terms of the motion of birds (the source domain). While this idea makes a metaphor (between patterns of notes and patterns of birds) explicit, it is also stated with the aid of another (perhaps less obvious) metaphor ("The larger theory ... is built on the idea that ..."). That other metaphor conceptualizes the structure of ideas ("The larger theory") in terms of the structure of architecture ("is built on"). This book follows recent conventions in publications on metaphor and capitalizes such metaphors – here, Ideas Are Buildings or, more basically, Organization Is Physical Structure.

Metaphors permeate our thinking. I claim that musical meaning arises in part through such cross-domain mappings when we "hear ... as" – that is, for example, when we hear sounds as motions (even something as simple as hearing a succession of tones as a melodic "ascent").

A metaphor is a special type of analogy. In this book I use the term "analogy" to describe any mapping that calls attention to similarities between two different things. Analogies include mappings within a single domain (say between two different melodic patterns, where the single domain is that of music). Analogies also include cross-domain mappings (such as "The larger theory is built on the idea that ...," where the different domains are ideas and architecture). In this book I reserve the term "metaphor" for cross-domain mappings. Thus, as this book uses the terms, all metaphors are analogies, but not all analogies are metaphors.

In its more detailed examination of each of these concepts – pattern, meaning, analogy, metaphor, and hierarchical levels – chapter 2 not only provides terms that are useful in understanding the idea of musical forces, but it also lays an important foundation for the larger theory of expressive meaning that includes the idea of musical forces.

MUSICAL MOTION

A central metaphor to be explored in this book is the idea that Musical Succession Is Physical Motion. Chapter 3 discusses this metaphor, arguing that we acquire our basic embodied understanding of physical motion in four different ways and that these four basic experiences of physical motion give rise, via metaphor, to the chief ways in which we conceptualize musical motion.

MUSICAL FORCES

A principal entailment of the metaphor of musical motion is the idea of "musical forces." By musical forces I mean tendencies we hear in, and attribute to, music – tendencies to move in certain ways.

I identify and define three such melodic forces: "melodic gravity" is the tendency of a note heard as above a reference platform to *descend,* "melodic magnetism" is the tendency of an unstable note to move to the *nearest* stable pitch (a tendency that grows stronger the closer we get to a goal), and "musical inertia" is the tendency of a pattern of pitches or durations, or both, to continue in the *same* fashion (where what is meant by "same" depends upon what that musical pattern is "heard as"). Chapter 6 defines two rhythmic forces: "metric magnetism" (the pull of a note on an unstable attack point to a subsequent and more stable attack point, a pull that grows stronger as the attracting attack point grows closer) and "rhythmic gravity" (that quality we attribute to a rhythm, when we map its flow onto a physical gesture, that reflects the impact physical gravity has on that physical gesture).

It is important to remember that these forces are metaphorical. They are not literally a property of sounds the way pitch and duration are. They are tendencies that our minds attribute to the sounds we hear.[7]

It is also important to stress that our immediate experience of musical motion is shaped primarily by our *embodied intuitive* understanding of physical motion – not by our *intellectual* understanding of physics. Here, by "embodied," I mean (following Lakoff and Johnson [1980, 1999) that our understanding is not the understanding of a mind totally separate from its body but, rather, that our understanding is shaped by the somatic "feel" of what we know – that we "know" with our bodies as well as with our minds.[8] For example, our embodied intuitive understanding of physical gravity is that it constantly pulls us toward the ground – and that we are more aware of it in some contexts than in others (gravity is a more important part of our experience when we are on a steep, tall roof than when we are swimming underwater). Physicists tell us that every object has a mass-dependent gravitational interaction with every other object (the moon is pulling on us right now). And although they may still speak of "gravitational force," physicists might also point out that (according to Einstein's theories) gravity is not strictly a force (it is the inertial tendency of an object within a four-dimensional space-time curved by the mass of another object). Physicists might also tell us that, technically speaking, the vernacular usage "force of inertia" is incorrect; inertia is not a force (it is a principle, or a property of an object, and thus cannot be quantified). Because it is our immediate intuitive understanding of physical gravity that shapes our experience of musical motion, I shall talk about a "gravitational force" that pulls us downward, ignoring such things as the gravitational pulls of other heavenly bodies and the curvature of four-dimensional space-time, and I shall use the vernacular "inertial force" to describe the tendency of patterns to continue. Likewise, because our bodies are unaware of the "strong and weak forces" that bind atomic nuclei, I shall not speak of musical analogues to such nuclear forces.

Chapter 4 illustrates the effect of each melodic force with simple musical examples, compares it to its analogous physical force, and draws hypotheses concerning that force from the comparison.

MELODIC EXPECTATION

Chapter 5 offers a theory of melodic expectation based on those forces. That theory claims that experienced listeners of tonal music have expectations about how melodic beginnings will be completed, and it claims that these expectations are shaped, in part, by the musical forces. Chapter 5 also provides a vocabulary for describing melodic expectation that allows us to capture that theory in the following summary statement:

> Experienced listeners of tonal music expect melodic completions in which the musical forces of gravity, magnetism, and inertia control operations on alphabets in hierarchies of elaboration whose stepwise displacements of auralized traces create simple closed shapes.

That chapter clarifies and expands on this statement and then restates portions of it in the form of specific rules. Although these terms may at first appear specialized, new, or difficult, chapter 5 makes them (and the ultimately simpler underlying cognitive processes they describe) easier to understand.

RHYTHM AND METER

Although the theory of musical forces appears primarily pitch oriented, it has much to say about rhythm and meter. Chapter 6 discusses the phenomenon of musical rhythm and shows its intimate connection with musical forces. It notes what is rhythmic about musical forces, describes "rhythmic forces" (rhythmic gravity and metrical magnetism) that are analogous to musical forces, explains analogies between pitch and durational patterns, and shows how the same embodied knowledge of physical forces that informs our understanding of musical forces also shapes our experience of musical rhythm. Chapter 6 suggests that the theory of musical forces can deepen our understanding of rhythm and meter.

ANALYSES

Part 1 concludes with a series of analyses in chapter 7. These analyses illustrate the ideas discussed in chapters 1–6 with longer passages of music. The pieces analyzed include the opening melody of a Schubert song ("Am Feierabend," from *Die schöne Müllerin*), a familiar folk song ("Hickory Dickory Dock"), and two jazz compositions (one by Toshiko Akioshi and one by Charlie Parker).

EVIDENCE

Part 2 (chapters 8–13) considers evidence for the theory from a variety of sources. Chapter 8 introduces part 2 by noting that writers on music have called upon metaphors of motion for millennia and upon metaphors of force for centuries, providing evidence that these metaphors shape the way we think *about* music. It then goes on to sketch the types of evidence presented in the remaining chapters that these metaphors also shape the way we think *in* music, and to suggest how that evidence might be approached. Chapter 9 finds support for the theory from experiments in visual perception and neuroscience, arguing that if experience of physical motion can shape expectation and experience in music, then it should shape expectation and experience in other modalities – such as visual perception – and shows how experiments in visual perception provide evidence of visual analogues to musical forces (and the chapter concludes by suggesting that recent findings in neuroscience describe underlying brain structures whose operation is consistent with that argument). Chapter 10 shows that the distribution of melodic patterns within compositions and improvisations of various styles may be explained well in terms of a model of constantly interacting musical forces. Chapter 11 argues that historical and contemporary music theorists have misunderstood musical forces in ways that parallel common misunderstandings about physical forces, and it thus provides further evidence of the analogy between physical and musical forces. Chapter 12 turns to psychological experiments that test the role of musical forces in participant ratings of melodic completions. Chapter 13 describes computer models that implement the theory of melodic expectation presented here, and it compares the behavior of those computer models with that of participants in psychological experiments involving the production of melodic completions.

Chapter 14 concludes the book with ideas about how the theory of musical forces might be further tested, suggestions about how continued work on this theory might proceed, questions about how ideas in this book might be applied to music of other world cultures, and thoughts about how implications of the theory might be pursued in other disciplines.

PART 1

A Theory of Musical Forces

2

Thinking *about* Music and Thinking *in* Music: Pattern, Meaning, Analogy, Metaphor, and Hierarchies

As noted in chapter 1, the central argument of this book is that our experience of physical motion shapes our experience of musical motion in specific and quantifiable ways – so that we not only *speak* about music as if it were shaped by musical analogs of physical gravity, magnetism, and inertia, but we also actually *experience* it in terms of "musical forces." Chapter 1 also suggested that the concepts of pattern, meaning, analogy, metaphor, and hierarchy provide useful tools for explaining how that experience arises. Chapter 2 explores each of these concepts in greater detail. To do so, it begins by distinguishing between "thinking *about* music" and "thinking *in* music."

We use our minds in many different ways. For example, we may think in words, but we can also think in pictures or in sounds. If to think in pictures is to "visualize," then to think in sounds is to "auralize."[1] When I write about "auralizing" in this book, I am referring to what happens when we hear music in our heads – especially when the music is not actually sounding. For example, if I ask you to hear the melody of "Happy Birthday" in your head, you will probably be able to auralize that tune. I use the term "thinking in music" to mean the same thing, because it is something we do with our minds; it is a kind of *thinking*. And because that thinking involves pitches and durations instead of something else (such as words or pictures), it is thinking *in music*.

Thinking in music is quintessential to musical experience. I hope that, as you read this book, you will auralize the musical examples. Playing the musical examples on the piano, getting someone else to play them, or listening to a recording can also help you to hear the examples in your head. This may lead you to recall other pieces of music. Trained musicians will be able to auralize the musical examples simply by looking at them. But auralizing is something that anyone who can remember a melody can do. I suppose that it would be possible to read this book and to think *about* music without this kind of thinking *in* music. But that runs the risk of turning it into a dry, intellectual exercise that lacks an important connection with the worlds of feeling, imagination, and movement so important in musical experience.

If we hear music in our heads when no music is actually sounding, then clearly we are auralizing. But I think that we also auralize – in some sense – when we listen attentively to music. When we are listening to music in a meaningful way, we are predicting what will happen next. If that prediction is verbalized (for example, as "I'll bet that melody will soon stop repeating that one note"), then we can call it thinking *about* music. But musical meaning seems to depend on our auralizing predictions – thinking *in* music. For example, we cannot appreciate the wonderful surprises in a Haydn string quartet if we do not have specific expectations about what will happen next.

Thinking *in* music is different from thinking *about* music. We think about music whenever we talk about how its harmonies relate to the key it is in, whenever we ask when it was composed, or whenever we describe its form in standard terms such as "ABA," "sonata-rondo," or "alap." When we respond to music aurally – by auralizing pitches and durations – we are thinking *in* music; when we respond to music intellectually, we are thinking *about* music.[2]

Of course, we may respond to music in other ways, too. These other ways include emotional, imaginative, and kinesthetic responses. We respond emotionally to music whenever we weep upon hearing music that touches our hearts, whenever we are soothed by recalling a calming melody, or whenever we smile at the humor in a passage we have just composed. We respond imaginatively to music whenever we see colors or shapes while hearing a symphony, whenever we imagine a story that fits a piece of music, or whenever we recall experiences that are triggered by a distinctive tone combination, an expressive chord, or an unusual turn of musical events. We respond kinesthetically to music whenever we dance to a piece, whenever we communicate the impact of a passage by making a gesture with our arms, or whenever we sway imperceptibly to an engaging rhythm.

When I write about "experiencing music" in this book, I mean to include all these responses – aural, intellectual, emotional, imaginative, and kinesthetic – and anything else we do that gives music meaning for us. In fact, part of the purpose of this book is to suggest how these experiences may be joined. For example, consider the metaphor Musical Succession Is Physical Motion, the topic of chapter 3. Whenever we talk about how a melody *moves,* how it *goes,* whether it moves by *step* or *leap,* about it going *up* or *down* – we use the metaphor Musical Succession Is Physical Motion. If we talk about music in terms of this metaphor (which, as we shall see, seems unavoidable), then our intellectual response to music may be joined to imagined kinesthetic responses. And as soon as we feel that "music moves us," our emotions join in as well. It appears that musical meaning emerges (at least in part) through analogies we make between one passage of music and another, through comparisons we make between one passage of music and patterns we have abstracted from other passages, and through metaphors we make by mapping musical events onto the hierarchical patterns of our intellectual, emotional, imaginative, and kinesthetic lives. These ideas – pattern, meaning, analogy, metaphor, and hierarchies – are fundamental to the project of this book, and are each discussed in turn in the remainder of this chapter.

PATTERN

Pattern is central to meaning. To help make this point clear to students in my music theory classes, I ask them to play the following game. I ask them to look at the following string of numbers for just three seconds with the intent of memorizing it.

78 9101 1121 314

Then I hide it and ask them to write it on another sheet of paper. We talk about what parts of it they think they got right, how confident they were that they had those parts right, and which parts were easiest to remember, and why.

Then I point out that some people find it difficult to memorize a string of random numbers; they find letters easier. So we try the same experiment with the following string of letters. This time I give them five seconds.

Thissen ten ceise asytome mori ze

Most of my students tend to remember the beginning or the end of the whole string but have trouble remembering the middle parts. Some people remember the beginnings and endings of each group of numbers or letters but have trouble remembering what comes in the middle of each group.

This suggests that the boundaries of groups – the beginnings and endings – stay in our minds more easily than the middles. And it suggests that the grouping of individual pieces of information is important. Notice how much easier it is to remember the same string of numbers if it is grouped as "7 8 9 10 11 12 13 14" or if the same string of letters is grouped as "This sentence is easy to memorize."

It doesn't require three to five seconds to memorize these strings if one simply understands them. In fact, if you understand them, they are hard to forget!

This experiment suggests some important things about *how* I want students to learn the content of courses they take with me. If what they learn seems like a random string of facts, they will have trouble remembering and using the ideas. So we make sure that they understand *why* each thing we study is as it is. This way, instead of memorizing (and then, inevitably, forgetting) music theory, they understand it (and thus cannot forget it).

This experiment also suggests some important things about *what* I hope they will learn in these courses. They learn to recognize common musical patterns, to see and hear how pitches and durations are grouped to form those patterns, and to understand how those patterns can be combined and transformed to create the remarkable variety of music.

We tend to use the word "pattern" to describe at least three sorts of things – and they all seem related to repetition. First, we may use the word "pattern" to describe a design or shape (such as a dress pattern used in sewing) that could serve as a model. Such a pattern is something we can imagine repeating. Second, we speak of a pattern when a single thing (such as a cross or a mandala) has some kind of internal symmetry or logic. Such a pattern may be said to contain repetition (of a shape or of a rule) within it. Third, we speak of a pattern (such as the rhythm of an engine or a pattern of behavior) when we notice something being repeated. Since this last sort of pattern may consist of things that would themselves be called patterns, we can also have higher-level patterns of patterns.

My main point here is to stress the connection between pattern and meaning. We have all had the experience of hearing music that seems meaningless. Music we are unfamiliar with may sound meaningless. Music that is composed badly, performed badly, or even heard badly can have the same effect as the strings "78 9101 1121 314" or "Thissen ten ceise asytome mori ze." The effect is like hearing bad actors pronounce lines mechanically or hearing people pronounce "correctly" the words of a foreign language they do not understand. The strings "7 8 9 10 11 12 13 14" and "This sentence is easy to memorize" are easier to remember because their individual characters are grouped into meaningful units – patterns – that we can understand.

MEANING

But I have been talking about "meaning" without saying what I mean by that word. What, after all, does "meaning" mean? In my view, meaning is something that our minds create when they group things into patterned relations. By itself, the world is not meaningful. By this I do not mean "life is meaningless." Life is full of meaning, but it is meaningful because our minds create meaning. We have a strong drive to find meanings in the world, but those meanings exist only in our minds. "Music simply does not exist independent of experience. Meaning is not something in the music itself, as many musicologists and music philosophers seem to believe, but something that arises through individual subjects' encounters with musical works" (Aksnes 2002, 28). Aspects of the world (and the limits of our imagination) constrain the meanings we give to things, but to find meaning in something is a creative act. Rudolf Arnheim (1974) argues this point persuasively by showing the myriad ways in which we create meaning in everything from looking at a complex painting to perceiving a simple shape.

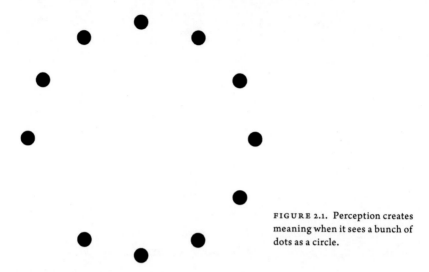

FIGURE 2.1. Perception creates meaning when it sees a bunch of dots as a circle.

Thus this creative attribution of meaning takes place on all different levels. We give meaning at one level to the lines in Shakespeare's *King Lear* when we connect the name "Edward" with one of the characters. We give meaning at another level when we see certain events in the play following the path of a circle. But even the perceptual act of seeing the dots in Example 2.1 as a circle creates meaning that was not there before. And meaning is hierarchical – each of these levels relies on or supports other levels of meaning. For example, seeing the path of Edward's fate in terms of a circle not only requires connecting the word "Edward" to the character it describes; it also relies on our perception of events in his life as discrete points that can be joined in the smooth figure of a circle. The lowest of these levels of meaning clearly involves finding a pattern in a percept (such as the circle in the dots). But I believe that patterns play an important role at all levels of meaning. Notice that, according to this definition, meaning is not purely (or even primarily) verbal. We are used to thinking of meaning in terms of words. Words are thought of as units that have meaning. We look for meanings in dictionaries and find strings of words there. But finding a circle in a bunch of dots or in the actions of a play does not necessarily involve thinking only in words. In the words of John Dewey ([1934] 1979, 74): "There are values and meanings that can be expressed only by visible and audible qualities, and to ask what they mean in the sense of something that can be put into words is to deny their distinctive existence." Mark Johnson's *The Meaning of the Body: Aesthetics of Human Understanding* (2007) makes this point – and shows its importance in aesthetics – well.

Whenever our minds group musical sounds into patterned relations we create meaning. Howard Margolis (1987) shows how pattern is central not only to meaning itself but also to the processes by which meanings are attributed. The process by which listeners create musical meaning is captured in the phrase "to hear as" – that is, "to *hear x as y*," where *x* is some sound and *y* is some meaning. For example, we may say that we *hear* a pattern of pitches *as* an ascending gesture or that we *hear* a pattern of durations *as* a syncopated rhythm. Again, aspects of specific passages of music constrain the meanings we give to them, but to find meaning in music is a creative act. Douglas Hofstadter has long held that this process of "seeing as" is central to all cognition, and he has described several projects in artificial intelligence based on this idea (Hofstadter et al. 1995). His insightful discussions about the central role of pattern in thinking, feeling, mind, and consciousness (see also Hofstadter 1979) have shaped my views on meaning in music. Recent (apparently somewhat independent) discussions of "hearing as" by a number of different authors (Boretz 1989, 107; Cumming 2000; Larson 1993e; Scruton 1997; and Spitzer 2004) suggest its appeal and importance.

In fact, I argue that our minds have a drive (that is strengthened by, if not a result of, evolution) to create meaning by grouping percepts into patterned relations. And I agree with the assertion by Gestalt psychologists that our minds also have a drive to see (or hear) percepts as based upon simple, complete shapes (this is one reason why we tend to see, and feel, that something is missing in Example 2.1). Taken together, these two principles imply that our minds "create" musical meaning by finding ways of completing things in the simplest possible way (an idea pursued in chapter 5, which presents a theory of melodic expectation). A further implication of these two principles is that, once we discover a pattern (or a way of making patterns), we have a creative drive to explore the "space" of all equally simple ways of making such patterns.

When we hear musical events as reflecting the patterns of our intellectual, emotional, imaginative, and kinesthetic lives, we may speak of
that musical meaning as "expressive meaning" – that quality that allows
music to suggest (for example) feelings, images, or actions (or even still-
ness, a special kind of action). That quality may not translate well into
words nor relate clearly to the emotions of a composer. And different
people may attribute different meanings to the same sounds (something that happens with language, too). But these mappings make music
meaningful according to the definitions of "meaning" and "expressive
meaning" offered here.

ANALOGY

Hofstadter's work also suggests that analogy is at the core of cognition.
If analogies are at the core of cognition, then musical analogies are at the
core of music cognition. I define an "analogy" (such as "If analogies are
at the core of cognition, then musical analogies are at the core of music
cognition") as a mapping that calls attention to similarities between two
different things – regardless of whether those things belong to the same
or to different domains (when the mapping is between things in different
domains, I call that analogy a "metaphor" – more on this below). The following discussion of a passage by Mozart illustrates some of the different
types of analogies listeners may make between one passage of music and
other bits of music, and it shows something of the relationships between
analogy and expressive meaning.

The music in Example 2.1 gives the opening of the "Adagio" from
Mozart's Piano Concerto in A major, K. 488. These twelve measures
form an "antecedent-consequent" period. Measures 1–4 (the antecedent) begin with a distinctive "motto" in the "Siciliano rhythm" ♪.♪♪ and
end with a half-cadence. The result is a musical "question." Measures
5–12 (the consequent) begin with the same distinctive motto (though at
a different pitch level) and end with an authentic cadence. The result is
a musical "answer."

When we describe the music in this way, we make an analogy between measures 1–4 and measures 5–12. (And when we describe these

EXAMPLE 2.1. Wolfgang Amadeus Mozart, "Adagio" from Piano Concerto in A major, K. 488, measures 1–12.

measures using the terms "question," "answer," "phrase," and "period," we invoke another analogy, the metaphor Music Is A Language – an idea to which we shall return shortly.) This analogy maps the motto in measure 1 onto the motto in measure 5, and the cadence of the question onto the cadence of the answer. Finding these similarities between measures 1–4 and measures 5–12 makes this analogy possible. And finding these similarities provides a context for noticing meaningful differences (such as the fact that the motto begins in measure 1 on C♯ and in measure 5 on D, that G♯ in measure 3 precedes the first cadence and that G in measure 9 precedes the second cadence, and that the first cadence is incomplete and the second one is complete).

Notice that making an analogy rests on the process of "hearing as." To hear measures 1–4 and 5–12 as analogous in this sense relies on hearing measures 1 and 5 as "the same" in some sense. Measures 1 and 5 have the same rhythm, and they share other features. They are not identical, however; one starts on C♯ and the other on D. Nevertheless, making this analogy means hearing them as equivalent. In fact, in music, because

EXAMPLE 2.2. An alternative continuation for Wolfgang Amadeus Mozart, "Adagio" from Piano Concerto in A major, K. 488; measures 1–4 as written and measures 5–8 as expected.

it takes place in time (like the moving stream one can never step into "in the same place"), no two bits are ever totally the same – even when they look identical on the page. What matters is how we experience them. And my points here are (1) that, when we experience an analogy between two bits of music, the analogy rests on *hearing* both bits *as* "the same" in some way, and (2) that the senses in which we experience bits of music as the same or different are an important part of musical meaning.

A related analogy arises when we compare measures 5–12 to what we expect as an answer to measures 1–4. Example 2.2 shows one expectation we might have.

If one hears this music without expecting a C♯ on the downbeat of measure 5, then one can still enjoy the D that sounds there. But if we expect C♯ on the downbeat of measure 5, the surprise we get when we hear D instead may add substantially to our experience of its beauty.

There is another reason to expect a C♯ at the beginning of measure 5. In measure 3 the melody leaps away from a D. That D is an unstable note that would normally resolve to C♯ at its first opportunity (which, because of the harmony, would be in measure 4). Because we do not get that C♯ in measure 4, a C♯ on the downbeat of measure 5 would seem the next-best opportunity.

EXAMPLE 2.3. An analogy between the motto and the first six measures of
Wolfgang Amadeus Mozart, "Adagio" from Piano Concerto in A major, K. 488.

Listeners familiar with this type of music will (at some level) expect
something like Example 2.3 because they recognize measures 1–4 as a
typical four-bar antecedent and because they expect it to be followed
by a typical consequent. (Notice that this requires only that they have
internalized these expectations – not that they know the terms such
as "antecedent" or "period" that music theorists use to describe those
expectations.) They can do this, in part, because they make analogies
between this passage and patterns (such as the antecedent-consequent
pattern) that they have abstracted from other passages. (At another level,
the same listeners may expect to have their expectations denied; more
about this later.)

Furthermore, there are subtleties of Mozart's writing here that
would seem to require that we listen with this expectation (of a return
to C♯ in measure 5) in order to appreciate them. Example 2.3 shows one
such subtlety. Example 2.3b reproduces the first six measures of Example
2.1. Example 2.2 compares these measures to a stretched-out version of
the motto of measure 1. But the notes shown in Example 2.3a are not just
the motto; they are also the notes that form the most basic structural
skeleton for these measures. Put another way, if we regard these measures as elaborating a simpler pattern (that elaborates a simpler pattern
and so on), then the simplest pattern elaborated in these measures is
the C♯–D–C♯ shown in Example 2.3a. (In other words, a Schenkerian
analysis of this phrase would show that the notes that appear in Example
2.3a are the basic structural pitches that are elaborated in Example 2.3b.
I shall have more to say about Schenker's theories below.) Example 2.3

EXAMPLE 2.4. A comparison between Wolfgang Amadeus Mozart,
"Adagio" from Piano Concerto in A major, K. 488, and the same
composer's Piano Sonata in A major, K. 331, first movement.

thus makes an analogy between the first half of measure 1 and the first
half of Mozart's phrase.

Of course, one can also make analogies between two *different* pieces.
Example 2.4 finds two similarities between Mozart's "Adagio" and the
"theme and variations" first movement of his Piano Sonata in A major,
K. 331. Examples 2.4a and b give the openings of both movements. Both
pieces begin with the same three melody notes – the C♯–D–C♯ Siciliano
motto. Examples 2.4c and d show another similarity. Example 2.4c gives
measure 6 of the "Adagio." Example 2.4d gives the beginning of the first
variation of the Mozart theme. The same notes (a B♯–C♯ appoggiatura
above an A–E fifth) occur in both pieces.

These two similarities make an interesting comparison. Both pieces
are written with a key signature of three sharps; but the Sonata movement is in A major, whereas the Concerto movement is in F♯ minor. Both
movements begin with the same three-note motto (C♯–D–C♯ in the Si-

EXAMPLES 2.5. A familiar blues-piano cliché.

ciliano rhythm); but the Sonata theme harmonizes that motto with a
tonic major chord, whereas the Concerto's "Adagio" harmonizes it with
a tonic minor chord. Both pieces are notated in $\frac{6}{8}$; but the Sonata theme
is usually performed at a faster tempo than the "Adagio." Both pieces
include the appoggiatura figure shown in Examples 2.4c and d; in the
Sonata, however, those notes come at the beginning of a gesture on the
tonic, while in the Adagio those notes come at the end of a gesture on a
nontonic harmony (and are undercut when the left hand changes just as
the right hand resolves).

Each similarity provides a context that makes some differences
meaningful. And those differences help shape the expressive meanings
of these passages. The use of minor and a slower tempo gives the "Adagio"
a deeper and more poignant affect. Hearing the B♯–C♯ appoggiatura as
a brisk beginning on a stable tonic harmony (in the Sonata movement)
gives them a direct and affable quality, whereas hearing them as a point
of temporary (and then undercut) arrival that is not in the home key (in
the Concerto movement) gives them a more dreamlike affect. And the
context of Mozart's style in general gives these notes a different meaning
than they might have in a different context (for example, in a jazz context
[see Example 2.5], they could sound like a familiar blues-piano cliché).
Of course, we could say much more about what makes these passages
different and how those differences create the distinctive affects we hear
in these pieces. The point here is that these analogies between different
passages by a single composer help us both appreciate and explain the
expressive meanings of these passages.

But we can just as readily compare pieces in different keys or by different composers. As Example 2.6 shows, the beginning of the "Adagio"

EXAMPLES 2.6. A comparison between Wolfgang Amadeus Mozart,
"Adagio" from Piano Concerto in A major, K. 488, measures 1–3 and 7–8,
and Chopin, Waltz in B minor, op. 69, no. 2, measures 5–9.

resembles part of Chopin's Waltz in B minor, op. 69, no. 2. Example 2.6a
gives the melody of that Waltz as Chopin wrote it. Example 2.6b trans-
poses these same measures down a fourth so that they are notated in the
same key as the "Adagio" (Example 2.6c).

Once again, finding the similarities highlights the differences. Comparing Examples 2.6b (the transposed version of the Chopin) and Example 2.6c, we see that, though many of the notes are the same, there are
important differences. Both passages begin on C♯; but whereas Mozart
begins on the beat, Chopin brings the C♯ in early (with a quarter-note
anticipation). Both passages circle around that C♯ with half-step neigh-
bor-note motion, but whereas Mozart uses only the (diatonic) upper
neighbor, Chopin uses both the upper and (chromatic) lower neighbors.
And, after almost identical upward arpeggios, both passages leap in sevenths and sixths back and forth between two stepwise descending lines
whose starting points are the high and low notes of that upward arpeggio
(A and C♯, respectively) and whose suspensions create beautiful dissonances; but whereas Mozart's lines descend diatonically, Chopin's lines
descend chromatically.

Once again, the differences may help us both to appreciate (and to begin to explain) the expressive meanings of these passages. Comparing these two passages highlights the simplicity and grace of Mozart's melody, and the rhythmic interest and sense of direction of Chopin's melody. And the role of anticipations, suspensions, and chromaticism in creating those effects is clearer when we compare these passages.

Such piece-to-piece comparisons can play a significant role in our musical experience. Recent scholarship focused on "intertextuality" explores such comparisons in depth (see, for example, Hatten 1985). However, I do not think that our primary experience of musical meaning lies in such specific piece-to-piece comparisons. Of course, we make such comparisons whenever one piece reminds us of another. And such comparisons provide one effective way to think *about* music. But, in my view, our thinking *in* music involves comparing a piece that we are hearing to *patterns* (that we have drawn from listening to other pieces) more often than it involves such specific piece-to-piece comparisons.

In fact, even the comparison just described (between the Chopin and Mozart melodies in Example 2.6) seems to rely on our sense of patterns and norms. Comparing Chopin's anticipation of the first C♯ (F♯ in Chopin's original key) to Mozart's downbeat beginning helps underscore the rhythmic interest of Chopin's melody. But we do not need Mozart's melody in order to appreciate the anticipations; we can compare Chopin's melody (Example 2.7b) to our expectation of a simpler pattern – the more normative (and less interesting) rhythm given in Example 2.7a. Likewise, we do not need Mozart's melody in order to appreciate the chromaticism in Chopin's melody; we seem (automatically!) to compare Chopin's chromatic lines to our expectation of simpler diatonic patterns. And it is important not to mistake this specific piece-to-piece comparison for a comparison between Mozart and Chopin (for one reason, Mozart's music is full of anticipations and chromaticism). Furthermore, our expectations for simpler patterns run deeper. Other aspects of musical meaning emerge when we compare Chopin's melody to a more regular pattern, such as the melody given in Example 2.7a. Upon hearing the first half of Example 2.7, one might expect the melody to continue by following the formula or recipe that generates Example 2.7a. That

EXAMPLE 2.7. An alternative version of Chopin, Waltz in B minor,
op. 69, no. 2, measures 1–8.

melody (which we might attribute to the hypothetical composer Frederic
Deadpan) is a perfect plausible melody. But Chopin's melody is much
more sophisticated and much more attractive. And we appreciate that
sophistication and beauty only when we compare the Chopin melody
to a simpler pattern like the Deadpan melody.

Heinrich Schenker ([1910] 1987) pointed out that when we listen to
music, we compare what we hear to a simpler, more normative, or more
predictable version of how that music might have gone. His writing also
suggests that the meanings we give to a passage of music are, in part,
shaped by that comparison.

Douglas Hofstadter suggests that such comparison is also central to
creativity itself. In a chapter titled "Variations on a Theme as the Crux
of Creativity," he writes: "Careful analysis leads one to see that what we
choose to call a new theme is itself always some sort of variation, on a

EXAMPLES 2.8. A comparison between Wolfgang Amadeus Mozart,
"Adagio" from Piano Concerto in A major, K. 488, measures 5–6 and 7–8.

deep level, of previous themes" (1985, 232). Our tendency to create meaning through such comparisons, together with the role that simplicity
and completeness play in percepts, goes hand in hand with what seems
to be a cognitive drive to explore the "space" of all equally simple ways
of making patterns.

Even analogies made between different parts of a *single* piece may
depend on our ability to abstract patterns from the music. Consider measures 5–8 of the "Adagio" (the music is reproduced in Example 2.8b).
Measures 1–4 are, as noted above, a question. That question may lead
us to expect a four-measure answer. But the four measures that follow
sound more like two pairs of measures.

Those two pairs of measures may be described as a sequence. The
left hand makes the sequence clear; the left hand of measures 5–6 is
repeated two steps lower in measures 7–8. The right hand of measures

5–6 is not repeated sequentially in measures 7–8, but its basic structural skeleton (and the use of a downbeat appoggiatura in measures 6 and 8) is sequential (see Example 2.8a). Thus a listener could (consciously or unconsciously) hear these pairs of measures in at least three increasingly deep ways: (1) because there is a longer stable note at the end of measures 6 and 8, but no cadence, they may be heard as equivalent pairs of measures (related to the beginning of a 2 + 2 + 4 phrase-rhythm pattern called a "sentence"); (2) because the left hand is sequenced, they may be heard as a familiar harmonic sequence (based on the harmonic pattern IV_5^6–V_5^6–I); (3) because both hands elaborate the same underlying melodic patterns (Example 2.9a), they may be heard as a sequence at a deeper level (based on the "linear intervallic pattern" 6–5–3). And at all of these levels, the hearing is based on perceiving an underlying pattern – whether it is a pattern of phrase rhythm, harmonic progression, or underlying counterpoint.

Whether we are thinking in music or thinking about music, we often make such analogies. Whether the analogies we make are between passages within a single piece, between passages from different pieces, between a passage and a pattern, or between a passage and our expectations for that passage, those analogies contribute to the meaning we give to the music.[3]

METAPHOR

The analogies just discussed are all within the domain of music. When an analogy maps one thing onto a different sort of thing, this book – following the theory of conceptual metaphor (Lakoff and Johnson 1980, 1999) – calls that cross-domain mapping a "metaphor."[4]

The theory of conceptual metaphor contradicts virtually all classical theories of metaphor, as well as many popular recent views of metaphor in linguistics, psychology, and philosophy. Traditional theories of language treat metaphor as a "figure of speech" having no serious cognitive import. Such theories are characterized by at least the following four tenets.

1. Classical theories claim that metaphor is a matter of words. It is a way of saying one thing and meaning something else.

2. They claim that a metaphor is a deviant use of a term, in which we take the proper ("literal") meaning of a given word or phrase and apply it to some object or event to which it does not properly apply.

3. They claim that the metaphorical transference of a term from one domain to a domain of a different kind is based on preexisting literal similarities holding between parts of the two different domains. Metaphors call our attention to those preexisting literal similarities, but they add nothing truly new.

4. Consequently, they claim that metaphor is in no way constitutive of our concepts. It is merely an alternative form for expressing what can be expressed in literal concepts.

According to this classical view, there could be nothing cognitively important about metaphor, beyond its rhetorical or didactic value. So, to grant that we use metaphorical language to talk about music would be to say nothing about how we experience and conceptualize music.

The theory of conceptual metaphor contradicts all four of these tenets by making the following claims.

1. Metaphor is conceptual. It is not merely a matter of words.

2. Metaphor is one of the basic, common devices we have for abstract conceptualization and reasoning. It permits us to use our knowledge of one domain of experience to construct an understanding of some other domain.

3. The metaphorical transference of a term from one domain to a domain of a different kind is based on experienced correlations between sensory-motor domains and domains involving subjective judgment and abstract thought. Metaphors do not necessarily call our attention to those correlations, but they always add new relationships and logical entailments to our experience and understanding of at least one of the domains involved.

4. Consequently, conceptual metaphors are actually constitutive of our understanding, conceptualization, and reasoning.

Empirical evidence emerging in the cognitive sciences over the past two decades reveals the central role metaphor plays in all our abstract conceptualization and reasoning. George Lakoff and Mark Johnson (1999) and Raymond Gibbs (1994) present psychological, linguistic, and philosophical evidence for conceptual metaphor theory. They argue that metaphors are indispensable to abstract concepts; if we try to discard one metaphor, we will necessarily adopt another.[5]

Metaphors are what Richard Dawkins (1976) calls "memes": mental constructs analogous to genes. Like genes, they live in a particular environment: our thoughts and our culture. Like genes, their survival depends on how well they fit in their environment. Thus metaphors are, to an extent, shaped by culture. And, like genes and in an equally circular fashion, they make up part of their environment. Thus culture is simultaneously, to an extent, shaped by metaphors.

Defining metaphor as a way of understanding one thing in terms of something from a different domain of experience raises an interesting question: "If everything is understood in terms of something else, how is that 'something else' understood?" What prevents an infinite circular regress? Metaphors form coherent webs of mutually reinforcing relationships, and so, to an extent, we do have an infinite circular regress. Yet, if metaphors help us to understand new things in terms of familiar things, then those familiar things will tend to belong to source domains that are more basic in our experience. And our most basic experiences are physical. Thus the answer appears to be that metaphors are understood in terms of more basic metaphors, and that basic metaphors are "grounded" in our physical experience. In other words, our most basic concepts – the simplest things we learn at the earliest ages – come from our experience of moving about in the world. For example, if we say "prices are rising," we make the metaphor More Is Higher. Prices are not literally "higher." But we use this metaphor in part because, in our most basic embodied experiences, more of something (more milk in a glass or more logs in a pile) rises higher. Lakoff and Johnson (1999) cite evidence from cognitive linguistics showing that source domains for conceptual metaphors are typically based on aspects of our bodily experience. Consequently our understanding and reasoning about the target domain is highly constrained by the structure of bodily experience.

Thus, although some of our conceptual metaphors are culturally shaped, their meaning is anything but arbitrary. In this book, when I refer to "embodiment," "embodied experience," or "embodied knowledge," I mean understanding that is thus physically grounded (regardless of how that knowledge was first acquired – that is, if we see someone move, the knowledge is visual, but once we understand that motion in terms of the motion connected with our own body, that knowledge becomes "embodied").

Philosophers, historians, and theorists have written with great insight on the central role of metaphor in music.[6] Others have explicitly called on the theory of conceptual metaphor to illuminate the theory and analysis of music.[7] Still others have focused on the embodied nature of musical meaning.[8]

This scholarship focuses primarily on Western concert music. But metaphor plays an important role in jazz, too. The central metaphors of jazz-as-language and jazz-as-motion figure in much nonanalytical writing and talk about jazz. It is common to hear jazz musicians speak of "telling a story," and this idea has been pursued in "serious" jazz scholarship by several authors (see, e.g., Gushee 1981; Larson 1996a; Monson 1996). When jazz musicians speak of "swing," I believe they are invoking the metaphor Musical Succession Is Physical Motion (Larson 1999b). And Janna Saslaw (2000) has explicitly applied the work of Lakoff and Johnson (1999) in her jazz scholarship.

Metaphor also plays an important role in non-Western music. The work of Steven Feld (1981) and others explicitly applies conceptual metaphor theory to musics of other world cultures. Metaphor theory has also been applied to fields other than music.[9]

Lakoff and Johnson (1999) argue that conceptual metaphors structure our thoughts so thoroughly that they influence our behavior in systematic ways. Their illustration, the conceptual metaphor Argument Is War, suggests that we do not just *talk* about arguments as if they were wars, we *behave* as if they were; we try to *win* them:

Argument Is War
Your claims are *indefensible.*
He *attacked every weak point* in my argument.
His criticisms were *right on target.*

I *demolished* his argument.
I've never *won* an argument with him.
You disagree? Okay, *shoot!*
If you use that *strategy,* he'll *wipe you out.*
He *shot down* all my arguments.

Likewise, the metaphor Musical Succession Is Physical Motion shapes the way we speak of musical motion. In fact, the mapping is remarkably complete. It is hard to imagine a term that describes physical motion that has not been, or could not be, applied to music:

Musical Succession Is Physical Motion
The D is a *passing* tone between C and E.
The last *passage pushes* toward a climax.
That part *went by* quickly.
Large *leaps* should be balanced by *steps* . . .
This part *moves* in *running* sixteenth notes . . .
The *pace quickens* in the coda.

Just as we tend to anthropomorphize physical motions, we attribute purpose to musical motions:

That dissonance really *wants to* resolve.
It *achieves* a climax in measure 106.
The French horn *intrudes* . . .
The music *climbs* relentlessly . . .

One way in which we commonly anthropomorphize musical motions is to call them "gestures," mapping musical succession onto intentional human motions. Chapter 6 discusses the rhythmic implications of thinking of music in terms of gesture.

The metaphor of musical motion goes beyond shaping the way we talk about music to shape our musical experience; we not only think *about* music but also think *in* music in terms of the metaphor Musical Succession Is Physical Motion. We not only talk about notes as passing tones, we experience them as traversing a path that connects points of departure and arrival. We not only talk about melodic leaps, we experience them as gathering energy, skipping over a more connected path, and landing somewhere. Furthermore, we not only talk about the dissonance that wants to resolve, we also experience a desire for it to resolve.

TABLE 2.1. THE ABSTRACT HIERARCHICAL STRUCTURE
OF DURATIONAL NOTATION

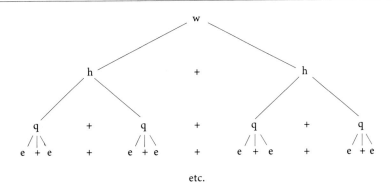

etc.

As Fred Maus ([1988] 1997) has pointed out, regardless of whether or
how we attribute agency to music, we may still experience it as purposeful action.

HIERARCHIES

I have already suggested that meaning is hierarchical. And I have defined "meaning" as something that our minds create when they group
things into patterned relations. This means that meanings themselves
can also be grouped into patterned relations to make higher-level meanings. In the example from *King Lear* mentioned above, lower-level meanings (such as connecting the name "Edward" to one of the characters or
seeing discrete points as a circle) can be grouped to make higher-level
meanings (such as understanding Edward's fate as following the path
of a circle).

Our minds seem particularly adept at (and even inclined toward)
forming hierarchies out of musical materials. Consider the symbols
used to represent durations in music. Table 2.1 shows that, in a measure
of $\frac{4}{4}$, a whole note is equal to two half notes, that a half note is equal to
two quarter notes, that a quarter note is equal to two eighth notes, and
so on.

Table 2.1 uses the "tree diagram" notation that is typically used to
depict hierarchies. However, some of the names given to the elements of

the hierarchy ("roots," "nodes," and "leaves") suggest that this picture is upside-down. The top level (here represented by a whole note) is called the "root." Each point at which the "tree" branches (here represented by each single note) is called a "node." The nodes at the bottom level (here represented by the eighth notes) are called the "leaves." (Actually, the "etc." suggests that there are other lower levels, so the eighth notes are not conceptually the leaves here.)

This hierarchy has a "whole-note level," a "half-note level," a "quarter-note level," and so on. Each level of this hierarchy is generated by following the same rules; each level may be thought of as grouping the level below it or dividing the level above it, and each note value represents twice the duration of some shorter value or half the duration of some longer value. (In order to represent groupings or divisions in threes and other numbers, our system of notation may use dotted notes or tuplets.) Table 2.1 thus describes the hierarchical relationship that exists between the *durations* represented by the symbols it depicts.

Table 2.1 may also be taken as a description of $\frac{4}{4}$ *meter*. Each level shows a whole measure worth of durations in $\frac{4}{4}$. The duple relationship between each adjacent level of Example 2.10 is implied by the meter signature for $\frac{4}{4}$, and many pieces in $\frac{4}{4}$ articulate these levels in various ways. One such passage is given in Example 2.9.

In J. S. Bach's Prelude in C minor, both hands (at the "surface" of the musical notation) articulate the level of the sixteenth note (see Example 2.9f). Changes in direction (clearer in the left hand) usually articulate the level of the eighth note (see Example 2.9e). The entrance of new chord tones may also be understood in relation to the level of the eighth note (see Example 2.9d). The pattern of chord tones and neighbor notes (which repeats every four sixteenth notes) articulates the level of the quarter note (see Example 2.9c). In the first measure, the appearance of the pitch class C in the right hand (which reappears every four sixteenth notes) could also be said to articulate the level of the quarter note (again see Example 2.9c). The exact repetition of each half bar articulates the level of the half note (see Example 2.9b). And the change of chord every bar articulates the level of the whole note (see Example 2.9a).

Musical form is often described in hierarchical terms. Sub-phrases may combine to form phrases, which may combine to form periods,

EXAMPLE 2.9. J. S. Bach's Prelude in C minor (from the *Well-Tempered Clavier,* Book 1) illustrates the articulation of metric levels.

which may combine to form subsections, which may combine to form sections, and so on.

Other musical elements may create hierarchical structures, too. For example, consider the relative stabilities of the degrees of the scale. Carol Krumhansl (Krumhansl 1990, 1995; Krumhansl and Kessler 1982) has done experiments in which listeners judge how well each different scale degree fits in a given context. In one of those experiments, listeners heard a bit of music that established a particular key. They then heard a single tone (called the "probe tone") and were asked to rate how well it fit that key. Graph 2.1 shows the average listener rating for each scale degree – the "probe-tone profile" (here, in the key of C major).

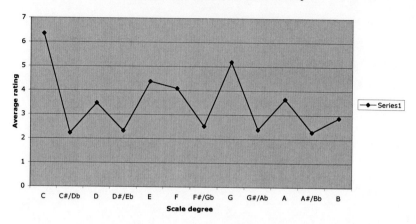

GRAPH 2.1. Krumhansl's probe-tone profile for C major.

Following Deutsch and Feroe's (1981) observations concerning the hierarchical relationships between the pitch collections they call "alphabets," Fred Lerdahl (1988, 2001) describes a "tonal pitch space" in which the degrees of the scale form a hierarchy that reflects Krumhansl's results: the twelve-note chromatic scale includes the seven-note diatonic scale, the diatonic scale includes the tonic triad, the tonic triad contains the tonic-dominant "frame," and the tonic-dominant frame includes the tonic pitch. Each of these is an "alphabet" as Deutsch and Feroe (1981) define that term (alphabets are defined and discussed in greater detail in chapter 5). Table 2.2 shows Lerdahl's (2001) basic pitch space for C major. The level of embedding of any pitch reflects the stability judgments reported by Krumhansl. Similar hierarchies have been described for the relative stabilities of different chords within a key or different tonal regions (key areas) within a piece.

The hierarchies described so far can be divided into two categories: synchronic and diachronic. A synchronic hierarchy is an ordering of elements with respect to some inherent quality rather than with respect to the time of a piece within which they occur. The relative lengths of durational symbols and the relative stabilities of scale degrees are two

TABLE 2.2. LERDAHL'S (2001) BASIC PITCH SPACE FOR C MAJOR

C												C
C		E		G				C				
C	D	E	F	G	A	B	C					
C	C♯	D	E♭	E	F	F♯	G	A♭	A	B♭	B	C

examples of synchronic hierarchies. These relative lengths and relative stabilities are presumed to be independent of the pieces in which they might occur. Jamshed Bharucha (1984b) calls synchronic hierarchies "tonal hierarchies." A diachronic hierarchy is an ordering of elements with respect to the time of a piece within which they occur. A description of the form of a piece in terms of nested sections and subsections is one example of a diachronic hierarchy. The analysis of Bach's Prelude in C minor in Example 2.9 is another. Bharucha (1984b) calls diachronic hierarchies "event hierarchies."

Hierarchies can also be distinguished in terms of how concrete the nodes are. In hierarchies of voters, where each level is made up of people, all the nodes are concrete. For example, the voters of the State of Oregon are a subset of all Oregonians (felons and minors are excluded), the Oregonian congressional delegates (representatives and senators) are a subset of Oregonian voters, and the Oregon senators are a subset of those delegates. Cohn and Dempster (1992) call hierarchies in which every node is concrete "robust." However, a biological classification of animals into categories such as "genus" and "species" has abstract nodes (only the leaves are concrete animals). Cohn and Dempster (1992) call hierarchies in which leaves are concrete and other nodes are abstract "inclusional."

Yet another way to characterize hierarchies is to ask if every level is a literal subset of the leaves. On the one hand, in a business organization, janitors may make up one level, while secretaries, managers, and CEOs make up other levels. In such a business-organization hierarchy, each person typically appears at only one node; thus no level is a literal subset of another level. On the other hand, in the hierarchy of Oregon voters mentioned above, every member of a given level of the hierarchy

EXAMPLE 2.10. Schenkerian analysis describes a passage of music as
an elaboration of an elaboration.

is present in the larger level that contains it; every level is a literal subset
of the levels closer to the leaves.

Heinrich Schenker ([1935] 1979) described music in terms of hierarchies of elaboration, embellishment, or ornamentation (Larson
1997c). Because the terms "embellishment" and "ornamentation" suggest something "extra" that is not central to meaning, I prefer the term
"elaboration." Schenker's theories now provide the dominant paradigm
for understanding tonal music.[10] According to those theories, a passage
such as that given in Example 2.10e may be understood as an elaboration of the simpler pattern given in Example 2.10d, which, in turn, may
be understood as an elaboration of the pattern given in Example 2.10c.
Schenker's notation depicts these relationships with the stems and slurs
shown in Examples 2.10a and b. Schenker claimed that all passages of
tonal music can be understood as such elaborations of elaborations. The
word "prolongation" is often used in place of "elaboration"; thus we can
say that Schenker claimed that all passages of tonal music prolong simpler patterns.

A Schenkerian analysis is a diachronic event hierarchy. Each node
of a Schenkerian analysis is concrete in the sense that it is a musical note
of specific pitch and corresponds to a certain duration of the piece it
represents. However, each node in the higher levels of a Schenkerian

analysis is also more abstract than the leaves. In a Schenkerian "voice-leading graph," one note of the analysis may stand for many notes in the passage analyzed. That note *stands for* other notes – it is not *selected from* those notes. Thus a given level may not be regarded as a literal subset of the level closer to the leaves. For instance, in a trill on a quarter note D, the D stands for the whole trill (including a possible *Nachschlag*); no single D in the trill is the "real D" (and, of course, none of the D's in the trill is a quarter note). In fact, Schenkerian analyses often include "implied tones," notes that are not literally present in the passage analyzed. Two additional examples include substitution (in which a $\hat{7}^{11}$ at a level closer to the foreground may "stand for" a $\hat{2}$) and chromatic transformation (in which a diatonic pitch at a level closer to the background is represented in the surface of the music by a chromatic pitch). William Benjamin (1984) has written on this topic and offers a nice example of a harmony that is prolonged but nowhere literally present in the musical surface.

Schenker's ideas play an important role in this book. In this sense I follow in the footsteps of Peter Westergaard (1975), Lerdahl and Jackendoff (1983), and others, who have recast Schenker's theories as rule-driven systems designed to account for the experience of listeners. To better understand how those ideas apply here, we must first talk about association, prolongation, and structural hearing.

ASSOCIATION, PROLONGATION, AND STRUCTURAL HEARING IN HIERARCHIES

When two events may be related to each other, I call that an "association." Associations typically involve relations of *sameness, similarity,* or *successorship.* Remember that these events may be abstract events rather than events selected from the surface of a piece. An association may exist, for example, between different notes, between motives, or between rhythms within a piece. Some associations structure events hierarchically, but some do not. For example, timbral and motivic associations do not necessarily produce hierarchical structures. But the mere existence of an association does not necessarily guarantee that it will be perceived.

The act of *hearing* a passage of music *as* containing an association I call "associative hearing." Knowing intellectually that an association exists is thinking *about* music. Associative hearing is thinking *in* music.

Prolongation is thus also a particular kind of association: it is an association between events at different hierarchical levels. This suggests that *sameness, similarity,* or *successorship* must play a role in prolongation, too. This is because prolongation results from "transformations" that turn notes on one level into notes on another level. And those transformations, to be understood as such, create similarity by preserving sameness in some element and by introducing differences through operations on alphabets, operations that are based on sameness or successorship (operations and alphabets are discussed in chapter 5). The act of *hearing* a passage of music *as* containing a prolongation I call (after Salzer 1952) "structural hearing." Accordingly, Schenker's term *Fernhören* means global structural hearing. These terms suggest a fruitful way of refocusing debates concerning the relation of Schenkerian analysis to the experience of listeners. Leonard B. Meyer (1967, 96) has often stressed that local and global levels are heard quite differently. Candace Brower (1993) marshals evidence concerning differences between long- and short-term memory to underscore this point. Meyer's view is that although we may hear shorter phrases in terms of prolongation (say, as elaborated linear progressions like $\hat{3}$–$\hat{2}$–$\hat{1}$), we more readily hear longer pieces in terms of their "formal structure" (say, as a string of formal sections like ABA).

Meyer's and Brower's comments might be taken as a criticism of Schenker's theories – or, more specifically, as a denial of the perceptual significance of the *Ursatz*. (The *Ursatz,* or "fundamental structure," is the simplest pattern of pitches underlying a piece of tonal music, and it is always a descending stepwise pattern that ends on the tonic, harmonized with an "authentic cadence.") But the terms offered here suggest a reconciliation: we might more accurately say that prolongation exists at all structural levels of all tonal pieces but that structural hearing may not. Knowing intellectually that a prolongation exists is thinking *about* music. Structural hearing is thinking *in* music. Looking at structural hearing as a listening skill leads us to recognize that different listeners will hear different levels of prolongation. A fruitful avenue of investigation for a cognitive science of music would be to recognize the existence of prolongation at all levels and to explore the conditions that make structural hearing more or less difficult. Those conditions might include absolute duration, pacing (perhaps measured in terms of a harmonic rhythm or, better yet, an "event rhythm"), cadential support for rival tonics, key distance, number of levels, and the presence of supporting or conflicting timbral or motivic associations.

HIERARCHIES IN TONALITY VS. ATONALITY, AND CONSONANCE VS. DISSONANCE

Those features that lead listeners to lose track of a tonic in tonal music are the same ones that make it difficult to hear atonal music in a key (Larson 1987a). To clarify this, consider why we would want to call a piece of music "atonal."

To say that a piece is in a certain key is to say a great deal. But one thing we mean is that we expect that piece to end on a certain note. Key determination is thus a function of melodic continuation – which is, in turn, partly a function of musical forces and thus dependent upon prolongation (Larson 1993a). Music that never does what we expect may so frustrate our expectations that we give up expecting things – and thus give up determining a key. Atonal music, according to this view, lacks a key because it implies so many keys, gives conflicting clues, or changes keys so often that listeners give up choosing one.

Linking prolongation and key determination suggests that atonal music lacks global prolongation. But if we are to understand music that seems to deny key centers, we must understand what features are making structural hearing difficult. My aim here is not so much to address atonal music analysis as to suggest that the terms and concepts offered here can shed light on these interesting and difficult topics. Elsewhere (Larson 1997c; see also the responses by Lerdahl and Straus in the same issue) I have shown how the same terms and concepts can also clarify debates about consonance and dissonance – debates that have a centuries-long history (Palisca and Spender 1980; Cazden 1980; and Tenney 1988).

Having discussed pattern, meaning, analogy, metaphor, and hierarchy, and having suggested the value of these ideas to clarify central questions about the experience of music, I turn in the next chapter to the central metaphor that underlies musical forces – the metaphor of musical motion.

3

Something in the Way She Moves: The Metaphor of Musical Motion

Music *moves*. And something in the way it moves *moves* us. The relative ease with which we talk about musical motion might fool us into thinking that we know quite well what musical motion is. But do we? This chapter suggests how the theory of conceptual metaphor described in chapter 2 can explain important aspects of our experience and understanding of musical motion. As we shall see, the logic of certain metaphors shapes our understanding of musical motion and constrains the inferences we make in reasoning about such motion. These metaphors define *what* moves, the *way* it can move, and *where* it moves.

This chapter, coauthored by Mark Johnson,[1] argues that we acquire our basic embodied understanding of physical motion in four different ways and that these four basic experiences of physical motion give rise, via metaphor, to the chief ways in which we conceptualize and experience musical motion. It claims that our understanding of musical motion rests on metaphors, and that the key metaphors are grounded in these basic bodily experiences of physical motion.

This chapter focuses exclusively on the ways in which we utilize body-based conceptual metaphors to comprehend and reason about musical motion within "common-practice tonal music" (the Western-European music of Bach to Brahms and some contemporary jazz and popular musics). Chapter 14 returns to the question of how metaphors grounded on apparently universal aspects of bodily functioning might still give rise to cultural differences in the understanding of music, differences based on diverse cultural values, interests, and practices.

WHAT IS MUSICAL MOTION?

Let us begin with a familiar and attractive song by the Beatles. If we try to explain how the opening line of "Something" (Harrison 1969) captures the meaning and sound of the words "Something in the way she moves," we immediately encounter two metaphorical senses of motion, one related to pitch and the other to rhythm. First, the pitches move. Before the word "moves," every note is sung to the same pitch. When we reach "moves," the pitch *moves* (down from C to B). Second, the rhythm moves. It moves in the same way that speech rhythms do, so that accented words are musically accented. Moreover, the words that are the most important to the song's message ("something," "way," and "moves") are emphasized through agogic and metric accents. To better appreciate this, consider Example 3.1. If one sings each of the words with notes of equal duration, as in Example 3.1a, the result is stiff, unmusical, and at odds with the rhythms and accents of speech – it does not *flow*. Putting the main words on the main beats, as in Example 3.1b, is an improvement, because it produces a more speech-like prosody. But as set by the Beatles, as in Example 3.1c, it is even better. Each of these three notes receives a different kind of accent, and those differences create an overall shape that leads to the word "moves" ("Some-" is a downbeat; "way" is an anticipated long note; and "moves" is both, which gives it special emphasis). To appreciate the "motion quality" of this overall shape, sing this melody and stop "up in the air" on the word "way." Suspended on the long note "way," we feel a strong anticipation of movement to the next downbeat ("moves"), to complete both the musical and semantic sense of the passage. And by anticipating that downbeat, the melody draws us strongly to it. In these ways, the music reflects the meaning of the words. But notice that the musical meaning does not depend on the words. Even without the lyrics, we would still speak of the melody *moving* from C to B or of the rhythm *moving* ahead.

This one brief musical passage is enough to suggest two of the many senses of musical motion that we use all the time to think and to talk about our musical experience. But although our discourse about music is filled with such references to motion, the idea of musical motion is a

EXAMPLE 3.1. George Harrison, "Something," measures 1–2.

profound enigma. In a section entitled "The Paradox of Tonal Motion," Victor Zuckerkandl (1956) reminded us that we know almost nothing about melodic motion. He surveyed a number of received ideas we have about tonal motion and then showed that they appear to have little to do with our ordinary literal understanding of motion. A typical passage conveys just one of the many enigmas of melodic motion. Zuckerkandl asked whether tones move, and he answered:

> Actually, they stand still! In the *Marseillaise,* for example, we hear the first tone E – it does not move; then comes A, another static tone; this one is repeated; then comes B; and so on. No tone, as long as it sounds, moves from its place. What has happened to the motion? Motion is the process that *conveys* the thing from here to there, in a continuous and never suspended traversal of the interval. If it stops anywhere, the motion is instantly abolished. But in a melody we have nothing but this, nothing but stops, a stringing together of static tones, and, between tone and tone, *no* connection, *no* transition, *no* filling up of intervals, nothing. It is the exact opposite of motion. (83)

Many writers (such as Davies 1994; Ferguson 1960; and Todd 1999) have addressed the problem of musical motion, but we still lack a clear answer to the question posed by Zuckerkandl.

So the concepts of musical motion that all of us use unreflectively to describe our musical experience turn out, under scrutiny, to be anything but clear, literal, and unproblematic. Musical motion must be some kind of metaphorical motion that takes place within a metaphorical space. One purpose of this chapter is to explain the metaphoric structure and logic of such motion and to ask what this means for how we experience and understand music. Just as the Beatles emphasize, in turn, different words in the lyric "Something in the way she moves," we have begun with the observation that something in the music *moves*. We shall next consider the question of what the *something* is that moves and will go on to look at the *way* music moves.

CONCEPTUAL METAPHOR AND TEMPORAL MOTION

In order to analyze our metaphorical concepts of tonal motion, we must first understand our concepts of time, all of which are profoundly metaphoric. We typically conceptualize the "passing" of time metaphorically – as motion through space. Robert Morgan (1980) has noted the inseparability of musical space and musical time, and Philip Alperson (1980) notes that our experience of musical motion depends upon "the familiar habit of regarding the properties of time as analogous to those of space" (409). Alperson cites Henri Bergson's claim that

> we set our states of consciousness side by side in such a way as to perceive them simultaneously, no longer in one another, but alongside one another; in a word we project time into space, we express duration in terms of extensity, and succession thus takes the form of a continuous line or chain, the parts of which touch without penetrating one another. (409)

Recent research in cognitive linguistics has revealed the marvelously complicated internal structure of such Western metaphorical conceptions of time, and it explains how we reason about time based on these inescapable, yet mostly invisible, metaphors. What this research shows is that there are two basic spatialization metaphors for time, and, as we shall see, each has a relevant counterpart in our conception of musical time and motion.(The following abbreviated analysis of spatial metaphors for time is based on a larger analysis found in Lakoff and Johnson [1999].)

Consider, first, how we are conceptualizing time when we speak of it as "flying," "dragging," and "rushing by us," and when we say things like *"Easter will soon be here"* and *"Christmas has long since passed."* Here we understand temporal change as a particular kind of motion through space. There is a spatial schema in which an observer is facing in a fixed direction (*"facing the future"*), is situated at "the present" (the *"here and now"*), and times are conceptualized as objects moving toward and then past the stationary observer. Elements and structures of this spatial schema are mapped onto our understanding of time to form the Moving Times metaphor. In the following diagram of this mapping, spatial motion is the "source domain" from which structure and relations are projected (as indicated by the direction of the arrow) onto the "target domain" (here, temporal change) that we understand via the mapping:

The Moving Times Metaphor

Source Domain (Space)		Target Domain (Time)
Objects	——>	Times
Motion of Objects Past the Observer	——>	The "Passage" of Time
Location of the Observer	——>	The Present
Space in Front of the Observer	——>	The Future
Space Behind the Observer	——>	The Past

Examples: The time will *come* when typewriters are obsolete. The days of inexpensive housing are long *gone.* The time for action *has arrived.* The deadline is *fast approaching.* Thanksgiving will *be here* before we know it. Christmas is *coming,* the goose is getting fat. The summer *flew by.* The time for end-of-summer sales *has passed.*

Notice the tight internal logic of this metaphor. We imaginatively project fronts and backs onto moving objects, and we conceptualize moving objects as facing in the direction of their motion (e.g., the "front" of the bus "faces" in the direction of its typical forward motion). Via the mapping of times as moving objects, times thus face the observer toward which they are moving, as in: I can see the *face* of things to come. I can't *face* the future. Let's meet the future *head-on.*

Because the metaphorical motion of particular times is toward the observer, Time B can *precede* Time C and can *follow* Time A. This gives rise to expressions such as: In the weeks *following* next Tuesday, nothing is scheduled. During the week *preceding* next Tuesday, things will be impossibly hectic. Wednesday *follows* Tuesday. Thursday *comes after* Wednesday. The *preceding* announcement was brought to you by the Department of Redundancy Dept.

The second major metaphorical system for time involves a different spatial schema, one in which the observer moves across a landscape and times are points or regions on that landscape.

The Moving Observer Metaphor (or "Time's Landscape")

Source Domain (Space)		Target Domain (Time)
Locations on Observer's Path	$\longrightarrow$	Times
Motion of the Observer	$\longrightarrow$	"Passage" of Time
Distance Moved by Observer	$\longrightarrow$	Amount of Time "Passed"
Location of the Observer	$\longrightarrow$	The Present
Space in Front of the Observer	$\longrightarrow$	The Future
Space Behind the Observer	$\longrightarrow$	The Past

Examples: I fear trouble *up ahead*. There's going to be profit for us *down the road*. Will you be staying a *long* time or a *short* time? Let's spread the conference *over* two weeks. We're *coming up on* Christmas. He'll retire *within* two years. We're *halfway* through June already. We've *reached* the final week of the term.

The two vast metaphor systems, Moving Times and Moving Observer, define most of our spatialization of time. Notice that they are figure-ground reversals of each other. In the Moving Times metaphor, the times are the figure moving relative to the stationary observer (as ground), whereas in the Moving Observer metaphor, the observer is the figure moving relative to the time landscape (as ground). Although the logic of each of these two metaphors is different, they both are based on the fundamental conception of the passage of time as relative spatial motion.

These two spatial metaphors for time both play a central role in our understanding of musical motion, to which we now turn.

CONCEPTUAL METAPHOR AND MUSICAL MOTION

This chapter claims that people have no robust way of conceptualizing musical motion without metaphor and that all reasoning about musical motion and musical space inherits the internal logic of such metaphors. If this claim is correct, and if the source domain for musical motion is *motion in space,* then the ways we learn about space and physical motion should be crucial to how we experience and think about musical motion. To see this, consider four of the most important ways in which we experience and learn about motion:

We move our bodies.
We feel our bodies being moved by forces.
We use our bodies to set other objects in motion.
We see (or hear) objects move.

Notice that all these fundamental and pervasive experiences of motion are, for the most part, nonconceptual and prereflective, and yet they give rise to a large body of knowledge that we have about motion. For example, we experience objects and we experience ourselves moving from one point to another along some path, and so we develop our sense of *locomo-*tion (movement from one place [*locus*] to another). We experience moving objects changing speed through the application of physical forces. We know, in an immediate bodily way, what it feels like to be moved by something else, to move ourselves, and to move other objects. It is this source-domain knowledge of physical motion that is carried over into the target domain (musical motion) via systematic metaphoric mappings.

The central claim of this chapter is that these four basic experiences of physical motion give rise, via metaphor, to the chief ways in which we conceptualize musical motion. Moreover, because musical motion, like physical motion, occurs over time, our two different metaphorical conceptualizations of time (Moving Times and Time's Landscape) are incorporated into the basic metaphors of musical motion. This chapter examines each of these four types of experience of motion, along with the metaphors based on them.

THE MOVING MUSIC METAPHOR

"*Here comes* the recapitulation," "The strings *slow down* now," and "The music *goes faster* here." In this way we describe the metaphorical motion of a musical event as moving toward and then past us. According to this orientation, which incorporates the Moving Times metaphor, a musical event is conceptualized as an object that moves past the stationary hearer from front to back. A future musical event – something that's "coming" in a piece of music we are listening to – exists in a musical space in front of the hearer and moves toward the hearer. When it reaches the stationary observer it is experienced (heard), because it now exists in the present moment. Once the musical event has occurred for us, it exists only in memory in the past, that is, in the metaphorical space behind the observer.

Because music is both a temporal and a tonal art, the Moving Music metaphor is a complex set of mappings that combines a notion of physical contours of motion with the Moving Times metaphor, as follows:

The Moving Music Metaphor

Source (Physical Motion)		Target (Music)
Physical Object	———>	Musical Event
Physical Motion	———>	Musical Motion
Speed of Motion	———>	Tempo
Location of Observer	———>	Present Musical Event
Objects in Front of Observer	———>	Future Musical Events
Objects Behind Observer	———>	Past Musical Events
Path of Motion	———>	Musical Passage
Starting/Ending Point of Motion	———>	Beginning/End of Passage
Temporary Cessation of Motion	———>	Rest, Caesura
Motion over Same Path Again	———>	Recapitulation, Repeat
Physical Forces	———>	"Musical Forces"

This mapping defines one of our most influential and pervasive ways of thinking in and thinking about musical motion, as we import some of the logical entailments of the source domain into our experience of the target domain. Thus the metaphorical logic of musical motion is based upon the spatial logic of physical motion. To test this claim, we shall consider three of the most important kinds of inferences we draw about physical motion: (1) that motion requires an *object* that moves, (2) that motion will take place along a *path*, and (3) that motion will have a *manner*. We then ask how those same structures of reasoning are present in our understanding of musical motion.

The analysis that follows explores how our experience and understanding of musical motion relies on our more basic experience and understanding of physical motion. The analysis begins with a relatively simple view of physical motion. Of course, a similar analysis could explore our concepts of physical motion and space. For example, Eric Pedersen and colleagues (1998) argue that some concepts of space and orientation that we might expect to be universal are, in fact, culturally shaped in that they systematically reflect the structures of that culture's language. Such an exploration would further illuminate the ways in which metaphor shapes all our abstract concepts. But such an analysis lies beyond the scope of this chapter.

First, physical motion requires an *object* that moves. Having observed that music *moves,* we turn now to the *something* in the music that moves. The logic of physical motion (here, the fact that there must be something that moves) generates a corresponding question about music, namely, what is it that "moves" in music? This is a deeply perplexing and, in fact, misleading question. When we speak of music in terms of the Moving Music metaphor, we mean that our experience of a bit of music shares something with our experience of seeing objects move in physical space. It is the metaphor that leads us to speak as if there must be musical objects. Notice that we do the same thing in the Moving Times metaphor, according to which we conceptualize times as moving objects, even though times are not objects in any physical sense.

Second, moving objects trace out an imaginary *path* of motion. In music, segments of a musical path are thus called "passages."

Third, physical motion will have a *manner.* There will thus be something in the *way* the music moves. Objects can move quickly or slowly, abruptly or smoothly, forcefully or gently. Via the Moving Music metaphor, then, this same logic carries over into our understanding of the music as moving at some speed. That metaphorical speed is the *tempo.* We describe music as *fast* or *slow.* The *manner* of the motion is marked by words like "creep," "crawl," "rush," "fly," "slow down," "speed up," "walk," "float," "stumble," and so on. The music can proceed *by steps,* or it can make *leaps* of various lengths. Virtually any concept of a particular manner of physical motion can be applied to music.

Notice that the word "way" is polysemous – it has multiple related meanings. "Way" can mean the literal *path* one takes to a destination (as in, "The Roman legions marched along the Appian *Way*"). It can also mean the *manner* (metaphorically understood) in which something is done (as in, "Play the piece this *way,* with vibrato"). Or it can mean the metaphorical path one takes to achieve an end (as in, "That's the best *way* to solve this equation"). So, when we say, for example, "The tune *goes this way,*" the "way" is the metaphorical path the music takes.

THE MUSICAL LANDSCAPE METAPHOR

A different basic experience of physical motion is the motion of our bodies through a spatial landscape. We have the experience of moving from a starting point through a series of intermediate steps to a destination. Such experiences are the basis for a second major conception of a musical work, as an extended three-dimensional landscape through which the hearer moves. The listener takes a journey over the path that defines the particular piece of music being heard. Just as in the Time's Landscape metaphor, the present moment is wherever the moving observer is; likewise, in the musical landscape, the present moment is where the listener is at a particular point along his or her journey. In other words, *where* the musical traveler is in the musical landscape is *what* the listener hears at that moment. Consequently, what has already been heard is conceptualized as points in the landscape that are behind the listener-traveler, whereas parts of the music not yet heard are future points on the path that one will encounter later. This explains expressions such as the following: We're *coming to* the coda. When we *get to* measure 57 we'll see how the dissonance is resolved. Let's see, *where are we* in the second movement? The melody *rises up ahead*. At measure 4 the horns *enter*. Once you *reach* the refrain, the dissonant part is *behind* you. We're *going faster here* (said in reference to a point in the score). Two voices *start*, but soon a third *enters (joins in)*. The soloist is waiting to *come in* seven measures *from here*.

Musical events are locations on a musical landscape, according to the following conceptual mapping:

The Musical Landscape Metaphor

Physical Space (Source)		Musical Space (Target)
Traveler	——>	Listener
Path Traversed	——>	Musical Work
Traveler's Present Location	——>	Present Musical Event
Path Already Traveled	——>	Music Already Heard
Path in Front of Traveler	——>	Music Not Yet Heard
Segments of the Path	——>	Elements of Musical Form
Speed of Traveler's Motion	——>	Tempo

TWO PERSPECTIVES: PARTICIPANT AND OBSERVER

One can take two perspectives on the musical landscape: that of the participant and that of the observer. In the "participant perspective" you, the listener, are moving over the musical landscape. As the listener, you are metaphorically *in* the piece; that is, you are traveling over the path that defines a particular musical piece, and you are actually hearing it (either in a live performance or on a recording). Imagine yourself, for example, listening to a Mozart string quartet and saying, "The cello comes in right *here!*" (where the word "here" is uttered just as the cello enters). The "here" is the place on the musical landscape where you are at the present moment. Notice also the strong tendency many people have to use a pointing gesture to accompany their uttering of the word "here," indicating the exact "location" at which the cello enters.

As you, the hearer, move through a musical space, you can stand in various spatial relations to different musical events (as locations) and you can notice various things along your journey. You can *approach* the refrain, *come to* a resolution, *look ahead* to measure 21, *pass* the dissonant part, and *see* where the melody stops.

Within this landscape framework, repetition is tracing out the same trajectory of motion again. In music one can repeat the same path of motion, but always *at a different time* from the original musical event. However, the experience of tracing the *same* musical path over again is so powerful that it can actually make you feel as though you are experiencing the *same time* over again. Such metaphorically understood experiences are not limited only to music. We say, for example, "Oh no, it's Monday again" or "Here comes the weekend again!" with the sense that there is something about Monday (or the weekend) that is experienced as *the same* every time it occurs. In music this effect appears to be even stronger. Some of the most striking effects in music come from its ability to make us feel as though we are experiencing the *same time* over again, as though we are "back home" (and back *now*) again. The film *Peggy Sue Got Married* (Coppola 1986) draws powerfully on this desire we have to live through certain moments and experiences one more time – to be able to return to what happened before and to relive it. In music, when you hear a certain motif once again, it may not merely be that something that occurred before is returning at a different time. Rather, you may feel that the *same time* is returning.

The second perspective on the musical landscape is an "observer perspective." Whereas the participant perspective arises from our experiences of the motion of our own bodies, the observer perspective arises from the experience of seeing other objects move. The observer perspective is conceived as a distant standpoint from which we can observe the path through a musical landscape that defines a particular work. Whereas the participant perspective seems more natural for the performer, the observer perspective seems more natural for the listener. The observer perspective is the one utilized most often by musicians who are analyzing a score. The score is one metaphorical representation of the imaginary path through an abstract musical space. Every expression that can be used when speaking from the participant perspective can also be used from the observer perspective, just as observers are traveling the musical journey in their imagination (in an imaginary space). The advantage that the allegedly "objective" observer perspective supplies is that one can see the entire musical piece at once, since it is an abstract object that can be viewed from afar. By contrast, from the participant perspective you ordinarily cannot see everything that is up ahead, because, according to the logic of the Musical Landscape metaphor, from a particular standpoint within the music, you may not be able to see the entire path ahead.

The observer perspective on the Musical Landscape is typically the preferred metaphor for music analysis, because it allows one to treat the entire musical work as an abstract object and to study its features. Those features can supposedly be measured, analyzed, and looked at from various perspectives – precisely what the "objective" music theorist is regarded as doing. Performers, listeners, and analysts, however, may all use different perspectives at different times.

We have argued that it is primarily our experience of seeing objects move that gives rise to the Moving Music metaphor and that it is primarily our experience of moving our own bodies from one place to another that gives rise to the Musical Landscape metaphor. Our central

EXAMPLE 3.2. George Harrison, "Something," measures 1–4.

claim has been that it is the specific spatial logic of each particular source domain that controls the entailments of our metaphors of musical motion. For example, when music is viewed as a moving object, its status as metaphorical object gives it an aura of permanence. Also, taking the participant perspective within the Musical Landscape introduces strong notions of intentional action within a piece of music. The music can "strive," "seek," "want to resolve," "push ahead," and so forth.

MOTION AND FORCES

Another important entailment shared by both of the central metaphors we have discussed so far is that motions are shaped by forces. Whether we are experiencing the physical motion of our bodies or of other objects, we learn that the motion is influenced by physical forces such as gravity, magnetism, and inertia. A central argument of this book is that musical motion is shaped by analogous "musical forces." Each of these metaphorical forces is discussed in detail in the following chapters, but a foretaste here will illustrate their connection with motion and expressive meaning.

When different physical forces act on a physical object, they may pull it in different directions. The same is true of musical forces. But at one point in the "Something," they all agree in a way that elegantly illustrates the meaning of the text "attracts me like no other lover." The line "Something in the way she moves" (Example 3.2a, beginning) may be heard as an elaboration of the simpler, whole-note melody given in Example 3.2b (that is, a C–B that begins a descending motion in half steps).

Musical inertia, the tendency of a pattern to continue in the *same* fashion, suggests that, after B♭, this whole-note motion will continue descending in half steps, as in Example 2b (that is, C–B–B♭–A). Melodic gravity, the tendency of a melody to *descend,* suggests that this whole-note motion will continue by going down. And melodic magnetism, the tendency of an unstable pitch to resolve to the *closest* stable pitch, suggests that B♭ will resolve to A. Thus all three of these musical forces here reinforce one another to powerfully embody the meaning of the text they set.

THE MUSIC AS MOVING FORCE METAPHOR

Yet another way in which we experience physical motion is when physical substances and entities such as wind, water, and large objects move us from one point to another. In music, the metaphorical force is the music itself, moving the hearer from one metaphorical location (state) to another (different state). If music is a force, then it has causal effects. This idea of music as a force is thus a special case, via metaphorical extension, of what Lakoff and Johnson (1999) have called the Location Event Structure metaphor. According to the metaphor, States Are Locations; that is, they are metaphorical places that an entity can be *in* or *at,* as when we say, "She was *in* a coma for three months" and "Jack is head over heals *in* love." Change of state is movement from one state-location to a different state-location, as in, "The water *went from* hot *to* cold in five minutes," where the states of being *hot* or *cold* are metaphorical locations, and the water is hot when it occupies the *hot* state-location and cold when it "moves" into the *cold* state-location. Causes of change are then metaphorical forces that move an entity from one location to another, as in "He *fell into* a depression, but therapy *brought him out* of it," "The psychological pressure *drove me to* drink," "Their taunting *pushed me over the edge,*" and "I was *forced* to go in a *different direction* with my life." In short, States Are Locations, Causes Are Physical Forces, and Causation Is Forced Motion (from one state-location to another).[2]

The Music As Moving Force Metaphor

Source (Physical Motion)		Target (Musical Experience)
Locations	——>	Emotional States
Movement (from Place to Place)	——>	Change of Emotional State
Physical Forces	——>	Causes
Forced Movement	——>	Causation
Intensity of Force	——>	Intensity of Musical Impact

Based on this generic metaphor for causation, music is conceived as a force acting on listeners to move them from one state-location to another along some path of metaphorical motion. You can actually feel yourself being *pushed, pulled,* and generally *moved* by the music. When music is a *moving* experience, it can *bowl you over, blow you away, carry you along, transport you, give you a lift,* and *take you on a roller coaster ride.* It can make you *float along* or it can *drag you down.* When the music *swings,* you *swing.* "Something in the way she moves, attracts me like no other lover," can be as much about music as it is about love.

So when we say that music moves and that music moves us, we do more than make a pun. This is another important instance of polysemy. Just as we noted above that "way" has multiple metaphorically related senses, so, too, does "move" in its application to musical experience. The Music As Moving Force metaphor helps to explain why we use the word "move" to mean these different, but related, things.

OTHER METONYMIES AND METAPHORS FOR MUSICAL MOTION

The four major ways of experiencing physical motion listed above, upon which our most important metaphors for musical motion are built, clearly do not exhaust our experience, knowledge, and conceptualization of motion. A comprehensive account would need to include additional metaphors and metonymies based on additional ways that we experience motion and causation. Here are some additional metaphors that would need to be investigated as part of an exhaustive analysis. For example, the Musical Landscape metaphor emphasizes only *movement over a landscape.* It does not focus explicitly on the *cause* of the motion. As with physical motion, I can either *move myself* (purposefully) over and through a landscape, or else I can *be moved* by forces beyond my control. These two different sources of motion will thus produce two different metaphoric scenarios, one in which *I move* over the landscape and the other in which *I am moved* over the landscape. Thus the Music As Moving Force metaphor might actually be treated as one partial set of sub-mappings of the Musical Landscape metaphor. We have included it as a separate metaphor system because of the way that it shows the embodied grounding in physical motion and also because it plays such a central role in our experience of music.

Other extensions and variations are possible, too. Consider the way that the metaphoric scenario in which I move through the musical land-scape can be combined with the basic metonymy, The Performer Is The Music Performed. The performer then creates the musical path as he or she moves. We can thus say to a performer, who is metonymically identified with the music she makes, "You *speed up* and *go higher,* just when he *slows down* and *goes lower,*" "You've got to *swing* in the second movement," and "This is where *you take over.*" Other extensions are also possible. Via the Instrument For The Performer metonymy, we can say "*the horns rushed at measure 34,*" "*the violins were sluggish,*" and "*the drums got lost.*"

Another extremely important dimension, which we have only touched upon here, involves our metaphorical conception of musical agency. In those metaphors where there is an agent who moves or is moved, such as in the Musical Landscape metaphor, we can attribute *in-tentions* and *purposes* to the agent, and thereby to the music. We will then experience and understand music as purposive in various ways – as "*going somewhere,*" "*trying to resolve,*" "*overcoming an obstacle,*" or "*wanting to move to the dominant.*" Such purposive agency has been much discussed.[3]

Writers on expressive meaning in music have long observed the rela-tionship between motion, emotion, and purpose. Davies (1994, 229–230) surveyed several sources that describe music in such terms, tying our experience of musical motion to our experience of physical motion at more than one level. He noted that "musical movement invites attention to expressiveness because, like human action and behavior (and unlike random process), it displays order and purposiveness" (229). This talk of musical movement as teleological brings into play – inevitably – the metaphor of musical forces: "Usually musical movement is heard as tele-ological, as organized around a target that exercises a 'gravitational pull' on other notes" (236–237). Our entire notion of agency is metaphorically shaped, and we cannot understand musical agency apart from one or more conceptual metaphors for event structure and causation.

IS MUSICAL MOTION REAL?

If most of what we can think and say about musical time and musical motion depends on metaphor and metonymy, then it might seem that there is no such thing as musical motion! Maybe it is just a fiction and a mere manner of speaking about music (Scruton 1997). Yet, we do seem to *experience* movement in music. So, is it real?

Eric Clarke observes that music can give us clues about the motion of "fictional" or "virtual" sources. He argues that "the sense of motion and gesture in music is a straightforwardly perceptual phenomenon, and that the process by which auditory information specifies motion in music is, broadly speaking, the same as the process by which motion is specified in everyday circumstances" (2005, 89). Although he claims that the experience of musical motion "is truly perceptual rather than metaphorical, symbolic, or analogical" (2005, 74), we believe that a close reading of his paper (and of Gjerdingen's 1994 discussion of "apparent motion"), rather than contradicting the arguments presented here, provides additional support for our argument.[4]

Our answer to the question "Is musical motion real?" is that musical motion is just as real as temporal motion, and just as completely defined by metaphor. Music *moves*. We *experience* musical events as fast or slow, rising or falling, creeping or leaping, pausing and stopping. The reason that musical motion is "real" is that, as Eduard Hanslick ([1891] 1986) said more than 150 years ago, music exists only in our "aural imagina-tion" – that is, only as experienced by us. Music is not the notes on the scores. Nor is it merely the vibrations of air that we hear as sounds. It is, rather, our whole vast rich experience of sounds synthesized by us into meaningful patterns that extend over time. This experience of musical motion is no less real for being a product of human imagination – which is our profound capacity to experience ordered, meaningful patterns of sensations. If there were no people like us, with bodies and brains like ours, then there would be no musical time and no musical motion. Music "exists" at the intersection of organized sounds with our sensory-motor apparatus, our bodies, our brains, our cultural values and practices, our music-historical conventions, our prior experiences, and a host of other social and cultural factors. Consequently musical motion is really experienced by us, albeit via our imaginative structuring of sounds.

On the basis of the kinds of analyses and evidence given above, how strong a conclusion can we draw about the constitutive role of metaphor in our experience and understanding? The safer, although still controversial, claim is that our understanding and conceptualization of musical experience, and therefore our thinking about music, are in large measure irreducibly structured by deep conceptual metaphors. There appears to be a compelling body of empirical evidence for the correctness of this claim, some of which we have examined here.

However, this book makes the even stronger, more polemical, claim that our thinking in music – our very *experience* of musical meaning – is fundamentally shaped by conceptual metaphors that are grounded in our bodily experience. There can be no robust experience of musical meaning without these conceptual metaphorical framings and their spatial and bodily logics. We cannot clearly separate our understanding and conceptualization of music from our experience of it. We do not merely experience a musical work and *then* understand it. There is not experience first, followed by our grasp of the meaning of that experience. Rather, our understanding is woven into the fabric of our experience. Our understanding is our way of being in and making sense of our experience. Thus the way we *experience* a piece of music will depend importantly on how we *understand* it, and our understanding is intimately tied to our embodiment – that is, to our sensory-motor capacities and to our emotional makeup. For example, we do not just listen to a musical passage that moves and then say "Hey, that piece really moves, and, by the way, I can see a similarity between the way the music moves and what happens when a person or object moves." If there were no physical motion, it is difficult to imagine how there could even *be* musical motion. It appears that we can experience musical motion only because of our embodied experience and our embodied understanding of physical motion.

THE PLURALISTIC ONTOLOGY OF MUSICAL MOTION

Another persistent worry surrounding the idea that conceptual meta-phors can be constitutive of our experience stems from the fact that typically there are multiple inconsistent (or even mutually exclusive) metaphors for any given phenomenon. In the Moving Music metaphor, for example, music moves and the perceiver is stationary, whereas in the Musical Landscape metaphor the musical landscape is stationary and the perceiver moves over and through it. In the first case musical events are *objects* that move, whereas in the second case they are *locations* on a musical landscape (and thus do not move). Consequently we have two different and mutually exclusive ontologies underlying these two differ-ent metaphors.

To some people, this incompatibility among various metaphori-cal structurings of our basic concepts for musical motion will be taken as evidence that the metaphors cannot really be constitutive and must rather be nothing but figures of speech.

On the contrary, we should begin by noting that what is true of musical motion is equally true of our incompatible conceptions of time and, generally, our inconsistent conceptions of a vast range of abstract concepts, including causation, morality, mind, self, love, ideas, thought, and knowledge. The claim of conceptual metaphor theory is that each of these different, and often inconsistent, metaphorical structurings of a concept gives us the different logics that we need to understand the rich-ness and complexity of our experience. However strong our desire for a monolithic, consistent ontology might be, the evidence does not support such a unified and simple view of human experience. The absence of any core literal concept of musical "events" should direct our attention to the ways in which we imaginatively conceive of the flow of our musical expe-rience by means of multiple metaphors that provide the relevant logics of our various conceptions of musical motion and space. There is no more a single, univocal notion of musical motion than there is of causation, and yet we have survived reasonably well by knowing when a specific metaphor for causation is appropriate for a specific context of inquiry.

The fact of multiple inconsistent metaphors for a single concept also sheds light on the important question of cultural difference and variation. The grounding of metaphors in bodily experience suggests possible universal structures (of bodily perception and movement) for understanding music. However, because there are multiple metaphors available, and because there may be differing cultural interpretations of bodily experience, metaphor provides one important avenue for exploring cultural and historical variation in significantly different conceptions of musical experience that might arise around the world.

THE PRIMACY OF MUSICAL MEANING

We would like to end by highlighting one important insight that comes from an examination of the role of metaphor in our understanding and experience of music, namely, that the mechanisms of human meaning extend far beyond the capacity for language. Philosophical reflection on music has often assumed that music is some kind of "language." There is a strong tendency among philosophers and music theorists to think that our "primary" experience of meaning is in language, so that whatever meaning music has must be measured against linguistic meaning. Moreover, these same theorists often adopt false views of linguistic meaning as tied solely to reference and to truth conditions. When music seems not to measure up to such mistaken referential criteria of linguistic meaning, it is then erroneously concluded that music is a second-class citizen of the intellectual world.

The problem here lies not so much in the idea of music as language but rather in overly narrow and restricted views of linguistic meaning as involving objective reference that is alleged to be completely independent of the nature of our bodies (see also Hatten 1994, chap. 10, esp. 247–257). What is left out are the embodied and affective dimensions of linguistic and musical meaning alike. Music is meaningful in specific ways that some language cannot be, but it shares in the general embodiment of meaning that underlies *all* forms of symbolic expression, including gesture, body language, ritual, spoken words, visual communication, and so on. Thinking about how music moves us is not going to explain everything we need to know about language, but it is an excellent place to begin to understand how all meaning emerges in the flesh, blood, and bone of our embodied experience.

EXAMPLE 3.3. George Harrison, "Something,"
last phrase with concluding guitar gesture.

This brings us back, finally, to where we began – with music of the Beatles. We have already admired some of their text painting and its relation to musical motion. We conclude this chapter by examining another piece of text painting that emphasizes the embodiment of musical meaning. The passage of music in Example 3.3 resembles a common musical pattern known as a "sentence."

In a sentence, a short bit of music ("I don't want to leave her now") is followed by a similar short bit of music ("You know I believe, and how"), which is then typically completed, and answered, by a longer, balancing unit. But here the balancing unit is stated by the guitar, not the voice. We expect a balancing unit of text to answer the two lines of text. In fact, we might expect words that will tell us, finally, what that "something in the way she moves" actually *is* that "attracts me like no other lover." By giving us that balancing unit only in the guitar, without words, the Beatles seem to be saying that, in the end, only music can say what needs to be said.[5] When the guitar "has the final word," its melodic line not only retraces the path of what has gone before (the essential pitches of the guitar line, A–B♭–B♮–C, reverse the essential pitches of the opening lines of text; see the whole notes in Example 3.2), but it also leads us back to the beginning of the piece. Where the text leaves off, embodied musical meaning answers.

4

Melodic Forces: Gravity, Magnetism, and Inertia

The metaphor Musical Succession Is Physical Motion, discussed in the previous chapter, suggests that an important entailment of that metaphor is the idea that musical motion is shaped by analogues of physical forces – melodic gravity, melodic magnetism, and musical inertia. (As noted in the introduction, it is our intuitive embodied understanding of these forces that concerns us here, not the latest intellectual understanding of physicists.)

This chapter examines each of these musical forces, illustrates the effect of that force by comparing it to its analogous physical force, and, from that comparison, draws hypotheses concerning that force. The first phrase of "Twinkle, Twinkle, Little Star" (Example 4.1) helps to illustrate the effects of the musical forces. Because this phrase was cited in chapter 1 as an example of the "hallelujah figure," it provides an opportunity to return to questions posed there concerning the expressive meaning of that figure and to compare it to the expressive meaning of "Dido's Lament."

According to the view presented in chapter 3, the melody of "Twinkle, Twinkle, Little Star" is not just a succession of pitches but may be heard in terms of physical motion. Thus we talk about how that melody *goes*. We talk about *high* and *low* notes. We describe its motion in terms of *steps* and *leaps*. We experience it as tracing out a *path* (whether following an existing path or blazing a new one). And we feel that the melody is pushed and pulled by various forces. Even though music does not *literally* move, experienced listeners of tonal music hear that music *metaphorically* as purposeful physical action – subject to musical forces that are analogous to the physical forces that shape physical motion.

EXAMPLE 4.1. "Twinkle, Twinkle, Little Star," first phrase.

One could say that we do not directly experience physical forces. Rather, we experience the effects of forces – that is, we do not experience gravity but we experience its effects when we fall. Likewise, we do not directly experience musical gravity, but we experience its effects when we hear a melody as "falling."

MELODIC GRAVITY

Melodic gravity is the tendency of a note (heard as "above a stable position") to descend. In "Twinkle, Twinkle, Little Star," the first note (C) provides a base for subsequent melodic action. Every other note is heard as *above* that C. And if we pause on any of those other notes, we may feel that the unfinished melody is "up in the air." In other words, melodic gravity pulls all those other notes down.

Furthermore, the overall shape of this melody reflects motion within a gravitational field in a way that helps to explain the expressive meaning of the "hallelujah figure" in general and this specific melody in particular. This melody has a prototypical shape. A large ascending leap is balanced by descending steps, creating an arching path. (It is because that leap is to an alternation between the fifth and sixth scale degrees that it is an example of the "hallelujah figure.") As in an analogous physical motion, the energy of the large ascending leap is dissipated in the following descending steps. To me, this leap suggests a quality of ease because it leaps from the most stable platform (the tonic) to the next-most-stable degree of the scale (the fifth scale degree). That ease, combined with the energy associated with an ascending leap of this size, suggests a kind of athletic quality that is effortless and secure. The specific pitches used (the tonic and dominant may remind us of tympani announcements and bugle calls) also give the opening gesture the quality of a straightforward call to attention. And the simple repetition of each note in the melody gives the line a kind of simpleminded momentum that I associate with skipping motions expressive of unconcerned contentment. Others may hear different expressive meanings in this melody, but if they hear an up-and-down motion in this melody, then they will hear it as motion within a gravitational field.

In the same way, the overall shapes of the melody and the bass of "Dido's Lament" (Example 1.1) reflect motion within a gravitational field in a way that helps to explain the expressive meaning of the "lamento bass" in general and this specific melody in particular. The downward motion of the bass reflects the sadness of death by giving in to gravity; people feeling the weight of sadness are pulled down by it (this is why we speak of feeling *low,* being *depressed, down* in the dumps, or *weighed down* by concerns). The slow tempo and the gradual but constant bass descent by half step map easily onto an experience of being pulled slowly and inevitably downward. Although beginning each new repetition of this bass pattern requires an ascent (to get back up to its first note), the primary motion of each gesture is a drooping or sighing one that gives in to gravity.

Of course, both "Twinkle, Twinkle, Little Star" and the lamento bass (when repeated) include ascending leaps and descending steps (and any melody that starts and ends on the same pitch will necessarily have a global balance of ascent and descent). But it is the specific ways in which steps and leaps are used that make it easy for us to "tell a story" about how the motion of the music reflects the motions of bodies experiencing the emotions we associate with these musical passages. For example, "Twinkle, Twinkle, Little Star" begins with an athletic leap, foregrounding that interval, so that the descending steps feel like an effortless return to its starting point. At the same time the lamento bass leaps up only in order to begin again, so that its descending steps are felt as the primary concern of its path (and the ascending leap only a result of beginning again). Whereas "Twinkle, Twinkle, Little Star" floats back down to its stable starting point (the tonic scale degree), the lamento bass descends ponderously below the same starting point (as if descending into the earth).

My point here is not to give a complete account of the expressive meanings of these passages. But I do want to suggest that, if listeners make sense of musical motions by mapping them onto their own experience of physical motion, then musical gravity will play a role in the way they interpret melodic ascent and descent.

Musicians in Western musical culture have long described melody in terms of high and low, ascent and descent. Melodic gravity is reflected in rules of composition (for example, fourth-species counterpoint requires the downward resolution of suspensions). And some theorists have explicitly related this tendency to physical gravity (e.g., Hindemith 1945; Roth 1926; Schachter 1995; and Toch 1948). Gary Karpinski (2000, 47) appeals to melodic gravity and the theory of musical forces in his explanations of, and recommendations concerning, the acquisition of aural skills.

As just noted, an initial ascending leap followed by one or more descending steps is a common melodic archetype (and creates a common type of melodic arch) and is consistent with the notion of melodic gravity. Studies suggest that this archetype is widespread. Piet Vos and Jim Troost (1989) studied a sample of Western classical music and another sample of mainly Western folk music (including Albanian, Bulgarian, Iberian, Irish, Macedonian, Norwegian, and African American folk songs). They found that large melodic intervals are more likely to ascend and that small melodic intervals are more likely to descend.[1] David Huron's laboratory has replicated this result for Australian aboriginal music, Chinese folk songs, traditional Korean music, and Ojibway, Pondo, Venda, and Zulu songs. Huron's study of several thousand Germanic folk songs in major keys (analyzing more than a quarter-million pairs of tones) shows that descending steps are more common than ascending steps.

Huron (2006) reports that Curt Sachs (1962) noted the tendency of certain cultures to produce what Sachs called "tumbling" melodies, in which phrases typically begin with an ascending leap and continue with mostly descending steps, and that others have noted the same tendency in Russian laments (Mazo 1994), Australian aboriginal music

(Ellis 1969), and Lakota (Sioux) music (Densmore 1926). Huron notes the similarity of such melodic contours to the typical intonation curve of vocal utterances. He goes on to suggest that "since singing requires sustained control of pitch height, it is unlikely that the tumbling melodic phrase pattern originates in the loss of subglottal air pressure" (77). This book does not take a position on the *origin* of this widespread pattern, but it suggests that the *meanings* that listeners attribute to tumbling melodies may draw on both their resemblance to the intonation patterns of speech and their resemblance to the behavior of physical objects in motion – and that the widespread popularity of this pattern of upward leaps and downward steps is consistent with the idea of musical gravity.

Huron (2006) notes the tendency of melodies to combine upward leaps and downward steps but adds that "the reason for this asymmetry is not yet known" (92). In a footnote (389 n. 3), however, he observes that (in a number of different cultures) descending contours are even more common in lullabies than they are within the music of that culture as a whole. In his words:

> Since lullabies are intended to soothe infants and encourage sleep, the preponderance of descending pitch contours might have an innate tendency to reduce physiological arousal. If infants are frequently exposed to lullabies or lullaby-like stimuli, then they might develop a general expectation for descending intervals that continues to shape their listening as adults.

This raises the interesting question of why "descending pitch contours might have an innate tendency to reduce physiological arousal" and whether this tendency is responsible for lullaby contour or is reinforced by the association of lullaby contours with other soothing behaviors. Even if we are unable to determine which is cause and which is effect, it seems clear that we come to associate a reduction in tension with a giving in to musical gravity.

Another popular pattern for melodic phrases (at least within Western tonal music) is the "melodic arch" – an up-then-down motion like that of a ball thrown in the air. Huron had a computer classify a large collection of European folk-song phrases into nine types (ascending, descending, arch, upside-down-arch, horizontal, horizontal-ascending, horizontal-descending, ascending-horizontal, and descending-horizontal) and count the number of each. The computer found that the melodic arch was the most common type. Furthermore, the next most common types (ascending and descending) tended to pair so as to form a two-phrase melodic arch (that is, ascending shapes tend to be followed by descending ones) but not an upside-down-arch (that is, descending shapes exhibited no marked tendency to be followed by ascending shapes). In other words, as we would expect in light of musical gravity, we can say of melodies "that which goes up must come down" but not "that which goes down must come up." Huron also found that this principle applies on other levels of melodic structure: "if one represents each phrase by the average pitch-height of all the notes within the phrase, then whole melodies also tend to exhibit an arch contour" (2006, 86–88).

Huron reports that, in a reaction-time study, Bret Aarden (2003) observed that Western musicians were no faster at identifying descending vs. ascending intervals within the first halves of tonal phrases but that they were faster at identifying descending intervals than they were at identifying ascending intervals within the second halves of phrases. Huron takes this as evidence that experienced listeners of tonal music expect descending intervals in the second halves of phrases.

Some scholars writing on melodic expectation, however, have ignored, or have been openly skeptical about, melodic gravity. The bottom-up component of Narmour's (1990) implication-realization model does not distinguish between ascending and descending motion. Lerdahl suggests that "gravity appears to be dispensable" (2001, 191). Margulis (2003) does not include gravity in her model of melodic expectation. Bharucha (1996) finds no evidence of "a preference for downward anchoring" in his study of the exposition of the first movement of Mozart's Sonata in E♭ major, K. 282 (but he does note that this may be simply because the small number of cases he counted may have limited the statistical significance of his findings). Eitan (1997) found, however, that registral direction does affect melodic implications.

If we experience musical gravity as analogous to its physical counterpart, then our experience of physical gravity may suggest hypotheses that could flow from the theory of musical forces. Sometimes (for example, when perched atop a high, exposed, and somewhat rickety ladder, or when careening down a ski slope) gravity can have a powerful effect on us. It is constantly acting on us, on the objects we move, and on the objects we see moving. Yet much of the time we tend not to be aware of it (especially when our bodies, or the objects we experience, are in a low, stable position). It may seem that we feel its influence less directly and less powerfully than we feel the impact of some other forces. As a result, we are more likely to observe its influence on the global, rather than the local, trajectories of our bodies and other objects.

Thus we may hypothesize that musical gravity affects the "strength" of melodic pattern completion and the frequencies with which patterns appear in compositions, improvisations, and analyses of music; that its effect is often less striking than that of other forces; that its effect is more significant for notes heard as above a stable platform; and that its effect is clearer in global than in local trajectories. Part 2 of this book offers evidence consistent with each of these hypotheses.

MELODIC MAGNETISM

Melodic magnetism is the tendency of an unstable note to move to the closest stable pitch, a tendency that grows stronger as we get closer to that goal. In Example 4.2, if C and G are heard as stable pitches, then B♭ is more strongly attracted to C (two half steps away) than to G (three half steps away). And B is even more strongly attracted to C (one half step away) than B♭ is.

In "Twinkle, Twinkle, Little Star," the stable pitches (C, E, and G – the members of the tonic triad) seem to pull the other notes toward them. As F moves to E (on the words "how I wonder"), the melody may be heard as giving in to melodic magnetism because the E is the closest stable pitch (one half step away from F).

Thinking about melodic magnetism helps to explain the expressive meaning of the hallelujah figure and how that differs from the meaning of the melody and the lamento bass of "Dido's Lament." In "Twinkle, Twinkle, Little Star," the G is poised above the tonic; as a relatively stable pitch, the G provides a good starting point for a secure motion down to C. Instead of descending directly to the C, however, the G is first elaborated with its upper neighbor A. The motion from G to A (scale degrees $\hat{5}$–$\hat{6}$ may be heard as implying continued ascent (that is, it could give in to

EXAMPLE 4.2. Magnetic attraction depends
on distance.

inertia and go on to B and C), but when it returns to G, it feels as though
it gives in to gravity (by going *down* to G) and as though it gives in to
magnetism (because G is closer than the C above). Because it moves just
a step above the relatively stable platform of the G, it does not feel like a
"risky" motion within its gravitational field (compare it to the physical
motion of taking an easy step up and back from a very broad and stable
platform, which is not at all as risky as leaping to or from an unstable
place). Because it moves a whole step as it resolves within a space where
the competing magnetic attractor (the C above) is even farther away, the
resolution does not feel "compelled" the way a half-step resolution would
(compare this to the physical motion of dancing in a large open space).
And because $\hat{6}$ (in "Twinkle, Twinkle, Little Star" and in the hallelujah
figure generally) is made contextually stable (when it is harmonized by
a IV chord), it is also less constrained in its resolution to G. This gives
the motion an ease and security that is enhanced by the simple naiveté
of the repeated notes on each degree.

If you compare this melody to the same notes in minor (C–C–G–
G–A♭–A♭–G), then the impact of the musical forces is clearer. Moving
only a half step up and back is a motion that feels more "weighed down"
by gravity (the analogous physical motion – a smaller instead of larger
step up and back – is one that you would make when carrying a heavier
load). And the stronger magnetic pull of A♭ to G (scale degrees b$\hat{6}$–$\hat{5}$)
makes the motion feel more "compelled" (the analogous physical motion with magnets – moving them back and forth but over a smaller
distance – allows one to feel the pull more intensely). All descending
half-step resolutions share this quality of giving in to gravity and being
more intensely drawn by magnetism (and, of course, different musical
contexts will give different expressive meanings to that quality). As may
be seen in Example 4.3b, the lamento bass in "Dido's Lament" may be
thought of as a series of such descending half-step resolutions – thus the

EXAMPLE 4.3. Half-step magnetism in "Dido's Lament."

quality of being continually and inevitably drawn downward by this bass line is enhanced by half-step magnetism. Dido's melody also exploits descending half-step resolutions at more than one level of musical structure. The first few gestures of this melody end with half-step resolutions, and the last couple of gestures elaborate a larger-scale motion that has the same motion (scale degrees b6̂–5̂) discussed above.

Although different listeners may hear different expressive meanings in these melodies, the evidence presented in part 2 of this book suggests that they all hear similar magnetic pulls – and that the expressive meanings they hear are related to those pulls.

Melodic magnetism is reflected in rules of composition (for example, species counterpoint requires the stepwise resolution of all dissonances). Musicians have long talked about the tendency of certain notes to attract other notes, and they have often used metaphors (such as attraction, magnetism, pulling, yearning, and "leading tone") to describe those dynamic tendencies (Lerdahl 2001 offers examples).

Melodic magnetism favors melodic motion by smaller intervals, a tendency that plays an important role in recent literature on music cognition and melodic expectation. Although David Huron notes that his account of statistical regularities in music is "biased primarily toward Western art and folk melodies," it also draws on "music from a number of cultures, including Albanian, American, Bulgarian, Chinese, English, German, Hassidic, Iberian, Irish, Japanese, Macedonian, Norwegian, Ojibway, Pondo, Venda, Xhosa, and Zulu" (2006, 74). Huron goes on to note that,

> One of the best generalizations one can make about melodies is that they typically employ sequences of tones that are close to one another in pitch. This tendency to use small intervals has been observed over the decades by many researchers.

As examples of researchers who have noted this tendency, he cites Ortmann (1926), Merriam, Whinery, and Fred (1956), and Dowling (1967). Huron notes that this statistical regularity does not guarantee that listeners expect melodic intervals to be small, but he notes psychological experiments by Deutsch (1978), Boomsliter and Creel (1979), and Aarden (2003) that show that listeners make accurate judgments more rapidly when pitches are closer, which suggests that listeners do indeed expect melodic intervals to be small.

The following discussion of work by Toch, Narmour, Arnheim, Bharucha, Lerdahl, Margulis, and Brower clarifies the relationship between their work and the theory of musical forces, notes the different terms that these authors have used to describe melodic magnetism, and uses a discussion of terminology to lead us back to the source domain of physical magnetism in a way that generates further hypotheses concerning musical magnetism.

Toch (1948) speaks of "shaping forces" in music and uses (among others) the terms "gravity," "magnetism," and "inertia." It is not clear, however, if he would define these terms the same way that I do. Nor does he offer a quantitative model of their interaction.

Narmour's (1990, 1992) implication-realization model suggests that melodic continuations result from the interaction of "bottom-up" and "top-down" components. If magnetism is regarded as a property of the tonal system, then it would appear to belong to the top-down component of Narmour's model. However, tests of the bottom-up component of his model (Cuddy and Lunney 1995; Krumhansl 1995; and Schellenberg

1996, 1997) quantify "proximity" as a tendency to move to a proximate pitch – one that varies inversely with the distance – so that it also incorporates an element of melodic magnetism.

Arnheim (1986) uses the term "magnetism" but limits its application to attractions exerted by the tonic pitch. He does not suggest that the strength of magnetism depends upon distance nor does he quantify it in any way. (Nor does he mention inertia; his discussion is limited to magnetism and gravity.)

I define magnetism so that it describes the attraction of any unstable pitch to the closest stable pitch, and have argued (Larson 1997c) that prolongational structures of the type described by Schenker ([1935] 1979) determine which notes are stable. The algorithm used by my computer models (Larson, 1993a, 1994b, 1999a, 2004) to evaluate the interaction of musical forces represents magnetism as the difference between the inverse squares of the semitone distances between opposing attractors (chapter 13 discusses my computer models in greater detail).

Bharucha (1996) describes the sum of all forces acting on a given note in a given context as its "yearning vector." He describes this net force as an expectation, and explains it in terms of attention (modeled by neural-net activations) and the "anchoring" of dissonances. He does not specify what all the components of such a vector might be. But if those forces were gravity, magnetism, and inertia, then his yearning vector would be equivalent to the algorithm used by my computer models. His article, however, describes only one force – melodic magnetism (which he calls the "tonal force vector"). Like me, Bharucha quantifies the net magnetic pull on a note as the difference between the pulls of the closest stable note above and the closest stable note below that note, and asserts that the magnetic pull on a note from either attractor is inversely proportional to the distance between that note and its attractor. (Whereas Bharucha offers a *linear* function, my computer algorithms model this pull as inversely proportional to the *square* of that distance.) He also suggests that the magnetic pull on a note from either attractor is directly proportional to the activation (which, in his article, is equated with the stability) of its attractor.

Lerdahl (1996, 2001) also offers an algorithm for the interaction of musical forces. That algorithm (called the "tendency algorithm"), like

TABLE 4.1. PROXIMITY VALUES USED FOR CALCULATING MUSICAL
MAGNETISM IN MARGULIS'S (2003) MODEL OF MELODIC EXPECTATION

PITCH DISTANCE IN SEMITONES	PROXIMITY RATING
1	36
2	32
3	25
4	20
5	16
6	12
7	9
8	6
9	4
10	2
11	1
12	.25
13	.02
=14	.01

the algorithm used by my computer models, quantifies the interaction
of magnetism (which he calls "attraction") and inertia. (As noted above,
however, Lerdahl omits gravity.) Like Bharucha and me, Lerdahl (1996)
quantifies the net magnetic pull on a note (which he calls the "resultant
attraction") as the difference between the pulls of the closest attractor
above and the closest attractor below that note.[2] Again like Bharucha
and me, he asserts that the magnetic pull on a note from either attractor
(both of which he calculates with his "attraction algorithm") is inversely
proportional to the distance between that note and its attractor. Like
me, Lerdahl quantifies this pull as inversely proportional to the square
of that distance. And like Bharucha, Lerdahl suggests that the magnetic
pull on an unstable note from either attractor is directly proportional to
the stability of its attractor. (However, whereas Bharucha considers only
the stability of the attractor, Lerdahl's "attraction algorithm" includes the
stabilities of both the unstable note and its stable attractor.)

Margulis (2003) incorporates a similar algorithm in her model of
melodic expectation. She also asserts that the magnetic pull on a note
is inversely proportional to the distance (in semitones) between that
note and its attractor. Rather than a simple formula, however, she offers

a complicated table of proximity values that reflect her intuitions about how melodic magnetism depends on distance in semitones. Table 4.1 reproduces these values.

According to Margulis, "the selected proximity curve, falling between the simple inverse and the inverse squared, can be produced by adding the appropriate constants to the terms in an equation of the form $(1/(x^5 + x^4 + x^3 + x^2 + x))$, where x is semitone distance" (126). Her dissertation does not tell us what those coefficients are. She does suggest, however, that the resultant values match experimental findings, and refers to a study of expectations in Indian classical music (Mukherji and Krumhansl, unpublished). Although such values seem more complicated than the inverse of distance in semitones (as Bharucha suggested) or the inverse square of distance in semitones (as in the algorithm used by my computer programs and in Lerdahl's similar algorithm), the use of such a table suggests that it could be adjusted further to reflect empirical results – if sufficiently consistent patterns attributable solely to distance arose.

Furthermore, like Bharucha and Lerdahl, Margulis suggests that the magnetic pull on an unstable note from an attractor is directly proportional to the stability of that attractor. (However, Margulis follows Bharucha rather than Lerdahl in considering the stability of the attractor but not the stability of the attracted note.) Like Lerdahl, she omits gravity from her model. She also replaces inertia with a factor (called "direction") that represents aspects of Narmour's implication-realization model.

Brower (1997–98, 2000) retains the terms "gravity" and "inertia," but, like Lerdahl, she suggests "attraction" as an alternative term for "magnetism." She also suggests that moving a heavy box end-over-end up or down an inclined plane may provide a better metaphor than physical magnetism for understanding musical magnetism.

While I find Brower's heavy-box analogy a poor metaphor for graceful and enjoyable music making, I do see multiple source domains for musical magnetism (including any goal-directed desire, such as hunger or thirst). The desire for any goal that grows stronger as that goal approaches may provide a source that can be mapped onto the target domain of musical attractions (of course, "attraction" itself is also a metaphor). Nevertheless, sensitive and thoughtful musicians, such as cellist Pablo Casals (Blum 1977), pianist Glenn Gould (Monsaingeon 1980), and jazz theorist Jerry Coker (Coker 1964) have relied on the metaphor of magnetism to describe these attractions, and I retain that term here. Thus, just as we speak of "personal magnetism," we shall also speak of "musical magnetism."

Further aspects of our experience of physical magnetism (and of our experiences with goal-directed desires) also suggest further hypotheses that might flow from the theory of musical forces. In particular, the pull of a magnet not only grows stronger as it gets closer and closer, it does so in an accelerating way that can be quantified. As a result, we are more likely to observe its influence on the local, rather than the global, trajectories of objects. We typically experience magnets later in life than we experience gravity and inertia (however, we do experience other goal-directed desires early in life). Magnets (if you reverse the poles) can also repel each other (the analogy to a string of 2–3 suspensions, in which two voices seem to push each other away each time they are a step apart, might be a good example of this phenomenon). Finally, although it is less obvious or less vivid, we may notice that some magnets are stronger than others and that this strength tends to correlate with other factors such as size and weight.

Thus we may hypothesize that musical magnetism affects the "strength" of melodic pattern completion and the frequencies with which patterns appear, that its effect is stronger than that of musical gravity, that its effect is clearer in local than in global trajectories, that its effect depends on proximity, that the proximity effect may accelerate with something like the inverse-square or inverse-cube law,[3] that there may be stronger and weaker magnetic attractors, that the strength of an attractor may correlate with other factors (such as stability, volume, or timbre), that the perception of musical magnetism may be more dependent on learning than is the perception of other musical forces, and that there may be some musical settings in which we can experience repulsion instead of attraction between musical objects. Part 2 of this book offers evidence consistent with each of these hypotheses.

EXAMPLE 4.4. Musical inertia depends on how patterns are internally represented.

MUSICAL INERTIA

Musical inertia is the tendency of a pattern of motion to continue in the same fashion, where the meaning of "same" depends on how that pattern is represented in musical memory. All "sequences" can be heard as giving in to inertia. If we hear the melodic beginning given in Example 4.4a as ending with a descending stepwise scale (as suggested by the notation in Example 4.4b), then inertia will imply continuing that stepwise descending pattern (as shown in Example 4.4c). If we hear the melodic beginning given in Example 4.4a as moving in triple meter with each measure ascending through the scale by step (as suggested by the notation in Example 4.4d – the first two notes being heard as pick-ups), then inertia will imply continuing that pattern of three notes in each successive measure (as shown in Example 4.4e). If we hear the melodic beginning given in Example 4.4a as moving in quadruple meter with each measure ascending by third (as suggested by the notation in Example 4.4f), then inertia will imply continuing that pattern of four notes in each successive measure (as shown in Example 4.4g).

The portion of "Twinkle, Twinkle, Little Star" given in Example 4.1 breaks into two halves. The second half may be heard as giving in to inertia by continuing in the same rhythm as the first half. If one hears measures 5 and 6 as "two notes per measure of the same pitch, each measure descending through the diatonic scale," then measure 7 may be heard as following inertia when it continues those same patterns of pitch and duration. If measures 3 and 5 are heard as resolving down by step into their following measures, then measure 7 may be heard as giving in to inertia when it continues that same pattern of resolution.

Thinking about musical inertia also helps to explain the expressive meaning of "Twinkle, Twinkle, Little Star" and how that differs from the meanings of the melody and the lamento bass of "Dido's Lament." In "Twinkle, Twinkle, Little Star," the melody begins with a sense of purpose in the form of an upward leap. It achieves its purpose quickly and effortlessly. Then a pattern takes over, and the melody ends by following inertia (as well as gravity and magnetism). Such a musical motion may be compared to a physical motion in which an uncomplicated initial impetus sets an object in motion, and in which that object "takes the path of least resistance" from there on, simply accumulating momentum as it gives in to gravity.

In Dido's melody, by contrast, a series of gestures are set in motion, and in most of them, instead of building up inertia in the direction suggested by the initial impetus of each gesture, the melody seems repeatedly overcome by gravity. This interpretation of the melody agrees well with the text, which struggles against the painful inevitability of death to make the plea "Remember me."

Each gesture begins with a stepwise ascent. The first gesture moves from G through A and then (following inertia) it continues upward. The melody, however, does not continue up in whole steps (to B); instead, gravity limits its ascent to a half step (to B♭ – of course, we expect the B♭ because we are in minor, but one can also say that the $\hat{1}$–$\hat{2}$–$\hat{3}$ gesture in minor reflects the influence of gravity in a way that contributes to its expressive meaning by making it feel "weighed down"). But this B♭ immediately becomes unstable (as the bass moves to F♯) and resolves back to A. The second gesture again begins by ascending; its B pulls us up magnetically to C, which may be heard as continuing the ascent begun by the first gesture. This results in a feeling of purposefully attempted ascent. But on reaching the C, the melody again falls. Such musical motions may be compared to physical motions in which a complicated series of purposeful attempts to ascend fail to generate inertia in that direction and succeed in climbing upward only with great effort.

Again, others may hear different expressive meanings in these melodies, but if they hear patterns of motion in these melodies, then the meanings that they attribute to these patterns will be shaped by a tendency they experience for those patterns to continue in the same fashion.

Inertia is not a new idea to musicians. Meyer (1956, 1973) described the phenomenon as "good continuation" and explains it in terms of the laws of perceptual organization proposed by Gestalt psychologists (Meyer's notion of good continuation is discussed in greater detail in chapter 11 of this volume). Inertia also appears central to the tonal expectancy model of Mari Riess Jones (1981a, 1981b). Gary Karpinski suggests that musical inertia as understood in the theory of musical forces may help explain consistent errors in recall of melodic contour (2000, 49).

Narmour's "process" may be thought of as a special case of inertia. His implication-realization model predicts that listeners expect intervals smaller than a tritone to be followed by intervals that are similar in size and direction. He argues, however, that larger intervals do not induce this same expectation. And his claim is restricted to the size and direction of a single interval produced by just two notes. The theory of musical forces claims that inertial expectations are based on internal representations, that they do not apply differently to small vs. large intervals, and that they are not limited to just the size and direction of intervals. For example, the theory of musical forces claims that: (a) if E–A is heard as individual notes descending by fifth, then it will induce the expectation of another descending fifth, A–D (when a performance of "Turkey in the Straw" presents these tones on the open strings of a fiddle, and harmonized with adjacent open strings, it tends to encourage such a hearing; see Example 4.5a); (b) if E–A is heard as a motion within

EXAMPLE 4.5. Different hearings of E–A suggest different
inertial continuations.

a chord (say, an A major chord), then it will induce the expectation of
continued motion with that chord (regardless of melodic direction; see
Example 4.5b); and (c) if E–A is heard as part of a larger pattern (say, one
in which the E is an upbeat prefix elaboration of A, which is itself part of
an ascending A minor scale; see Example 4.5c), then it will induce the
expectation of the same pattern continuing (in this case, with an upbeat
prefix elaboration to B).

Paul von Hippel (2002) uses the term "step inertia" to refer to a tendency for steps (whole steps and half steps) to continue in the same
direction, but he restricts the idea to note-to-note connections and to
intervals smaller than a minor third. In an experiment, von Hippel presented listeners with a randomly generated twelve-tone row and then
asked them whether they expected the melody to continue by ascending
or descending. He found that when the row ended with a descending
step, listeners expected another descending step (giving in to both inertia and gravity). He also found that when the row ended with an ascending step, listeners expected another ascending step (giving in to inertia),
even though his statistical analyses suggest that ascending steps are just
as likely to be followed by a descending step. Bret Aarden (2003) asked
listeners to indicate the direction in which a folk-song melody moved
(up, down, or remained the same). He found that listeners answered
more quickly and more accurately when stepwise melodies continued
by giving in to inertia.

Margulis's model of melodic expectation replaces inertia with a
factor (called "direction") that combines aspects of Narmour's (1990,
1992) implication-realization model (for small intervals, Margulis's "di-

rection," like Narmour's "process," is equivalent to inertia; for larger intervals, Margulis's "direction" produces something like Narmour's "reversal").

Returning once again to the source domain of physical motion, we note that inertia is *both* the tendency of an object in motion to remain in motion *and* the tendency of an object at rest to remain at rest, that inertia has an impact that is stronger than gravity and more pervasive than magnetism, that inertia tends to carry motion beyond the points of stability to which other forces draw objects, that inertia may act in concert with other forces, and that, in so doing, it creates smooth motions that tend toward a state in which those forces are in equilibrium.

Thus we may hypothesize that musical inertia affects the "strength" of melodic pattern completion and the frequencies with which patterns appear, that its effect is stronger than that of other forces, that the perception of musical inertia may be less dependent on learning than is the perception of other musical forces, that inertia tends to carry musical motions beyond the stable positions that serve as goals for other forces, and that it may thus combine with other forces to create smooth motions that tend toward a state of equilibrium with other forces. Part 2 of this book offers evidence consistent with each of these hypotheses.

STABILITY

Stability plays an important role in the theory of musical forces. The definition of magnetism (as the tendency of an *unstable* tone to move to the closest *stable* pitch) depends on the idea of stability. The algorithms for magnetic attraction offered by Bharucha, Lerdahl, and Margulis (described above) quantify magnetic pulls in terms of stability.

Stability is a comparative quality that we attribute to a note. We hear a note as unstable to the degree that it leads us to auralize another (more stable) pitch – and a path that will take the melody to that pitch. In "Twinkle, Twinkle, Little Star," the As are less stable than the Gs that follow because we experience the A as resolving to the G.

Thus we may hypothesize that stability values (such as Krumhansl's probe-tone profiles, Lerdahl's levels of pitch-space embedding, and Margulis's stability ratings) may correlate with judgments of the "strength"

TABLE 4.2. PROBE-TONE PROFILES FOR MAJOR- AND MINOR-KEY CONTEXTS
(Krumhansl & Kessler 1982), Levels of Pitch-Space Embedding in Lerdahl's (1988)
"Basic Tonal Space," Levels of Pitch-Space Embedding in Lerdahl's (1996)
Algorithm, and Stability Values in Margulis's (2003) Model of Melodic Expectation

MAJOR SCALE DEGREE	KRUMHANSL & KESSLER (1982)	LERDAHL (1988)	LERDAHL (1996)	MARGULIS (2003)
C	6.35	5	4	6
C♯/D♭	2.23	1	1	2
D	3.48	2	2	4
D♯/E♭	2.33	1	1	2
E	4.38	3	3	5–6*
F	4.09	2	2	4
F♯/G♭	2.52	1	1	2
G	5.19	4	3	5
G♯/A♭	2.39	1	1	2
A	3.66	2	2	4
A♯/B♭	2.29	1	1	2
B	2.88	2	2	4

*In Margulis's model, when preceded by its dominant seventh,
the stability rating of the third of a chord is elevated from 5 to 6.

of melodic pattern completion and the frequencies with which patterns
appear, and that their effect may be more relevant in explaining the experience of listeners in situations in which the tonic is unambiguously
prolonged than in situations in which other chords exert control or the
control of the tonic is less clear.

Stability can be quantified or modeled in several ways. Table 4.2 lists
the stability values according to Krumhansl and Kessler (1982), Lerdahl
(1988), Lerdahl (1996), and Margulis (2003).

In Table 4.2, the column labeled "Krumhansl and Kessler (1982)"
gives stability values that were experimentally derived (they are the
probe-tone profiles given in Graph 2.1).

The other columns of Table 4.2 give values that were theoretically
generated. In his original article on tonal pitch space (1988), Lerdahl
suggests that the stability of each tone in the scale might be described in
terms of its level of embedding in his basic space. These are given in the
third column of Table 4.2.

However, Lerdahl's (1996 and 2001) algorithm uses a different pitch space. The difference is that the 1988 pitch space distinguishes between the stability of mediant and dominant, and the 1996 pitch space does not. He explains that "the calculations work out better if the fifth level, necessary for harmonic and regional modeling, is suppressed for melodic modeling; this places $\hat{3}$ and $\hat{5}$ at the same level" (2001, 161–162; 1996, 343). The resultant stability values are given in the fourth column of Table 4.2.

The stability values used by Margulis (in a context where the tonic triad in major is elaborated) are given in the fifth column of Table 4.2. These values are quite similar to those used in Lerdahl's tonal attraction algorithm. Margulis's values, however, are modified in particular contexts. For example, in a context where the controlling harmony is V7 and the expectation is for a following event that will be harmonized by I, the third of the following I chord has a higher stability value than it would in other circumstances.[4]

Like Lerdahl, Margulis omits gravity from her model. Also like Lerdahl, however, she uses stability values that favor downward resolutions. Example 4.6 clarifies how these stability values favor downward resolutions. This example shows scale degrees (depicted in the key of C) and their single-note resolutions. According to the theory of musical forces, experienced listeners of tonal music expect melodic completions that move through a specific alphabet to a more stable pitch (an alphabet is a basic collection of pitches, such as the chromatic scale, the diatonic scale, the tonic triad, etc.). (In three cases this results in motions that require more than one note to reach a more stable pitch: A goes through B to get to C, B goes through A to get to G, and E goes through G to ascend to C. Such longer paths are not shown in Example 4.6.) In Example 4.6 each system is labeled according to Margulis's stability value (given in Table 4.2) for the notes on that system: 2 for the nondiatonic pitches, 4 for the diatonic nontriadic tones, 5 for the fifth scale degree, 5–6 for the third scale degree (which is promoted from 5 to 6 when it is preceded by V7), and 6 for the tonic. Each solid or dashed slur or line shows a possible single-note resolution to a more stable pitch. Now we ask which path is favored if we consider only stabil-

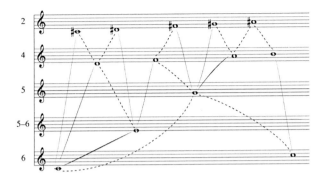

EXAMPLE 4.6. Single-note resolutions.

ity. In two cases we cannot answer the question – A♯ (= B♭) resolves to
A or B (which are equally stable) and G resolves to a lower or a higher
C (which are equally stable). But from all other pitches, stability favors
one direction over the other. The favored paths are shown with solid
lines or slurs in Example 4.6. Notice that most (six out of nine) of the
favored paths descend. (In fact, the three exceptions have something in
common; they are the pitches that lie a half step below each of the tonic-
triadic tones. Especially for F♯ and B, it is true that these pitches tend to
ascend more often than they descend, but the theory of musical forces
would argue that these notes may be regarded as using the magnetism
of a half-step resolution to overcome gravity.)

Lerdahl's 1996 stability values favor downward resolutions more
than his 1988 values do. And Margulis's stability values favor downward
resolutions even more than either of Lerdahl's sets of values.

Thus, even though Lerdahl and Margulis do not explicitly include
a factor called "melodic gravity," their models produce tendencies for
downward motion as a by-product of the stability values and other factors in their models. The theory of musical forces, however, regards musical gravity not as a mere "by-product" but as a fundamental force – as
basic to musical experience and as viscerally real as musical magnetism
and musical inertia. As we shall see in part 2, the evidence concerning
musical forces and stability is best understood when we regard stability
and gravity as separate factors.

INTERACTING FORCES

Physical motion is shaped by the interaction of constantly acting physical forces. The smooth, arch-like path taken by a thrown ball shows the interaction of various factors, including impetus, inertia, wind resistance, and gravity. As it ascends, inertia and gravity oppose each other. As it descends, inertia and gravity work together. The path of the ball has a predictable quality that comes from the fact that the interaction of these forces can be quantified. If musical motion inherits the entailments of physical motion, then the interaction of constantly acting musical forces might be similarly quantifiable.

In some situations the musical forces agree: in a context where we expect melodies to move within the major scale and where we experience the members of the tonic triad as stable pitches, melodic gravity suggests that the melodic beginning $\hat{5}$–$\hat{4}$–? will continue by going *down*, $\hat{5}$–$\hat{4}$–$\hat{3}$; melodic magnetism suggests that the same beginning will continue by going to the *nearest* stable pitch, $\hat{5}$–$\hat{4}$–$\hat{3}$; and musical inertia suggests that the same beginning will continue by going in the *same* direction, $\hat{5}$–$\hat{4}$–$\hat{3}$. (Chapter 3 discusses such an agreement of forces in Harrison's "Something," where that agreement elegantly illustrates the meaning of the text "attracts me like no other lover"; see Example 3.2.)

In other situations the forces may disagree: in a context where we expect melodies to move within the major scale and where we experience the members of the tonic triad as stable pitches, gravity and magnetism suggest that the melodic beginning $\hat{5}$–$\hat{6}$–? will continue by going *down* and to the *nearest* stable pitch, $\hat{5}$–$\hat{6}$–$\hat{5}$; but inertia suggests that the same beginning will continue by going in the *same* direction, $\hat{5}$–$\hat{6}$–$\hat{7}$–$\hat{8}$.

The interaction of the forces may be contextually determined (for example, it could be that a specific context might heighten listener attention to the effects of gravity while another context might lessen the impact of the same force). But if musical forces are analogous to physical forces, then we should expect them to act in a consistent and quantifiable way.

Paul von Hippel (2002) examined a large sample of melodies from a broad range of cultures and asked what happened when one melodic step is immediately followed by another melodic step. There are, of course, four possibilities: up-up, up-down, down-up, and down-down. If we assume that melodies give in to the musical forces more often than they go against them, then we would expect the most common pattern to be down-down (which gives in to both gravity and inertia), and we would expect the least common pattern to be down-up (which gives in to neither force). This is exactly what von Hippel found.

The remaining section of this chapter deals with the interaction of musical forces from a mathematical perspective. Readers who find this section too detailed or technical may wish to skip ahead to chapter 5.

<h2>ALGORITHMS FOR QUANTIFYING THE
INTERACTION OF MUSICAL FORCES</h2>

One way to quantify the interaction of these forces is to use an algorithm of the type used in my computer models (Larson 1993a, 1994b, 1999a, 2004). The general form of that algorithm is

$$F = w_G + w_M + w_I$$

This equation shows how, for a particular note in a particular context, the computer can represent the forces felt to impel that note to another specified note. It combines the scores it gives to gravity (G is 1 for patterns that give in to gravity and 0 for motions that do not), magnetism (M is calculated according to a formula discussed in more detail below), and inertia (I is 1 for patterns that give in to inertia, −1 for patterns that go against inertia, and 0 if there are no inertial implications) in a proportion (represented by the weights w_G, w_M, and w_I, respectively) to represent their cumulative effect (F). Just as we experience physical motions as shaped by an interaction of constantly acting but contextually determined physical forces, so, the theory argues, we experience musical motions as shaped by an interaction of constantly acting but contextually determined musical forces.

As noted above, my computer models of musical forces represent the magnetic pull toward the closest stable pitch as the difference between the pull of that pitch (expressed as the inverse square of its distance in semitones) minus the pull of the closest pitch in the other direction (also expressed as the inverse square of its distance in semitones). In this way, the algorithm models the human tendency to be more strongly drawn to closer goals. Theoretically one could calculate magnetic pulls from all stable pitches, but, as a practical matter, only the closest notes in each direction are considered in this calculation. Thus the computer models represent magnetism as

$$M = 1/d_{to}^2 - 1/d_{from}^2$$

where M indicates the magnetic pull on a given note in a given context in the direction of a specified goal; d_{to} is the distance in semitones to that goal; and d_{from} is the distance in semitones to the closest stable pitch (the potential goal or attractor) in the other direction. In the context described above (where we expect melodies to move within the major scale and where we experience the members of the tonic triad as stable pitches), the distance (d) from $\hat{4}$ to $\hat{5}$ is 2 semitones, and the distance from $\hat{4}$ to $\hat{3}$ is 1 semitone. Thus the magnetic pull exerted on $\hat{4}$ by $\hat{5}$ is represented as .25 $(1/d^2 = 1/2^2 = \frac{1}{4})$, the magnetic pull exerted on $\hat{4}$ by $\hat{3}$ is represented as 1 $(1/d^2 = 1/1^2 = 1)$, and their combined magnetic effect on $\hat{4}$ is .75 in the direction of $\hat{3}$ $(1/d_{to}^2 - 1/d_{from}^2 = 1/1^2 - 1/2^2 = 1 - \frac{1}{4} = \frac{3}{4})$. In the same context, the magnetic pull exerted on $\hat{6}$ by $\hat{8}$ is represented as .11 $(1/d^2 = 1/3^2 = \frac{1}{9})$, the magnetic pull exerted on $\hat{6}$ by $\hat{5}$ is represented as .25 $(1/d^2 = 1/2^2 = \frac{1}{4})$, and the combined magnetic effect on $\hat{6}$ is .14 in the direction of $\hat{5}$ $(1/d_{to}^2 - 1/d_{from}^2 = 1/2^2 - 1/3^2 = \frac{1}{4} - \frac{1}{9} = 5/36)$. Again the computer model considers only the effects of the two closest stable pitches (above and below the unstable note).

If we take the general algorithm given above and substitute this more specific representation of magnetism, then we get the first of the five following algorithms.

$$F = w_G G + w_M (1/d_{to}^2 - 1/d_{from}^2) + w_I I \text{(Larson 1993a)}$$
$$F = w_M (s_{to}/d_{to} - s_{from}/d_{from}) + \ldots \text{(Bharucha 1996)}$$
$$F = w_M (s_{to}/d_{from}^2 - s_{from}/d_{from}^2) + w_I I \text{(Lerdahl 1996)}$$
$$E_{to} = s_{to} p_{to} + r_{to} \text{(Margulis 2003)}$$
$$E_{from} - E_{to} = s_{from} p_{from} - s_{to} p_{to} + (r_{from} - r_{to}) \text{(Margulis 2003)}$$

The first of these algorithms (Larson 1993a) is the one used by my computer models.

The second is Bharucha's (1996) "yearning vector," with magnetism described by his "tonal force vector" (the ellipsis indicates that there may be other unspecified forces). In Bharucha's algorithm, the magnetic pulls on a note depend on the stabilities (s_{to} and s_{from}) of the pitches to which that note is attracted.

The third is Lerdahl's (1996) "tendency algorithm," which also quantifies the net magnetic pull on a note (which he calls "the resultant attraction") as the difference between the pulls of the closest note above and the closest note below that note. In Lerdahl's algorithm, the magnetic pull on a note depends on both the stabilities of its attractors and the stability of the attracted note itself (s_{to} is the ratio of levels of embedding in a tonal pitch space between the closest stable pitch and the unstable note; s_{from} is the ratio of levels of embedding between the closest pitch in the other direction and the unstable note). This requires calculating the stability values for three pitches: the unstable pitch and the attractors in both directions. Instead of using the basic pitch space given in his original article (1988), Lerdahl's (1996) algorithm uses a different pitch space – one that does not distinguish between the stability of the mediant and that of the dominant. He omits gravity. Inertia (which he calls "directed motion") is modeled in similar ways in both our algorithms (my algorithm, however, allows for three cases: patterns that give in to inertia score 1, patterns that go against inertia score –1, and patterns that do not have inertial implications score 0 – Lerdahl's algorithm only considers the first two of these cases).

The fourth is an algorithm proposed by Elizabeth Margulis (2003). Margulis theorizes that the degree to which a pitch is expected (E_{to}) is a sum of two scores. The first score is the product of the stability of the expected note (s_{to}, similar to the ratings in Lerdahl 1996) and its proximity score (p_{to}). Margulis gives her proximity scores in a table. They may be thought of as falling between w_M/d and w_M/d.[2] Thus Margulis's first score has much in common with the magnetism scores of Larson, Bharucha, and Lerdahl. In place of a score for inertia, however, Margulis suggests her "direction" scores. These are also given in a table. She labels these scores d, but since the other algorithms are shown here using d for semitone distance, I show her direction score here as r_{to}. Because these direction scores favor continuation in the same direction for small intervals and reversal of direction for larger intervals, this part of her algorithm may be seen as incorporating an element of Narmour's implication-realization model. Following Lerdahl (2001), Margulis also defines a measure of "implicative denial" – the extent to which a given realization denies the strongest expectation at that point. Thus, if a melody moves toward its weaker magnetic attractor, the implicative denial is computed as $E_{from} - E_{to}$. Using Margulis's measure of implicative denial and regrouping the terms gives the fifth algorithm above.

A comparison of these algorithms suggests six more hypotheses concerning the ways in which the expectations of experienced listeners might reflect their intuitions about musical forces: (1) expectations are influenced by the stability of the unstable note (the attracted note); (2) expectations are influenced by the stability of the goal to which that unstable note is most strongly attracted (the attractor); (3) expectations are influenced by the stability of the closest stable pitch in the other direction (the opposing attractor); (4) substituting Lerdahl's 1996 for his 1988 stability values for pitch-space embedding, or substituting Margulis's stability values, will yield higher correlations with experimental data; (5) magnetic pulls are better represented as inversely proportional to distance rather than inversely proportional to the square of distance; and (6) gravity does not play a necessary role in understanding melodic expectations. Each of these six hypotheses may be regarded as refining (or, in the case of the sixth hypothesis, contradicting) some aspect of the theory of musical forces. Part 2 of this book returns to each of these hypotheses, reviewing the evidence we now have concerning each of them.

Lerdahl makes the last of these hypotheses explicit (2001, 191):

> However, gravity appears to be dispensable: in the major scale, except for the leading tone, the strongest virtual attractions of nonchordal diatonic pitches are by stepwise descent anyway. If there is any downward tendency beyond what is accounted for by attractions, it may reside in the fact that the most relaxed register for vocal production lies in a rather low range (though not at the bottom) – that is, the cause may be more physical than cognitive. Besides, what is "down" to us may be "up" or "away" in another culture. The use of spatial metaphors is universal in talking about music, but spatial orientations are not. There is reason, then, to drop gravity as a musical force.

Notice that Lerdahl does not deny the tendency of tonal melodies to descend. He just questions whether our explanations of musical forces need to call upon the idea of melodic gravity (suggesting that, since descent is a by-product of his attraction algorithm, it is unnecessary to regard gravity as a separate factor and theoretically simpler to ignore it).

There is an interesting restatement of this last hypothesis. If, as Lerdahl suggests, the relative stabilities of each of the tones in the tonal system result in a tendency for less stable tones to descend, then we might ask whether the tonal system itself has evolved so that its magnetic pulls imitate the effects of physical gravity. (One could, of course, answer this question in the affirmative and still find that gravity retains explanatory value as a separate musical force.)

The recent attention given to musical forces (and their role in melodic expectation) suggests the compelling interest of the idea. And the detailed attempts to quantify their interaction – in algorithms that turn out to be remarkably similar – suggest a general acceptance of the idea that musical forces are enough like physical forces so that they interact in an analogous (and even quantifiable) fashion. Part 2 of this book offers strong evidence supporting the idea of constantly acting and mathematically quantifiable musical gravity, magnetism, and inertia. Although the similarities between the predictions of the different algorithms make it difficult to distinguish between them experimentally, the evidence in part 2 of this book seems to give strongest support to the first of those algorithms (Larson 1993a).

5

A Theory of
Melodic Expectation

Chapters 1–4 argue that listening to music is a creative process in which we shape the sounds we hear into meanings tempered by our biology, culture, and experience. When we are engaged in that process, experienced listeners of tonal music make predictions about what will happen next – about "where the music is going." In this sense the recent growth of interest in melodic expectation, both in theoretical and experimental research, responds to central questions about musical experience – questions about meaning and motion. Chapter 5 offers a theory of melodic expectation built on the ideas set out in the previous four chapters.

The theory of melodic expectation presented here claims that experienced listeners of tonal music have expectations about how melodic beginnings will be completed, and it claims that important aspects of those expectations are captured in the following summary statement:

> Experienced listeners of tonal music expect melodic completions in which the musical forces of gravity, magnetism, and inertia control operations on alphabets in hierarchies of elaboration whose stepwise displacements of auralized traces create simple closed shapes.

The following paragraphs explain what is meant by this summary statement and then restate portions of it as specific rules.

ENTIRE COMPLETIONS VS. MERE CONTINUATIONS

The first claim in this summary statement is that listeners expect *completions*. This emphasis on completions, as opposed to mere continuations, separates this claim from many current experimental and theoretical studies of music perception. Notice also that this summary statement talks about completions (plural) instead of just one possible completion; it claims that incomplete melodic beginnings may imply more than one possible completion.

Some experimental work in music perception restricts attention to the first new note that listeners expect in a melodic continuation. James Carlsen and his collaborators asked participants to sing continuations of two-note beginnings (Carlsen, Divenyi, and Taylor 1970; Carlsen 1981; Unyk and Carlsen 1987). Lola Cuddy and her collaborators have tested listener judgments (Cuddy and Lunney 1995) and continuations (Thompson, Cuddy, and Plaus 1997) of two-note beginnings. William Lake (1987) and Dirk-Jan Povel (1996) also asked participants to produce continuations of (respectively) two- or one-note beginnings, but for each beginning they first established a major-key context. In Povel's experiment, participants played their continuation on a synthesizer but were allowed to add only one note. In the rest of these experiments in which participants produced continuations, the participants often added more than one new note, but the experimenters analyzed only the first added note.

Experiments by Carol Krumhansl and others that ask listeners to judge how well a single probe tone or chord fits an established context may also be regarded as asking listeners to rate the degree to which that tone or chord is expected in that context (Krumhansl 1990). Some of these studies (Cuddy and Lunney 1995; Krumhansl 1995; Schellenberg 1996, 1997) used the probe-tone technique to test predictions of the bottom-up component of Eugene Narmour's (1990, 1992) implication-realization model of melodic expectancy. Such probe-tone experiments also typically limit analysis to only the first new element expected by listeners.

Other experiments (Larson 1997a) suggest, however, that we should regard the melodic expectations of participants as expectations not so much for *continuations*, but as expectations for *entire completions*. (By "entire completions," I mean *all* the notes sung by an experimental participant.) In these experiments most participant responses agreed note-for-note with another participant's *entire* response – and the total number of different entire responses was small. (Some responses failed to agree note-for-note with another response, but since our interest lies in shared musical intuitions, the elimination of such outliers may be regarded as a positive feature of considering entire completions.) Furthermore, these other experiments (Larson 1997a) demonstrate that sorting responses by just the first added notes can confuse the data – by making clearly similar responses look different and by making clearly different responses look similar. For example, responses that end in the same key and have the same essential structure can have different first added notes, and responses in different keys and ending on different notes can have the same first added notes.

All these different experiments have produced a number of interesting results. But the three clearest conclusions that one can draw by looking at those experiments seem to be, first, that experienced listeners of tonal music have expectations not only about how a melody will continue but also about how it will end; second, that the same melodic beginning may produce different expectations (perhaps of different length) for different listeners; and, third, that such listeners typically show a high level of agreement on a small number of favored completions.

Despite these fairly clear conclusions, earlier theories of melodic expectation do not offer a testable explanation of how listeners generate entire completions. For example, Narmour's "implication-realization model" suggests that melodic continuations result from the interaction of "bottom-up" and "top-down" components. But tests of the bottom-up component of the implication-realization model (cited above) suggest that it is little more than a description of what is statistically true of first added notes in general – like claiming that "added notes are usually close in pitch to one of the two preceding notes" and "large leaps are usually followed by a change in direction." In fact, the work of Glenn Schellenberg (1996, 1997) and Paul von Hippel (2002) suggests that the bottom-up component of Narmour's model can be simplified to something like these two statements without any loss of accuracy in describing experimental results.

It might appear that including the top-down component of Narmour's model would allow it to generate entire completions. In fact, Krumhansl (1995) found that, in order to account well for the data in one of her tests of Narmour's model, she had to add a factor she called "tonality" (which she modeled with her major-key profile) – and that factor turned out to be one of the most important in explaining the data. (In her experiment with tonal melodies, this was true even though the experiment considered only diatonic continuations. Had a more complete test been done, also considering nondiatonic tones, this factor may well have played an even greater role.) But a close reading of Narmour's books suggests that the top-down component – including factors like "the influence of intra-opus style" and "the influence of extra-opus style" – includes more than Krumhansl's "tonality." Despite the elegance of Krumhansl's experiments, the top-down component of Narmour's model is still not codified as a set of rules capable of generating entire completions.[1]

Ideally, then, a theory of melodic expectation would have three features: first, it would generate entire *completions* (instead of just the next note of a *continuation*); second, it would be capable of generating more than one completion for some beginnings (preferably indicating the relative likelihood or strength of each completion); and, third, it would produce specific, testable results. The theory described in this chapter is the first that has all three of these features. The theory is stated as a set of rules that generates completions (of varying lengths) that achieve a degree of closure, instead of mere (single-note or unending) continuations. For each beginning, the rule set produces a list of one or more possible completions – together with a weight or rating for each completion, suggesting how likely or how strong that completion is. Because those rules are detailed enough to be implemented as a computer program, the theory can be tested by comparing the output of the computer to the results of independent experiments (the closer that program comes to matching note-for-note all and only the completions produced or approved by experimental participants, the more successful it appears; and the closer the ratings attached to the computer-generated responses correlate with the frequency with which those responses are produced, or with the judgments made about them, the more successful it appears). Chapter 13 describes two computer models that have implemented aspects of that theory, and shows that a comparison of the results of those models with the results of psychological experiments offers strong support for that theory.

MUSICAL FORCES

The summary statement given above claims that "musical forces" play an important role in generating melodic completions. Chapter 4 defines and illustrates the musical forces. To review: "melodic gravity" is the tendency of a note that is heard as above a stable platform to descend; "melodic magnetism" is the tendency of an unstable note to move to the nearest stable pitch, a tendency that grows stronger the closer we get to a goal; and "musical inertia" is the tendency of a pattern of musical motion to continue in the same fashion, where what is meant by "same" depends upon what that musical pattern is "heard as."

OPERATIONS ON ALPHABETS

The summary statement above claims that musical forces "control operations on alphabets." Diana Deutsch and John Feroe (1981), drawing on the work of Simon and Sumner (1968), advance a model of music cognition that describes musical passages in terms of alphabets and operations, and they claim that such representations have a cognitive "economy of means" – that is, that such representations allow our musical memories to store melodies more easily this way than in other ways. The theory of musical forces adopts aspects of their model for describing sequences of pitches.

Alphabets are basic collections of pitches (such as the chromatic scale, the major scale, and specific chords) in terms of which listeners understand passages of music, and which may be economically described as complete, theoretically well-defined pitch collections. Listeners infer alphabets from passages of music aurally. For example, after hearing a bit of a melody in C major (such as the opening phrase of "Twinkle, Twinkle, Little Star"; see Example 4.1), experienced listeners of tonal music will easily sing the whole C major scale (including a B, even though the melody has no B in it). Karpinski (2000, 39–44) discusses this "collection inference" and its role in the acquisition of aural skills, as well as citing other relevant psychological literature. Alphabets are also typically easy to describe; that is, some simple rule allows us to say which notes are in an alphabet and which notes are not. For example, the major scale can be defined in a number of different straightforward ways, as can the major triad.[2]

Operations are simple ways of moving within an alphabet (such as repetition or motion to the next higher or lower member). Because of this simplicity, they may be rigorously and unambiguously defined. Deutsch and Feroe (1981) give a notation that depicts each of the operations they define. This book and the computer implementations it describes limits themselves to operations that transform a single note by adding one note (an affix) before it (a prefix) or after it (a suffix), or that transform a pair of notes by adding all the appropriate notes between (connectives). Furthermore, every operation specifies the alphabet from which it draws these notes, and it adds them in such a way that the transformed notes either repeat a pitch from that alphabet or move in one direction within that alphabet. In other words, each transformation results in a motion that stays (repeats the same member of the alphabet), goes up (moves to the next higher member of the alphabet), or goes down (moves to the next lower member of the alphabet).

Operations also appear basic to music listening, can be economically described, may be applied to any alphabet, and always produce a unique result. Listeners infer operations from passages of music aurally. For example, after hearing the opening phrase of "Twinkle, Twinkle, Little Star" (see Example 4.1), many listeners (even many who could not tell us which scale degrees are sung) could describe most of its motion using the terms "repeat a note," "leap up," "step up," and "step down." Three of these terms ("repeat a note," "step up," and "step down") describe operations ("leap up" is not an operation because it does not tell us how far to leap, but there are other ways to describe this specific leap in terms of alphabets and operations). Karpinski's discussion of memory for melodic contour (2000, 48–50) illustrates the centrality of such basic operations in music listening, as well as citing other relevant psychological literature. Example 5.1 shows that a simple operation (repeating the note started on and then descending to the next lower member of the collection, done three times – plus an additional operation that lengthens the final note) can be applied to different collections to produce different results. In Example 5.1a, the collection is the major scale (starting on $\hat{4}$), and the result is the second four measures of "Twinkle, Twinkle, Little

EXAMPLE 5.1. A simple operation can be applied to different collections to produce different results.

Star." In Example 5.1b, the collection is the chromatic scale (starting on $\hat{5}$), and the result is a common pattern (typically harmonized by I–V7/V–V7–I). In Example 5.1c, the collection is the major triad, and the result is a simple arpeggio.

Example 5.2, taken from Deutsch and Feroe's 1981 article, shows a passage of music and a representation in pitch names of its derivation (top to bottom) or its encoding (bottom to top). This derivation suggests that the passage may be viewed as the result of starting with a middle C, making three applications of one operation (go up to the next higher member of the alphabet) to a specified alphabet (the C major triad), and then taking the resultant C–E–G–C and applying to each of its elements a second operation (adding a prefix before each note that

EXAMPLE 5.2. Deutsch and Feroe (1981) describe passages in terms of alphabets and operations.

EXAMPLE 5.3. A typical jazz lick (from Charlie Parker's
1946 performance of "Oh, Lady Be Good!").

is the next lower member of the alphabet) on a second alphabet (the
chromatic scale).

It is easy to see how a typical jazz "lick" may be thought of as generated by operations on alphabets. Example 5.3 shows a lick from Charlie
Parker's 1946 performance of "Oh, Lady Be Good!"[3] This passage may
be described as the result of two operations (the addition of a prefix that
ascends through the chromatic alphabet and the addition of a suffix that
repeats tones) on a descending arpeggiation of a G-major chord (itself
the result of another operation: descending through the alphabet of the
tonic triad). But it also possible to describe any passage of music in terms
of such operations on alphabets.

As Deutsch and Feroe (1981) note, these alphabets can relate to one
another in hierarchical fashion. Fred Lerdahl (1988, 2001) uses the hierarchical nesting of such alphabets to describe the relative stability of
tones in his "tonal pitch space" (see Table 2.2). My computer models of
melodic expectation (described in chapter 13) use pairs of alphabets to
show how musical forces create motion within one alphabet (called a
"reference alphabet") toward notes of greater stability (members of a
subset alphabet called a "goal alphabet").

But jazz theory precedes all these authors. George Russell's (1959)
Lydian Chromatic Concept inaugurated an important stream of jazz theory called "chord-scale theory" (Amuedo 1996; Gonda 1971–72; Jungbluth
1983; Pressing 1978). Chord-scale theory associates with each chord one
or more chord-scales that project the sound of that chord well. And, as
Russell described the hierarchical nesting of these alphabets in 1959, the
chromatic scale provides motion through the more stable "parent" chord-
scale, which in turn provides motion through the more stable chord.

For the improviser, to say that one alphabet (for example, a whole-
tone chord-scale) provides motion through another (for example, a

certain seventh chord) can be a useful way of thinking. It provides a recipe that identifies and helpfully limits the materials to be used, and that suggests ways of using those materials. Assume one has the task of improvising over a given chord (the same seventh chord just mentioned). If one also knows an alphabet (the same whole-tone scale just mentioned) that can be used to connect the members of that chord, then the task is helpfully reconceived of as starting a melody on some note of that seventh chord, continuing in a simple pattern-driven (probably stepwise) motion, and ending with a note of that seventh chord. Of course, improvising well involves a great deal more than thinking in this way, but thinking in this way can be very useful to the improviser. The computer models of melodic expectation described in chapter 13 may be thought of as solving this task in a similar fashion. And one claim of this book is that listeners do something similar: they tend to hear melodic successions as motions within one alphabet (like our whole-tone scale) that connect pitches of a more basic alphabet (like our seventh chord).

Example 5.4 illustrates the idea of chord-scales with a passage from a three-piano performance of "Stella by Starlight" by Bill Evans.[4] In Example 5.4, the piano labeled "Right" (in the right channel of the album's stereo mix) plays the melody. The piano labeled "Left" plays arpeggiated chords. These chords may be thought of as based upon more basic four-note harmonies.[5] But these arpeggiations also introduce "tensions" or "extensions" typical of these harmonies in this context.[6] The result is chords of six and seven notes. If those same notes are placed in a single octave, the result is a scale.[7] We may think of these chord voicings as subsets of these scales; we may think of these melodies as being built from such scales; or we may regard such chord-scales as a theoretical abstraction useful in understanding such chords and scales. In any case, the piano labeled "Center" exploits this collapsed distinction between chord and scale by playing chords that are essentially scale fragments.

Although a complete specification of the theory might say more about how alphabets might be chosen and internally represented, the present description simply assumes that we hear passages in terms of these collections.[8]

EXAMPLE 5.4. A passage from a three-piano performance of
"Stella by Starlight" by Bill Evans.

HIERARCHIES OF ELABORATION

The summary statement of the theory given above claims that these
operations on alphabets create "hierarchies of elaboration." Deutsch and
Feroe (1981) note that the operations on alphabets they describe create hierarchical structures like those described by Heinrich Schenker
([1935] 1979) – what Bharucha (1984b) calls "event hierarchies." Whereas
Schenker's claims about relationships between distant pitches have

proven controversial, some more recent authors have recast his claims as claims about the perceptions of skilled listeners (Larson 1997c; Lerdahl and Jackendoff 1983; Westergaard 1975). Others report experiments that support these claims about perception (Dibben 1994; Marvin and Brinkman 1999).

As noted in chapter 2, Schenkerian analysis represents a hierarchy of *elaborations*. Furthermore, the theory of musical forces claims that the *way* in which those elaborations are internally represented influences the way in which we expect melodies to be completed.

THE STEPWISE DISPLACEMENT OF AURALIZED TRACES

The general statement above claims that in these hierarchies of elaboration, "stepwise displacements of auralized traces create simple closed shapes." As noted in chapter 2, to "auralize" means to hear sounds internally that are not physically present. The term "trace" means the internal representation of a note that is still melodically active. In a melodic "step" (meaning a half step or a whole step), the second note tends to displace the trace of the first, leaving one trace in musical memory; in a melodic "leap" (meaning a minor third or larger), the second note tends to support the trace of the first, leaving two traces in musical memory.

The displacement of traces is related to what Bharucha (1984a) calls "melodic anchoring" (the tendency of unstable pitches to resolve by step). Albert Bregman (1990) offers evidence that auditory streaming (the way in which we hear notes divide into different "streams," such as melody and accompaniment, or the different strands that make up a "compound melody") depends, at least in part, on the step/leap distinction (so that notes a step apart tend to belong to the same stream, and notes a leap apart tend to belong to different streams). And some theories of tonal music (Bharucha 1984a; Dembski 1988; Komar 1971; Westergaard 1975) grant important status to this distinction. Robert Gjerdingen ([1994] 1999) has explored how neural-net models of aural perception may explain how we hear discrete pitches as forming a single melody or a compound melody. But the questions "How do these notes

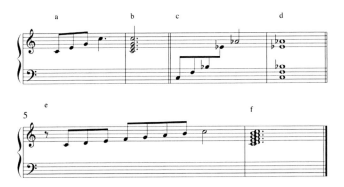

EXAMPLE 5.5. Leaps leave traces; steps displace them.

break into different groups?" and "How do these notes displace the tensions represented by traces?" though related, are not identical.

Regardless of whether hearing this distinction between steps and leaps is learned, innate, or some combination of the two, it is clearly an important part of how experienced listeners give meaning to tonal music. To make this more vivid, consider Example 5.5. Because leaps leave traces, there is a sense in which Example 5.5a (a collection of leaps) leaves something like Example 5.5b sounding in our musical memories. And this is because it is a stack of *leaps,* not because it is triadic; Example 5.5c (a nontriadic collection of leaps) likewise tends to leave something like Example 5.5d sounding in our musical memories. Because melodic steps tend to displace traces, however, Example 5.5e does not leave something like Example 5.5f sounding in our musical memories.

Our ability to hear music in terms of hierarchies of elaboration (what Schenker called "prolongations") means that the displacement of traces also operates on various levels of musical structure. Consider the melodic pattern shown in Example 5.6b. On the surface each new note displaces the trace of the preceding note (from which it lies a step away). If, however, in the context of Example 5.6b, we hear the first measure as prolonging E and the second measure as prolonging D, then we hear the traces of those notes lasting through their respective measures (see Example 5.6a). Thus the trace of the E (at the level of Example 5.6a) is not displaced until the D sounds on the downbeat of the second measure.

EXAMPLE 5.6. The displacement of traces operates on all
hierarchical levels.

Specific factors (such as meter, harmonic rhythm, and melodic patterning) contribute to our hearing of this passage. But it is important to note
that no one of these factors can be said to create prolongations. Any one
of them can override another in a specific example.

Example 5.7 illustrates how "compound melody" (the tendency of a
single melody to be heard as based upon a number of different melodic
"strands," "parts," or "lines" – a centrally important aspect of melodies)
relies on the stepwise displacement of such traces. The passage shown in
Example 5.7d is from Bill Evans's *Town Hall* performance of "Who Can I
Turn To?"[9] The discussion of this example is fairly detailed; some readers may wish to skip over this discussion and continue with the section
below, titled "Step Collections and Leap Collections."

The passage in Example 5.7d is written in traditional notation (also
called "durational notation," because the appearance of each note tells
us how long it lasts). All the notes in Example 5.7d appear in Example
5.7c, but there they are depicted in a restricted form of Schenkerian analytic notation called "strict use of analytic notation."[10] In a Schenkerian
analysis, the appearance of each note tells us whether (at that level) it is
a basic pitch (a stemmed note in strict use) or a note (unstemmed) that
elaborates a more basic pitch.

In Example 5.7c, stem direction shows how the line improvised by
Evans may be understood as alternating between at least two parts (unstemmed notes are notes of elaboration – here only the suffix repetitions
are unstemmed). The upper part, shown with stems up, moves down by
step in a single motion that extends over the whole passage. Every time a
note of that part is leapt away from, it leaves a trace in our musical memo-

EXAMPLE 5.7. Compound melody in Bill Evans's *Town Hall* performance of "Who Can I Turn To?"

ries. That trace is displaced only when it is followed by another note a step away. The same thing happens with the lower parts. The lower parts, however, shown with stems down, are somewhat more complicated. The lower parts make a number of repeated upward motions. Each of these motions eventually converges with the upper part. Every time two parts converge on a single pitch, the total number of parts leaving traces (at the hierarchic level on which the parts converge) is reduced. The result is a reduction in complexity. In each case, this reduction in complexity accompanies a resolution of dissonance. (Although this subtle coordination between the reduction of traces and the resolution of dissonance is remarkably beautiful, it seems to be a relatively common feature of lines improvised by Evans.) Each convergence of parts is shown with a set of converging lines in Example 5.7c.

Example 5.7b offers a more detailed explanation of the lower parts. The notes that connect D♭5 (in the first measure of this example) to A♭5 are heard as passing tones; that is, the more stable (and thus stemmed) D♭5 and A♭5 belong to a deeper level of structure than the elaborating (and thus unstemmed) passing tones that connect them.

That deeper level of structure is shown in Example 5.7a, which includes only the stemmed notes of Example 5.7b. As Example 5.7a suggests, D♭5 belongs to a "structural alto." (A second alto – G as sustained through mm. 4–6 of Example 5.7b – is suggested by the dashed slur in Example 5.7b but is not shown in Example 5.7a. The E♭4 with the flagged stem in Example 5.7b is shown as a structural tenor in Example 5.7a.) The use of durational notation in Example 5.7a also suggests that both the structural alto and the structural soprano leave traces that keep them present in musical memory throughout the passage. After the lower part converges with the upper part on A♭5, it leaps back down to C5, the next note of that structural alto. As this leaping between parts continues, the idea of converging lines becomes central to their rhetorical and gestural meaning. Here the ability of experienced listeners to make sense of the music – to hear it not as a disjointed succession of pointless leaps but as a coherent compound melodic structure – relies on their hearing the traces left by melodic leaps.

STEP COLLECTIONS AND LEAP COLLECTIONS

The theory of musical forces claims that the step/leap distinction not only shapes our experience of melodies in this way but that it also leads us to hear passages of music in terms of a special group of alphabets (Larson 1992; Hurwitz and Larson 1994); those alphabets are called "step collections." A "step collection" is a group of notes that can be arranged in ascending pitch order to satisfy the following two conditions: (1) every adjacent pair of notes is a step (that is, a half step or a whole step) apart; and (2) no nonadjacent pair of notes is a step apart (that is, the collection contains no consecutive semitones). The second condition can be modified slightly to produce a third condition, true of all "proper" step collections: (3) no two pitches – nor any of their octave equivalents – that are not adjacent in the list (except the first and last) are a step apart. And the first condition can be modified in a similar way to produce a fourth condition, true of all "closed" step collections: (4) every adjacent pair of notes – including octave equivalents – is a step apart.

If no other pitches can be added to a proper step collection and still create a step collection, then it is also called "complete." The first condition ensures that the collection can be heard as a complete filling in of a musical space (this follows from recognizing that melodic leaps tend to leave the "trace" of a note "hanging" in our musical memories). The second condition ensures that no note will be heard as redundant in the filling of that space (this also reflects our desire to avoid confusion and the fact that either a whole step or half step can be heard as a step). The third and fourth conditions grant a role to octave equivalence, ensuring that adding octave equivalents to a proper step collection can result in a proper step collection.[11]

The theory of musical forces also claims that we hear passages of music in terms of "leap collections" (whose definition also depends on the step/leap distinction). A leap collection is a group of notes in which no two notes are a step apart. A "proper" leap collection is one in which no two notes – nor any of their octave equivalents – are a step apart. If no other pitches can be added to a proper leap collection, then it is also called "complete." Proper complete leap collections can be further distinguished on the basis of whether they contain a perfect fifth (those that do, the major and minor triads, play a central role in tonal music).

Furthermore, the theory of musical forces claims that the nature of the step/leap distinction supports our tendency to hear melodies in terms of voice-leading strands based on pairs of alphabets. That pair of alphabets includes a "reference collection" (the basic notes from which the melody is drawn, for example, a major scale) and a "goal collection" (the notes on which the melody comes to rest, for example, the notes of the chord harmonizing that melody). The goal collection is a subset of the reference collection. Voice-leading strands typically create a sense of connection by moving successively through a reference collection. The points they connect are members of the goal collection. As noted above, our minds rely in part on the step/leap distinction in order to organize melodies in terms of voice-leading strands. The same distinction explains why reference collections are typically step collections and why goal collections are typically leap collections.

Because they play a central role in music cognition, the step collections play a central role in the computer models described chapter 13. Most of the reference alphabets are step collections, and the programs encourage their selection as reference alphabets.

THE THEORY AS A SET OF INSTRUCTIONS

To give an idea of what a complete implementation of this theory of melodic expectation might look like, it may be restated as a set of instructions – like a recipe – for producing a completion from a cue. Such a set of instructions, when made explicit enough, allows us to test the theory by turning it into a computer model. Here is such a set of instructions:

1. Build up an internal representation of the cue (the "analysis") that includes the key, the mode, the meter, and a hierarchical representation of the elaboration functions and rhythmic attributes of each note or group of notes and the traces they leave. Evaluate the quality of that analysis in terms of its simplicity and order – a kind of confidence rating.

2. For each appropriate level of that hierarchy, determine the alphabet within which motion might continue (the "reference alphabet") and allow more basic levels of structure to determine the alphabet of pitches that will serve as potential goals of that motion (the "goal alphabet").

3. List inertia predictions by continuing successorship motion within the reference alphabet until a member of the goal alphabet is reached. Preserve musical patterns in inertia predictions by applying the same elaboration structures at analogous levels of structure. Consider alternative descriptions of structure wherever these may facilitate the creation of analogous structures.

4. For gravity predictions, allow pitches that are described as "above stable reference points" to descend within their reference alphabet until that reference point or a member of the goal alphabet is reached.

5. For magnetism predictions, move through the reference alphabet to the closest member of the goal alphabet.

6. Evaluate potential completions according to the degree that they give in to the musical forces (their "rating") and enter them into a lottery in which their chance of being chosen is a reflection of their rating, the confidence rating of the current analysis, and other factors affecting the urgency of choosing a completion.

Although I have numbered these instructions, we should consider them as taking place in parallel, and influencing one another, until a potential completion is chosen.

Chapter 13 describes two computer models I have built implementing central parts of this recipe. Although those computer programs do not implement all these instructions, they do allow us to test the workability of certain of these instructions. The complete recipe resembles computer models of analogous cognitive tasks (pattern finding, sequence extrapolation, and analogy making) created at the Center for Research on Concepts and Cognition (CRCC) (Hofstadter et al. 1995). The success and sophistication of programs already created at CRCC suggest that a complete implementation of this set of instructions, though a very complex task, is possible and will likely be quite informative about music cognition. In fact, at this writing, Eric Nichols is working on a more complete implementation of the recipe given above.

REPETITION, BROWNE'S "RETROSPECTION OF ANTICIPATION," AND SCHENKER'S "HIDDEN REPETITION"

Another important claim in the theory of musical forces is that, after hearing a bit of music, experienced listeners tend to say to themselves (albeit usually not consciously) something like "I knew it would go that way!" The first clear exposition of this idea may have come from Richmond Browne (1982). In a presentation on saxophonist Gerry Mulligan, Browne described this as the "retrospection of anticipation" (he also speaks of the "anticipation of retrospection"; more on this in chapter 7).

Consider the short melodic successions in Example 5.8. Assume that we are hearing each in the key of C minor. After hearing Example 5.8b, a listener might say, "I knew it would go that way – gravity pulled the D down to C." After hearing Example 5.8c, a listener might say, "I knew it would go that way – magnetism pulled the D up to E♭." (Or the same listener might hear the pattern as giving in to inertia by continuing the ascending stepwise motion.) And after hearing Example 5.8d, a listener

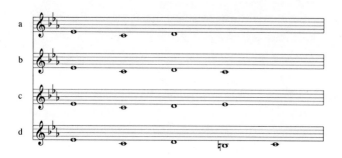

EXAMPLE 5.8. Different continuations for the same melodic beginning illustrate the "retrospection of anticipation" concept.

might say, "I knew it would go that way – inertia continued the pattern of downward leaps and upward steps."

In other words, Examples 5.8b, c, and d – even though they all begin the same way (with the notes given in Example 5.8a) – all end differently. Yet the musical forces allow listeners to say to themselves, for any one of those endings, that they "knew it had to go that way." In this sense, experienced and involved listeners are like jazz improvisers; both are making up the music (or the musical meaning) as they go along – and both do it in a way that makes the best possible sense out of the preceding music.[12]

Of course, in music as in language, expectation and retrospection may continuously reshape the meanings we give to what we hear. David Lewin (1986) offers a model of music perception that grants an important role to such real-time processing of musical meaning. Hallgjerd Aksnes (2002) discusses "the constant reinterpretation that goes on during the listening act" as "an important aspect of musical meaning" (23) and relates that aspect to the work of philosophers Edmund Husserl and William James, as well as music theorists Lewin, Narmour, and Clifton. In Schenker's view, the meanings that we give to music change as we listen, depend on our expectations, and may be revised in retrospect.[13]

It is important to keep in mind this difference between analysis and perception. Schenker's later writings dwell on *analysis* – so they insist on showing one and only one interpretation of a passage. But Schenker had a different view of *perception* – he recognized its multivalent and context-changing character. As I have pointed out elsewhere (1987b, 1997c), the best way to show that one event may be conceived in contradictory ways is to use different analyses – so that the univalent clarity of contradictory Schenkerian analyses can show how a given passage may be perceived in different ways.

Furthermore, we like to *feel* that we "knew it had to go that way" – even when we may *know* that it did not. Like the fox (who decided that he didn't really want the grapes that he couldn't reach – because they must be sour), we make up stories about our (listening) experience that allow us to feel good about ourselves. We experience the "retrospection of anticipation."

The retrospection of anticipation involves the attribution of a single expectation where we might have had no expectation (or might first have seen multiple possible paths). We not only attribute those expectations to ourselves, however, but we also tend to attribute those expectations to the music itself; that is, we tend to make up stories that attribute tendencies to the music – and the musical forces I have described are some of the tendencies we attribute to the music itself. In fact, as noted in chapter 3, we talk about music in a way that suggests that we not only attribute tendencies to the music, we also attribute intentions to the music, as if the music were an animate agent (who wanted, for example, to resolve in a certain way, because impelled to do so). In other words, we anthropomorphize the music.

Of course, we make sense of the physical world in the same way. That we anthropomorphize the physical world, attributing intentions to inanimate objects, is a commonplace observation; roads "climb" up mountains, rocks "want" to fall, and water "seeks" its level. Rudolf Arnheim (1966, 1974) shows nicely how this anthropomorphizing relies on our propensity to attribute dynamic tendencies to the objects of our perceptions, and argues (1986) that musical forces allow us to do the same thing with music. Schenker, who devotes a series of essays (1921–24) to what he calls *Tonwille* ("the will of the tones"), makes such anthropomorphic attributions frequently. When we make these attributions after the fact, we are experiencing the retrospection of anticipation.

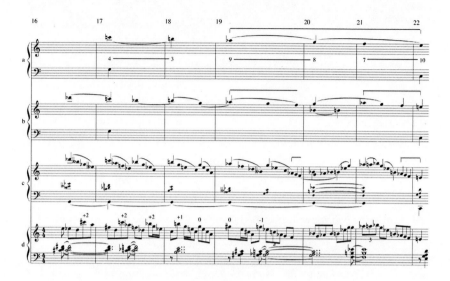

EXAMPLE 5.9. A confirmation in a passage improvised by Bill Evans.

I believe that this is one reason why we derive so much pleasure from repetition in music.[14] Repetition rewards listeners who want to feel that they "knew it had to go that way." The same is true for varied repetitions.

As I have pointed out elsewhere (Larson 1987b), a special type of repetition that exploits our pleasure in the retrospection of anticipation is the type of "hidden repetition" that I call a "confirmation." "Hidden repetition" is Heinrich Schenker's term for what happens when a musical idea occurs on two different levels of musical structure (Burkhart 1978) or its function changes so that it is not clearly heard as a repetition. A "confirmation" is my term for a hidden repetition in which two versions of a single melodic idea, on two different levels of musical structure, are completed at the same time (I also call the shorter, more foreground idea itself "the confirmation"). Example 5.9 shows a confirmation in another passage improvised by Bill Evans.

This figure reproduces part of an analysis (from Larson 2006b) of an improvisation on Cole Porter's song "All of You." The brackets show that the pattern A♭–G–F–E appears on three different levels of musical structure. In each case, the pattern is preceded by a B (albeit in different octaves), so we might speak of the pattern as B–A♭–G–F–E. Because the final E completes all three patterns at the same time, we have a confirmation. The last four or five notes of this passage thus summarize, or retrace the steps of, the preceding music.

In a confirmation, the simultaneous completion of different versions encourages the listener to attribute a kind of inevitability to that completion. And the fact that two (in this case, three!) versions are the same encourages the listener to retrospectively attribute to the longer version(s) the same predictability experienced in the shorter version.

SCHENKER, MUSICAL FORCES, AND MUSICAL IMPLICATIONS AND REALIZATIONS

The passage cited above from Schenker's *Counterpoint* suggests his interest in musical implications and realizations. But the theory of musical forces goes further, claiming that listeners expect music to complete the kinds of hierarchical structures that Schenker described.

To some readers, my reliance on Schenkerian theory may seem at odds with my emphasis on expectation. Perhaps this is because some theorists who have written about expectation in music (especially Leonard Meyer and Eugene Narmour) have distanced themselves from Schenker's theories. In fact, Narmour (1977) initially described his implication-realization model as an alternative to Schenker's theories. My purpose in this and the following section is to hint at the strong connections between Schenker's theories and work in music cognition, melodic expectation, and musical forces.

Narmour's work on melodic complexity (1992) argues that expectations create hierarchical structures that resemble Schenkerian analyses. But a more recent article (Narmour 1996) may be read as a more plausible case for the reverse argument: that expectations arise on all perceived hierarchical levels of musical structure, that those levels are best described with Schenkerian analyses, and that Schenker's theories provide a necessary underpinning for any successful implication-realization model. That article, devoted to understanding a movement by Mozart in terms of Narmour's implication-realization model, begins by presenting a Schenkerian analysis of that movement.

The theory of musical forces claims that part of the way in which we give meaning to music is to hear the notes as relating to one another in hierarchies of elaboration – that is, in terms of (at least at some levels of) a Schenkerian analysis – and that such hierarchies are central to melodic expectation. In other words, like the theories of Westergaard (1975) and Lerdahl and Jackendoff (1983), it claims that experienced listeners of tonal music not only perform (unconscious) aural Schenkerian analyses but also expect the music to continue in such a way that it creates the types of hierarchical patterns that occur in such analyses.[15]

KEY DETERMINATION, POSITION FINDING, MULTIPLE MECHANISMS, AND MELODIC EXPECTATION

Taken together, these ideas suggest two interesting paradoxes. The first concerns the "chicken and egg" nature of key determination and melodic expectation. The second concerns the multiple mechanisms and the unitary experience of key.

As noted in chapter 2, key determination and melodic continuation are related. Melodic continuation depends on the operation of musical forces, which depend on stability conditions, which depend on key determination; thus melodic continuation depends on key determination. Yet chapter 5 argues that key determination answers the question "What is the (ultimately most stable) note on which this passage will end?"; thus key determination appears to depend on melodic continuation. In other words, it is difficult (and perhaps misleading) to answer the question "Which comes first, key determination or melodic continuation?" Such "chicken and egg" dilemmas are common in trying to explain how the mind launches the various programs it runs. Somehow these processes of key determination and melodic implication "pull themselves up by their own bootstraps." (In fact, the reason we say that we "boot" a computer when we start it is that, before it can execute a program, it must execute a program that allows it to execute programs – originally called a "boot-strapping" program.)

Chapter 1 noted another interesting paradox concerning causal and mental mechanisms. In complex systems, effects often have multiple causes. One of those complex systems is the mind.[16] Yet the multiple mechanisms of our minds have evolved a strong drive to seek simple explanations (potential ancestors who favored more complex reasoning tended not to pass on the genes for such elaborate thinking when that slower thinking led them to become another animal's lunch). Thus we seek single-mechanism explanations.

In the latter part of the twentieth century, researchers in music cognition sought single-mechanism explanations for key determination. Key determination seems to have an "all or nothing" quality that may have encouraged this search for a single mechanism. As this chapter argues, when we hear something in a certain key, it is because we auralize a melodic completion that creates a simple shape that closes on a relatively stable pitch. When we get our tonal bearings in this way, I believe that we usually (at least in common-practice tonal music) experience a passage of music as being in one and only one key. In other words, our minds seek a single-key experience.

Perhaps this single-key experience led researchers to think that there must be a single-mechanism explanation. Different researchers proposed different mechanisms. I suspect that our musical minds can employ any or all of them, but published descriptions and arguments about key finding give the impression that at least some researchers thought they were describing the one and only key-finding mechanism. Three important mechanisms may be summarized under the rubrics of "rare intervals," "tone profiles," and "order effects." The following paragraphs describe each of these in turn, relating each to aspects of the theory described in this chapter.

The "rare interval hypothesis" (also called the "intervallic rivalry theory") followed Richmond Browne's (1981) observation that subsets of the diatonic collection occur with varying frequencies and that the musical mind could thus use the rarest subsets in "position finding." In experiments by Helen Brown and David Butler (1981), when participants heard rare subsets they had higher levels of agreement on which note was the tonic (even when that note was not in the subset heard) than when they heard common subsets (even when the putative tonic was in the subset).

Notice, by the way, that although many writers seem initially to have taken "position finding" as equivalent to "key finding," they are not the same thing. Rare subsets tell us where we are in a diatonic collection,

but they only tell us what key we are in if we make two additional assumptions: first, that we are in a diatonic collection; and, second, that
the collection is major (rather than minor or a different mode).[17] These
assumptions are related to what I call "reference levels" and "goal levels";
for example, for the diatonic collection without sharps or flats (C D E F
G A B), the specification of one goal level (D–F–A) would make it one
diatonic mode (Dorian), whereas the specification of a different goal
level (G–B–D) would make it a different diatonic mode (Mixolydian).[18]
I use the term "key" to refer to the note on which we expect melodies
to end, "mode" to refer to the step collection that we hear as reference
collection for that passage, and "diatonic collection position" to refer
to the position within that collection that we find via rare intervals (so
that D in D Dorian is the same "diatonic collection position" as the D
in G Mixolydian, even though the first functions as $\hat{1}$ and the second
functions as $\hat{5}$).

The "tone profiles" (also called "tonal hierarchies") of Carol Krumhansl and colleagues (Krumhansl 1990; Krumhansl and Kessler 1982)
have led to "key-finding algorithms" that allow a computer to determine
the key of a passage of music by comparing its distribution of pitches
to the distribution of pitches in Krumhansl's probe-tone profiles (described in chapter 2, in the section titled "Metaphor").[19] Although these
algorithms have done well with some passages, they produce a list of
correlations with the various keys that may fluctuate over time (even
on a note-to-note basis); my experience of key is an "all or nothing" one
(not a sense that I am 30% in F and 20% in B♭), and that experience does
not typically fluctuate with each new added note.

The work of Helen Brown (Brown 1988; Brown, Butler, and Jones
1994) shows "order effects" in key determination. Her experiments
clearly show that temporal re-orderings of a given string of pitches can
systematically and consistently change the key that experimental participants attribute to those notes.

When I first presented these ideas on key determination, melodic
continuation, Schenkerian analysis, and their mutual dependence (Larson 1993a describes each and refers to the "bootstrapping" involved),
the music-cognition community was very interested in all three topics,
treated each one polemically, and did not speak of connections between

any of them. Now it would appear that multiple-mechanism explanations have displaced the polemics to a degree (Butler [1998] discusses "tonal bootstrapping" in a way that argues for the co-generation of aural key recognition through multiple cognitive mechanisms, and recent updates to the Krumhansl-Kessler key-finding algorithm may be viewed as attempts to incorporate Brown's ideas about order effects). I claim that all three are intimately tied, that key attribution is part of how tonal listeners create musical meaning, that we have a drive to attribute a single key (and a reluctance to change keys without substantial contrary-key evidence) and it is this drive that helps make modulation both interesting and challenging to us, that key attribution is a form of melodic expectation that brings with it a whole set of metaphorical entailments (such as hearing a return to tonic as a "coming home"), that key attribution and melodic continuation both involve a kind of aural Schenkerian analysis, and that this bootstrapping process is best described in the summary statement repeated below.

SUMMARY

This chapter has presented a theory of melodic expectation (and key finding) in tonal music. The theory claims that experienced listeners of tonal music have expectations about how melodic beginnings will be completed, and it claims that important aspects of those expectations are captured by the musical forces theorized in chapter 4:

> Experienced listeners of tonal music expect melodic completions in which the musical forces of gravity, magnetism, and inertia control operations on alphabets in hierarchies of elaboration whose stepwise displacements of auralized traces create simple closed shapes.

Our prospective expectations depend on the attribution of meanings (especially involving metaphorical motion and forces) and intention to the music we are currently hearing. At the same time our retrospective understanding of musical meaning depends on the attribution of expectations and intentionality to the music we have just heard.

6

Rhythm, Meter, and Musical Forces

Chapters 1–5 presented a theory of musical forces, including a model of melodic expectation (and key determination) based on gravity, magnetism, and inertia. Chapter 6 expands upon that theory by showing how it can illuminate aspects of rhythm and meter. In doing so, this chapter notes what is rhythmic about musical forces, describes "rhythmic forces" that are analogous to musical forces, explains analogies between pitch and durational patterns, and shows how the same embodied knowledge of physical forces that informs our understanding of melodic expectation also shapes our experience of musical rhythm. It appears that the theory of musical forces can deeply enhance our ideas about meter and rhythm.

MEANING, MOTION, AND METER

Many published studies of rhythm begin with the observation that a series of identical, equally spaced, un-pitched clicks (like the ticks of a clock or metronome, for example) tend to be heard in groups, usually in twos or threes. Different listeners may hear different groupings, or they may hear the groups beginning and ending with different clicks. But once they hear a given grouping, they tend to hear the remaining clicks as continuing in that same grouping. Beginning with this observation allows theorists to start with what seem like the most basic rhythmic phenomena, allows them to introduce and define terms through an uncomplicated example, and allows them to remind us that rhythmic phenomena are mental.

The same example can provide a convenient starting point for our discussion of rhythm and musical forces. Note that the definition of "meaning" offered in chapter 2 captures what happens when we hear those undifferentiated clicks in groups. Chapter 2 defined "meaning" as "something that our minds create when they group things into patterned relations," and it notes how the phrase "to hear as" reflects that meaning-making process. When we *hear* undifferentiated clicks *as* grouped in twos, our minds create musical meaning. That different listeners may hear different groupings, or groups beginning and ending with different clicks, underscores the point that it is our minds, not just the stimuli, that shape the meaning that is created. Of course, there is typically a lot more to musical meaning than whether events are grouped in twos or in threes (especially when we are dealing with musical sounds that are more sophisticated than a series of undifferentiated clicks), but the points here are that these meanings are created by our minds, that meaning and grouping are related (a point underscored in chapter 2 with the example of "Thissen ten ceise asytome morize" or, rather, "This sentence is easy to memorize"), and that one of the fundamental ways in which we create musical meaning involves rhythmic phenomena.

Chapter 3 noted that one important way in which we give meaning to musical sounds is to hear them in terms of the metaphor of musical motion. That chapter argued that we acquire our basic embodied understanding of physical motion in four different ways and that these four basic experiences of physical motion give rise, via metaphor, to the chief ways we conceptualize musical motion. Extended to the example of hearing undifferentiated clicks as groups of clicks, the argument of chapter 3 suggested that when we hear those clicks, we take them as evidence of motion – the motion of a (musical) object we observe, the motion of an object we move, or the motion of our own bodies.

Chapter 3 went on to observe that many aspects of physical motion are imported into our experience of music as motion. Thus we tend not only to hear those clicks as groups of clicks but also in terms of an object or objects moving along a particular path in a particular manner. This "manner of motion" that we attribute to successions of sounds depends in part on the way we experience those sounds. Hearing those undifferentiated clicks grouped in twos instead of threes affects how one might hear the character of their movement; clicks heard in twos will be easier to hear as march-like motions than clicks grouped in threes. The time between clicks (their "inter-onset interval," or IOI) will affect the speed we attribute to the motion we hear in them; other things being equal, less time between clicks is understood as "faster." In fact, this may seem so obvious that it might escape our notice that mapping shorter IOIs onto increased speed is also a metaphorical attribution of meaning – a nice example of how metaphors of motion can be both powerful and invisible. But other things are not necessarily equal. If those undifferentiated clicks have an IOI close to 125 ms (equivalent to sixteenth notes at 120 beats per minute), one listener may hear them as a chugging train sound whereas another listener hears them as the sound of the rhythm typically played on a hi-hat cymbal in disco music. These two listeners might have a different sense of how fast that motion is, depending upon their expectations about the speeds of trains or typical dance-music tempos. A third listener who grouped the same clicks in threes might have a completely different experience of how "fast" those clicks are moving. In other words, rhythmic experiences like tempo and pace are dependent upon the nature of the physical motions in terms of which those clicks are experienced. Different listeners, when hearing those clicks, may experience different degrees of effort, massiveness, inevitability, location, immediacy, attractiveness, threat, and many other such "meanings." But the meanings that they attribute to those sounds are, at least in part, a function of their tendency to hear musical successions as physical motions. And this is just for a set of undifferentiated clicks. Rich musical contexts provide many other means of creating rhythmic character.

Some discussions of rhythm and meter reflect our experience of music by referring to such rhythmic character. Justin London begins his book *Hearing in Time* (2004) by noting that musicians asked to define "meter" are likely to count, give examples, or perhaps talk about "rhythmic feel" or "groove." Such practical definitions (or illustrations) resonate with the etymology of "rhythm" – the Greek ρυθμός means "flow" or "style"; they reflect an embodied understanding of rhythm and meter. Disembodied discussions of rhythm and meter have the potential to derail attempts to understand the *experience* of these phenomena.

In the sections that follow I consider the problems created by treating rhythm as a solely musical phenomenon, and by conflating "rhythm" and "duration."

RHYTHM IS NOT SOLELY A MUSICAL PHENOMENON

Rhythm, as defined in this book, is not a purely musical phenomenon. In this chapter I argue that rhythm is an embodied meaning – part of the meaning we attribute to music when we hear a musical succession in terms of physical motion – and I define the rhythm of music as the quality of motion we experience in it, a quality that is only partly dependent on its timing, and a quality that includes grouping and meter. When we use adjectives such as "fast," "slow," "flowing," "stately," "eager," or "awkward" to describe a bit of music, we are discussing aspects of its rhythm. As Maury Yeston notes, "The theory of musical rhythm has always been concerned with the elucidation of musical motion" (1976, 1).

To use the word "rhythm" in this way does not restrict the term to music. It is common to speak of the rhythm of poetry, the rhythm of one's workday, or the rhythm of life. To do so is to speak of the quality of motion we attribute to that of poetry, the workday, or life – by relating it to our experience of physical motion. In fact, because we can even experience static forms (such as architecture or painting) in terms of physical change (for example, by "reading" them from left to right as enacting a physical or musical process), people also speak of the rhythm of architecture or the rhythm of a painting. John Dewey captures this larger sense of rhythm when he writes that "all interactions that effect stability and order in the whirling flux of change are rhythms" ([1934] 1979, 16).

It might seem that focusing only on what is distinctively musical about rhythm and meter might be the best path to a better understanding. Such a focus would exclude considerations of poetry and workdays, painting and architecture, or physical motions and the paths of our lives outside of music. It is easy to imagine why such a specialized focus might seem reasonable. After all, a popular image of modern science is that it is such specialization that allows it to "divide and conquer" its subject matter (notice that the metaphor of "divide and conquer" suggests that popular images of military science also shape such thinking). But in my view science is most interesting when it finds connections between apparently different phenomena. I also think that it is our interest in "all interactions that effect stability and order in the whirling flux of change" (Dewey [1934] 1979, 16) that leads us to want to understand musical rhythms in the first place.

Furthermore, focusing only on what is distinctively musical about rhythm would run counter to the approach of this book. "Meaning," as noted above, is defined in chapter 2 as "something that our minds create when they group things into patterned relations." If we limit our investigation to asking how musical events group into patterned relations with one another, then we appear to restrict our study to what is distinctively musical about rhythm. Chapters 1 and 2, however, also position the theory of musical forces within a larger theory of expressive meaning in music. And they note that such expressive meanings arise metaphorically "when we hear musical events as reflecting the patterns of our intellectual, emotional, imaginative, and kinesthetic lives." I believe that one of the attractions of musical rhythm is the way that it leads us to create expressive meanings by mapping musical motions onto other life experiences.

RHYTHM IS MORE THAN MERE DURATION

This view of rhythm (as the quality of motion we experience in music) does not conflate rhythm with duration. To indicate the durations in a musical event is to say only how long that event (and each element of it) lasts. Returning to "Twinkle, Twinkle, Little Star" (see Example 6.1a), we might describe the durations by saying that all the notes (except the seventh and fourteenth) last one quarter note. Or we could say that, at the tempo q = 120, the first through sixth and eighth through thirteenth notes all last 500 ms. Another way of providing the same information is to state when each element in a musical rhythm occurs. For example, if the tempo is q = 120, then the fifth note enters two seconds after the first one. If we speak of deviations from the notated timing (say, to give two examples, if the fifth note occurs 20 ms later than the two-second mark just mentioned, or if an extra 30 ms is added before the last three notes) we can still restrict ourselves to observations about duration – as opposed to rhythm.

EXAMPLE 6.1. Two passages that have the same patterns of durations but different rhythms.

One way to underscore the difference between duration (or timing) and rhythm is to note that two passages can have the same patterns of duration but be experienced as having two different rhythms. Example 6.1b gives notation for a variation on "Twinkle, Twinkle, Little Star." In Example 6.1a, the repetition of each note in measures 1, 2, 3, 5, 6, and 7 creates two-note groups within these bars. At the same time the rhythmically unstable upbeats can also be heard to lead into the next bar. In Example 6.1b, the A♭ in the third measure and the D♭ in the seventh measure make the third and seventh measures flow more smoothly and more purposefully into the following measure. The quality of flow has changed because we experience the musical succession in terms of physical motion, and because the musical forces act differently on A♭ than they do on A (in part because melodic magnetism draws A♭ to G more strongly than it draws A to G). Because the quality of flow has changed, the rhythm has changed – even though the durations are the same. Remember, of course, that all these musical meanings (flow, motion, and forces) – although they tend to be experienced as if they were inherent in the music – are not literally a part of the music; they are created in the mind of the listener, who then attributes them to the music.

Actually, there are two senses in which we might speak of the durations having changed. First of all, reflect on the differences in how you would sing these two melodies. I believe that many musicians, if they sang the original melody with the notes somewhat detached, would tend to lengthen the sixth note when it is changed to A♭. This might not affect the "inter-onset durations" (the time between note beginnings), but it could lengthen the A♭ (and shorten the space between it and the onset of the following G). But even if the notes are performed with precisely the same length, the A♭ still flows more smoothly and more purposefully into the following G than the A does. In fact, the tendency to lengthen that A♭ may be regarded as the musician's intuitive way of responding to that smoother, more purposeful flow. In other words, altering the duration of the note might enhance the effect – but it is still the pitch of that note and the way the musical forces act upon it that makes it flow differently.

Another sense in which we might speak of the durations having changed would be to talk about the duration of pitch change. In Example 6.1a, we hear a new note every two beats, but in Example 6.1b, the A♭ makes the pitch change more often, introducing a new note every single beat. In other words, the durations of the "surface" of the music have not changed, but the durations at a deeper level, or the durations of a different aspect of the music, have changed – but it is still the pitch of that note and the way the musical forces act upon it that creates a different rhythmic effect.

We have seen that confusing "rhythm" and "duration" may mislead us by inappropriately discounting the role of pitch (and musical forces) in rhythmic experience. It may also mislead us to regard rhythm as something quantified, intellectual, and disembodied.

Gottfried Wilhelm Leibniz (who, along with Sir Isaac Newton, invented calculus) wrote that "music is a secret exercise in arithmetic of the soul, unaware of its act of counting." Of course, Leibniz's observation is most useful when we think of that counting as a part of – rather than a complete account of – musical experience. In an article that begins with this quotation from Leibniz, Joanne Cavanaugh (1998) also quotes Peabody Conservatory musicologist Susan Weiss as saying that, for the ancient Greeks, "music was not emotional. It was based on solid evidence of how the moon, the sun, and the stars worked, more than on the localized, anecdotal experience of hearing sound." If Weiss means that, for the

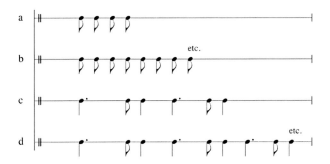

EXAMPLE 6.2. Inertia (the tendency of a pattern to continue in the same fashion) applies to patterns of durations.

ancient Greeks, the term "music" meant the intellectual study of music rather than its experience, then we may accept her point – as long as we also remember that the writings of some ancient Greeks show that they were also very interested in the emotional aspects of the experience of music. But when rhythm is thought of as *only* an arithmetical counting, then we confuse rhythm with mere duration.

We began this chapter by thinking about the grouping of undifferentiated clicks. Such thinking shows us that duration, by itself, can do much to shape our experience of rhythm. But if rhythm is the way that notes flow into one another, then pitch and musical forces also shape rhythm.

INERTIA AND RHYTHM

Musical inertia (the tendency of a pattern to continue in the same fashion) is central to musical rhythm. If we hear a pattern of durations, then inertia leads us to expect that pattern to continue. Consider the rhythms in Example 6.2. If we hear the notes in Example 6.2a as a string of eighth notes (like the undifferentiated clicks discussed just above), then inertia leads us to expect that pattern of eighth notes to continue (as in Example 6.2b). If Example 6.2c is heard as repeating the pattern ♩.♪♪, then inertia leads us to expect the next three notes to have the same durational pattern (as in Example 6.2d).

EXAMPLE 6.3. Inertial expectations depend on the way in which
patterns are internally represented.

The way in which a pattern is heard shapes the inertial expectations
we experience. Consider the melodies in Example 6.3. If we were to hear
the notes in Example 6.3a as repeating the durational pattern ♩.♪♩ – and
as independent from any pitch pattern in those notes – then our inertial
expectation would be limited to expecting the pattern of durations to
continue (as suggested in Example 6.3b); that is, we would accept Example 6.3c as giving in to inertia. However, if we were to hear the notes
in Example 6.3a as repeating the pitch pattern of a descending stepwise
third – and as independent from the durations of those notes – then our
inertial expectation would be limited to expecting the pattern of pitches
to continue (as suggested in Example 6.3d); that is, we would accept
Example 6.3e (but not Example 6.3c) as giving in to inertia. And if we
were to hear the notes in Example 6.3a as repeating both the durational
pattern notated in Example 6.3b and the pitch pattern notated in Example
6.3d, then our inertial expectation would be that both patterns would
continue; that is, we would accept Example 6.3f (but not Examples 6.3c
or e) as giving in to inertia.

Example 6.3 also illustrates the retrospection of anticipation (discussed in chapter 5). After hearing any of the continuations suggested
in that example, listeners might feel that they heard something that they
had predicted, thus experiencing the retrospection of anticipation.

INERTIA AND HIERARCHICAL PHYSICAL MOTIONS

If we hear musical motions as analogous to physical motions, and if we experience physical motions as hierarchical, then durational patterns will also tend to be heard as hierarchical. And because this knowledge comes from our experience of physical motions, we expect those musical motions to be combined in hierarchies that are constrained by the same tendencies that constrain the combinations of physical motions. (As argued in chapter 3, and in agreement with contemporary cognitive metaphor theory, our experience of musical motion seems to borrow not just selective features of physical motion but any aspect of physical motion that can be mapped onto musical succession, including the constraints such as physical forces.) One of those constraints is that physical motions tend to have beginnings, middles, and ends that move from stability through instability then back again to stability.

Like many musicians, I often refer to such a motion (one with a beginning, middle, and end) as a "gesture." Robert Hatten defines musical gesture as meaningful and expressive "significant energetic shaping of sound through time" (2004, esp. 93–132). Hatten's theory of gesture draws on the theory of musical forces (2004, esp. 115–117) in order to describe what he calls the "virtual environmental forces" that contribute to the shape and meaning of musical gestures, and he notes that "their expressive effects exploit potential contrasts or energetic expenditure with respect to the forces in their field/space" (2004, 110). As Hatten notes, "Gestures may also be hierarchically organized, in that larger gestures can be comprised of smaller gestures" (2004, 94).[1]

Consider the melodies in Example 6.4. If we were to hear the notes in Example 6.4a (which is the same as Example 6.3a) as repeating the pattern ♩.♪♪, then we would be hearing a pattern that lasts for a dotted half note. Example 6.4b gives that dotted-half-note "pattern length" to the pitches that the pattern elaborates. Example 6.4b thus shows a deeper level of structure contained within Example 6.4a – a level that we experience as an "underlying rhythm." And if we experience Example 6.4b as a stepwise descent in dotted half notes, then inertia leads us to expect it to continue as shown in Example 6.4c. Of course, the claim here is that we hear Example 6.4b because we hear the ♩.♪♪ pattern. This

EXAMPLE 6.4. Hearing patterns of durations in terms of physical motions leads us to hear beginnings, middles, and ends.

suggests that if inertia turns Example 6.4b into Example 6.4c, then it turns Example 6.4a into Example 6.4d – each dotted half note being elaborated with the same ♩.♪♩ pattern. However, Example 6.4e – without an elaboration of the final dotted half note – sounds perfectly acceptable as a way of realizing the implications of Example 6.4a. In fact, no matter how many times inertia leads us to repeat the ♩.♪♩ pattern, we will prefer the melody to end with ♩.♪♩♩., with its metrically stable final dotted half note. This suggests that we are not hearing the melody of Example 6.4 as a series of three-note ♩.♪♩ patterns; instead, we are hearing it as a series of elided four-note ♩.♪♩♩. gestures. (Patterns are "elided" when the last note of the first pattern is shared by the first note of the second pattern.) In other words, just as physical gestures tend to have beginnings, middles, and ends that move from stability through instability and back again to stability, so, too, do musical motions. (Notice also that successive patterns are combined by eliding a stable ending with a stable beginning.) Example 6.4f uses stem direction and slurs to show this.

Experienced performers know intuitively that it is often helpful to think of rhythms as elided in this way. Yet our notational system, with its bar lines that typically separate a downbeat from the upbeats that lead to it, often disguises such elided rhythms. Thurmond's (1982) performance

EXAMPLE 6.5. Rhythmic and tonal stability.

manual encourages performers to feel the way in which upbeats (at various rhythmic levels) lead to the following downbeats and to emphasize those connections with dynamics or slurring, or both. Performers who follow his advice tend to produce interpretations in which listeners hear a stronger sense of forward motion. And when they do, the result is often that their performance projects those elisions more strongly.

METRIC STABILITY AND RHYTHMIC MAGNETISM

If we think of musical successions in terms of physical motion, then this last observation seems easy to explain. Physical motions, when complete, begin and end in stable positions. Chapter 4 defined "melodic magnetism" (the tendency of an unstable note to move to the closest stable pitch, a tendency that grows stronger as we get closer to the goal) in terms of the pitch stability described in Schenkerian theory. But what is stability within the domain of rhythm? Rhythmic stability is a quality that listeners attribute to points in time and, as a result, also to the notes that articulate those points in time.

Of course, rhythmic stability differs from tonal stability. Traditional theory might illustrate this point with the appoggiatura in Example 6.5b, measure 3. When we hear the first two measures of Examples 6.5a, we expect it to continue with the third measure of Example 6.5a. The C on that downbeat is tonally stable – it does not need to resolve. To say that we hear a note as tonally unstable means that we auralize a more stable note to which it could resolve and a path that would take it there (displacing the trace of that unstable note), and that we experience a desire to hear that resolution. It is also metrically stable – it starts on the downbeat instead of on a less stable part of the bar. If, instead of that C, we hear the D in Example 6.5b, then we hear that D as an appoggiatura – a note that is rhythmically stable (because it is on a downbeat) yet tonally unstable (because it needs to resolve).[2]

Like tonal stability, metric stability is comparative; no moment possesses absolutely metrical stability. Rather, we experience one moment as more or less metrically stable than another – that is, we hear rhythmic moments in terms of other rhythmic moments. We feel, for example, that this beat moves to that one, or that this upbeat connects those downbeats. Thus we say that to hear a note or time point as rhythmically unstable means that we auralize a more stable note or time point to which, or from which, it moves.

Like tonal stability, metric stability creates hierarchical levels. To say that a pitch is more tonally stable is to say that it belongs to deeper levels of pitch structure (in a Schenkerian analysis). To say that a time point is more rhythmically stable is to say that it belongs to deeper levels of meter (where, for example, in four-four, the quarter-note level is deeper than the eighth-note level but not as deep as the half-note level).

Like tonal stability, metric stability gives a note or moment the quality of a goal. Because our desire to move to that goal grows stronger the closer we get to that goal, we experience a "metric magnetism" that parallels our experience of melodic magnetism.[3]

RHYTHMIC GRAVITY

Our embodied experience of musical rhythm also suggests that we might experience something that could be called "rhythmic gravity." Rhythmic stability maps onto physical stability, and our most stable physical positions involve rest on a stable platform or base. The terms "downbeat" and "upbeat" reflect the simplest ways in which dance-like motions associate downward physical motions with musical motions toward metrically stable points. Conducting motions reflect this mapping by showing "downbeats" with downward motions. Effort, opening, and similar qualities associated with an upward (against gravity) motion are, according to this mapping, associated with upbeats. This idea (that a single mapping, such as rhythm as gesture, brings with it a whole system of metaphorical entailments, such as a resultant "rhythmic gravity") is consistent with the contemporary cognitive theory of metaphor.

This suggests that we might define "rhythmic gravity" as that quality we attribute to a rhythm (when we map its flow onto a physical gesture) that reflects the impact physical gravity has on the physical gesture onto which we map that rhythm. Thus, if we hear a musical gesture as "falling in to a downbeat," then we experience rhythmic gravity as a force which pulls that musical gesture "down" (regardless of whether the pitch ascends or descends as it does). And if we hear a different gesture as moving up and away from a downbeat, then the musical meaning that gesture has for us is related to the way in which it relates to the downward pull of rhythmic gravity. That musical meaning could vary. We might hear that rhythm as moving up and away with effort, as if feeling pulled down by its own weight as it strives to overcome rhythmic gravity. Or we might hear that rhythm as floating effortlessly up and away, as if having easily liberated itself (like a balloon), escaping rhythmic gravity.

The result is that "up and down" map onto musical motion in two very different ways. In the domain of musical pitch, "down" means pitches with "lower" frequencies. In the domain of meter, "down" beats are moments of greater metric stability. The two need not agree, and they can interact in interesting ways.

ELIDED PATTERNS OF DURATIONS

As noted above, our tendency to hear elided patterns of durations is an important fact about musical rhythm that depends upon our understanding of musical motions in terms of hierarchies of physical motions. Example 6.6 illustrates this point. Example 6.6a returns to the pattern discussed in connection with Example 6.4, and Example 6.6c shows the dotted-half-note pattern contained within it. In between, Example 6.6b shows a pattern in half notes and quarter notes. If the eighth notes in Example 6.6a are heard as passing tones, then they are heard as con-

EXAMPLE 6.6. Hearing hierarchical patterns of durations in terms of physical motions with beginnings, middles, and ends.

necting and elaborating the notes shown in Example 6.6b. If we hear the pattern in Example 6.6b, then we have the inertial expectation that it will continue, and we could hear continuations such as those given in Examples 6.6d and (rhythmically) e as giving in to that inertial impulse.

A further important claim about our experience of musical rhythm is that it does not just *reflect* physical motions (for example, when we hear musical rhythms as hierarchies of elided durational patterns joined the way physical motions are, as noted above); our rhythmic experience also reflects our (physically grounded and culturally shaped) *values*. For example, in contexts where our culture places a high value on equanimity, balance, and calm reflection, music tends to move in ways that reflect those values: it tends to move smoothly in usually smaller motions, to balance expansive gestures with compensating motions that restore equilibrium, to avoid sudden or exaggerated motions, and so on.

Music for worship in the Catholic Church of the sixteenth century seems to support this claim. Valuing equanimity, balance, and calm reflection, it seems that the Church sought music reflecting those values. I am not claiming that these are the only values motivating what the Church sought. Nor am I claiming that all musical preferences sought by the Church at that time were entirely consistent. But it does appear that the Catholic Church, at least to a degree, sought music consistent with those values. Sixteenth-century sacred polyphony (as a result, according to this claim) tends to emphasize smooth and graceful motion. Textbooks that teach students how to emulate this style, including both early and modern counterpoint treatises, may (according to this view) be viewed as collections of rules that are at least partly designed to produce smoothly elided rhythmic patterns.[4] Such rule collections can be quite extensive (and, as is inevitably the case, agree in varying degrees with the actual practices of specific composers). Thus it is quite beyond the scope of this book to consider more than a small portion of them in any detail. Looking at just a few such rules, however, can usefully illustrate the basic argument here: that both physical embodiment and cultural values may shape rhythmic choices and rhythmic experience.

One example concerns restrictions on the use of the rhythm notated as quarter-quarter-half (that is, when the quarter notes occupy a more metrically stable part of the bar than the half note does). Unless the last note is tied over into the following measure, this rhythm is usually prohibited (except in the penultimate measure). The equivalent (twice as fast) rhythm eighth-eighth-quarter (that is, when the eighth notes occupy a more metrically stable part of the bar than the quarter note does) is also prohibited. One could rightly note that these prohibitions are designed to make the underlying meter clear; they result in an agreement between agogic (or durational) accent and metric stability (that is, the long notes happen on the more stable beats). But if such agreement were the only reason for this rule, then the syncopations allowed in fourth and fifth species would also be outlawed. Further, the use of the quarter-quarter-half rhythm in the penultimate bar is not explained by this preference for agogic and metric agreement.

When one tries to explain these rhythmic preferences in terms of physical motion and musical forces, it becomes easier. If we hear, in a species counterpoint exercise, a series of half notes as dividing (for example) measure 4 into stable downbeats and unstable upbeats, then the entry in measure 5 of what I call the "momentum rhythm" (half-quarter-quarter) means that the quarter note at the end of measure 5 enters too late for us to think of measure 5 as subdivided. Musical inertia carries our interpretation of measure 4 into measure 5. But if those quarter notes then continue in measure 6, we hear the inertia of that quarter-note motion carry into measure 6 – the same way that we use the inertia of a preparatory bounce before jumping. By contrast, if measure 5 is all half notes and measure 6 is all quarter notes, then the abruptness we experience is akin to jumping without a preparatory bounce.

Such embodied explanations help to explain why the quarter-quarter-half rhythm usually occurs only in the penultimate bar, why it is typically allowed elsewhere only if the half note is tied into the following bar, and why syncopations are the most graceful way to move from quarter notes to half notes in species-counterpoint exercises. The quarter-quarter-half rhythm subdivides the first half of a bar into two quarter notes and then pauses on a half note in the second half of the same bar. The result resembles a physical motion that accelerates away from a rhythmically stable jumping-off point and then pauses ("up in the air") on the rhythmically unstable part of the bar. If this rhythm were to continue by articulating the beginning of the next bar (without a tie), then its analogous physical motion might land quite squarely on that downbeat, with the upbeat half note heard as "putting on the brakes" – as if one took a few running steps, leaped from an unstable platform, and then landed with both feet on a more stable platform. With such a deceleration and stop, such a physical motion would make a suitable ending for a series of physical motions. And since it makes such a good ending, it works less well for the middle of a passage that is supposed to create the sense of a single motion. But if the rhythm quarter-quarter-half ties its half note over into the following bar, then it more strongly resembles a physical motion that, leaping into the air, sails beyond a stable landing point (the downbeat over which it is tied), touching lightly on the next (less stable) location – continuing the forward motion and smoothly joining musical gestures. In fact, such a motion seems the smoothest way, in the middle of a passage of species counterpoint, to connect the running quarter notes of third species back to the slower motions of the other species.[5]

Counterpoint treatises give long lists of rules for acceptable and unacceptable rhythms in this type of music. One argument I am making here is that thinking of these rhythms in terms of physical motions gives us a more economical way of understanding them. If this argument were a good one, one way to test it would be in the classroom. My experience teaching counterpoint (though hardly as "scientific" as the studies cited in part 2 of this book) is consistent with this idea. My students seem to have achieved very good results (and shown substantial improvements) every time they have moved away from trying to work from long lists of rules about acceptable and unacceptable rhythms and toward conceptualizing those rules as based on principles grounded in physical motion. For example, students who think of melodic leaps as analogous to physical leaping motions (and especially students who make analogous physical gestures as they sing what they are composing) tend to do a better job of following such rules (like "when making upward leaps, prefer to leap from stable rather than unstable pitches, or from downbeats rather than upbeats" and "usually follow large leaps by stepwise motion in the opposite direction") than do students who actually consult rules lists while composing.

A related argument is that thinking of rhythms in terms of physical motions is economical *because* the grounding of rhythmic experience in our embodied understanding of physical motion is so thoroughly consistent that it *necessarily* results in consistent webs of entailments. Musical rhythm reflects the flow of physical motions; melodic leaps and melodic steps have the same rhythmic character as physical leaps and physical steps; melodic leaps relate to pitch and metric stability in ways that are analogous to the ways in which physical leaps relate to physical stability; melodic flow tends to combine motions in ways that reflect combinations of physical gestures; and so on.

The diagram in Figure 6.1 helps to illustrate this point. This diagram encapsulates one set of rules for strict fifth-species counterpoint. Rather than stating rules in terms of durations, it represents the ideas discussed here in terms of patterns elided at stable points. A flow chart, it suggests that a passage of fifth-species counterpoint should begin with a half rest followed by a (preferably tied) half note (second species or fourth species), that quarter notes (third species) should be saved for the middle of an exercise, that such quarter notes should lead back to other durations via tied half notes (fourth species) by using the rhythm quarter-quarter-half in which the half note is tied into the following bar, that the quarter-quarter-half rhythm (if the half note is not tied) should be used only in the penultimate bar, and that the exercise should end with a whole note (first species). The rhythm in Example 6.7b, which

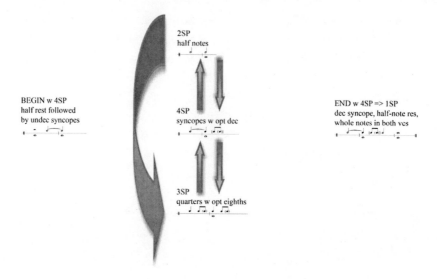

FIGURE 6.1. A map of durational patterns for fifth-species counterpoint (from Larson manuscript).

follows this flow chart, is shorter than a typical species-counterpoint exercise, but its smooth quality exemplifies the type of motion valued in sixteenth-century sacred polyphony and species-counterpoint exercises. The rhythm Example 6.7c, in part because it does not follow this flow chart, starts abruptly, has a halting quality, and does not "change gears" smoothly.

It is possible to find sixteenth-century sacred polyphony that uses rhythms that cannot be generated by following this flow chart, but following this chart tends to ensure that the rhythm of a species exercise obeys important guidelines. My students have found that they can improvise stylistically and musically persuasive rhythms by following this flow chart.

Notice also that this chart, like a map of train routes, invokes further metaphors of musical rhythm as physical motion. It represents the overall path of a passage of music as a journey. That journey takes us into rhythmic spaces of varying activity levels, moves smoothly from one rhythmic space to another, and concludes by bringing us home to the most stable rhythmic state.

EXAMPLE 6.7. (b) rhythms that follow the map, (c) rhythms that do not follow the map.

Although sixteenth-century sacred polyphony is quintessentially smooth, there are other musical styles that place a positive value on effects that are decidedly not smooth. David Huron (2006) suggests, however, that (at least at some level) evolution guarantees that we derive pleasure from smoothness – or, to be precise, from predictability. The essence of his argument is that there is survival value in making correct predictions ("Is this animal a friend or foe?" "Is this situation dangerous?" "Does this path lead to food?") and that natural selection has created systems within our bodies that reward us (by releasing chemicals that make us feel good) simply for making correct predictions. Thus, even if we have other reasons for deriving pleasure from surprises or from musical events that are not smooth, it would appear that if smoothness by itself is an underlying value in many different styles, this could be for the reasons Huron gives.

One result of valuing smoothness, as Heinrich Schenker ([1923] 1987) noted, is that composers tend to introduce subdivisions on upbeats rather than on downbeats. The rhythms in Example 6.7b (which follow the map in Figure 6.1) sound smoother than the rhythms in Example 6.7c (which do not follow the map) in part because they introduce subdivisions on upbeats. Staying with one rhythm continues the sense of forward momentum (giving in to musical inertia).

RHYTHMIC FLOW IN PITCH PATTERNS

The ideas presented so far (that rhythm is not a purely musical phenomenon, that it is more than the timing or durations of notes, that it arises from the mental attribution of embodied meaning involving patterns, that it is informed by the logic of physical motion, that it involves a map-

TABLE 6.1. FORCE-DRIVEN STEPWISE CONNECTIONS
BETWEEN TONIC-TRIAD PITCHES

	$\hat{5}$–$\hat{6}$–$\hat{5}$	$\hat{5}$–$\hat{4}$–$\hat{3}$		$\hat{5}$–$\hat{6}$–$\hat{7}$–$\hat{8}$
$\hat{3}$–$\hat{4}$–$\hat{5}$	$\hat{3}$–$\hat{4}$–$\hat{3}$	$\hat{3}$–$\hat{2}$–$\hat{1}$		
$\hat{1}$–$\hat{2}$–$\hat{3}$	$\hat{1}$–$\hat{2}$–$\hat{1}$		$\hat{1}$–$\hat{7}$–$\hat{1}$	$\hat{8}$–$\hat{7}$–$\hat{6}$–$\hat{5}$

Note: Integers refer to degrees of the scale.

ping of physical stability onto both metric and tonal stability, and that it combines patterns of pitches and durations in the same ways that physical motions join physical patterns), if taken together, can help generate a set of patterns and pattern combinations that are accorded a privileged status within the theory of musical forces.

In an earlier discussion of patterns in music (Larson 1993e), I generated such a list of patterns by using the following assumptions. A single physical motion may be represented by a pattern that begins on a stable note, moves through an unstable note, ends with a stable note, and ends by giving in to one or more of the musical forces. Let a tonic major triad define the stable pitches (the "goal level" as defined in chapter 5): $\hat{1}$, $\hat{3}$, and $\hat{5}$. Let the unstable pitch create a connection by step within that triad's tonic major scale (the "reference level" as defined in chapter 5). Eliminate any patterns that do not follow the musical forces. (When I speak of a three-note pattern following, or giving in to, a certain force, I mean that the second note of the pattern resolves to the third by moving in the direction determined by that force.) These assumptions generate the patterns of pitches shown in Table 6.1.

Notice that not all possible stepwise patterns are listed in Table 6.1. For instance, $\hat{5}$–$\hat{4}$–$\hat{5}$ is not included. After $\hat{5}$–$\hat{4}$–, gravity predicts continuation *down:* to $\hat{3}$. Magnetism predicts continuation *to the closest stable pitch:* to $\hat{3}$. And inertia predicts continuation *in the same direction:* to $\hat{3}$. All forces predict continuation to $\hat{3}$, none to $\hat{5}$. Thus $\hat{5}$–$\hat{4}$–$\hat{5}$ is excluded from our list. Similar lists of patterns may be found in other theoretical or pedagogical discussions (Komar 1992; Neumeyer 1987), but these do not explicitly consider the question of musical forces.

The list is also diatonic in major. We would get a different set of patterns if we chose other alphabets as the reference and goal levels.

For example, the chromatic scale could be used as reference level to connect elements of the tonic triad or to connect elements of the major scale. But, as noted in chapter 5, tonal music seems to privilege motions in which the reference level is a "step collection" and the goal level is a "leap collection."

All the *diatonic* upper-neighbor patterns are included (they all give in to gravity). Only the *half-step* lower-neighbor pattern ($\hat{8}$–$\hat{7}$–$\hat{8}$) is included. Lower-neighbor patterns defy both gravity and inertia, so they need the magnetic pull of half-step magnetism to overcome gravity and inertia. Elsewhere (Larson 1994a, 1999b) I have discussed the prevalent combination of *diatonic* (sometimes whole-step) upper neighbors and *half-step* (often chromatic) lower neighbors (for example, in $\hat{5}$–$\sharp\hat{4}$–$\hat{5}$, magnetism overcomes the gravitational and inertial tendencies to descend). Although $\hat{3}$–$\hat{2}$–$\hat{3}$ in major is excluded for this reason, the same pattern in minor would be included (because of the half-step magnetism).

The list is organized in a particular way, too. The rows are organized by starting pitch: patterns that begin on $\hat{5}$ are listed in the first row, those beginning on $\hat{3}$ in the second, and those beginning on $\hat{1}$ (= $\hat{8}$) in the last. Furthermore, the columns are organized by pattern type: those in the first column are three-note ascending-passing-tone patterns, those in the second column are upper-neighbor patterns, those in the third column are three-note descending-passing-tone patterns, the one in the third column is a half-step lower-neighbor pattern, and those in the last column are four-note passing-tone patterns. These patterns combine in various ways, but because the list is set up as it is, those three-note patterns that are next to each other in a column are often combined simultaneously.

THE RHYTHM OF COMBINING PHYSICAL MOTIONS

How might successive combinations of these patterns be created according to rules that reflect our embodied understanding of smoothly connected physical motions? Recall the central argument of chapter 3 – that we acquire our basic embodied understanding of physical motion in four different ways (we move our bodies, we see or hear objects move, we use our bodies to move other objects, and we feel our bodies moved by forces). A consideration of examples that represent these ways of understanding physical motion suggests ways of combining musical patterns.

When we move our bodies in ways that skillfully take into account the interaction of physical forces, the motions are more graceful than they would otherwise be. For example, consider how we prepare to jump. The extra effort required to overcome gravity means that, instead of leaping from a standing position, we first go into a crouch. But as a "wind up" we typically bob upward before dipping into that pre-jump crouch, as if we were on a springboard. In this way we gather momentum so that inertia can overcome gravity. Consider also what happens when you jump down from a height. If you were to land suddenly in the posture that you have when you are standing still, it would hurt. In a more graceful landing, you flex your knees as you land so that inertia carries you beyond the ultimately most stable position, cushioning your deceleration by circling around your arrival point.

These preparatory and conclusive circling motions imitate what we observe when we see some physical objects in motion or feel our bodies moved by an outside force. Consider what happens when we watch a pendulum or sit in a park swing as it comes to rest. Gravity pulls it toward its most stable position, but inertia carries it beyond that point. Because these separate forces (and friction) are constantly acting, the pendulum or swing tends toward a state in which those forces are in equilibrium. Note that, as the pendulum or swing comes to rest, it moves through smaller and smaller arcs of motion.

Consider what happens when you catch a ball and then toss it back to someone. If the motions remain separate but still graceful, you may pause in a stable position and then change direction. If you catch the ball and throw it back in one graceful, smoothly joined motion (as also happens in juggling), you will move continuously, changing direction at a point of instability, so that inertia carries motions through stable points.

Notice that these combinations of physical movements are rhythmic phenomena. The joining of events concerns the way one event *flows* into another. And the pacing of events determines whether changes of direction will happen at stable or unstable moments.

Thus, when *physical* gestures combine gracefully, we may expect one or more of (at least) five things to happen: (1) in evenly paced combinations, the first gesture continues smoothly into the second (so that inertia carries motion through the stable point of elision at which one gesture ends and the other begins); (2) such an evenly paced combination of an upward bob and a downward crouch makes a springboard-like motion, which is then followed by an upward leap; (3) gesture(s) circle around an arrival point before settling there; (4) changes in direction or type of motion will be introduced prior to the stable beginning of the next gesture; or (5) the first gesture pauses at a stable point of elision before changing direction to begin the second gesture. There are other possibilities, of course, but these five illustrate the point well enough for our purposes.

COMBINING MUSICAL PATTERNS

If successive combinations of *musical* patterns were created according to rules that reflect our embodied understanding of smoothly connected *physical* motions, then we might expect to find musical pattern combinations analogous to these same five physical pattern combinations. The following discussion generates a list of musical pattern combinations that are analogous to these physical pattern combinations, and are thus accorded a special status by the theory of musical forces.

To generate a representative list of examples of the first type (in which the pacing is even), we could follow two rules: first, the two patterns to be combined are elided (the last pitch of the first pattern is the same as the first pitch of the second pattern); second, inertia continues through the shared pitch (the direction at the end of the first pattern is the same as the direction at the beginning of the second pattern). In this way, $\hat{5}$–$\hat{6}$–$\hat{5}$ may be combined with $\hat{5}$–$\hat{4}$–$\hat{3}$ to create $\hat{5}$–$\hat{6}$–$\hat{5}$–$\hat{4}$–$\hat{3}$; the first pattern ends on the same pitch ($\hat{5}$) that begins the second pattern (first rule), and the inertia of the last two notes of the first pattern ($\hat{6}$–$\hat{5}$, that is, down) predicts the direction (down) of the first two notes ($\hat{5}$–$\hat{4}$) of the second pattern (second rule). One result of these rules is that successive pattern combinations either continue in the same direction or change direction in the middle of one of the patterns (not on a shared pitch).

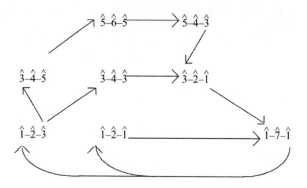

CHART 6.1. Connecting the three-note patterns of Table 6.1.

Chart 6.1 shows how the three-note patterns given in Table 6.1 may by combined successively so that inertia carries through stable points of elision. Notice that all but two of the patterns lead to only one other pattern (the other two both lead to either of two patterns).

The eight three-note patterns thus produce only ten unique five-note patterns. All but one of these patterns are listed in Table 6.2. The one possible five-note pattern not listed is the "backward turn figure" ($\hat{1}$–$\hat{7}$–$\hat{1}$–$\hat{2}$–$\hat{1}$). It and the standard turn figure ($\hat{1}$–$\hat{2}$–$\hat{1}$–$\hat{7}$–$\hat{1}$) are the only two of these patterns that start and end on the same pitch. Table 6.2 also lists all the seven-note patterns produced in the same way (omitting those seven-note patterns that include the "backward turn" or that start and end on the same pitch).

Viewing these melodic motions as a mapping of physical gestures onto musical motions suggests why we think of the $\hat{1}$–$\hat{7}$–$\hat{1}$–$\hat{2}$–$\hat{1}$ turn as common enough to deserve its own name and think of $\hat{1}$–$\hat{2}$–$\hat{1}$–$\hat{7}$–$\hat{1}$ as "backward." The turn figure is often used as a way to gather momentum. As C. P. E. Bach observed ([1753] 1949, 115), turn figures point upward – but he did not explain why. The theory of musical forces allows us to do that. The musical turn is like a crouch (prepared with an upward bounce) before a leap (one can crouch down to pick up something, but when one bounces up in preparation for a crouch, it is usually to gather momentum for a more energetic upward motion). Thus the turn, like a springboard, uses inertia to overcome gravity.

TABLE 6.2. THREE-NOTE PATTERNS AND THEIR FIVE- AND
SEVEN-NOTE COMBINATIONS, DERIVED FROM RULES
REFLECTING THE METAPHOR OF MUSICAL MOTION

$\hat{5}$–$\hat{6}$–$\hat{5}$	$\hat{5}$–$\hat{6}$–$\hat{5}$–$\hat{4}$–$\hat{3}$	$\hat{5}$–$\hat{6}$–$\hat{5}$–$\hat{4}$–$\hat{3}$–$\hat{2}$–$\hat{1}$
$\hat{5}$–$\hat{4}$–$\hat{3}$	$\hat{5}$–$\hat{4}$–$\hat{3}$–$\hat{2}$–$\hat{1}$	$\hat{5}$–$\hat{4}$–$\hat{3}$–$\hat{2}$–$\hat{1}$–$\hat{7}$–$\hat{1}$
$\hat{3}$–$\hat{4}$–$\hat{5}$	$\hat{3}$–$\hat{4}$–$\hat{5}$–$\hat{6}$–$\hat{5}$	
$\hat{3}$–$\hat{4}$–$\hat{3}$	$\hat{3}$–$\hat{4}$–$\hat{3}$–$\hat{2}$–$\hat{1}$	$\hat{3}$–$\hat{4}$–$\hat{3}$–$\hat{2}$–$\hat{1}$–$\hat{7}$–$\hat{1}$
$\hat{3}$–$\hat{2}$–$\hat{1}$	$\hat{3}$–$\hat{2}$–$\hat{1}$–$\hat{7}$–$\hat{1}$	
$\hat{1}$–$\hat{2}$–$\hat{3}$	$\hat{1}$–$\hat{2}$–$\hat{3}$–$\hat{4}$–$\hat{5}$	$\hat{1}$–$\hat{2}$–$\hat{3}$–$\hat{4}$–$\hat{5}$–$\hat{6}$–$\hat{5}$
	$\hat{1}$–$\hat{2}$–$\hat{3}$–$\hat{4}$–$\hat{3}$	
$\hat{1}$–$\hat{2}$–$\hat{1}$	$\hat{1}$–$\hat{2}$–$\hat{1}$–$\hat{7}$–$\hat{1}$	$\hat{1}$–$\hat{2}$–$\hat{1}$–$\hat{7}$–$\hat{1}$–$\hat{2}$–$\hat{3}$
$\hat{1}$–$\hat{7}$–$\hat{1}$	$\hat{1}$–$\hat{7}$–$\hat{1}$–$\hat{2}$–$\hat{3}$	$\hat{1}$–$\hat{7}$–$\hat{1}$–$\hat{2}$–$\hat{3}$–$\hat{4}$–$\hat{5}$
		$\hat{1}$–$\hat{7}$–$\hat{1}$–$\hat{2}$–$\hat{3}$–$\hat{4}$–$\hat{3}$

To begin this turn on $\hat{1}$ makes sense; it gathers momentum for a more energetic upward motion (often a leap) from the most stable position. The "backward turn figure" on $\hat{1}$, however, lacks this sense. It turns around a stable note but in a way which suggests that a descent will follow. This is not impossible (in fact, the familiar third movement of Boccherini's String Quintet in E major begins this way; see Example 6.8).[6] But it makes the interpretation of gathering momentum for a leap inappropriate. Instead, the motion seems to crouch, return, move up, and then end by giving in to gravity. The main effect – that of arriving in a satisfactory way on $\hat{1}$, *twice*, without promising anything further – is redundant. For this reason Table 6.2 omits the backward turn figure.

Table 6.2 thus lists all the three-, five-, and seven-note patterns that follow these simple rules, derived from viewing musical motion as a metaphor for physical gesture:

EXAMPLE 6.8. Boccherini, String Quintet in E major.

1. All three-note patterns connect stable pitches by step and give in to the musical forces.

2. All five- and seven-note patterns are successive elided combinations of the three-note patterns in which the inertia carries through the shared pitch.

3. Five- and seven-note patterns (except the $\hat{1}$–$\hat{2}$–$\hat{1}$–$\hat{7}$–$\hat{1}$ turn) that start and end on the same pitch and/or include the "backward turn" ($\hat{1}$–$\hat{7}$–$\hat{1}$–$\hat{2}$–$\hat{1}$) are omitted. (This also has the effect of eliminating all longer patterns that contain a single three-note pattern more than once.)

The claims here, then, are: (1) that our experience of the rhythm of graceful musical gestures will depend on the timing *and* the pitch content of the patterns that make them up; (2) that we will tend to experience equally paced gestures as more graceful when they elide patterns as do the patterns combinations in Table 6.2 (so that inertia carries through the elided pitch, and direction changes on an unstable pitch); (3) that the turn figure will typically lead to the expectation of an upward leap; (4) that circling motions will be experienced as "easing" arrival on the "goal" pitch of a passage; and (5) that we will tend to experience gestures that change direction on an elided stable pitch as more graceful when they pause on that pitch before changing direction. Each of these claims is about musical rhythm (despite the presentation of these scale degrees without any particular durations), and each affords musical forces a central role in our experience of rhythm. And, as we shall see in part 2, a substantial body of evidence from a variety of sources is consistent with these claims.

METER AS RHYTHM AND METER AS EXPECTATION

I believe that it is this same way of hearing (our embodied tendency to attribute inertia to musical motions with hierarchies of beginnings, middles, and ends) that gives rise to what we usually call "meter." According to this view, we could define meter as the expectation that a pattern of physical motion (think of conducting or dancing) that reflects the movement quality and fluctuations in rhythmic stability of the patterns heard in a passage of music will, upon repetition, continue to reflect the qualities of the passage that follows – experienced as "in the same meter."

According to this view, $\frac{3}{4}$ is not a single meter; that is, not all pieces in $\frac{3}{4}$ are in the same meter. Rather, each piece in $\frac{3}{4}$ creates expectations for continued hierarchical patterns of durations, each with its own characteristic way of capturing or implying a physical motion. For example, the pieces in Example 6.9–11 are all notated with the same meter signature; all are written in $\frac{3}{4}$. But there is an important sense in which each one is felt to be in a different meter. The opening of the Sarabande of Bach's English Suite in G minor is given in Example 6.9a. It moves slowly enough so that Bach could write the ornaments given in Example 6.9b. As in many Sarabandes, the second beat of the measure has a special character (other Sarabandes have pairs of measures with an underlying rhythm like ♩♩.♪|♩.♩♪). The opening of Chopin's Scherzo in E major is given in Example 6.10. It is much faster than the Bach Sarabande; it is easy to find performances of this piece whose measures last one-sixth as long as the measures in some performances of the Bach Sarabande. As in all of Chopin's Scherzos, a complete discussion of the meter of this example would note the way that the measures group in fours and eights (creating a higher-level meter called "hypermeter"). The Courante from Bach's French Suite in E♭ major, BWV 815, is given in Example 6.11. Whereas the Sarabande has duple subdivisions, this piece has triple subdivisions and could have been written in $\frac{9}{8}$ (as the editors note, the rhythm ♪.♪ is intended to be played so that the first note lands on the beat and the second is the third eighth note of an eighth-note triplet). All these examples have the same meter signature, but each is in a different meter.

I doubt that anything I have said in this chapter would strike an experienced musician as controversial. In fact, the points I have made have important intersections with several recent theories of rhythm and meter – for example, the idea of meter as a type of expectation intersects with the work of Christopher Hasty (1997) and Justin London (2004). The point here is that these aspects of rhythm and meter may be seen as derived from our experience of analogous physical motions and physical forces.

EXAMPLE 6.9. (a) The Sarabande of Bach's English Suite
in G minor (BWV 808); (b) Bach's notation of how the
same piece might be ornamented.

EXAMPLE 6.10. Chopin's Scherzo No. 4 in E major, op 54.

EXAMPLE 6.11. The Courante of Bach's French Suite in
E♭ major (BWV 815).

ANALOGIES BETWEEN PITCH PATTERNS
AND DURATIONAL PATTERNS

Considering analogies between pitch and duration can further under-score the central argument of this book (that our experience of physical motion shapes our experience of musical motion in specific and quantifiable ways – so that we not only *speak* about music as if it were shaped by musical analogs of physical gravity, magnetism, and inertia, but we also actually *experience* it in terms of musical forces). Here I explore three such analogies: the idea of "metric dissonance," the "cognitive isomorphism" between diatonic scales and African "time lines," and the analogy between key determination and meter finding.

METRIC DISSONANCE

Harald Krebs and others have discussed the idea of "metrical disso-nance."[7] To use the term "dissonance" (from the domain of musical pitch) to describe meter (the domain of musical duration) is to make an analogy – and (if we regard pitch and duration as different domains here) it is also a metaphor. When two durational patterns are simply nested so that one is a subset of the other (for example, with eighth notes and quarter notes in a given meter), the patterns are said to be "consonant." When they do not coincide in this way (for example, in syncopated patterns or with the pattern combination called "two against three"), the patterns are said to be "dissonant." Notice that this metaphor "feels right"; we easily understand what is meant, and (more to the point) we have a visceral sense of what is intended – the idea is that metrical dissonance feels like tonal dissonance. This is because the metaphor not only maps one experience in the domain of rhythm (say, a syncopation) onto one experience in the domain of pitch (say, an unresolved chord), it also brings with it a whole set of entailments. If a metrical dissonance is like a tonal dissonance, then it relies on a sense of stability (so stability in pitch maps onto stability in meter); if a metrical dissonance is like a tonal dissonance, then we may expect it to resolve to a more stable state (that is, we expect conflicting rhythms to be followed by durational patterns that are more simply nested); if a metrical dissonance is like a tonal dissonance, then we may expect to find both being used to express similar types of movement qualities or emotional states; and so on. Krebs (1999) makes explicit the varied ways in which the idea of "metric dissonance" suggests productive analogies between pitch and duration.

My point here is that "metric dissonance" is a metaphor that (like other metaphors described in this book) brings with it a whole set of entailments – including the notion that we experience motion not only within patterns of pitches but also within patterns of durations, the notion that we experience that motion as shaped by states of stability and types of forces that are analogous to physical stability and physical forces, the notion that we experience that motion as creating paths and journeys, and the notion that those paths and journeys map onto our life experiences in a way that helps create musical meaning.

MORE "DS"

A further consideration of three phenomena related to this metaphor of "metric dissonance" illustrates how the ideas presented in this book can further illuminate rhythm and meter.[8] Here are the three phenomena, all involving some sort of rhythmic "disagreement": metric dissonance of the types discussed by Krebs and others, the use of a consistent discrepancy between articulated and perceived beat "location," and "microtiming deviations."

Before we consider each of these ideas in turn, notice that each can be described with words that begin with the letter D – "disagreement," "dissonance," "displacement," "discrepancy," and "deviation" – so I will refer to these phenomena collectively as "Ds." Such words have negative connotations, but I shall argue that engaged aesthetic judgments rely on the embodied nature of the meanings we attribute to these Ds, that these negative connotations are misleading, and that these Ds are part of what gives positive value to some listening experiences.

The first category of Ds includes the types of metric dissonances discussed by Krebs and others: "grouping dissonance" and "displacement dissonance." In a grouping dissonance (such as a hemiola), one layer of music may (for example) group pulses in twos whereas another groups them in threes. In a displacement dissonance (like a string of syncopations), one layer of music may sound like it starts earlier or later than another layer by a certain number of pulses. In both cases we may think of one layer as "disagreeing" with another (a term which invokes the metaphor Music Is Language). But we may also think of (and experience) the two layers as "moving" in different ways (invoking the metaphor Musical Succession Is Physical Motion). And I believe that the meanings and values we attach to such Ds depend on (at least in part) the ways in which we understand and experience them in terms of this embodied metaphor of music as motion.

Second, a part played by one ensemble member may be "located" a consistent "distance" away from the perceived referential beat. Jazz musicians use terms such as "behind the beat" or "laid back" (meaning consistently later than the perceived reference pulse), "on the beat" or "in the pocket" (meaning consistently in agreement), or "ahead" or "on top of the beat" (meaning consistently early). These terms all invoke a specific kind of metaphor of musical time as physical space, in which the referential beat is an unchanging location in space and one player is conceptualized as situated a consistent distance behind (or in front of) that beat. The musical effect of "placing" one part consistently early or late is sometimes regarded as a positive one and always contributes to the particular character of a performance. Notice that this spatial metaphor takes on another dimension when musicians speak of the "depth" of the "groove."

Third, a part played by one performer may be heard as having "micro-timing deviations." These Ds are also sometimes referred to with terms such as "rubato" and "expressive timing." Ds of this third category, like those of the second, result in notes being attacked earlier or later than the referential beat (or earlier or later than their durational notation, if written down, might suggest). In the taxonomy presented here, however, and unlike the consistent Ds of the second category, deviations of this third category are not consistently early (or late); different notes will typically be delayed (or anticipated) by different amounts. Although a positive value may be attached to such deviations (and music without them is often said to be "lifeless"), such deviations can also make music sound sloppy and inelegant.

This taxonomy does not have mutually exclusive categories. The "participatory discrepancies" to which Charles Keil and Steven Feld (1994) refer belong to both the second and third categories. Manfred Clynes (1995) has studied timing (and loudness) patterns in the performances of gifted pianists. He describes "composer's pulses," consistent patterns of deviations from strict timing. Though one might argue that Clynes oversimplifies such patterns, they seem to be an important part of valued performances. To the extent that they consistently place notes before or after a referential pulse, they belong to the second category. At the same time their use of expressive micro-timing deviations seems to put them in the third category as well.

These Ds may also interact. The way in which two players "lock up" (perhaps with one playing consistently ahead of the other's beat) may enhance (or detract) from our engagement with the metric dissonances or expressive deviations in their playing.

All these Ds may be considered in relation with two separate phenomena, both of which are called "swing." One use of the term (which is specific and technical) distinguishes "swing eighth notes" from "straight eighth notes" (such that downbeat eighths are about twice as long as upbeat eighths). A different use of the term (which is general and aesthetic) valorizes performances that are so rhythmically engaging that they tend to induce kinesthetic responses, such as foot tapping or dancing in time with the music. Elsewhere (Larson 1999b) I have argued that this latter use of the term "swing" may be best understood in terms of musical forces, by comparing swinging music to swinging physical motions and by comparing the musical forces that shape swinging music with the physical forces that shape swinging physical motions.

Both kinds of swing raise interesting questions about all three types of Ds. For instance, when swung eighth notes are grouped in threes, we get a common grouping dissonance; that is, it may appear (from the notation, but also from the way musicians talk about this common D), that we are hearing a pulse layer of three eighth notes that is dissonant with the grouping in twos suggested by the underlying meter. But to describe it this way, or to call it $\frac{3}{8}$ (as some jazz musicians do), assumes that the swing eighth notes are equal in duration. Actually, if the eighth notes are swung, they are not equal in duration. In such a rhythm, if the down-beat eighth notes are twice as long (two units) as the upbeat eighth notes (one unit), then we hear groups of four (up-down-up = 1+2+1 units) and five (down-up-down = 2+1+2 units) in alternation. Nevertheless (as argued in chapter 2), musical meanings rest on hierarchies of "hearing as." Swung eighth notes may be *heard as* equivalent (just as diatonic steps may be *heard as* equivalent even when some are whole steps and some are half steps, and just as two C♯s may be *heard as* equivalent even when they are tuned differently). Both kinds of swing also have an important and dynamic relationship with Ds of the second and third categories.

Performers and theorists alike discuss these Ds in detail. My purpose is not to provide a complete explanation of these phenomena.[9] Rather, my point here is to show how the theory of musical forces can illuminate these interesting and useful discussions.

I believe that one important element of how we make aesthetic judgments about such Ds is the (usually subconscious) feeling we have about the qualities of physical motion that are reflective of, or implied by, those Ds. Of course, different listeners may make different judgments at different times about the value of such Ds. I believe, however, that we share a tendency to make positive judgments about the rhythm of a musical passage when we hear all aspects of it as reflective of physical motions we favor. According to this belief, the mere presence (or absence) of any of the three types of Ds neither guarantees not excludes a positive aesthetic response. We might say with approval, for example, that two different jazz artists both "swing hard" even though they use radically different amounts and types of all three of the Ds described above. We might hear a rubato as elegantly appropriate if the "distortions" in timing are consistent with the experienced "weight" and "direction" of notes within the gesture shaped by it. The same rubato with a different set of pitches, articulations, or dynamics might seem awkward. But it is possible that a different rubato with the same set of pitches and notated durations might also seem "just right" – if and only if the articulations and dynamics also work together with that expressive timing to create the sense of a physical motion in terms of which the listener experiences the music, and about which the listener feels positively.

Thinking about the relationships between these Ds and physical motions (such as walking, dancing, or juggling) can thus illuminate the complexity of questions about whether such "dissonances" require resolution and how they shape our aesthetic judgments. In walking, for example, certain motions are repeated at regular intervals. We might experience a number of different moments in our gait – when our foot strikes the ground, when the weight is transferred, or when we push off – as "the beat." But most important is that these things do not happen all at once. In fact, walking would be less graceful, more effortful, and downright awkward if certain walking motions did not happen consistently before or after "the beat." A (globally) stable gait may depend on such (locally) repeated Ds.

In my experience some Ds feel very unstable and in great need of resolution. Most typically these Ds are "special events." In a baroque dance suite movement, for instance, a hemiola may feel like it has the same urgency to resolve that a climactic appoggiatura might possess. That urgency can be highly enjoyable (especially when the music seems to provide or delay the expected resolution in ways that reward listening for such resolutions). But it can also be aesthetically disappointing (especially when the music seems too predictable or not predictable enough, but also when the physical motions I associate with those resolutions seem awkward or plodding).

In my experience other Ds lack or lose any great need for resolution. Most typically these are Ds that occur frequently within a passage, but their resolutions appear infrequently. For example, metrical and tonal instability in some twentieth-century concert music may suggest resolutions that change so frequently and yet are realized so infrequently that I give up making predictions. Elsewhere (Larson 1997c) I have argued that it is this tendency to give up making predictions that makes us experience some music as "atonal." That lack of urgency can be highly enjoyable (especially when it creates a sense of suspended time that focuses my attention on attractive sonorities or intriguing gestures). But it can also be aesthetically disappointing (especially when the avoidance of predictability negates both the pleasure of short-term gratification that I get from pleasurably repetitive motion as well as the longer-term engagement that narrative structures can afford).

And, in my experience, yet other Ds feel less urgent but still quite satisfying. Most typically these are Ds that occur frequently within a passage, and their resolutions appear frequently and reliably. Repetitive dance music, for example, may be driven by Ds that (like the tonal dissonances in a Telemann sequence or the rich harmonies of some modern jazz) are predictably but satisfyingly resolved by subsequent Ds. Again the effect can be aesthetically positive (as when a repetitive dance groove transports me to a delightful sense of bodily engaged timelessness) or aesthetically negative (as when a similar groove seems boring).

But these are my personal musical values. I am not claiming here that others "should" experience things the same way or that such experience is inherently more valuable. Instead, my point is that the theory of musical forces gives us useful terminology for talking about such important issues of musical experience and value.

COGNITIVE ISOMORPHISMS

Jeff Pressing (1983) has described "cognitive isomorphisms" between pitch and durational patterns in his studies of world music. For example, certain repeated patterns found in African musics are called "time lines" or "bell patterns." One can make a relatively complete set of such patterns for meters that have twelve pulses. Each member of the set may be labeled by the name of the culture in which it is common (for example, the "standard pattern" in Ewe drumming differs slightly from the pattern called "Yoruba"). And each member of the set, although different in some ways, may be thought of as a rotation of another member of the set. Example 6.12 shows how the Yoruba pattern may be thought of as a rotation of the Ewe pattern; that is, if you play the Ewe pattern beginning with its fifth note, you get the Yoruba pattern. The "isomorphism" is an interesting parallel between this set of patterns and the diatonic modes. If the "standard pattern" of the Ewe is represented with the durations between attack points, it is 2 2 1 2 2 2 1 (see the numbers below the pat-

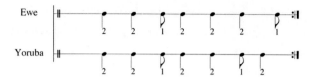

EXAMPLE 6.12. The "standard pattern" in Ewe drumming and a
bell pattern from Yoruba.

terns) – and if the major scale is represented with the half steps between
adjacent pitches, it is the same 2 2 1 2 2 2 1; the rotations of the bell patterns
can be seen to correspond to the varieties of the diatonic modes.

The basic points articulated by Pressing and others are (1) that minds
(or collective minds, called cultures) create referential durational patterns (like the African bell patterns) and referential pitch patterns (like
the diatonic collections); (2) that these referential patterns are isomorphic with respect to structure (so that two sizes of durations, expressed
as 1s and 2s, map directly onto two sizes of scale steps, also expressed
as 1s and 2s); (3) that these patterns tend to form *complete* families, as if
our minds sought *all* those patterns that were isomorphic (that is, every
possible rotation of the standard pattern is also used as a bell pattern, and
every possible rotation of the diatonic collection is also used as a diatonic
collection); (4) that these patterns also tend to form *exclusive* families,
as if our minds sought *only* those patterns that were isomorphic (that is,
bell patterns that are not rotations of the standard pattern are rare, and
referential tonal collections that are not rotations of the diatonic collection are also rare); (5) that the consistency and completeness of this
isomorphism reflects the operation of the minds that created these referential collections; and (6) that differences in the uses of these patterns
reflect differences in cultures, whereas similarities in their structures
reflect similarities in fundamental aspects of the mind.

Even a cursory glance suggests that each of these points is consistent
with claims of this book. The following paragraphs take such a cursory
glance. A deeper exploration of the same analogy then follows.

The point that minds create these referential patterns agrees with
the claims in chapter 2, which argued that meaning does not exist inde-

pendently in the world but is a creation of minds. That point also defines "meaning" as something that minds create when they group things into patterned relations.

The idea that these referential patterns are isomorphic makes an analogy. Chapter 2 noted that analogy is central to musical meaning. It also argued that to hear bits of music as analogous rests on hearing some parts as "the same," even though they are not identical. (In this case it may make more sense to talk about "seeing as" instead of "hearing as"; drawing an analogy between the structures of abstract pitch patterns and abstract durational successions seems to me more like thinking *about* music than thinking *in* music. But the same principles of analogy making apply.) Consider the half steps and whole steps being compared to durations, which, for the sake of illustration, we might notate as eighth notes and quarter notes. Calling all half steps "1" and all whole steps "2" assumes that all the half steps in a given collection are equal in size and that the whole steps are precisely twice that size. Likewise, calling all eighth notes "1" and all quarter notes "2" assumes that all the eighths are equal in size and that the quarters are precisely twice that size. We know, from studies of tuning and temperament, that this is the case only in the abstract.[10] We also know, from measurements of recorded performances, that notes which are notated as if they should last the same amount of time are rarely performed with precisely equal durations.

The point that these patterns tend to form *complete* and *exclusive* families is related to the notion that this isomorphism reflects the operation of the minds that created these referential collections. As noted in chapter 2, once we discover a pattern (or a way of making patterns) we have a creative drive to explore the "space" of all equally simple ways of making such patterns. The tendency of the human mind to explore the complete and exclusive families of diatonic-collection rotations and bell-pattern rotations can be seen as an expression of that drive.

The point that differences in the uses of these patterns reflect differences in cultures and that similarities in their structures reflect similarities in fundamental aspects of the mind is consistent with assertions made in chapter 1 (in the section "Convention and Culture").

Thus, at first glance, each of these basic points articulated by Pressing and others seems consistent with claims of this book. The ideas of this book, however, also make possible a deeper examination of the analogy between diatonic collections and bell patterns, which further illuminates this chapter's claims – that rhythm is not a purely musical phenomenon, that it is more than the timing or duration of notes, that it arises from the mental attribution of embodied meaning involving patterns, that it is informed by the logic of physical motion, that it involves a mapping of physical stability onto both metric and tonal stability, and that it combines patterns of pitches and durations in the same ways in which physical motions join physical patterns.

As noted in chapter 5, tonal music seems to privilege motions in which the reference level is a step collection and the goal level is a leap collection. The diatonic collections are all step collections. But there is one other proper closed step collection: the melodic minor scale and its rotations (also called the "acoustic collection"). The claim of chapter 5 (that tonal music privileges step collections as reference levels) together with the claim of chapter 2 (that we seek all equally simple ways of completing patterns) suggests that we should find bell patterns isomorphic to all rotations of the acoustic collection, too. Recent work by Jay Rahn (2010) suggests that this is indeed the case.

In the language of the theory of musical forces, it is the association of a goal level (a leap collection) with a diatonic collection that determines which rotation of that diatonic collection is said to function as referential for a given passage. For example, for the diatonic collection without sharps or flats (C D E F G A B), the specification of one goal level (D–F–A) makes it one diatonic mode (Dorian), and the specification of a different goal level (G–B–D) makes it a different diatonic mode (Mixolydian).[11] Thus it is the relationship between levels that determines mode. This observation is analogous to Maury Yeston's point (1976) that meter arises from the interaction of levels of durational patterning.

The idea that mode and meter both arise from such relationships suggests, however, a slightly different analogy. The notion that mode arises from relationships between levels is elegantly captured by Fred Lerdahl's (2001) "basic space." Table 6.3 shows the basic space for two

TABLE 6.3. LERDAHL'S (2001) "BASIC SPACE" FOR TWO DIFFERENT
DIATONIC COLLECTIONS

DORIAN

D												D
D							A					D
D			F				A					D
D		E	F		G		A		B	C		D
D	E♭	E	F	F♯	G	A♭	A	B♭	B	C	C♯	D

MIXOLYDIAN

G												G
G							D					G
G				B			D					G
G		A		B	C		D		E	F		G
G	A♭	A	B♭	B	C	C♯	D	E♭	E	F	F♯	G

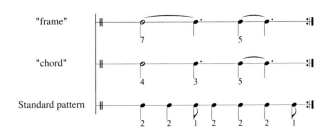

EXAMPLE 6.13. Subsets of the standard bell pattern.

different diatonic collections. If the analogy were simple and direct, an analogous depiction of the meter of the standard bell pattern would look like Example 6.13 – but I do not think that this is what we would call a "metrical hearing" of the bell pattern.[12] Writers on African music have debated about whether the standard bell pattern is heard in a meter that divides its twelve beats into four groups of three or three groups of four (two groups of six or six groups of two also seem possible). Others have suggested that African meter is purely "additive" (that the twelve beats of the bell pattern should not be thought of as grouped or divided in *any* consistent and meaningful way). Example 6.14 depicts a reading

Ewe

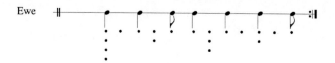

EXAMPLE 6.14. The standard bell pattern in four groups of three.

Ewe

EXAMPLE 6.15. The standard bell pattern in three groups of four.

of the bell pattern in four groups of three pulses. Example 6.15 depicts three groups of four. The claim that the bell-pattern meter is "additive" is equivalent to saying that neither of these readings are appropriate.

If we seek an explanation of how mode and meter arise from relationships between levels, then the approach of this book suggests that we should also explore the analogy between key determination (described in chapter 6) and meter induction. As noted in chapter 5, the asymmetry of the diatonic collection is only part of what helps us orient ourselves; although it helps us find our position within the diatonic collection, it does not, by itself, tell us the key.[13] Likewise, the asymmetry of any bell pattern is only part of what helps listeners (and musicians and dancers) orient themselves; although it helps them find their position within its succession of short and long durations, it does not, by itself, tell them where the downbeat is. As noted in chapter 5, we have a drive to attribute a single key (and a reluctance to change keys without substantial contrary-key evidence), and it is this drive that helps make modulation both interesting and challenging to us. Similarly, we may ask if we have a drive to attribute a single meter (and a reluctance to change meters without substantial contrary-meter evidence) and if this drive helps make metric conflict or ambiguity both interesting and challenging to us (and how this might vary from culture to culture). As noted in chapter 5, key attribution is a form of melodic expectation that brings with it a whole set of metaphorical entailments (such as hearing a return to tonic as a "coming home"). Likewise, chapter 6 has argued that meter is also a form of expectation with similar motion-based metaphorical entailments. As pointed out in chapter 5, key attribution and melodic continuation both involve a kind of aural Schenkerian analysis. Chapter 6 similarly argues that to get our metric bearings means to induce an entire multi-level hierarchy (one that reflects the hierarchies of physical motions and physical structures).

Returning to the question of what meter the bell pattern is heard in, I find the argument of Kofi Agawu (2006) most interesting in light of the ideas in this book. Agawu builds his arguments on the ideas that there are different ways to look at the issue and that no perspective should be discounted a priori (solely because it is, for example, an insider or outsider perspective). But he does go on to note that if we watch Ewe dancers dancing to music with the bell pattern, it is clear from the motion of their feet that they are hearing the pattern in four groups of three (as in Example 6.14). For Agawu, part of the *meaning* of this music arises from the way in which its sounds are mapped onto physical motions such as dance. My point here is not to take sides.[14] Rather, I contend that our understanding of rhythm and meter is improved when we take into account their embodied nature and their source in human physical movement such as dancing.

If the step collections and the bell patterns are what chapter 2 called successful "memes" (following Dawkins 1976), it is because the cultures in which they evolved favored their selection. Another way of making the same point is to say that, within the cultures that spawned them, these memes survived because they were "fit." What is it about these memes that makes them attractive to the minds that perpetuate them? Why did the minds that favored some of the rotations of these patterns discover and incorporate all (and only) the other rotations?

Chapter 1 claimed that culture plays a central role in shaping the associations we make between material and meaning, but that it is not the sole determinant of such associations. The chapter noted that single-mechanism explanations make a mistake when they assume that locating a single "cause" for such associations rules out all other potentially relevant factors. It also claimed that such associations rest on our tendency (a drive related to the creative drive mentioned above) to understand the world in terms of abstract categories based on nonarbitrary coordination of features and underlying simple organization. As noted in chapter 5, modern scale theory shows us *many* fascinating mathematical properties possessed by diatonic scales (and their subsets and supersets);[15] there appears to be more than one mechanism to explain why these pitch collections crop up in cultures around the world. Each of these properties of diatonic collections may be regarded as a nonarbitrary underlying principle. Pressing's analogy suggests that each of these fascinating properties is thus also a property of African bell patterns. Such properties need not be taken as an indication of the artistic "superiority" of diatonic and acoustic pitch collections or of African bell patterns, but they may help explain why these structures have survived as "memes" in their musical cultures.

Mathematical features of the abstract structure common to both the diatonic collections and the bell patterns may be taken as one explanation. According to such an explanation, the human mind favors the elegant and simple relationships that theorists have noted (such as unique multiplicity, maximal evenness, and the nonconsecutive semitone constraint). As noted in chapter 2, the theory avoids "single-mechanism explanations"; there is no need to assume that there is only one reason why this structure should be favored. But this chapter suggests that we seek an (additional) explanation grounded in our experience of physical motion. In explaining step collections (chapter 5), I noted that avoiding consecutive half steps means that we can hear each step as functionally equivalent (consecutive half steps would allow us to hear one note as filling another larger whole step). Put in physical terms, if I am walking in steps and take two consecutive half steps, it can feel as though an extra step connected two "basic" steps. For the bell patterns there is a similarly physical constraint. If the pattern is to be performed at a sufficiently rapid tempo, it is physically more difficult to play two adjacent shorter durations; hence their avoidance.[16]

SUMMARY

This chapter has shown that inertia has a rhythmic component that is central to meter. It has described metric magnetism and rhythmic gravity as analogous to the musical forces described in chapter 4. It has shown how the same embodied knowledge of physical forces that informs our understanding of melodic expectation also shapes our experience of musical rhythm. It has illustrated how musical gestures (even when not tied to specific durational patterns) tend to combine according to rules that reflect our embodied understanding of the combination of analogous physical gestures (so that inertia carries through equally paced elided figures, so that figures that change direction on their elided stable pitches typically pause there before changing direction, so that turn figures initiate ascents the way springboards do, and so that passages often end with the same circling motion that brings physical motions to rest). The chapter has argued that if we really think about what is meant by "meter" and by "rhythm," then we find that the theory of musical forces can help us better understand both. And it has noted other interesting and deep analogies between pitch and durational patterns.

While such analogies are fascinating at the systematic and intellectual level (and have rightly led authors like Pressing to inquire into the fascinating "cognitive isomorphisms" they illuminate), they are also analogies that we feel directly with our bodies. As Robert Hatten (2004, 124) notes, "Meter and tonality each afford analogies to gravitation or dynamic vectoral space, making possible the experience of *embodied motion* subject to dynamics and constraints comparable to those affecting the body in a natural environment."

7

Analyses

Chapters 1–6 offered a theory of musical forces and related that theory to our experiences of expressive meaning, melodic expectation, and musical rhythm. Chapter 7 illustrates aspects of the theory with analyses of additional musical examples. Because the theory of musical forces illuminates such fundamental aspects of music, it offers a powerful tool for music analysis. Or (because the theory draws so deeply from Schenker's ideas) it might be better to say that Schenkerian analysis, when supported by this theory of musical forces, offers a powerful tool for illuminating motion, meaning, and metaphor in music. This chapter, however, is not intended as a thorough introduction to such an analysis. To show the real value of such an analytic approach would require another book (and, in fact, I plan a sequel to this volume with that purpose). Instead, this chapter concludes part 1 by showing how some of its ideas are manifested in four musical excerpts. The focus here is on illustrating the theory rather than giving a complete account of any of the excerpts.

Readers less familiar with (or less enthusiastic about) detailed musical analysis might like to know that each example is successively longer and discussed in successively greater depth. The first example is only a few measures long (the beginning of a Schubert song). The second is a whole eight-bar phrase (a folk song). The third is the "head" of a twelve-bar blues (by Toshikio Akiyoshi). And the fourth is an entire thirty-two-bar jazz tune (by Charlie Parker). Thus I invite my readers to read as much of this chapter as they are comfortable with and then skip ahead to the concluding section of the chapter.

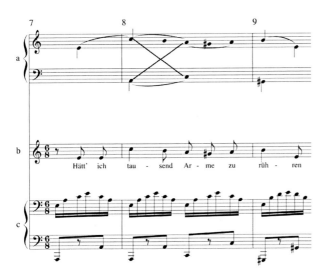

EXAMPLE 7.1. Schubert "Am Feierabend" from *Die schöne Müllerin,*
measures 7–9.

SCHUBERT'S "AM FEIERABEND,"
FROM *DIE SCHÖNE MÜLLERIN*

Example 7.1 is the opening vocal line of Schubert's "Am Feierabend,"
the fifth song from *Die schöne Müllerin.* This passage can be heard as
embodying the prosody and meaning of its text with a shape that flows
like a graceful physical gesture. The following analysis first considers the
meter projected by the piano part (considering the important role played
by inertia, as well as the ways in which hearing the passage in terms of
elided combinations of physical gestures illuminates distinctive qualities of that meter) and then turns to the vocal melody (suggesting how
force-driven patterns are used in ways that can be related to the text set
by that melody).

Consider the piano part in Example 7.1c. If we hear the first six right-
hand notes as a group, then the second group of six notes may be heard
as giving in to inertia (because they are the same six notes in the same
rhythm). The third right-hand group again gives in to inertia. But the
left hand changes its pattern for the third group (moving from the root

of the tonic chord to its third as the melody moves from its third to its root – the resultant "voice exchange" is shown with crossed lines in Example 7.1a). Thus, if the left-hand pattern is heard as *changing* the *inversion* of the chord, then it goes against inertia; but if it is heard as *preserving* the *quality* of the chord (or heard as a repeated succession of durations, as a repeated shape, or as some other pattern that does continue), then it gives in to inertia. Likewise, if the downbeat of measure 9 is heard as a change of chord, then it goes against inertia; but if it is heard as preserving the figuration, then it gives in to inertia.

As noted in chapter 6, our embodied understanding of rhythms leads us to hear them in terms of hierarchies of elided physical gestures. Here the notation shows the left hand as repeating the rhythm "eighth note, eighth rest, eighth note," but we tend to hear it as a series of elided motions "starting eighth note, eighth rest, eighth note, ending eighth note," such that the lower notes both begin and end patterns connecting each half of the bar. (The same could be said of the right hand, whose repeated six-note patterns could be heard as elided seven-note patterns.)

Heard together, the right and left hand of the piano articulate some of the hierarchical levels of meter that we experience. The right hand articulates the level of the sixteenth note by sounding a new pitch on every sixteenth. The right hand also articulates the level of the dotted quarter note by repeating its pattern every half measure. At the same time there are two other levels, which lie between the sixteenth-note and the dotted-quarter-note levels.

One of these is the level of the eighth note. Although the left hand is notated in eighth notes (eighth, eighth rest, eighth), its attack points sound like an alternation of quarters and eighths; no event is heard to articulate the second and fifth eighth notes of the bar. Nevertheless, that quarter-eighth pattern may be said to imply an underlying eighth-note succession. A cognitively based music theory might claim that if our minds seek to organize percepts in the simplest possible way, and if it is easier to think of an alternation of left-hand quarter notes and eighth notes in terms of the simplest regular metric level, then our minds infer the eighth-note level. The theory of musical forces further claims that if our embodied minds also seek to understand musical motion in terms of physical motion, and if the inertia of each "up" eighth note moving to a "down" eighth note implies continued motion in eighth notes, then force-driven expectations generate the eighth-note level. Note, in any case, that the vocal part explicitly articulates the eighth-note level when it enters.

Another of these metric levels is one that is ignored (or simply not granted equivalent status) in some theoretical accounts of triple-beat division. One could speak of a level of meter that is an alternation of quarter notes and eighth notes. According to some theories of meter, such as Lerdahl and Jackendoff's (1983) generative theory of tonal music, this is not a "well-formed" level (their theory requires that all levels consist of equal durations). One could object that such a level is common in pieces notated with triple-meter signatures or compound-meter signatures. One could also point to "swing eighth notes" in jazz, which are notated as conceptually equivalent (and in some respects experientially equivalent) strings of eighth notes, and which may be performed in this same 2:1 ratio. But one could also describe the left hand's rhythmic pattern as an element of the meter of "Am Feierabend" – without using the word "level." This repeated pattern of durations (proportionately 2:1, literally 4:2 as it groups the right-hand sixteenth notes) gives agogic accents (an emphasis of length) to what we experience as the two main beats of each bar. The left hand expresses the notated meter in another way – its up-down motion in pitch space (with the quarter notes in a lower register than the eighth notes) agrees with our experience of "upbeats" and "downbeats," mapping pitch space onto metric space in a straightforward way. Recall that chapter 6 defined meter as "the expectation that a pattern of physical motion . . . that reflects the movement quality and fluctuations in rhythmic stability of the patterns heard in a passage of music will, upon repetition, continue to reflect the qualities of the passage that follows." In Example 7.1, the pianist's left hand executes a pattern of physical motion that embodies the movement quality of that passage. To define meter as the expectation that this same motion will "fit" the following music suggests that the quarter-eighth alternation of the left hand is an important element of our experience of its meter – whether we call it a "level" or something else.

Defining meter in this way suggests that our experience of the meter of this piece might be (at least partly) shaped by the way in which it is performed. Different choices of (and different manipulations of) tempo might change the visceral quality of the physical motion experienced. Different relative weights given to the first half (as compared to the second half) of the bar might change the degree to which larger levels of meter are reflected in the physical motions experienced.

This analysis underscores two claims of the theory of musical forces. First, it argues that inertia plays a fundamental role in establishing and confirming each of those levels or elements of meter. Second, it illustrates the point, noted in chapter 6, that the meter we experience in an individual piece is more distinctive than its meter signature.

Now consider the vocal part. The opening three notes leap from E to C. This leap can be heard as an expression of strength, in part because of its large size and because in leaping upward it may be heard as striving against, or freeing itself from, melodic gravity. Yet, because it leaps from a note that is tonally stable yet rhythmically unstable and lands with agogic emphasis on the note that initiates the primary structure of this line, it can also be heard as an expression of both the passionate and emphatic beginning of a longer thought as well as a reflection of both the meaning and the prosody of the text. Upward leaps, whether in physical or musical space, heighten one's awareness of gravity and are thus usually followed by descent.

Here the leap to C is balanced by a descent through B to A. These three notes are heard as a specific elaboration of C: the "embellishing leap" to A (a suffix) is filled with the passing tone B (a connective). The relative structural weight of each note is the relative "contextual stability" of each note: C is the most stable, A the next most stable, and B the least stable. The relative contextual stability of each pitch in this three-note pattern thus agrees with its relative rhythmic stability. This agreement may be heard as imparting a natural grace to the pattern. The pattern completes itself (that is, answers C–B–? with A) by giving in both to melodic gravity (by descending) and to musical inertia (by continuing in the same fashion – down by step). This giving in to gravity and inertia also imparts a sense of inevitability to the line. But the line does not land with a "thud" on A; the descent after the leap is cushioned by a crouching recovery (A–G$\sharp$–A) that absorbs its energy, reversing direction smoothly in order to ascend to B on the downbeat of the next measure. The eighth notes A–G$\sharp$–A form another three-note pattern, this one a specific elaboration of A: the second A repeats the first (a suffix) and is filled with the neighbor note G$\sharp$ (a connective). Again the relative contextual stability of each pitch in this three-note pattern agrees with its relative rhythmic stability (this is clearest here if we recognize three metric levels: the eighth-note level, the quarter-eighth "level" discussed above, and the dotted-quarter-note level). But this pattern completes itself (that is, answers A–G$\sharp$–? with A) by giving in to melodic magnetism (moving to the closest stable pitch) rather than following inertia or gravity – in fact, one might say that the G$\sharp$ (instead of G) is used in this (and in analogous situations) so that magnetism can overcome gravity and inertia.

The five notes of this measure thus comprise two elided three-note patterns that are combined according to the observations in chapter 6 concerning rhythmic flow. The inertia of the last two notes of the first pattern carries into the direction of the first two notes of the second pattern (that is, the descent by step B–A continues as the descent by step A–G$\sharp$). The result is that $\hat{3}$–$\hat{2}$–$\hat{1}$ is elided with $\hat{1}$–$\hat{7}$–$\hat{1}$ to create $\hat{3}$–$\hat{2}$–$\hat{1}$–$\hat{7}$–$\hat{1}$ – one of the pattern combinations discussed in chapter 6. Whereas the first of these three-note patterns connects the metrically more stable first and fourth eighth notes of the measure, the second is completed on the rhythmically unstable final eighth note of the measure, allowing inertia to lead naturally across the bar line to the B, itself elaborated by an "embellishing leap" to E (a suffix) that recalls the first note of this melody.

This shows how the musical forces interact with one another to join smaller motions (through pitch space and metric space) into larger ones in ways that not only resemble graceful physical motions but also allow for a mapping between musical motions and expressive meanings.

"HICKORY DICKORY DOCK"

In the examples we have studied so far, force-driven patterns have elaborated tonic harmony, and have occurred essentially at one level of struc-

EXAMPLE 7.2. "Hickory Dickory Dock."

ture. In "Hickory Dickory Dock," these patterns not only occur in different harmonic contexts, they also appear at different levels of structure. Example 7.2 gives the melody and a Schenkerian analysis. The discussion that follows shows not only how the piece is composed of the same force-driven patterns derived in chapter 6 but also how those patterns are combined in the same ways predicted in that chapter. Furthermore, those combinations reflect the combination of physical gestures in ways that can easily be mapped onto a simple story line that helps us attribute meaning to that melody.

The first three notes (on the word "Hickory") make one of our patterns: $\hat{3}$–$\hat{4}$–$\hat{5}$. As Example 7.2a shows, this same pattern spans most of the melody. In fact, if we view the appearance of this pattern in the surface of the music (Example 7.2c, measure 1) as a prediction of the course of the melody (Example 7.2a, measures 1, 6, and 7), we may find an interesting relationship between the text and the music. Heard in this way, the first three notes are the mouse's first attempt to run up the clock, where "to run up the clock" means to get from $\hat{3}$ up to $\hat{5}$.

But this first attempt fails. In order to make a complete motion, the final pitch must be both tonally and metrically stable. The fifth scale degree is metrically unstable and falls back to $\hat{4}$. We then hear (on the word "Dickory") the "dominant third" $\hat{4}$–$\hat{3}$–$\hat{2}$. The melody approaches this $\hat{4}$

from above, and it descends through it, so we may experience musical inertia carrying us *into* that pattern (down to $\hat{4}$ and down from $\hat{4}$) and *through* that pattern ($\hat{4}$–$\hat{3}$–$\hat{2}$).

The result, at the deeper level of the half measure, is that we have moved from $\hat{3}$ to $\hat{4}$; this deeper motion is shown in Example 7.2b. We hear this deeper-level pattern in part because of the musical forces. When "Hickory" is followed by "Dickory," the rhyming words reflect the way the music has given in to inertia. Notice that we can hear the pattern of pitches on "Hickory" in a number of different ways, such that the pattern on "Dickory" is the same (that is, so that it gives in to inertia). This is true if we hear it as a succession of three eighth notes (assuming notation in $\frac{6}{8}$ meter), if we hear those eighth notes in the accentual scheme of the notated meter (leading to a fourth attack point), if we hear them as a stepwise pattern, if we hear them as filling a chordal third with a passing tone, and so on. The theory claims that (because we seek to understand music in terms of physical motion) we have a drive to hear force-driven patterns whenever we can. Here that means that to hear the first measure in terms of any or all of these patterns is favored because it is rewarded by a retrospection of successful anticipation.

But if we now pay attention to the mouse's progress at this deeper level, we see another unsuccessful attempt at $\hat{5}$; at this level, $\hat{3}$–$\hat{4}$ falls back to $\hat{3}$ (on the word "Dock") in measure 2, creating the resultant $\hat{3}$–$\hat{4}$–$\hat{3}$ (shown in Example 7.2b). We saw both these patterns in chapter 6. The longer duration of "Dock" gives an agogic accent to that note that confirms the meter, and its metric stability joins with its pitch stability to help us hear the music that sets the words "Hickory Dickory Dock" as a single gesture. The rapid scampering motion of this line suggests that the mouse is scurrying about, ready to gather energy for another try.

The next attempt is introduced with a pick-up note ("the" at the end of measure 2). As noted in chapter 6, introducing such smaller note values on the upbeat is recommended in theory treatises, creates a more graceful effect, and reflects our embodied understanding of the way in which musical motions are joined like physical ones, with inertia carrying through points of stability in patterns of evenly paced events. Singing the melody without this pick-up note helps to clarify the contribution that this pick-up note makes to the rhythmic flow of the phrase. This pick-up note also introduces leaps into the melody. It is as if the mouse, after failing to run up to its goal by step, tries again by leaping. (Or perhaps this is a Schenkerian mouse, and it is showing us that, if we take out the passing tone, then we can analytically reduce measures 1–2 to measures 3–4). At the half-measure level, however, measures 3–4 present the same failed attempt: instead of $\hat{3}$–$\hat{4}$–$\hat{3}$–$\hat{5}$, we again hear $\hat{3}$–$\hat{4}$–$\hat{3}$ (again, see Example 7.2b).

This bit of the song "Hickory Dickory Dock" is like a lot of music. Once we hear a bit of it, if we listen actively, we think we know what the melody is going to do. As mentioned in chapter 5, experienced listeners experience the "retrospection of anticipation"; after hearing a bit of "Hickory Dickory Dock," we may say to ourselves (perhaps subconsciously) "I knew that was going to happen."

Measures 1–4 of "Hickory Dickory Dock" help us say to ourselves "I knew that was going to happen"; these measures provide good reasons for expecting $\hat{3}$–$\hat{4}$–? to be completed as $\hat{3}$–$\hat{4}$–$\hat{3}$. The musical forces of gravity and magnetism both pull $\hat{4}$ down to $\hat{3}$. And moving to the embellishing leap (a lower third) of that $\hat{4}$ (the $\hat{2}$ in the second half of measures 1 and 3) means that the melody circles $\hat{3}$ in a way that leads the melody to that note. With such obstacles, we are not surprised that the mouse repeatedly falls back to $\hat{3}$.[1]

Although we are not surprised when it falls back to $\hat{3}$, the melody also gives us reasons to regard these $\hat{3}$–$\hat{4}$–$\hat{3}$ motions as unsuccessful attempts to go $\hat{3}$–$\hat{4}$–$\hat{5}$. Having heard two similar short bits, we expect a longer balancing bit (that is, we expect a pattern of 2+2+4 measures to create a "sentence"; see Caplin 1998). Furthermore, we expect phrases to have a climax (followed by a cadential descent to $\hat{1}$). Since a climax is a single highest note, and since we have ascended twice to $\hat{4}$, we now expect that longer balancing bit to ascend further, at least to $\hat{5}$ (and then to fall to $\hat{1}$).

In measure 5 the mouse makes a more determined effort to get to its goal. And it is successful in part because it overcomes the obstacles already mentioned. Beginning in measure 5, we get a new scale step every measure instead of every half measure ($\hat{3}$ in measure 5, $\hat{4}$ in measure 6, and our goal of $\hat{5}$ in measure 7; see Example 7.2b). The more deliberate

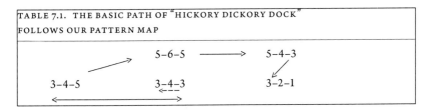

TABLE 7.1. THE BASIC PATH OF "HICKORY DICKORY DOCK" FOLLOWS OUR PATTERN MAP

quality of this ascent is underscored by stretching out the upper thirds (in the second half of measure 5 and in the second half of measure 6) and repeating each note (I see the mouse climbing deliberately, by putting both front and back paws on each note). The $\hat{4}$, instead of being harmonized by V7, is harmonized in measure 6 by IV (no longer a chordal seventh, it is freed of its obligation to resolve down). And $\hat{4}$, instead of being elaborated by a *lower* third (as in the second half of measure 1 and the second half of measure 3), is now elaborated by an *upper* third (the climactic A of the second half of measure 6), which circles around the $\hat{5}$ to which the line is directed.

Having finally reached its goal of $\hat{5}$ in measure 7, the melody gives in to all the forces with the pattern $\hat{5}$–$\hat{6}$–$\hat{5}$–$\hat{4}$–$\hat{3}$–$\hat{2}$–$\hat{1}$, a seven-note pattern that is an elision of three of our three-note patterns (see Table 6.2, upper right sequence, and compare Table 7.1).

The musical forces, operating on patterns of pitches and patterns of durations, allow us to "tell a story" about how those patterns add up to musical meanings. I am not claiming that all listeners experience this piece in terms of the story I have just told. Nor do I claim that this is the only story in terms of which one can experience this piece. But I do believe that we speak of "musical meaning" because, at some level and in some ways, we map musical patterns onto the patterns of our lives – and when, as often happens, those life patterns are patterns of physical motion, then we import our knowledge of physical forces into the musical meanings that our embodied minds create.

TWO JAZZ COMPOSITIONS

The practice of improvisation in general, the specific content of many different recorded jazz performances, and the testimony of jazz musicians all suggest that Schenker's ideas provide a natural – in fact, essential – way of understanding not only the technical features of recorded jazz performances but also of illuminating their artistic content.[2]

The analyses that follow (of a blues head by Toshiko Akiyoshi and an AABA bop head by Charlie Parker) illustrate the operation of the musical forces; they demonstrate that such forces operate on rhythmic as well as pitch patterns; they offer examples of hidden repetitions that include the "confirmation" type;[3] they exemplify the retrospection of anticipation and the anticipation of retrospection; they show the importance of Schenkerian analysis in understanding jazz melody, musical forces, and the perception of musical patterns; and they illuminate the rhetorical and gestural shapes of these pieces. These analyses illustrate how musical forces allow us to "tell a story" about how we might experience the music. Furthermore, these same pieces provide the basis for a study presented in chapter 9 that provides statistical evidence for some of the hypotheses generated by the theory of musical forces.

TOSHIKO AKIYOSHI'S "I AIN'T GONNA ASK NO MORE"

Toshiko Akiyoshi's "I Ain't Gonna Ask No More" is a slow, twelve-bar blues in B♭.[4] The first twelve-bar chorus is a melody played on bass trombone. The trombone part is not improvised; Akiyoshi has written it out note for note. This first chorus is accompanied only by light fills on the drums. Then the trombone restates essentially this same melody over a thicker accompaniment that includes brass and rhythm–section parts. Example 7.3 gives that melody and the chords given in Akiyoshi's score. The example also includes my transcription of the bass line played on the recording.

Examples 7.4 and 7.5 give a Schenkerian analysis of the same passage (in these examples, the bass trombone part has been transposed for ease of reading). The comments that follow are informed by these figures.

Upon hearing the opening gesture and the chord that comes on the downbeat of the second measure, experienced listeners will suspect that they are hearing a blues. This means that they will expect a certain kind of twelve-bar harmonic progression (something like | B♭7 | E♭7 E°7 | B♭7

EXAMPLE 7.3. Toshiko Akiyoshi, "I Ain't Gonna Ask No More," measures 1–12.

| Fm7 B♭7 | E♭7 | E♭o7 | B♭7 | G7 | Cm7 | F7 | B♭7 D7 | Gm7 C7 ‖) and a certain kind of melodic construction.

The harmonic progression in Example 7.4 is a twelve-bar bebop blues. In fact, it does not differ in any significant way from what an experienced listener would expect. This harmonic predictability provides a good frame for the violations of melodic expectations that it accompanies.

While harmonic predictability provides an excellent balance for melodic unpredictability here, jazz harmony can also depart from our predictions. For example, Charlie Parker's solo on "Oh, Lady Be Good!" a portion of which is quoted in Example 5.3, also begins with a similarly

EXAMPLE 7.4. Toshiko Akiyoshi, "I Ain't Gonna Ask No More," measures 1–12, Schenkerian analysis (detail).

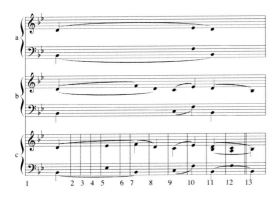

EXAMPLE 7.5. Toshiko Akiyoshi, "I Ain't Gonna Ask No More,"
measures 1–12, Schenkerian analysis (overview).

"bluesy" lick, and has the same harmonic progression from tonic in measure 1 to a "major-minor seventh chord" on IV in measure 2, and yet it is
not a twelve-bar blues. But in "I Ain't Gonna Ask No More," we do have
a standard bebop blues with its typical harmonic progression.

Examples 7.6a and b show a couple of the simpler possible melodic
continuations that might be imagined by experienced listeners. Both
these examples are based, in part, on the idea of musical inertia – the
idea that a pattern of musical motion, once perceived as a pattern, will
continue in the same way. Hofstadter and his colleagues (1995) have
described the importance to cognitive science of understanding what
it means to "do the same thing" in contexts that are different. In these
examples the melody repeatedly "does the same thing," even though the
harmonic contexts change. According to the theory of musical forces,
the meaning of "same" depends on how patterns are internally represented (that is, what they are "heard as") in musical memory. If the pattern of measure 1 is heard as an elaboration of the third scale degree, then
we expect a continuation that gives us a D♭ (the appropriately altered
third scale degree) in measure 5 (as in Example 7.6a). If the same pattern is heard as an elaboration of the third of its chord, then we expect
a continuation that gives us a G (the third of the appropriate chord) in
measure 5 (as in Example 7.6b).

EXAMPLE 7.6. Two possible continuations for the opening of
Toshiko Akiyoshi's "I Ain't Gonna Ask No More."

Note that each of these continuations has specific rhythmic profiles. If inertia were the only factor building these imagined continuations, then the pattern of durations in each measure would be the same.
There are additional factors, however, that suggest other possibilities.
For example, in both Example 7.6a and Example 7.6b, the third and
fourth measures have a pattern of durations that joins those measures.
One factor that leads to such an expectation is the general musical archetype (not specifically tied to the blues) called a "sentence," which
joins measures into this kind of 1+1+2 pattern (perhaps combined with
the knowledge that blues pieces often use that pattern for their first four
measures). Although I suspect that one could tell a convincing story
that ties our expectation for sentence-like patterns to patterns of physical motion (perhaps to dance?), one of my points here is that there are
other source domains for expectations (here the name "sentence" itself
suggests that the rhythms of speech may be a source domain for some of
our expectations about durational patterns in the blues). Another point

is that our expectations rely on knowledge about tonal music in general and about specific blues styles (and that different listeners may mix this general and specific knowledge in different proportions). The B♭–A–A♭ motion in measures 3–4 of Example 7.6a is a cliché of bebop blues that is itself a reference to earlier blues styles. But this motion, and the D–E♭–F motion in the analogous measures of Example 7.6b, may be thought of as resulting from a more general expectation that the melodic line will progress by step to the G of measure 5 (in the lower register for Example 7.6a and in the upper register for Example 7.6b).

Other musical forces shape these expectations, too. When, in measure 1, we hear D–E♭–D in the context of B♭ major, we may say to ourselves "I knew it would go that way – gravity and magnetism both pulled the melodic beginning $\hat{3}$–$\hat{4}$–? back to $\hat{3}$." The same pattern $\hat{3}$–$\hat{4}$–$\hat{3}$ provides the overall structure of the continuations listed in Example 7.6 as well as of Akiyoshi's melody (in all cases, measures 1–8 elaborate $\hat{3}$, measures 9–10 elaborate $\hat{4}$, and measure 11 resolves back to $\hat{3}$). But when the same beginning continues in a different way as $\hat{3}$–$\hat{4}$–$\hat{5}$ (in Example 7.6b, measure 4, and, as we shall see below, in Akiyoshi's melody, measures 1–5), we can still say to ourselves "I knew it would go that way – inertia pulled the melodic beginning $\hat{3}$–$\hat{4}$–? up to $\hat{5}$."

But the melodies in Example 7.6 are "too predictable." According to the argument advanced here concerning the anticipation of retrospection, listeners familiar with modern jazz in general or with Akiyoshi's writing in particular, in addition to expecting something like these continuations, will also expect the melody to depart from their expectations. In other words, we expect to be fooled. We even anticipate looking back and saying "I knew that I would be fooled that way" (perhaps this would be an example of the "anticipation of retrospection of anticipation"). The theory of musical forces suggests that we will expect the melody to depend for its rhetorical and gestural meanings upon the specific ways in which it departs from expectations that we will be happy in the end to attribute to some fictional listener who is "almost as hip" as we are.

One way that we might expect to be fooled involves the device of rhythmic displacement (Folio 1995; Larson 1997–98b, 2006; Strunk 1998; Waters 1996). Two ways of creating rhythmic displacement are "accentual shifting" and "polymeter." In measure 3–5, we hear both. As

EXAMPLE 7.7. Polymeter in Toshiko Akiyoshi's "I Ain't Gonna Ask No More."

Example 7.7 shows, those measures present a lick (B♭–D♭–E♭ as eighth-quarter-quarter) that we can hear as a modified version of the opening motive. The pitch modification (D♭ for D) is one we can tell ourselves we expected (see Example 7.6a, measure 2), but the final note is omitted. And because that lick is repeated every three beats, it implies a triple meter that conflicts with the underlying quadruple meter.

Example 7.7 shows this polymeter. The numbers below the staff show the underlying quadruple meter. The higher row of numbers above the staff shows the implicit triple meter that listeners might first attribute to these measures upon recognizing the repetition. The lower row of numbers above the staff shows a different hearing of the implicit triple meter that listener might retrospectively attribute to these measures upon hearing the repeated lick as a variation of the opening motive (that is, with the final note accented but withheld until the third statement of the motive).

Inertia leads us to expect such polymeters to continue indefinitely. But our desire for metric stability and our preference for simple shapes lead us to expect that the implicit triple meter will bring us back in line with the underlying quadruple meter. For these reasons, and because we can hear this lick as an incomplete version of the opening motive, we may expect a descending D♭–B♭ in eighth notes on the downbeat of measure 5.

Instead, Akiyoshi gives us E–B♭. The effect is a wonderful one. As with many musically effective surprises, the music not only departs from a single "most expected" continuation (a D♭ on the downbeat of measure 5), it also offers us a way to say to ourselves (in retrospect) that we antici-pated the surprise. Here the musical force of inertia (to which our atten-tion has been heightened through the riff-like repetition of the motive) suggests that the ascending D♭–E♭ should continue its ascent (recall the discussion of Example 7.6b, measure 4, above). Although the anticipated tone of such an ascent would be F, the E♮ that Akiyoshi wrote may be heard either as an inflected F (as an F♭) or as a note still on its way to F (as an E♮). Example 7.4c shows how Akiyoshi's melody realizes this second interpretation at a deeper level of musical structure (see the beamed notes in measures 3–7, D♭–E♭–E♮–F). At the same time a confirmation appears in the surface of the music (see the beamed notes in Example 7.4d, measures 6–7, D♭–E♭–E♮–F) that retraces the steps of this pattern as it is completed at the deeper level.

At the same time the melodic line "reaches over" with G–G♭–F so that two lines converge on the target F of measure 7. Note that Schenker's term "reaching over" (meaning that a "new voice" appears above those shown as more basic in the analysis) captures well the character of this gesture and reflects the metaphor of music as motion. Note also that this motion leads into measure 7 with a descending motion whose inertia carries into the descent that begins in measure 7 (F–E♭–D) so that, once again, patterns flow rhythmically into one another in the ways described in chapter 6.

Example 7.8 shows the similarities between the opening motive, the lick that leads into measure 7, and the lick that immediately follows. But there is more here than mere similarity – the "developing variation" (Schoenberg 1975) that connects these lines also tell a story. As suggested above, the music in measures 6–7 sounds like a version of the opening motive: transformed by the inflection of D to D♭, changed so that it ascends to F instead of descending to D, and elaborated with a reaching over G–G♭–F. If this is how we understand the relationship between measures 6 and 7, the resemblance shown between Example 7.8a and b is a coincidence – a kind of musical pun that we probably don't "get" when we first hear it. So when Example 7.8b is further developed through the modification of its pick-ups and the sequential extension of its stepwise descending third as Example 7.8c, it will seem like it is, in one sense, even further from the opening motive. Yet, at the same time, these changes transform it into something almost identical to the opening motive.

In terms of the metaphor of music as motion, we seem to have traveled to more and more distant places, only to discover that we are back

(a) m1

(b) m6-7

(c) m7-8

EXAMPLE 7.8. Toshiko Akiyoshi, "I Ain't Gonna Ask No More"; similarities between the opening motive, the lick that leads into measure 7, and the lick that immediately follows.

where we started. In terms of the metaphor of music as language, we seem to hear a series of logically connected arguments that takes us back to our original idea. Haydn, of course, has a well-deserved reputation for effectively exploiting this trick of "surprising us with something we originally expected" (see Larson 2003). But Akiyoshi is not alone among jazz musicians in exploiting this trick.[5]

We could ask more questions regarding, for example, how the bass part in measures 1 and 3 anticipates and then echoes the trombone part in measure 2. We could ask about how the bass part in measure 2 anticipates the E♭–E–F of the trombone part in measures 4–7. We could ask about how the bass part in measures 7–10 uses the musical forces to create a sense of inevitable momentum with the compound melody shown by the pair of beams in the lower system of Example 7.4c. We could ask about how the climax of Akiyoshi's melody in measures 9–11 refers to the opening motive on more than one structural level. Or we could ask about how the turnaround in measures 11–13 is a confirmation that seems to echo the basic structure of the whole chorus. But I hope that enough has been said to suggest how the theory of musical forces may enhance the analysis of "I Ain't Gonna Ask No More."

CHARLIE PARKER'S "CONFIRMATION"

Having introduced the concept of "confirmation," I can't resist asking how these ideas would apply to the Charlie Parker composition "Confirmation." First, I offer a few remarks about how choosing the text on

EXAMPLE 7.9. Different versions of the "same" passage.

which the analysis is based reflects principles of Schenkerian analysis. Then I point out how that analysis reveals a number of hidden repetitions of the "confirmation" type. (As noted above, a "hidden repetition" is the appearance of a single musical pattern on more than one structural level of a piece of music. A "confirmation" is a hidden repetition in which two different versions of a hidden repetition are completed at the same time.)

My analysis is based on two recordings (Parker 1947, 1953) of Parker's melody. To create a transcription, I first rendered the opening and closing choruses of both recordings cited into detailed musical notation. Those four choruses are quite a bit alike. In most cases the differences may be described as the inclusion or omission of embellishments. Example 7.9 illustrates this point.

Example 7.9a is taken from the first chorus of the live recording (1947). Example 7.9b is taken from the first chorus of the studio recording (1953). Example 7.9a does not include the turn or trill on B♭ that is included in Example 7.9b, and Example 7.9b omits the repetition of the final F. Example 7.9c shows another way to notate Example 7.9b; it represents the embellishment on B♭ as such through the use of a conventional symbol, and it suggests that the final note is optional (Parker seems to omit it in favor of beginning his solo on that recording a little earlier – he puts it back in at the end of the final chorus of the same recording). In other words, in order to make a transcription, one must answer the following questions: "Should the notation include this elaboration?" "Should the notation indicate that this elaboration as an ornament?" and "Should we consider this note as an implied tone?" In fact, a Schenkerian analysis may be regarded as a way to answer these questions for every note of the performance.[6]

Example 7.10 provides my transcription (Example 7.10d) of measures 1–4, together with a detailed Schenkerian analysis of the same measures (Examples 7.10a–c).[7]

"Confirmation" begins with a passage that is based on the descending third A–G–F; see Example 7.10a, the bracket labeled "a." That third is elaborated as a six-note motive A–G–B♭–A–G–F; see Example 7.10b, the bracket labeled "b." But that six-note motive ends with the same A–G–F; see Example 7.10b, the brackets labeled "a." Thus it ends with a confirmation; both versions of the three-note motive end together. Although this hidden repetition may add to the perceived momentum of the line and contribute to its logic by rewarding the retrospection of anticipation, it is, by itself, neither unusual nor particularly astonishing. More remarkable is that the music that immediately follows presents (as a kind of parenthetical aside) the same embedded structures in a completely different rhythm; see the brackets above Example 7.10b and c, measures 3–4. Further examination of the remainder of the piece (Larson 2002) confirms that these motives play important roles throughout.

CONCLUSION

Looking at a short passage from "Am Feierabend" in terms of musical forces showed that the melody may be heard as moving gracefully in part because its patterns of pitches and durations (the same patterns and types of pattern combinations discussed in chapter 6) can easily be mapped onto graceful physical gestures. Those mappings suggest that meter (understood as the expectation that physical motions capturing movement qualities of a passage will continue to do so) reflects the hierarchical nature of elided physical gestures, that inertia plays a fundamental role in establishing and confirming metric "levels" (some of which may not be "well formed" according to some traditional theories), and that the meter of an individual passage is more distinctive than its meter signature. Those mappings also show that rhythmic meaning depends on pitch content, on the operation of the musical forces, and

EXAMPLE 7.10. Charlie Parker, "Confirmation," Schenkerian
analysis, measures 1–4.

on the ways in which different patterns of motion are combined. And
those mappings support not only the prosody of the text of this song
but also its meaning.

In "Hickory Dickory Dock," we saw how the same patterns described
in chapter 6 can occur in different harmonic contexts and at different
levels of structure. Looking at the entire song in terms of musical forces
allowed us to see how the individual motions of shorter (measure-long)
gestures add up to create the path of the whole – and suggest a kind of
musical journey. In fact, it is possible to relate that musical journey to
the physical journey of a mouse climbing up a clock described in the
text of this song.

This raises an interesting question: What if we sing "Am Feieira-
bend" or "Hickory Dickory Dock" with a different set of lyrics? My
guess is that (if the texts were well chosen) we could easily find other
(perhaps equally persuasive) ways to map musical patterns onto physical motions. The point here is *not* that there is only one mapping between the patterns of a piece and its musical meaning. Rather, when

we do find persuasive musical meanings, they rely on mapping musical patterns onto life experiences – and when those mappings involve physical motion, the meanings they create rest on the operation of musical forces at various levels.

Looking at Toshiko Akiyoshi's "I Ain't Gonna Ask No More" in terms of musical forces showed how layers of sophisticated meaning can be based (in part) on sophisticated layers of expectations generated by those forces. We saw that the musical forces generate low-level expectations and participate in more sophisticated networks of higher-level expectations. We saw that our desire to understand the music in terms of such forces allows us to enjoy the surprises that come when the music departs from our expectations. We saw that higher-level expectations (including the expectation that we will be surprised by departures from our expectations) can also draw on our understanding of motion in terms of forces. We saw how such higher-level expectations can invoke not only a "retrospection of anticipation" but also an "anticipation of retrospection." And we saw that the musical forces can be relevant to meanings (like ones based on speech) drawn from other source domains besides physical motion.

Looking at Charlie Parker's "Confirmation" in terms of musical forces reinforced all these points. And the analysis revealed a number of "hidden repetitions" (of the type called "confirmations") in which the appearance of patterns (related to those discussed in chapter 6) on different levels of musical structure not only contributes to its sophisticated elegance but also draws the "retrospection of anticipation" and the "anticipation of retrospection" into our embodied experience of the improvisation's swinging momentum.

PART 2

Evidence for Musical Forces

8

Converging Evidence:
An Introduction to Part 2

Part 1 of this book (chapters 1–7) presented a theory of musical forces and related that theory to our experiences of expressive meaning, melodic expectation, key determination, and musical rhythm. The central claim of this theory is that musical forces shape not only our thinking *about* music but also our thinking *in* music.

The first part of this claim (that forces shape thinking *about* music) is already well documented. Lee Rothfarb (2002) has shown that writers on music have, for millennia, described music in terms of motion. He has also shown that writers on tonal music have, for centuries, increasingly turned to metaphors of force as important in explaining all aspects of music, and he describes in detail a school of "energetics," in which "analogies with force, power, or similar concepts from the domain of physics" appear "first with regularity in the decades straddling 1900" (927). The remainder of this chapter (which draws heavily on Rothfarb)[1] relates this first claim to central ideas of this book: that the idea of musical forces has long been connected with understanding psychological experience, ethical effects, and emotions; that the idea of musical forces seems necessarily to entail the idea of musical expectations and naturally to lead to attributions of agency and desire to music; and that everyday musical talk continues to reflect our understanding of music in terms of motion and forces.

The second part of this claim (that forces shape thinking *in* music) requires a different kind of evidence. Thus this chapter concludes with a discussion of the role of converging evidence in cognitive science and an overview of the types of evidence to be presented in the remainder of part 2.

DISCOURSE ABOUT MUSICAL MOTION

Chapter 3 explored metaphor systems that structure our thinking about music in terms of physical motion. The argument there was that we acquire our understanding of physical motion in four different ways and that these basic experiences of physical motion give rise, via metaphor, to the chief ways in which we conceptualize musical motion. If that is true, then we should expect to find evidence that the tendency to conceptualize music in terms of motion has a long history.

Rothfarb, as mentioned above, notes that metaphors of motion have shaped discourse about music for millennia: "ever since ancient times authors have identified motion as a fundamental aspect of music" (2002, 927). Kathi Meyer-Baer ([1930] 1975) suggests that music has long been regarded as extraordinarily powerful because, in symbolizing motion (245–256) and time (257–264), it was linked to the origin and movement of the cosmos – symbolism that she traces back to the Pythagoreans.

In fact, music has long been regarded as providing an ideal insight into motion. St. Augustine ([391] 1962, bk. 1, chap. 2) defines music as "*scientia bene modulandi*," (knowledge of correct movement) and explains that *modulandi* "means the process of motion, the flow of tones, and is nowhere better applied than in music."

DISCOURSE ABOUT MUSICAL FORCES

As scientists began to explain the world in terms of physical forces, musicians adopted the same vocabulary to explain music. They used this vocabulary to describe many different aspects of music.

Thomas Christensen (1993, 105) suggests that one of Rameau's greatest insights was to offer a mechanistic explanation of musical motion. In his *Treatise on Harmony* ([1722] 1971), Rameau noted that his description of the "collisions" of musical sounds (all steps in Rameau's examples) resembled the descriptions of solids given in a seventeenth-century physics text by Ignace-Gaston Pardies (see, too, Gur 2008).

Christensen also writes that Rameau's later description ([1737] 1974) of "tonal attraction" reflects Rameau's more recent acquaintance with Newton's theory of gravity. This suggests that, as Rameau rewrote his theories, he also used different analogies. Notice, however, that even as he changed the details, Rameau's metaphors still involved physical forces.

François-Joseph Fétis ([1844] 1994) and J.-J. Momigny (1806) also spoke of the "attraction" of some tones for others. One student of Fétis, Albert-Joseph Vivier ([1862] 1890), extended this view of tones to larger units (intervals, chords, and tonality) in a way that anticipates important aspects of the theory of musical forces described in this book. Chapter 11 returns to Momigny's ideas.

Ernst Kurth begins one of his books ([1917] 1946) with the assertions that "melody is motion" and "melody is streaming force" (translated in Rothfarb 2002, 940). Rothfarb's discussion of Kurth's contemporaries, Arnold Schering and Hans Mersmann, refers repeatedly to their concern with musical forces (944–947).

Rothfarb writes that, in the early twentieth century, music theorists August Halm and Heinrich Schenker gave central roles to musical forces.

> Musical forces are for Halm and Schenker not mere metaphors invoked for poetic or heuristic purposes. Both theorists explain in detail harmonic and melodic techniques, means by which forces manifest themselves, and the logic that governs them. (2002, 937)

Other aspects of music have also been described in terms of forces. Heinrich Christoph Koch ([1787] 1969) describes musical form in terms of melodic sections that "flow more forcefully [*stärker fortströmen*]" (quoted in Rothfarb 2002, 932). Janna Saslaw (1996) explicitly calls on the theories of Lakoff and Johnson to show how Riemann's explanations of modulation incorporate the source-path-goal schema to describe musical motion in modulations, and how those explanations incorporate the container schema to describe the interaction of opposing forces acting in modulatory motions. In a different essay, Saslaw (1997–98, 18) argues that "both Heinrich Schenker's *Free Composition* and Arnold Schoenberg's *Musical Idea* show significant evidence of underlying force schemas in their authors' conceptions of music."

Clearly the metaphor of musical forces has a long and distinguished history within western European music. Furthermore, many different aspects of music have been characterized in terms of such forces. As noted above, Momigny and Fétis talked about melody in terms of attractions; Vivier extended the idea to intervals and chords; Koch and Westphal spoke of form in terms of forces; Schering seems to find forces in all elements of music; Riemann spoke of modulations in terms of motion and forces; Schoenberg found forces central to "the musical idea"; and Schenker found forces operating at deeper levels of hierarchical structure.

EMPATHY, ETHICS, AND EXPRESSION

As discussed in chapter 3, there is a fundamental connection between saying that "music moves" and that "music moves us." As it turns out, this connection between motion in music and emotion in music is also a long and distinguished one.[2] Rothfarb notes that for Kurth, Schering, and Zuckerkandl, musical forces are psychological; they derive from or create resonances of psychic energy, tension and release, or dynamic fields. He also concludes that,

> for Schering, our enjoyment and understanding of music depend on empathy [*Einfühlung*], a dominant theme in aesthetics in the late nineteenth and early twentieth centuries. Kurth, too, relies on empathy as a vehicle for analysis. (2002, 946)

He further writes that,

> Westphal's theory of form, like Schering's, Kurth's, and Halm's, relies on listeners' resonance with, and mental processing of, musically intrinsic, shaping forces. We are drawn into and empathically participate in the musical flow. (948)

Arnheim's (1986) views on expressive meaning (in music and other artistic domains) and Cox's (1999b) "mimetic hypothesis" may be viewed as modern versions of empathy theory. Both authors find that listeners give meaning to music by participating in the metaphorical motions they attribute to melodies. And both authors speak of musical forces when they describe this meaningful participation.

EXPECTATION AND DESIRE

Chapter 5 builds its theory of melodic expectation on the metaphors of motion and force described in chapters 3 and 4. The history of theory suggests that this connection (between motion, forces, and expectation) has long shaped the way in which musicians conceptualize musical expectation.

Rothfarb notes that, once theorists began to talk about motion and energy, the idea of force became connected with the goal-directed nature of musical motion. As this chapter argues, it was natural for theorists to adopt the language of physicists in attempting to explain musical experience. But metaphor theory may also be seen as suggesting that the specific connection between forces and expectations is an inevitable one. In our experience of the physical world, the application of force causes change. And we apply force to bring about purposeful and predictable change. Lakoff and Johnson (1999) show how our metaphors for causation rely heavily on the idea of motion and forces. As Rothfarb (2002) notes, "The forces we hear in tones are, according to Zuckerkandl, directional tendencies (the symbolic 'pointing' attribute), which result in a continuous sense of expectancy." David Temperley (2003) expands on this relationship between forces and expectations.

Metaphor theory also helps explain a further connection. Understanding and experiencing musical expectation in terms of goals and forces leads naturally to the attribution of agency and desire to music. According to Lakoff and Johnson, to understand causation in terms of forced movement means that we naturally import other entailments of that metaphor into our thinking about causation. In our experience of other types of movement (especially movement to a goal), the motion may be attributed to the action of an animate agent. Thus, if we understand musical motion as goal-directed or shaped by musical forces, then we will tend to read that motion as caused by an animate agent – an agent driven by desire.[3] Rothfarb provides some nice examples which suggest that the attribution of agency and desire to music also has a long history:

> Jacques of Liège is explicit on the matter (*Speculum musicae,* 1321–25): "an imperfect concord strives (*nititur*) to attain a more perfect concord"; and Ugolino of Orvieto (*Declaratio musicae disiplinae*) speaks of how an imperfect consonance "ardently burns" to achieve perfection, "to which it is driven (*coacta movetur*)." (2002, 931)

ORDINARY DISCOURSE ABOUT MUSIC

References to forces are not isolated to the writings of historical music theorists. The following examples of everyday talk about music suggest that these forces continue to be important in how we think about music:

> GRAVITY
> The soprano's *high* notes rang *above*.
> The *rising* melodic line *climbed higher*.
> MAGNETISM
> The music is *drawn to* this stable note.
> The *leading tone* is *pulled* to the tonic.
> INERTIA
> The accompanimental figure, *once set in motion,* . . .
> This dance rhythm generates such *momentum* that . . .

THINKING *ABOUT* MUSIC AND THINKING *IN* MUSIC – CONVERGING EVIDENCE

This chapter has reviewed evidence for the first part of this central claim of the theory of musical forces (that forces shape thinking *about* music). Writers have spoken for millennia about musical motion and for centuries about musical forces. And the links between musical forces, expressive meaning, and melodic expectation are as clear in everyday speech as they are in the history of music theory.

But what of the second part of this claim (that musical forces shape our thinking *in* music)? To find evidence that musical forces shape our musical experience, we need the kind of evidence that cognitive science inevitably requires: evidence about what is going on "in our heads" (about "internal representations").

This raises interesting questions about the nature of evidence and the possibility of "proof" within the cognitive sciences. We often say something like "While it may be possible to *prove* things within mathematics, empirical science can only *disprove* things." This book cannot *prove* that forces shape our thinking *in* music. But it will show that "converging evidence" from a variety of sources is consistent with this claim. Chapter 9 finds further support for the theory from experiments in visual perception and neuroscience, arguing that if experience of physical motion can shape expectation and experience in music, then it should shape expectation and experience in other modalities – such as visual perception. This chapter also recounts how experiments in visual perception provide evidence of visual analogues to musical forces, and concludes by suggesting that recent findings in neuroscience reveal underlying brain structures whose operation is consistent with that argument. Chapter 10 shows correlations between predictions of the theory and the distribution of patterns within compositions and improvisations—correlations that seem too high to be a chance occurrence. Chapter 11 argues that historical and contemporary music theorists have misunderstood musical forces in ways that parallel common misunderstandings about physical forces, providing further evidence of the analogy between physical and musical forces. Chapter 12 turns to psychological experiments that test the role of musical forces in participant ratings of melodic completions. Chapter 13 describes computer models that implement the theory of melodic expectation presented here, and it compares the behavior of those computer models with that of participants in psychological experiments involving the production of melodic completions. Although none of these types of evidence, by themselves, can *prove* that forces shape musical experience, the cumulative weight of this converging evidence does a great deal to support that claim.

9

Evidence from Experiments in Visual Perception and Neuroscience

The theory of musical forces claims that our embodied knowledge of physical motion shapes not only our thinking *about* music but also our thinking *in* music. It also claims that this happens because of a process of "cross-domain mapping," in which our knowledge of one domain (physical motion) shapes our experience in another (music). If such cross-domain mapping connects these two domains, then it raises the interesting question of whether it might also connect other analogous domains. This chapter suggests that it does, and offers evidence that "visual forces" analogous to gravity, magnetism, and inertia shape visual perception. The idea that analogous domains call on similar mappings raises a further question about underlying brain structures that might support these mappings, and so the chapter concludes with some observations on how recent findings in neuroscience are consistent with the theory of musical forces.

In reviewing the evidence of experiments on visual perception, recall that the theory of musical forces claims that our musical experience incorporates our embodied experience of physical motion in ways that are immediately intuitive and logically consistent. The following paragraphs expand on what I mean by "immediately intuitive and logically consistent."

By "immediately intuitive" I mean that experienced listeners of tonal music feel – without conscious intellectual thought – the impact of musical forces. In fact, some people will deny the existence of musical forces at the same time that they are clearly feeling them in their bodies; I have heard musicians scoff at melodic gravity or claim that musical "up and

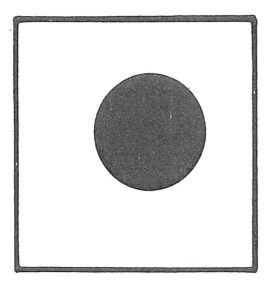

FIGURE 9.1. Off-center image induces kinetic interpretation (Arnheim 1974, Figure 1).

down" are meaningless conventions – and then seen them respond to psychological tests in ways that clearly suggest that they experience a consistent expectation that melodies will descend.

By "logically consistent" I mean that experienced listeners of tonal music import not only the idea or feeling of physical forces to their experience of music, but they also import associated entailments. For example, they know (at least intuitively) that it takes a while to stop a moving object. They know (at least intuitively) that the faster an object is moving, the longer it takes to stop. They know (at least intuitively) that smooth motions are less effortful than abruptly changing ones. And they know (at least intuitively) that if progress to a desired goal is blocked, then increased effort – or an alternative path – may be required to reach that goal.

As noted in the acknowledgements, Rudolf Arnheim's applications of Gestalt psychology to the experience of visual art provided a starting point for my questions about the experience of music. Arnheim (1974) argued that we experience visual shapes as imbued with directed tensions. Of Figure 9.1 (his Figure 1) he wrote:

> The disk in Figure 1 [Figure 9.1] is not simply displaced with regard to the center of the square. There is something restless about it. It looks as though it had been at

the center and wished to return, or as though it wants to move away even farther. And the disk's relations to the edges of the square are a similar play of attraction and repulsion. . . . What a person or animal perceives is not only an arrangement of objects, of colors and shapes, of movements and sizes. It is, perhaps first of all, an interplay of directed tensions. These tensions are not something the observer adds, for reasons of his own, to static images. Rather, these tensions are as inherent in any percept as size, shape, location, or color. Because they have magnitude and direction, these tensions can be described as psychological "forces."

Arnheim notes that we find directed tensions between objects we see as well as tensions between elements of a scene and the (relatively stable) lines of symmetry that structure that scene – analogous to musical magnetism. He also describes an "anisotropy" of visual space that leads us to experience an "up and down" in paintings (whether representational or abstract) and that makes us more comfortable with larger objects being lower in their visual space (notice that, in some typefaces, this fact leads, for example, to characters such as the "3 & B" in Table 9.1a–c, which look decidedly lopsided when inverted) – analogous to musical gravity. The analogy between these "visual forces" and the musical forces of magnetism and gravity is clear (and it is one that Arnheim himself notes.)

Before moving on, we should consider a possible counterargument. As noted in chapter 1, one (anonymous) reviewer of an earlier draft of this book reacted to its argument concerning associations between material and meaning by saying, "Musical association is culturally determined – symbolic – and that is why just any association is not possible." The introductory chapter responds at length to that reaction. In a similar and consistent way, the same reviewer reacted to Table 9.1a–c by writing, "Long experience of 3 and B in their conventional position would, all on its own, make them seem lopsided when upside down." I believe that my comments in chapter 1 also respond well to this reaction. But a simple "thought experiment" can further illuminate the reviewer's reaction, so I have added Table 9.1d and e. If our experience of lopsidedness were solely a result of convention, then the situation represented in Table 9.1d and e could just as well have arisen: what we now regard as a typical 3 would feel normal and its inversion would feel lopsided, and at the same time what we now regard as the inversion of B would be standard and its inversion (our now typical B) would look lopsided (in the opposite way).

TABLE 9.1a

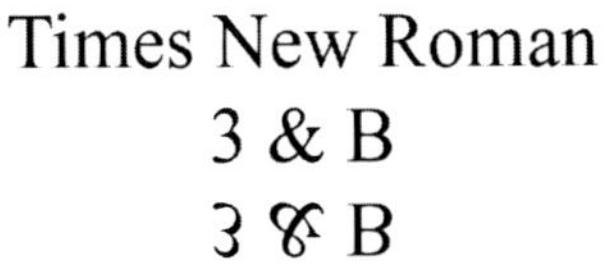

Times New Roman
3 & B
3 ℬ B

TABLE 9.1b

Century Gothic
3 & B
3 ℬ B

TABLE 9.1c

TRAJAN PRO
3 & B
3 ℰ B

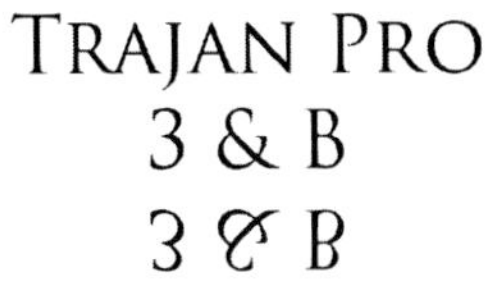

TABLE 9.1d. A Thought-Experiment Typeface. If the feeling of lopsidedness were entirely the result of convention, then the following typeface could have evolved – and *neither* its B nor 3 would feel lopsided.

ABC & 123

Table 9.1e. The Same Thought-Experiment Typeface Upside Down. And if the feeling of lopsidedness were entirely the result of convention, then in the same typeface, when inverted, *both* B and 3 would feel lopsided.

∀BC ℰ 1ꓭ3

I find it hard to imagine that such a situation would evolve (and I use the word "evolve" on purpose) – a situation in which we would experience both the B and 3 in Table 9.1d as "right" and would look at both the B and 3 in Table 9.1e and feel that they were "wrong." I find it hard to imagine, in other words, that the art of typeface creation would evolve typefaces that were consistently "illogical" in this way. If Table 9.1d and e strike one as "illogical," that suggests that there is a logic guiding typefaces. If there is a logic, then our experience is not the result of purely arbitrary convention.

If musical forces arise for the reasons claimed in this book (see chapter 2 on analogy, pattern, metaphor, and meaning), then we might expect analogous forces to arise in visual perception. And the appearance of something like "visual gravity," "visual magnetism," and "visual inertia" in visual perception might be seen as further evidence for the theory described in this book.

As noted, Arnheim makes a persuasive case for just such forces. And Roger Shepard (1984) has argued that the automatic operations of our perceptual systems have evolved "internal representations" that reflect "environmental invariants" – so that the constraints of our perceptions correspond to constraints in the physical world. Shepard also argues that his work on visual perception points to important analogies between apparent physical motion and apparent motion in pitch space (Sheppard and Cooper 1982, 319–321).

MUSICAL INERTIA AND "REPRESENTATIONAL MOMENTUM"

As it turns out, recent experiments in visual perception provide evidence that just such visual forces shape visual perception in an immediately intuitive and logically consistent manner. Those experiments have led to a body of work on what Jennifer Freyd calls "representational momentum."[1] Freyd (1993) notes connections between her work and that of Rudolf Arnheim. One experiment (Freyd and Finke 1984) involves an apparently rotating rectangle. Participants in this experiment saw an "inducing display" that presented three successive rotations of the same rectangle followed by a "probe" – a fourth (possibly differently rotated) presentation of that same rectangle (see Figure 9.2).[2] Participants were asked if the probe was in the same position as the third rectangle. What Freyd and Finke noticed was that participants often said that the probe was in the same position when it was actually rotated further beyond the final inducing rectangle (in the same direction as the inducing rotations) but were less likely to make this mistake when the probe was actually rotated the same amount in the opposite direction. Other experiments have presented continuous motions, asking participants to judge where

a.

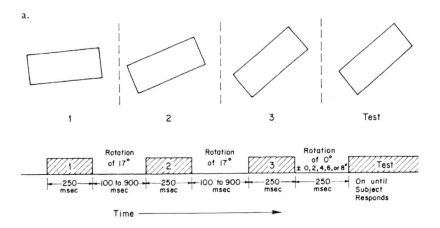

b.

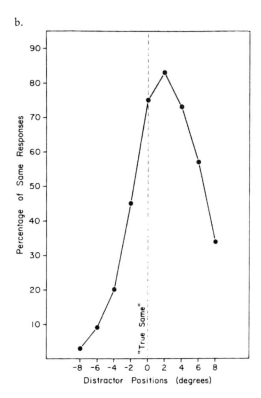

FIGURE 9.2a and b. Schematic depiction of stimuli and results from a representational momentum experiment (Freyd and Finke 1985).

a stimulus unexpectedly disappeared (Hubbard 1990), or have studied implied motion in static images (Freyd 1983). When asked to recall where a moving object (or apparently moving image) was when last viewed, observers consistently misremember that location as being farther along its path than the object had actually traveled. It appears that our perceptual system has internalized our knowledge of motion in the physical world in such an immediately intuitive way that our mental representations have their own momentum – one that operates without conscious intellectual thought. What has emerged is a substantial body of empirical work that finds evidence in participant response times as well as consistent discrepancies between actual and remembered stimuli.

Further experiments suggest that representational momentum is logically consistent with our embodied experience of physical motion. Representational momentum appears to depend on velocity (Freyd and Finke 1985; Hubbard and Bharucha 1988), acceleration or deceleration (Finke, Freyd, and Shyi 1986), direction (Halpern and Kelly 1993; Hubbard 1990; Munger et al. 1999), perceived weight (Hubbard 1997), and apparent friction (Hubbard 1995a, 1998). The relationship between representational momentum and the perceiver's conceptual knowledge about the nature or behavior of the object has also been explored (Freyd and Finke 1984; Hubbard 1994; Hubbard and Bharucha 1988; Kelly and Freyd 1987; Finke and Freyd 1989; Nagai and Yagi 2001; Reed and Vinson 1996; Verfaillie and d'Ydewalle 1991). Thus, representational momentum appears analogous to musical inertia in a number of ways.

Finke and Freyd (1985) explain representational momentum in a way that seems consistent with the argument of this book:

> Our explanation for this effect is that the human mind has internalized the properties of physical momentum, with the consequence that representational momentum and physical momentum obey some of the same laws.

Freyd and colleagues found that the results were not only logically consistent but also clearly quantifiable. Physicists can predict the final position of a physical object moving through consistent friction by knowing its mass, its velocity at a certain point, and the coefficient of drag. In a similar way Freyd and Johnson (1987) found that analogous equations could help them predict the final position of a perceptual object. (Freyd and Johnson also note that, over longer periods of time, an additional factor called "memory averaging" leads to errors in the other direction. But they were also able to quantify this effect in a consistent way.)

MUSICAL GRAVITY AND "REPRESENTATIONAL GRAVITY"

Experiments in visual perception have also discovered memory effects analogous to musical gravity. In one set of experiments Timothy Hubbard (1990) asked participants to judge the vanishing point of a target moving in various directions. In all those experiments Hubbard found that memory for the vanishing point was displaced in two directions – in the direction of travel (reflecting the effect of inertia) and in a downward direction (reflecting the effect of gravity). In another set of experiments Hubbard (2001, 235) found similar results but also noted that effects depended on the height within the visual field in a way that was "consistent with the hypothesis that memory for the location of ascending or descending targets is biased by the effects of implied gravitational attraction." Hubbard calls this effect "representational gravity" (1997, 1491).

MUSICAL MAGNETISM AND THE "LANDMARK ATTRACTION EFFECT"

If the analogy ran even deeper, we would expect to find a kind of "visual magnetism" in which a heavy "landmark" led viewers to mistakenly remember targets as being closer to the landmark than they actually were – as if a "visual magnetism" pulled the target toward the landmark. This is exactly what researchers have found (Hubbard and Ruppel [2000] cite a number of relevant studies). Bryant and Subbiah (1994) call this the "landmark attraction effect."

Also relevant here is the confirmation that these experiments give to Arnheim's claims about structural "skeletons" – the lines of symmetry associated with a landmark or enclosure of a scene. Hubbard and associates have found that the landmark attraction effect also distorts memory of a target's position toward such lines of symmetry.

Furthermore, the theory of musical forces claims that gravity, mag-netism, and inertia are constantly acting forces whose effects combine. As it turns out, experiments in visual perception show that representa-tional momentum, representational gravity, and the landmark attraction effect also combine like vectors – reinforcing one another when their effects are in the same direction and countering one another when their directions differ (Hubbard and Ruppel 2000).

FORCES IN STATIC SITUATIONS

However, if the claims of this book concerning musical forces were to find a thorough analog in visual perception, then we would expect to find something analogous to the claims that stasis is a special kind of motion and that musical forces contribute to the meaning of static (as well as changing) sounds. Of course, this is Arnheim's claim about visual im-ages – that "visual forces" contribute to the expressive meaning of images (whether they imply motion or not). In looking at a flower pot "resting" on a table, for instance, Arnheim would claim that our tendency to at-tribute dynamic tendencies to that static object (such as weight being pulled down by a "visual gravity") is part of how our creative imagination gives meaning to such objects.

In fact, Freyd's work also finds empirical evidence that pictures of objects at rest are mentally represented in terms of balanced physical forces operating on them, that these forces shape the way in which such images are remembered, and that the effects of these forces are immedi-ately intuitive and logically consistent with our experience of physical forces. Freyd, Pantzer, and Cheng (1988) showed a series of drawings as reproduced in Figure 9.3 to participants in their experiments. In one set of drawings (the "stand condition") the first drawing shows a flower pot resting on a stand. In another set (the "hook condition") the first drawing shows the same flower pot suspended from a hook. In both sets the second drawing shows the flower pot in the same location (with respect to the border of the picture and with respect to a window that provides a stable reference point) but removes the stand or hook. And in both sets the third and final drawing is either the same as the

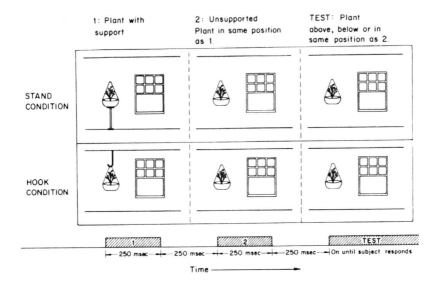

FIGURE 9.3. Freyd, Pantzer, and Cheng (1988) found that viewers experience static images in terms of balanced opposing "visual forces" that are analogous to physical forces.

second drawing or differs only in that the flower pot is slightly higher or slightly lower than it was in the second drawing. In both the stand condition and the hook condition, participants in this experiment were more likely to mistake lower positions of the flower pot as the "same" than they were to mistake higher positions of the flower pot as the "same."

Freyd and her colleagues claim that when we view the first drawing we experience the static flower pot as pushing down on the table because of gravity, and we experience the stand or hook as resisting that force. And they also claim that when we view the second drawing (with the stand or hook removed) we continue to experience the flower pot as being drawn down by gravity, but we no longer experience the resistance of the stand or hook. Thus they claim that when we view the third drawing and are asked if it depicts the flower pot in the same position, we mistake a lower position for being the same because our internal representation of the flower pot has been drawn to a lower position by the force of gravity that we experience as pulling the flower pot down.

PROCEDURAL VS. DECLARATIVE KNOWLEDGE, NAÏVE PHYSICS, AND AURAL-PERCEPTION EXPERIMENTS

These experiments are also interesting from the point of view of conscious knowledge. Typically people are not consciously aware that gravity is pulling down on an object resting on a table. Freyd, Pantzer, and Cheng (1988) suggest that their experiments reflect perceptual (rather than cognitive) understanding of physical forces. Such cognitive knowledge (things we know with our minds and which we can verbalize) is sometimes called "declarative knowledge" and corresponds to what this book has been calling "thinking *about* music." By contrast, perceptual knowledge (things we know with our bodies and which we express in what we do rather than in what we say) is sometimes called "procedural knowledge" and corresponds to what this book has been calling "thinking *in* music."

Apparently most people understand some aspects of the world better with their bodies than they do with their minds. People are more accurate in telling whether perceived motions accurately reflect gravitational acceleration than they are in describing what is happening conceptually (Shanon 1976), and they show a more accurate gauging of linear momentum when viewing filmed motions than in answering written questionnaires (McCloskey, Caramazza, and Green 1980).

Recognizing that declarative and procedural knowledge can differ, and recognizing that immediately intuitive experiences can have the logical consistency of cross-domain mappings and still be difficult to consciously (or even correctly) verbalize, intersects in interesting ways with what scientists call "naïve physics."

Studies of naïve physics by McCloskey and colleagues (McCloskey, Caramazza, and Green 1980; McCloskey and Kohl 1983) show that people have mistaken ideas about how physical objects will travel. Many people mistakenly believe that a ball traveling in a curved tube will continue to follow a curving path after it leaves the tube. Finke, Freyd, and Shyi (1986) argue that their findings concerning representational momentum and extrapolation are consistent with McCloskey's. Freyd and Jones (1994) found that representational momentum memory shift for a ball exiting a spiral tube was greater along a spiral path of the same curvature as the tube than it was along the physically correct straight path. That our representational momentum works in different ways than actual physical motion, they conjecture, may help account for some of the mistakes in "naïve physics."

On what seems like a related note, participant errors in studies of representational momentum were highly resistant to practice or feedback or both – in other words, the effect involves not just "thinking about motion" but actually also "thinking in motion." And the effects are immediate (they have been observed just 20 ms after the inducing stimuli are removed). Whereas studies of representational momentum deal with memory displacements after very short (less than one second) intervals, this book discusses musical inertia as a property of melodic expectations over both short and longer periods of time. Nevertheless, the results suggest that cross-domain mapping may be a fundamental part of the way we learn to deal with the world.

Ranney (1989) noted that the size of the effects found in experiments on representational momentum (and visual gravity) is much smaller than the actual effects of physical inertia (and gravity), suggesting that this argues against viewing these effects as having internalized physical laws. But one might argue, as Hubbard (1995b, 331) responded,

> that the magnitude of biases attributable to environmental invariants such as momentum and gravity should be smaller than the actual effects of momentum and gravity because a partial or smaller displacement would reflect the best compromise between the benefits of accurately extrapolating a target and the costs of inaccurately extrapolating a target that deviates from the expected course or position.

Scientists working in this area have explored the relationship between their work and auditory perception. Kelly and Freyd (1987) explored "auditory momentum." Their 1987 experiment excluded musically trained participants (who made no errors). And the stimuli they used were chosen because the computer could only generate tones 81.38 Hz apart (which means that the upper notes were, in musical terms, closer than the lower ones). Nevertheless, they noticed analogous effects. Freyd, Kelly, and DeKay (1990) replicated the experiment but used tones that were closer together. They chose tones three octaves above middle C "separated by equal-Hertz intervals" rather than by (perceptually equal) equal-cents intervals (perceptually the result is that the chosen tones seem closer together the higher one goes). And they did find an effect of "auditory momentum" for musicians as well as nonmusicians. They also found velocity and acceleration effects. Heather Johnston and Mari Riess Jones (2004) suggest that experiments concerning representational momentum in the aural domain provide evidence not only for musical inertia but also for musical gravity and musical magnetism.

FINDINGS FROM NEUROSCIENCE

These analogies (between audition and vision) suggest that there may be shared underlying brain mechanisms and raise questions about how the effects studied may be reflected in specific brain activity.

Two studies indicate that the experience of representational momentum is accompanied by observable differences in brain activity. Senior et al. (2002) found that transcranial magnetic stimulation can disrupt representational momentum. Lorteije et al. (2006, 158) found that "viewing static photographs of objects in motion evokes higher fMRI activation in the human medial temporal complex (MT+) than looking at similar photographs without this implied motion."

Neuroscientists have also studied brain activation in those listening to music (Janata et al. 2002; Levitin 2009; Miranda and Overy 2009; Peretz and Zatorre 2005), and their work suggests that melodic expectation and hearing basic rhythms activate the same part of the brain that is activated in the planning and execution of movement – a finding consistent with the claims of the theory of musical forces.

Studies of "mirror neurons" are particularly intriguing in light of these claims. In 1996 a group of Italian researchers under the direction of Giacomo Rizzolatti discovered a special group of neurons they called "mirror neurons" (Rizzolatti et al. 1996). They noticed that a certain area of a monkey's premotor cortex (area F5) and a certain part of the inferior parietal lobule (IPL) was activated when that monkey performed a certain action – and that the same area was activated when that monkey simply watched another monkey perform the same action. Subsequent studies (Rizzolatti and Craighero 2004) provide strong evidence that similar mirror-neuron systems can be found in the human brain.[3] Mirror neurons may thus be part of the underlying brain mechanisms by which we understand music as motion and music as emotion.

SUMMARY

The claim that analogies between physical motion and musical succession lead us to import our knowledge of physical gravity, magnetism, and inertia as "musical forces" is supported by the writings of theorists and experimenters working in visual perception. They have found visual forces that are analogous to physical and musical forces. Like musical gravity, "representational gravity" seems to pull down on visual images, distorting our memory of their location downward. Like musical magnetism, the "landmark attraction effect" seems to pull visual targets toward more massive visual landmarks, distorting our memory of the target's location in the direction of the landmark. And, like musical inertia, "representational momentum" seems to carry visual images in the same direction that they were moving, distorting our memory of their location in that same direction. Experiments also show that viewers of both moving and static visual images understand them in terms of constantly acting forces whose interaction can be quantified. And they show that this understanding of forces – whether or not it can be accurately verbalized – appears to be immediately intuitive and logically consistent.[4]

Because that immediately intuitive and logically consistent understanding constitutes a procedural and embodied knowledge that can differ from the declarative knowledge we put into words, it helps us understand the phenomenon of "naïve physics." In turning to the topic of naïve physics, the following chapter shows that the analogies between physical and musical motion run even deeper.

10

Evidence from Compositions and Improvisations

Chapter 8 noted that musical forces shape musical discourse. That (by itself), however, does not guarantee that music will reflect the operation of the musical forces. In other words, chapter 8 tells us that musical forces inform our thinking *about* music, but it does not prove that musical forces shape our thinking *in* music. Thus this chapter will focus on the content of individual pieces of music by summarizing three studies of patterns in musical compositions and improvisations.

All three studies tested predictions of the theory of musical forces by looking at a well-defined body of pieces and asking how well the distribution of patterns in those pieces agrees with distributions predicted by the theory. The first study (Larson 1997–98a) looked at all the pieces that had been analyzed in published articles on "hidden repetition" in tonal music. The second study (Larson 2002) looked at all published jazz transcriptions that had been analyzed according to a particular type of Schenkerian analysis (that type of analysis, explained earlier, is called "strict use" and is further described in Larson 1996c). The third study (Larson and VanHandel 2005) looked at all the pieces analyzed in Schenker's ([1932] 1969) *Five Graphic Music Analyses*.

Beginning with such well-defined bodies of pieces is an essential aspect of empirical research. The theory makes specific claims about the frequencies with which patterns will occur in pieces (and about how those frequencies reflect the operation of musical forces). Considering all and only the patterns (within all and only the pieces) of a body of pieces defined by external criteria (as is the case in all three of these studies) makes it more likely that high correlations between the predictions of the theory and the distribution of patterns within the pieces are not the result of chance or coincidence.

All three studies cataloged the patterns found in the body of pieces they looked at and then compared the number or type of those patterns to predictions made by the theory of musical forces. The first study (Larson 1997–98a) compared the patterns identified as "hidden repetitions" with a list of three-, five-, and seven-note patterns generated by assumptions of the theory of musical forces. (As noted in chapter 7, a "hidden repetition" is the appearance of a single musical pattern on more than one structural level of a piece of music.) That study also commented on the appearance of similar sets of patterns in what William Renwick (1991) called "fugue paradigms" and in Schenkerian background and middleground structures. The second study (Larson 2002) counted all the analytically identified three-note patterns that connect tones of seventh chords in selected jazz improvisations and compared the distribution of those patterns to the distribution predicted by the theory of musical forces of all such patterns. The third study (Larson and VanHandel 2005) counted all the analytically identified three-note patterns that connect tones of major and minor triads and compared the distribution of those patterns to the distribution predicted by the theory of musical forces of all such patterns.

All three studies found significant support for the theory of musical forces.

A STUDY OF HIDDEN REPETITION IN
TONAL MUSIC (LARSON 1997–98A)

The first study (Larson 1997–98a) began with an earlier discussion of patterns in music (Larson 1993e), reproduced in Table 6.2.

Experienced Schenkerian analysts will recognize this list as a collection of important "tonic-prolongation patterns." But published accounts of hidden repetition in tonal music allow us to quantify this intuition. In this study (Larson 1997–98a) I took twenty-five articles from 1978 to 1996 that discussed hidden repetition in tonal music.[1] To compile this list, I began with Charles Burkhart's seminal 1978 article on this topic and chose all subsequent articles (up until 1996, the year of my survey) that (1) appeared in major juried theory journals and in book collections

TABLE 10.1. PITCH PATTERNS FORMING HIDDEN REPETITIONS DISCUSSED
IN SELECTED THEORY ARTICLES PUBLISHED FROM 1978 TO 1996

generic descriptions	descending thirds	√√√√√√√√
	descending fourth	√
	descending fifth	√
	upper neighbors	√√√√
	turn	√√
patterns from Example 6.10	$\hat{5}$–$\hat{6}$–$\hat{5}$	√√√√√√√√
	$\hat{5}$–$\hat{4}$–$\hat{3}$	√√√
	$\hat{3}$–$\hat{4}$–$\hat{5}$	√
	$\hat{3}$–$\hat{4}$–$\hat{3}$	√√
	$\hat{3}$–$\hat{2}$–$\hat{1}$	√√
	$\hat{1}$–$\hat{2}$–$\hat{3}$	√
	$\hat{1}$–$\hat{2}$–$\hat{1}$	
	$\hat{1}$–$\hat{7}$–$\hat{1}$	
	$\hat{5}$–$\hat{6}$–$\hat{5}$–$\hat{4}$–$\hat{3}$	√√√
	$\hat{5}$–$\hat{4}$–$\hat{3}$–$\hat{2}$–$\hat{1}$	√√
	$\hat{3}$–$\hat{4}$–$\hat{5}$–$\hat{6}$–$\hat{5}$	
	$\hat{3}$–$\hat{4}$–$\hat{3}$–$\hat{2}$–$\hat{1}$	√√√
	$\hat{3}$–$\hat{2}$–$\hat{1}$–$\hat{7}$–$\hat{1}$	√
	$\hat{1}$–$\hat{2}$–$\hat{3}$–$\hat{4}$–$\hat{5}$	√
	$\hat{1}$–$\hat{2}$–$\hat{3}$–$\hat{4}$–$\hat{3}$	
	$\hat{1}$–$\hat{2}$–$\hat{1}$–$\hat{7}$–$\hat{1}$	√
	$\hat{1}$–$\hat{7}$–$\hat{1}$–$\hat{2}$–$\hat{3}$	
	$\hat{5}$–$\hat{6}$–$\hat{5}$–$\hat{4}$–$\hat{3}$–$\hat{2}$–$\hat{1}$	√√
	$\hat{5}$–$\hat{4}$–$\hat{3}$–$\hat{2}$–$\hat{1}$–$\hat{7}$–$\hat{1}$	√
	$\hat{3}$–$\hat{4}$–$\hat{3}$–$\hat{2}$–$\hat{1}$–$\hat{7}$–$\hat{1}$	
	$\hat{1}$–$\hat{2}$–$\hat{3}$–$\hat{4}$–$\hat{5}$–$\hat{6}$–$\hat{5}$	√
	$\hat{1}$–$\hat{2}$–$\hat{1}$–$\hat{7}$–$\hat{1}$–$\hat{2}$–$\hat{3}$	√
	$\hat{1}$–$\hat{7}$–$\hat{1}$–$\hat{2}$–$\hat{3}$–$\hat{4}$–$\hat{5}$	
	$\hat{1}$–$\hat{7}$–$\hat{1}$–$\hat{2}$–$\hat{3}$–$\hat{4}$–$\hat{3}$	
other patterns	$\hat{3}$–$\hat{4}$–$\hat{3}$–$\hat{2}$–$\hat{3}$ (minor)	√
	$\hat{5}$–$\hat{3}$–$\hat{1}$	√√
	$\hat{5}$–$\hat{3}$ & $\hat{5}$–$\hat{3}$–$\hat{5}$	√
	$\hat{3}$–$\hat{5}$–$\hat{3}$	√
	$\hat{5}$–$\hat{1}$–$\hat{3}$	√
	$\hat{3}$–$\hat{4}$–$\hat{5}$–$\hat{4}$–$\hat{5}$–$\hat{6}$–$\hat{5}$–$\hat{4}$–$\hat{3}$	√
	$\hat{6}$–$\hat{5}$ in minor and $\hat{4}$–$\hat{3}$ in major	√
	$\hat{5}$–b$\hat{7}$–b$\hat{6}$–$\hat{5}$	√
	$\hat{5}$–$\hat{6}$–($\hat{4}$)–$\hat{3}$	√
	$\hat{6}$–$\hat{5}$–$\hat{2}$	√

Note: Each check represents an article; a single article may be referenced by more than
one pattern.

of Schenkerian analysis,[2] (2) identified hidden repetitions appearing on different levels of musical structure, and (3) were not my own articles or translations of earlier articles. I then compiled a list of the patterns of pitches that are cited as hidden repetitions in those articles. Table 10.1 summarizes the results.

Some of the patterns discussed in these articles are described in generic terms not related to the key (see the first five rows of Table 10.1). All these generic patterns follow one or more of the musical forces. The first three patterns are descending linear progressions; all descending linear progressions give in to gravity by descending, and they give in to inertia by continuing in the same direction. The fourth pattern is the diatonic upper neighbor, which gives in to gravity by descending. The fifth pattern is the turn, which I have discussed in chapter 6.

The remaining patterns are expressed as scale degrees. The next twenty-four patterns are those listed in Example 6.10. Almost every one of these patterns is followed by a check, representing an article. In fact, it is harder than it may appear to say which patterns are *not* represented by an article discussing that pattern as a hidden repetition. The only three-note patterns not followed by a check are $\hat{1}$–$\hat{2}$–$\hat{1}$ and $\hat{1}$–$\hat{7}$–$\hat{1}$, but the elision of those two patterns (the $\hat{1}$–$\hat{2}$–$\hat{1}$–$\hat{7}$–$\hat{1}$ turn) is followed by a check. The five-note pattern $\hat{1}$–$\hat{7}$–$\hat{1}$–$\hat{2}$–$\hat{3}$ is not represented by a check, but it is contained in the seven-note pattern $\hat{1}$–$\hat{2}$–$\hat{1}$–$\hat{7}$–$\hat{1}$–$\hat{2}$–$\hat{3}$, which is represented by a check.

The theory of musical forces may be taken as predicting that some of these patterns (such as $\hat{1}$–$\hat{2}$–$\hat{3}$–$\hat{4}$–$\hat{3}$) will be discussed as hidden repetitions or otherwise acknowledged in subsequent publications by music theorists. For example, $\hat{5}$–$\hat{6}$–$\hat{5}$–$\hat{4}$–$\hat{3}$–$\hat{2}$–$\hat{1}$ is multiply represented. In fact, this is an important melodic archetype ("Twinkle, Twinkle, Little Star" is an obvious example, but a survey of folk tunes quickly turns up many more examples). This pattern is often accompanied by $\hat{3}$–$\hat{4}$–$\hat{3}$–$\hat{2}$–$\hat{1}$–$\hat{7}$–$\hat{1}$, one of the few patterns in Table 10.1 that lacks a check. When I published this work (1997–98a), I also added the observation that

its melodic inversion $\hat{1}$–$\hat{7}$–$\hat{1}$–$\hat{2}$–$\hat{3}$–$\hat{4}$–$\hat{5}$, though not followed by a check in Example 10.1, is another obvious companion (think of the third movement of the Third Brandenburg Concerto [see Example 10.2], which starts with an elision of these two seven-note patterns, $\hat{1}$–$\hat{7}$–$\hat{1}$–$\hat{2}$–$\hat{3}$–$\hat{4}$–$\hat{5}$ + $\hat{5}$–$\hat{6}$–$\hat{5}$–$\hat{4}$–$\hat{3}$–$\hat{2}$–[$\hat{1}$] = $\hat{1}$–$\hat{7}$–$\hat{1}$–$\hat{2}$–$\hat{3}$–$\hat{4}$–$\hat{5}$–$\hat{6}$–$\hat{5}$–$\hat{4}$–$\hat{3}$–$\hat{2}$–[$\hat{1}$]).

EXAMPLE 10.1. J. S. Bach, Third Brandenberg Concerto,
third movement, beginning.

Since that time, I have analyzed the entire Brandenberg movement and
found hidden repetitions, at a variety of pitch and structural levels, of
significant portions of the motive that begins the movement, as well as
passages that elaborate a slightly transformed version of this entire motive in augmentation.[3]

Thus nearly all the patterns generated in this way appear in published accounts of hidden repetition in tonal music. And most of the
patterns that appear in published accounts are in this list. The last nine
rows of Table 10.1 list the few patterns that appear in published accounts
that are not in Table 6.2. Their number is small.

Furthermore, a closer look reveals that most of these nine remaining patterns may be viewed as based on the same ideas that built the list
of patterns in Table 6.2. The first of these, $\hat{3}$–$\hat{4}$–$\hat{3}$–$\hat{2}$–$\hat{3}$ in minor, is a turn
on the third scale degree. This pattern was excluded from our original
list only because we restricted ourselves to cases in which the diatonic
scale was major; but in minor the half step between $\hat{2}$ and $\hat{3}$ allows magnetism to draw $\hat{2}$ back up to $\hat{3}$ and overcome gravity and inertia. This
pattern is thus an example of applying the same operations to a different alphabet. The next four of these also apply the same operations to
different alphabets; they are patterns of motion within the tonic triad
(rather than within the diatonic scale). The long pattern cited by David
Beach, $\hat{3}$–$\hat{4}$–$\hat{5}$–$\hat{4}$–$\hat{5}$–$\hat{6}$–$\hat{5}$–$\hat{4}$–$\hat{3}$, might be considered an elaboration of one
or more of the patterns given in Table 6.2. (This pattern, in other words,
is really a set of three patterns. First we hear $\hat{3}$–$\hat{4}$–$\hat{5}$. Then, in more rapid
notes, $\hat{4}$–$\hat{5}$–$\hat{6}$. Finally, we hear $\hat{5}$–$\hat{4}$–$\hat{3}$. Because the more rapid notes are a
kind of elaboration of $\hat{6}$, the more basic pattern is one of our seven-note
patterns $\hat{3}$–$\hat{4}$–$\hat{5}$–$\hat{6}$–$\hat{5}$–$\hat{4}$–$\hat{3}$, itself an elision of $\hat{3}$–$\hat{4}$–$\hat{5}$ + $\hat{5}$–$\hat{6}$–$\hat{5}$ + $\hat{5}$–$\hat{4}$–$\hat{3}$).
The four remaining patterns, though easily rationalized in terms of the
musical forces and their application to different contexts, constitute a
very small set of apparent exceptions.

Gjerdingen (1996, 2007) lists many examples in which two melodic patterns, $\hat{6}-\hat{5}-\hat{4}-\hat{3}$ and $\hat{4}-\hat{3}-\hat{2}-\hat{1}$, harmonize each other to form what he calls a "Prinner Riposte." Because these patterns are a response to an opening gambit, most Schenkerians may be tempted to describe the opening and the riposte together as the patterns $\hat{5}-\hat{6}-\hat{5}-\hat{4}-\hat{3}$ and $\hat{3}-\hat{4}-\hat{3}-\hat{2}-\hat{1}$, both of which appear in Table 10.1. Although Gjerdingen does not represent his analyses as Schenkerian, he does describe patterns of pitches that are elaborated by a musical surface. Despite the support his work gives to my argument here and the wealth of examples he cites, I have not represented his article with a check in Table 10.1.

The sample used to compile Table 10.1 does not include any articles or books by Schenker. Burkhart (1978) includes a summary of patterns that appear as hidden repetitions in Schenker's own writings.

> Perhaps the most frequent are the filled-in third, the turn, and, especially, the upper neighbor-tone formula. Another frequently found one is, like the Mozart example just discussed, that which starts with the upper neighbor tone, then continues to fall in steps; e.g., $\hat{5}-\hat{6}-\hat{5}-\hat{4}-\hat{3}$.

Thus the patterns Burkhart cites as common in Schenker's analyses of hidden repetitions are also typical of those listed in Table 6.2.

We have compared the list of patterns generated in chapter 6 (by our assumptions about musical motion as a metaphorical mapping of physical gestures onto musical patterns) with the list of patterns discussed in published accounts of hidden repetition. The striking similarity lends support to the assertion that patterns generated by musical forces enjoy a privileged status in tonal music.

Additional support for this assertion comes from a study of fugue expositions by William Renwick (1991). Renwick found that certain patterns provided the underlying structure for many of Bach's fugue expositions. Table 10.2 lists all six of these patterns, which he calls "subject paradigms." It also lists the three additional patterns that occur in combination with the subject paradigms, as well as the four additional important patterns cited in Renwick's article. Again, the striking similarity between this list and the patterns discussed above lends additional weight to the assertion that these patterns (and the principles behind them) enjoy a privileged status in tonal music.

TABLE 10.2. IMPORTANT PATTERNS IN BACH'S FUGUE EXPOSITIONS
(RENWICK 1991)

SUBJECT PARADIGMS	IN COMBINATION	ADDITIONAL IMPORTANT PATTERNS
$\hat{5}$–$\hat{4}$–$\hat{3}$	$\hat{3}$–$\hat{4}$–$\hat{5}$	$\hat{5}$–$\hat{6}$–$\hat{5}$–$\hat{4}$–$\hat{3}$–$\hat{2}$–$\hat{1}$
$\hat{1}$–$\hat{2}$–$\hat{3}$	$\hat{8}$–$\hat{7}$–$\hat{6}$–$\hat{5}$	$\hat{6}$–$\hat{5}$–$\hat{4}$–$\hat{3}$–$\hat{2}$–$\hat{1}$
$\hat{5}$–$\hat{4}$–$\hat{3}$–$\hat{2}$–$\hat{1}$	$\hat{8}$–$\hat{7}$–$\hat{8}$	$\hat{5}$–$\hat{6}$–$\hat{5}$–$\hat{4}$–$\hat{3}$
$\hat{3}$–$\hat{2}$–$\hat{1}$		$\hat{6}$–$\hat{5}$–$\hat{4}$–$\hat{3}$
$\hat{1}$–$\hat{2}$–$\hat{3}$–$\hat{4}$–$\hat{5}$		
$\hat{5}$–$\hat{6}$–$\hat{7}$–$\hat{8}$		

Schenkerian backgrounds (the most basic patterns that Schenkerian analyses find underlying tonal pieces, $\hat{8}$–$\hat{7}$–$\hat{6}$–$\hat{5}$–$\hat{4}$–$\hat{3}$–$\hat{2}$–$\hat{1}$, $\hat{5}$–$\hat{4}$–$\hat{3}$–$\hat{2}$–$\hat{1}$ and $\hat{3}$–$\hat{2}$–$\hat{1}$) constitute another well-defined class of patterns. All the Schenkerian backgrounds (in fact, all descending linear progressions) give in to the musical forces.

What about middlegrounds (the next most basic patterns)? Schenker's discussion in *Free Composition* ([1935] 1979) of the first level of the middleground is supported by a number of examples, all of which show patterns giving in to the musical forces and combined according to the principles given in chapter 6. Consider a few of his assertions about the first-level middleground. The assertion that "the descending line takes precedence over the ascending line" (44) reflects the force of gravity. The assertion that "only the upper neighboring note is possible at the first level" (42) reflects the interaction of forces in neighbor patterns (discussed above). Because this first-order upper neighbor is applied only to the primary tone, it creates the patterns $\hat{5}$–$\hat{6}$–$\hat{5}$–$\hat{4}$–$\hat{3}$–$\hat{2}$–$\hat{1}$ and $\hat{3}$–$\hat{4}$–$\hat{3}$–$\hat{2}$–$\hat{1}$ described above (in which patterns are elided with inertia carrying through the shared pitch). First-order arpeggiations (46–47) may be viewed as the use of a triad as the reference level with the goal defined by the tone of the background to which the arpeggiation moves. And reaching over (47–49) may be described as a way of using the "natural" tendency of musical motion to descend (giving in to gravity) in order to achieve an ascending motion.

All the examples cited so far, whenever they are described in terms of scale degrees, may be understood as tonic prolongations. But in different prolongational contexts, such as the prolongation of a dominant or a neighbor chord, notes other than $\hat{1}$, $\hat{3}$, and $\hat{5}$ may be stable. Neverthe-less, melodic patterns in all prolongational contexts and at all levels of the middleground usually share three things: they metaphorically map physical gestures onto musical patterns; they give in to one or more of the musical forces; and (especially when they are equally paced) they join patterns so that inertia carries through the elided pitch.

To summarize the first study (Larson 1997–98a), the idea that we hear tonal music as purposeful action within a dynamic field of musi-cal forces (gravity, magnetism, and inertia) suggests a method of gen-erating a well-defined set of patterns (Table 6.2). That set of patterns bears a striking resemblance to the set of patterns found in published descriptions of hidden repetition in tonal music, the set of patterns un-derlying fugue expositions, and the set of patterns found in Schenkerian backgrounds and first-level middlegrounds. This suggests that this set of patterns – and the musical forces on which they are based – enjoy a privileged status in tonal music.

A STUDY OF JAZZ MELODY

The second study appeared in an article (Larson 2002) that related the theory of musical forces to important trends in jazz theory and that il-lustrated aspects of the theory by using musical examples drawn from compositions and improvisations by jazz artists Toshiko Akiyoshi, Bill Evans, and Charlie Parker. The musical examples included Akiyoshi's composition "I Ain't Gonna Ask No More" and Parker's composition "Confirmation" (which have been incorporated into chapter 7 above), as well as improvisations by Parker on "Oh, Lady Be Good!" (Larson 1996a) and by Evans on "Who Can I Turn To?" and "All of You" (Larson 2006).

That study also compiled a list of all the dissonance resolutions in those passages occurring within patterns in which we can meaningfully compare the effects of the musical forces. Thus, in these examples, the patterns meet the following criteria: (1) every pattern moves entirely by step (within a step collection that is the chord-scale for the chord that supports that pattern); (2) every pattern is three notes long; (3) every pattern begins on a chord tone, moves to a non-chord tone, and ends with a chord tone – and the chord is always a triad or seventh chord; (4) every pattern's second note (the non-chord tone) lies between two chord tones that are a third apart.

There are three ways to fill a third with a step collection (these are called "species of thirds" in Larson 1992 and Hurwitz and Larson 1994). A major third must be filled with two whole steps. We describe this shape with the nomenclature of pitch-class-set analysis as "0 2 4" (meaning a collection of notes 0, 2, and 4 semitones above a given pitch). A minor third must be filled with one half step and one whole step. If the half step is below the whole step, then we have "0 1 3." If the whole step is below the half step, then we have "0 2 3." Thus there are three such "species of thirds."

In order to count those patterns, the second study (Larson 2002) regarded the first two notes of any of our three-note patterns as a question, with the third note regarded as the answer. For any species of third, there are two possible questions (starting on the upper note of the third or starting on the lower note). Given our three species of thirds, this makes six possible questions. Each question has two possible answers (ending on the upper note of the third or ending on the lower note). Given our six possible questions, this makes twelve possible patterns. Table 10.3 lists all twelve patterns that meet the criteria listed above.

The analytic approach used in the analyses discussed in this second study is called "strict use of analytic notation" (see chapter 5, the section titled "The Stepwise Displacement of Auralized Traces," for a quick description; see Larson 1996c for a more detailed account). One advantage of strict use is that each note of elaboration appears as an unstemmed notehead in a slurred figure at one, and only one, level of structure. As a result, the identification of patterns that meet the three criteria listed above is relatively straightforward. In the analyses listed above, there are forty-four such patterns. (Where a pattern appears two or three times verbatim because of a repetition demanded by the AABA form of the piece, the pattern is counted only once.) The sixth column of Table 10.3 shows the distribution of the patterns.

We then ask how well we can predict the distribution of those patterns by using the following formula (note its resemblance to the algorithms described in chapter 4): $F = w_G G + w_M M + w_I I + K$

TABLE 10.3. TWELVE PATTERNS (LARSON 2002)

SIZE OF THIRD	SPECIES OF THIRD	QUESTION	PATTERN (QUESTION + ANSWER)	CONTOUR	NUMBER OF PATTERNS IN SAMPLE	GRAVITY SCORE	MAGNETISM SCORE (HALF STEP)	INERTIA SCORE
minor	0 1 3	0 1	0 1 0	up-down	6	1	1	0
			0 1 3	up-up	1	0	0	1
		3 1	3 1 0	down-down	13	1	1	1
			3 1 3	down-up	0	0	0	0
	0 2 3	0 2	0 2 0	up-down	0	1	0	0
			0 2 3	up-up	3	0	1	1
		3 2	3 2 0	down-down	9	1	0	1
			3 2 3	down-up	1	0	1	0
major	0 2 4	0 2	0 2 0	up-down	1	1	0	0
			0 2 4	up-up	3	0	0	1
		4 2	4 2 0	down-down	7	1	0	1
			4 2 4	down-up	0	0	0	0

TABLE 10.4. THE RESULTS OF THE MULTIPLE-REGRESSION ANALYSIS

Summary of multiple-regression analysis	$R = .897$
	$p = .003$
	$N = 12$
Gravity	$w_G = 4.667$
	$\beta = .579$
	$p = .006$
Magnetism (half step)	$w_M = 3.125$
	$\beta = .366$
	$p = .047$
Inertia	$w_I = 4.667$
	$\beta = .579$
	$p = .006$
Constant	$K = -2.042$
	$p = .121$

In this formula, F is the sum of musical forces acting on the second note in the pattern; G is its gravity score (1 if it descends and 0 if it ascends); M is its magnetism score (1 if it resolves by half step, 0 if it does not); I is its inertia score (1 if it continues in the same direction and 0 if it does not); K is a constant; and the coefficients w_G, w_M, and w_I are weights that describe the relative contributions of each force, respectively. (The last three columns of Table 10.3 give these scores for each of our twelve patterns.) Most statistical packages include multiple-regression software that will solve this equation by finding the values of the weights (represented by the coefficients w_G, w_M, and w_I in the formula above) that produce the best correlation between F and the number of occurrences of all the twelve patterns. Another way to look at multiple regression is to say that it asks "How well can we predict the popularity (within a sample) of each pattern by assuming that it is a result of a recipe (such as two parts gravity, one part magnetism, and three parts inertia) – and what exactly is the recipe that makes the most accurate predictions?"

Table 10.4 shows the results of the multiple-regression analysis.

The results provide striking support for the theory of musical forces. The high R value (.897) means that the three forces, taken together, can account for a great deal of the variation in the data. (R quantifies the correlation between two different sets of numbers of the same length. An *R* of +1 means that the first set of numbers changes in the same way as the second set – that is, corresponding numbers go up or down in proportionate amounts. An *R* of 0 means that there is no relationship between the two sets of numbers. And an *R* of −1 means that they change in opposite directions.) The weights are all large enough to suggest that each force contributes significantly to explaining the result (the *b* values are "standardized coefficients," which provide the best way to compare the significance of each factor). (The similarity in weights for gravity and magnetism is a coincidence; there is no reason these numbers should be precisely the same.) The low *p* values mean that *R* and *b* values this high for data sets of this size are unlikely to have occurred by chance. (The *p* for a given *R* is the probability that an *R* at least this high would occur by chance – that is, the chance that the same or higher *R* would occur if one of the sets consisted of random numbers. By convention, *p* values below .05 are considered statistically significant.)

The sample of jazz melodies from which these patterns have been drawn is small and may not be representative of all jazz melody. Thus one should be cautious in extending the findings described here to a broader repertoire. As more jazz melodies are transcribed and analyzed, researchers can ask how well the model offered here describes the distribution of patterns within those melodies. But the fact that these data can be modeled so well by the interaction of constantly acting but contextually determined musical forces adds support to the growing body of evidence that we experience musical motions metaphorically in terms of our experience of physical motions.

A STUDY OF PATTERNS IN SCHENKER'S
FIVE GRAPHIC MUSIC ANALYSES

The third study (Larson and VanHandel 2005) counted all the well-defined patterns on all levels of all five analyses in Heinrich Schenker's *Five Graphic Music Analyses* ([1932] 1969). This collection of analyses represents the culmination of Schenker's graphic analytic technique. In it, he offers analyses of five pieces by three composers (Bach's "Ich bin's, ich sollte büssen" from the St. Matthew Passion; his Prelude Number 1 in C major from the Well-Tempered Clavier, Book I; the development section of the first movement of Haydn's Piano Sonata in E♭ major, H. XVI:49; Chopin's "Revolutionary" Etude in C minor, op. 10, no. 12; and his Etude in F major, op. 10, no. 8). It thus represents an excellent sample for a content analysis of the distribution of patterns within a body of pieces chosen and analyzed by an independent and respected music theorist.

The melodic patterns in this third study meet five criteria: (1) they are three notes long (hereafter called x, y, and z); (2) they are diatonic; (3) they move by step; (4) they begin and end on a stable pitch (meaning a member of a single major or minor triad; x and y are thus 1, 3, or 5 – where "1" means the root of that chord, "3" means its third, etc. – the numbers do not necessarily indicate degrees of the scale); and (5) they are paired so that each question has two possible answers, both of which are included in a pattern presented (that is, their second note is one that could subsequently ascend or descend by step to another member of the same chord – y is thus 2 or 4). Sixteen patterns (eight in major and eight in minor) fit these criteria: 1–2–1, 1–2–3, 3–2–1, 3–2–3, 3–4–3, 3–4–5, 5–4–3, and 5–4–5.

These criteria ensured that the third study would consider all and only those patterns in which the musical forces could be systematically and unambiguously quantified. The following paragraphs explain why this is so.

1. *The patterns are three notes long.* Thus each pattern may be heard as a single statement in which x and y form a "question" and z provides the "answer" (the closest stable pitch in the direction not taken will be called z'). A one-note question could imply an answer that gave in to gravity or magnetism, but a one-note question could not generate musical inertia. In longer patterns, the boundary between question and answer would not be clear. For example, 5–6–7–8 could be viewed as answering the question 5–6–?, but it could also be considered as answering the question 5–6–7–.

2. *The patterns are diatonic.* Thus the choice of "reference and goal alphabets" is straightforward; the patterns are heard as moving

C & D

C & Eb

A & D

EXAMPLE 10.2. Context alters the choice of reference alphabets (possible paths) and goal alphabets (opposing attractors).

within a diatonic scale (the reference alphabet) and resolving to chord tones (the goal alphabet). (For a discussion of the role of "reference and goal alphabets" within the theory of musical forces, see chapter 5.) The inclusion of chromaticism would make that choice ambiguous.

To understand why avoiding chromaticism is important, consider the patterns in Example 10.2. It shows, as an example, the issues that would arise if a question in the key of C major ended with $C\sharp/D\flat$.

According to the theory of musical forces, we expect motion within a reference alphabet until a member of the goal alphabet is reached. The choice of reference and goal alphabets determines the way in which the musical forces are quantified (the calculation of magnetic pulls requires that we determine the competing attractors – the closest stable pitches above and below the unstable y). If we heard the $C\sharp/D\flat$ as an unstable member of the chromatic scale, then C and D could be the competing magnetic attractors (Example 10.2, top stave). If we heard the $C\sharp/D\flat$ as an instance of "modal borrowing" (and thus as a member of the Phrygian mode, in which case it would be spelled $D\flat$), then C and $E\flat$ could be the competing magnetic attractors (Example 10.2, second stave). If we heard the $C\sharp/D\flat$ as a member of an "applied chord" (such as V7/ii, in which case it would be spelled $C\sharp$), then A and D could be the competing magnetic attractors (Example 10.2, third stave). Quantifying the interaction of musical forces requires identifying the competing magnetic attractors, but, as this example shows, that identification is problematic for chromatic notes.[4]

3. *The patterns move by step.* Because the patterns move entirely by step, we need only consider one strand of voice-leading structure. The inclusion of leaps would introduce the complexity of "compound melody." Furthermore, the step at the beginning of every pattern (from its *x* to its *y*) ensures that every pattern generates an inertial expectation (for motion by step in the same direction – in half the patterns, this expectation is satisfied; in the other half, it is denied because the pattern changes direction).

4. *The patterns begin and end on a stable pitch.* Thus every pattern tends to confirm the chord it elaborates. For each pattern, the competing magnetic attractors (the closest stable pitches in both directions) are 1 and 3 or 3 and 5.

5. *The patterns are paired.* This is necessary so that our consideration of magnetic pulls may take into account the attractors in both directions. For example, although the pattern 5–6–5 meets all the other criteria, it was excluded from the third study because of the ambiguity that would arise in comparing it to 5–6–7–8.

The resultant collection of patterns resembles those in the first two studies, but they are not identical. The third study uses only three-note patterns; the first study included three-, five-, and seven-note patterns. Furthermore, the first study included only those patterns in which the musical forces were best represented. For example, 5–4–5 was excluded from that list because it does not give in to any of the musical forces. However, because one can clearly quantify the interaction of forces in this pattern, it is included in the third study. The second study considered all possible patterns that fill a third within the seventh chords of selected jazz compositions and transcribed jazz improvisations. Because, in those modern-jazz contexts, the chords were all seventh chords, that list included patterns like 5–6–7 that are excluded from the third study. Furthermore, the second study distinguished patterns only on the basis of interval content, not on the basis of chord membership (thus the pattern C–D–E was considered the same pattern when it was 1–2–3 in major and when it was 3–4–5 in minor). The third study distinguished

TABLE 10.5. DIATONIC PATTERNS AND FACTORS TO BE ASSESSED

| | PATTERNS | | | FORCES | | |
Triad	Question $(x\,y)$	+Answer $(x\,y\,z)$	Gravity Score	Magnetism Score (Half Step y to z)	Opposing Attractor Score (Half Step y to z')	Inertia Score
minor	1 2	1 2 1	1	0	1	0
		1 2 3	0	1	0	1
	3 2	3 2 1	1	0	1	1
		3 2 3	0	1	0	0
	3 4	3 4 3	1	0	0	0
		3 4 5	0	0	0	1
	5 4	5 4 3	1	0	0	1
		5 4 5	0	0	0	0
major	1 2	1 2 1	1	0	0	0
		1 2 3	0	0	0	1
	3 2	3 2 1	1	0	0	1
		3 2 3	0	0	0	0
	3 4	3 4 3	1	1	0	0
		3 4 5	0	0	1	1
	5 4	5 4 3	1	1	0	1
		5 4 5	0	0	1	0

patterns on the bases of interval content *and* chord membership (so that the pattern C–D–E was considered different depending on whether it was $\hat{1}$–$\hat{2}$–$\hat{3}$ in C major or $\hat{3}$–$\hat{4}$–$\hat{5}$ in A minor).

Having chosen all and only those sixteen melodic patterns in which the musical forces may be systematically and unambiguously quantified, the third study then asked whether gravity, magnetism, and inertia – or any other factors – could help explain the distribution of those patterns within the pieces in *Five Graphic Music Analyses*. To do so, the study first scored each of the patterns on the basis of each factor it wished to investigate. Table 10.5 shows the result.

The first column of Table 10.5 divides the patterns into major- and minor-mode patterns. The second column, by listing the question (the notes *x* and *y*), groups the patterns in pairs having the same question. The third column lists each pattern. The numbers (all 1s and 0s) in the remaining columns indicate, for each pattern, something about the forces acting on that pattern.

Every pattern that descends gets a gravity score of 1; the rest get a gravity score of 0. This score in displayed in the fourth column of Table 10.5.

Every pattern that resolves to the closest stable pitch gets a magnetism score of 1; the rest get a magnetism score of 0 – regardless of whether they resolve to a further stable pitch (in the "wrong direction") or whether their rival attractors are equidistant. This score is displayed in the fifth column of Table 10.5. For this set of patterns, this same coding also answers the question "Does the pattern resolve by half step?" (1 for "yes," 0 for "no"). It may also be seen as coding Narmour's principle of proximity (1 for half step, 0 for whole step).

The quantifications of magnetic pulls in the algorithms of Larson, Bharucha, Lerdahl, and Margulis could also be used to produce scores for magnetism. It is difficult to compare these algorithms directly, however, because different numbers of factors are involved. Larson's, Bharucha's, and Lerdahl's algorithms take into account not only the semitone distance from y to z but also the distance from y to z'. In order to test the hypothesis that the distance from y to z' is relevant, its score (1 for half step, 0 for whole step) is displayed in the sixth column of Table 10.5. Bharucha's, Lerdahl's, and Margulis's algorithms also include factors based on the stabilities of y, z, and/or z'. Stability is discussed below.

Every pattern that gives in to inertia by continuing in the same direction gets an inertia score of 1; every pattern that goes against inertia by changing direction gets an inertia score of 0. This score is displayed in the seventh column of Table 10.5. For the patterns we have chosen (because all the questions are stepwise, and we assume that they are internally represented as such), "inertia" is coded the same way that Narmour's "process" and Margulis's "direction" would be. (Another of Narmour's factors, "registral return," makes precisely the opposite predictions for all our patterns; that is, for this set of patterns, every pattern that does not satisfy the prediction of Narmour's "process" satisfies the prediction of his "registral return." This would not be true of every set of patterns. What it means here is that these two principles are not independent for these data.)

TABLE 10.6. THE STABILITIES OF X, Y, AND Z', ACCORDING TO KRUMHANSL AND KESSLER (1982; REPORTED IN KRUMHANSL 1990), LERDAHL (1988), AND LERDAHL (1996)

PATTERN			STABILITY OF Y			STABILITY OF Z			STABILITY OF Z'		
Triad	Question (x y)	+ Answer (x y z)	Krumhansl and Kessler (1982)	Lerdahl (1988)	Lerdahl (1996)	Krumhansl and Kessler (1982)	Lerdahl (1988)	Lerdahl (1996)	Krumhansl and Kessler (1982)	Lerdahl (1988)	Lerdahl (1996)
minor	1 2	1 2 1	3.52	2	2	6.33	5	4	5.38	3	3
		1 2 3	3.52	2	2	5.38	3	3	6.33	5	4
	3 2	3 2 1	3.52	2	2	6.33	5	4	5.38	3	3
		3 2 3	3.52	2	2	5.38	3	3	6.33	5	4
	3 4	3 4 3	3.53	2	2	5.38	3	3	4.75	4	3
		3 4 5	3.53	2	2	4.75	4	3	5.38	3	3
	5 4	5 4 3	3.53	2	2	5.38	3	3	4.75	4	3
		5 4 5	3.53	2	2	4.75	4	3	5.38	3	3
major	1 2	1 2 1	3.48	2	2	6.35	5	4	4.38	3	3
		1 2 3	3.48	2	2	4.38	3	3	6.35	5	4
	3 2	3 2 1	3.48	2	2	6.35	5	4	4.38	3	3
		3 2 3	3.48	2	2	4.38	3	3	6.35	5	4
	3 4	3 4 3	4.09	2	2	4.38	3	3	5.19	4	3
		3 4 5	4.09	2	2	5.19	4	3	4.38	3	3
	5 4	5 4 3	4.09	2	2	4.38	3	3	5.19	4	3
		5 4 5	4.09	2	2	5.19	4	3	4.38	3	3

Table 10.6 gives various values for the stabilities of y, z, and z'. This table scores each pattern as if its triad were a temporary tonic. This approach is consistent with the approach of Lerdahl's analyses of magnetic attractions (1996, 2001), but it should be remembered that each of these triads may have a different meaning within its larger context.

Notice that in Table 10.6 the values for the stability of y given by Lerdahl's basic space (1988) and by his algorithm (1996) are the same for every pattern; in both pitch spaces, y (which is always 2 or 4) is always embedded at level 2. The same is true for Margulis's values (see Table 4.2). Since this factor is the same for each pattern, it will not account for any differences in the judgments or frequencies of these patterns. (This does not mean that these factors – Lerdahl's and Margulis's values for the stability of y – are irrelevant in listener judgments of all patterns; it just means that they cannot be relevant in explaining these particular patterns.) According to Krumhansl's profiles, however, y can assume four different values. (That these values are numerically very close does not prevent them from accounting for variance in the data – the technique of statistical analysis that we will use scales those values so that what is important is their relative size, not the absolute size of their differences.) Thus, with these patterns, Krumhansl's values for the stability of y can be assessed but Lerdahl's cannot.

Notice also that, for these patterns, Lerdahl's 1996 stability ratings of z and z' assume only two different values: 3 or 4. Lerdahl (1996, 2001) uses the root-and-fifth level for calculating chordal distance but removes it for figuring melodic stability so as to make 3 and 5 equally stable chord members. Every pattern that ends on 1 earns a 4; all others earn a 3. That means that those ratings provide the same information as asking the question, "Is there a preference for ending on the root?"

In fact, multiple-regression statistical analysis allows us to explore further hypotheses about stability by considering the stability of each chord member to be a separate factor. Table 10.7 shows how these factors are scored. The factor in the fourth column is called "ending on 1"; every pattern that ends on its chord root scores a 1 for this factor, and every pattern that does not scores a 0 for this factor. As noted above, this factor is equivalent to Lerdahl's 1996 stability ratings of z (and is equivalent to the stability ratings used by Margulis in some contexts). The factors in the

TABLE 10.7. THE STABILITIES OF INDIVIDUAL SCALE DEGREES
AS SEPARATE FACTORS

PATTERN			STABILITY OF Z			
Triad $(x\,y)$	Question $(x\,y\,z)$	+ Answer	Ending on $\hat{1}$	Ending on $\hat{3}$	Ending on $b\hat{3}$	Ending on $\hat{5}$
minor	1 2	1 2 1	1	0	0	0
		1 2 3	0	0	1	0
	3 2	3 2 1	1	0	0	0
		3 2 3	0	0	1	0
	3 4	3 4 3	0	0	1	0
		3 4 5	0	0	0	1
	5 4	5 4 3	0	0	1	0
		5 4 5	0	0	0	1
major	1 2	1 2 1	1	0	0	0
		1 2 3	0	1	0	0
	3 2	3 2 1	1	0	0	0
		3 2 3	0	1	0	0
	3 4	3 4 3	0	1	0	0
		3 4 5	0	0	0	1
	5 4	5 4 3	0	1	0	0
		5 4 5	0	0	0	1

remaining columns represent what happens when z is any of the other possible final chord members in our patterns. Thus, whereas the factors in Table 10.6 allow us to assess the explanatory value of specific ways of quantifying stability, the factors in Table 10.7 allow us to ask, "What (if any) quantification of stability by chord membership might help explain our experimental results?"

Before leaving the topic of stability, however, note that, with these patterns, a preference for ending on 1 also means a preference for downward motion. In other words, as factors in explaining listener judgments, the tendency to descend and the tendency to end on a chord root are not independent.

The theory of musical forces claims that gravity, magnetism, and inertia operate on all levels of musical structure. Schenker's analyses show patterns on different levels of musical structure. To clarify what this

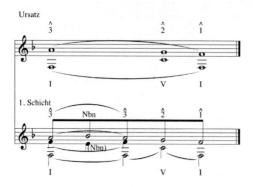

EXAMPLE 10.3. Fundamental structure (*Ursatz*) and
first-level middleground (*1. Schicht*) of Chopin's Etude
in F major, op. 10, no. 8.

means, a portion of one of the analyses from *Five Graphic Music Analyses*
is excerpted in Example 10.3. Example 10.3 gives the fundamental structure (*Ursatz*) and first-level middleground (*1. Schicht*) of Chopin's Etude
in F major, op. 10, no. 8. Schenker's analysis suggests that the first tone of
the fundamental structure is elaborated by neighbor notes (the soprano
B♭ and the alto E, both marked "Nbn") to create the first-level middleground. Through a series of such recursive elaborations, the fundamental
structure becomes a series of increasingly more detailed levels, leading
ultimately to the piece itself. Each time such an elaboration creates one of
our patterns, we add that occurrence to our tally. For example, the pattern
3–2–1 appears in the upper voice of the fundamental structure; we count
that as one appearance of that pattern (at the same time the bass has the
pattern 1–5–1, but that is not one of the patterns we are counting). The
three notes of that 3–2–1 pattern correspond (respectively) to the first
event in the piece (measure 1), to the upper voice of the cadential dominant (measure 71), and to the upper voice at the cadential tonic (measure
75). More patterns appear in the first-level middleground. The upper voice
adds the pattern 3–4–3, which is one of our patterns. This is followed by
3–2–1, but since it represents the same events in the piece (measures 1, 71,
and 75) as the 3–2–1 pattern that we counted in the fundamental structure, we do not count this as a new pattern. The inner voice also adds the
pattern 8–7–8, but that is not one of the patterns we are counting.

TABLE 10.8. THE DISTRIBUTION OF MELODIC PATTERNS WITHIN
HEINRICH SCHENKER'S *FIVE GRAPHIC MUSIC ANALYSES* (1932/1969)

PATTERNS			NUMBER OF TIMES IN SCHENKER (1932/1969)
Triad	Question ($x\,y$)	+ Answer ($x\,y\,z$)	
minor	1 2	1 2 1	2
		1 2 3	12
	3 2	3 2 1	4
		3 2 3	0
	3 4	3 4 3	0
		3 4 5	1
	5 4	5 4 3	2
		5 4 5	0
major	1 2	1 2 1	6
		1 2 3	6
	3 2	3 2 1	18
		3 2 3	3
	3 4	3 4 3	20
		3 4 5	12
	5 4	5 4 3	20
		5 4 5	0

Table 10.8 lists the number of times each of our patterns appears in the graphs of *Five Graphic Music Analyses*. We now perform another statistical analysis, this time asking how our model can account for the distribution of these patterns in the analytic graphs of *Five Graphic Music Analyses*. The results are given in Table 10.9. Graph 10.1 compares the number of appearances of each pattern with the predictions produced by the values shown in Table 10.9.

Table 10.9 includes a factor called "major vs. minor." The distribution of patterns within a piece is partly determined by the relative number of major and minor triads (there are many more major than minor triads in these pieces). Major triads may also be more prototypical; the idea that we understand minor by comparing it to its parallel major is a commonly made observation. The inclusion of the factor "major vs. minor" allows us to control for these differences between major and minor patterns.

TABLE 10.9. SUMMARY OF MULTIPLE-REGRESSION ANALYSIS FOR PATTERN DIS-
TRIBUTION IN *FIVE GRAPHIC MUSIC ANALYSES* (SCHENKER 1932/1969)

Summary of multiple-regression analysis	$R = .916$
	$p < .001$
	$N = 16$
Gravity	$w_G = 4.750$
	$\beta = .333$
	$p = .019$
Magnetism	$w_M = 8.500$
	$\beta = .515$
	$p < .001$
Inertia	$w_I = 5.500$
	$\beta = .385$
	$p = .009$
Major vs. minor	$w_{maj} = 8.000$
	$\beta = .560$
	$p < .001$

Note: Weights marked w are nonstandardized coefficients; weights
marked β are standardized coefficients.

The results provide striking support for the theory of musical forces.
The high correlation ($R = .916$) means that the theory of musical forces
can account for a great deal of the variation in the data. The probability
that a correlation this high could have occurred by chance is very low
($p < .001$). A closer look at the individual forces shows that gravity, magnetism, and inertia all make significant contributions to the model. The
weights attached to these forces also suggest that inertia has a greater impact on the ratings than gravity does but that magnetism has the greatest
impact. Additional tests show, moreover, that none of the other factors
listed in Tables 10.5, 10.6, and 10.7 appears to be statistically significant
(this includes the distance from y to z', as well as the stabilities of y, z,
and z' – regardless of how they are coded).

The distribution of patterns in the third study provides strong evidence that all three forces shape the frequency with which those patterns
occur. Thus, our results converge with those of previous studies, which
find good evidence for all three musical forces.

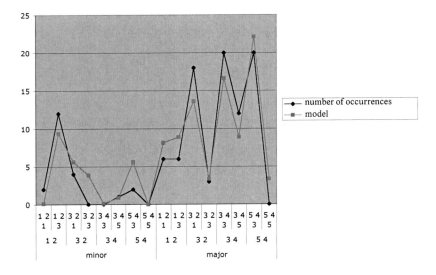

GRAPH 10.1. A graph that compares the number of appearances of sixteen patterns in Schenker's *Five Graphic Music Analyses* ([1932] 1969) with the predictions of a model based on gravity, magnetism, inertia, and "major vs. minor" (cf. Tables 10.8 and 10.9). (In the one case where the model generates a negative value, that prediction is graphed as zero.)

The hypotheses advanced in chapter 4 concerning the relative ranking of the musical forces received only partial support. We hypothesized that gravity is the weakest, that magnetism is stronger, and that inertia is the strongest force. In the content analysis, gravity is the weakest, but magnetism appears to be considerably stronger than inertia.

We have defined magnetism as a preference for proximate resolutions and found evidence for a proximity effect. The patterns that we studied, however, limit the conclusions that we can draw about the inverse-square or inverse-cube laws.

The third study found no evidence in favor of any stability profile to account for the distribution of patterns within *Five Graphic Music Analyses*. This finding would seem to agree with a recent study by Vega (2003, 35), which found that "a low correlation between Lerdahl's model and the attraction judgments demonstrated that distance in semitones is a more influential factor than anchoring strength in the perception of melodic attraction." It is possible, however, that a different sample of musical patterns would better show the impact of stability on listener judgments of the strength of pattern completion.

The third study is limited to diatonic tonal music. The absence of chromaticism in these patterns may further limit the conclusions that can be drawn.

CONCLUSION

All three studies reported in this chapter explore the distribution of patterns within analyses of specific pieces of music. All three studies find that certain patterns occur more often. The patterns that happen more often are those in which the musical forces have a greater impact. For each study, a simple "recipe" that combines gravity, magnetism, and inertia comes very close to predicting the frequency with which each pattern occurs. Together, these three studies support the claim of this book that tonal music moves as if shaped by constantly acting forces of musical gravity, magnetism, and inertia.

11

Evidence from Music-Theoretical Misunderstandings

Chapter 10 provided evidence that pieces of tonal music are shaped by musical forces. It found that the distributions of melodic patterns within the compositions and improvisations analyzed can be explained through a simple formula that combines gravity, magnetism, and inertia. But to play "devil's advocate" for a moment, one could object that chapter 10, by explaining the distributions of patterns within analyses, told us something about *analyses* – or about the *theories* behind them – but did not necessarily tell us anything about the *experience* of music.

Such an objection seems to assume that Schenker's theories favor the discovery of patterns that give in to the musical forces. Because I am sympathetic to Schenker's theories (which now provide the dominant paradigm for the analysis of tonal music), and because I feel that musical forces shape my experience of music, I expect Schenker's theories to favor the discovery of patterns that give in to musical forces. My intuition, in fact, is that any musically sensitive approach to analysis will tend to reflect the importance of musical forces. In other words, because I believe that Schenker's analyses reflect important aspects of my experience of music, I believe that chapter 10, by telling us something about Schenkerian analyses, also told us something about the experience of music.

Another objection might be, however, that music theories are "just theories" – and that theories can involve misunderstandings. Thus chapter 11 considers the question of misunderstandings in music theory. (Chapters 12 and 13 use methods from psychology and artificial intelligence to provide evidence that bears more directly on musical experience and musical behaviors.) The argument of this chapter is that some theorists actually do misunderstand musical forces – and that these misunderstandings are analogous to the kinds of misunderstandings that people have about physical forces – the "naïve physics" referred to in chapter 9. In fact, these misunderstandings become a part of the converging evidence that supports the analogy between musical forces and physical forces.

This chapter thus extends the analogy between physical forces and musical forces in the following way:

Some people misunderstand the operation of physical forces.	Some musicians misunderstand the operation of musical forces.
Nevertheless, the paths of physical objects are shaped by those forces.	Nevertheless, the paths of melodies are shaped by those forces.
Therefore, graceful physical gestures reflect their skillful balancing of physical forces.	Therefore, graceful melodic gestures reflect their skillful balancing of musical forces.

Physicists tell us that some people misunderstand the operation of physical forces. For example, some people will say things like "the ball continued to rise until its inertia gave out, and then gravity started to pull it down more and more" – as if physical forces took turns, acting one at a time.

Nevertheless, the paths of physical objects are shaped by the interaction of constantly acting forces. The ball just referred to is being pulled down constantly by gravity. And it is the constant interaction of gravity and inertia (as well as wind resistance) that shapes the path of the ball.

Chapter 6 noted that graceful physical gestures are shaped in ways that reflect this interaction, and it gave some examples. That chapter also suggested five analogous ways in which musical patterns can be combined so that they reflect the interaction of musical forces: (1) circling around a point of approaching repose; (2) combining two patterns in even pacing so that inertia carries through the relatively stable point of elision (and thus changing direction at relatively less stable points); (3) pausing when changing direction at a relatively stable juncture; (4) a turn followed by an upward leap; and (5) the introduction of changes in direction or type of motion on upbeats.

If the hypothesis suggested by this analogy is a good one, then we may find that theorists make statements which contradict (or are contradicted by) the theory of musical forces in the same ways that people misunderstand physical forces; that melodic expectations nevertheless obey musical forces; and that graceful melodic gestures contradict those statements by balancing musical forces in musical analogues of at least the five types of graceful physical gestures just listed.

This chapter continues by finding just such statements (which seem to misunderstand musical forces in the same ways that people misunderstand physical forces) in the writings of two leading music theorists. It then offers analyses showing how melodies in several different styles of tonal music contradict those misunderstandings by moving in the five types of pattern combination just listed.

TWO THEORISTS

The two theorists upon whose work I shall comment are central figures in the history of music theory. Jérôme-Joseph Momigny was an innovative and influential music theorist who wrote about music two hundred years ago. Leonard B. Meyer is one of the most respected contemporary music theorists. What follows is not intended as a criticism of either of these writers. I admire them both. Instead, what I hope to show is that even these respected scholars talk about musical forces in ways that echo the misunderstandings of "naïve physics."

A HISTORICAL MUSIC THEORIST

The following passage from Momigny (1806; quoted in Lerdahl 2001) pursues the analogy between physical and musical forces.

> There exists a true attraction or affinity between these notes . . . Like the attraction recognized in physics in relation to the inertia of bodies, this attraction acts in inverse relation to distance: a tone that is only half a step away from the one that has to follow it is much more powerfully attracted by it, than were it [separated] by a whole step . . . Since it is sometimes the lower tone that attracts the higher tone, and sometimes the higher that attracts the lower one, it follows that the attraction is not due to gravity but to proximity.

This quote provides further evidence that musicians have long conceived of music in terms of motion and forces. But it also contains some striking mistakes. It confuses physical attraction and physical inertia. It mistakenly attributes to physical inertia an "inverse relation to distance." And it apparently assumes that causation must have only one force at a time ("not due to gravity but to proximity") – what chapter 1 termed the "single-mechanism explanation."

Nevertheless, as chapter 10 showed, the distribution of melodic patterns suggests that all the musical forces are constantly acting on melodies rather than taking turns with one another. The analyses below suggest some of the ways in which music exploits the constant interaction of musical forces. But first let us consider the writings of a more recent music theorist.

A CONTEMPORARY THEORIST

Meyer's books include *Emotion and Meaning in Music* (1956) and *Explaining Music* (1973). These books provided an inspiration for the book you are now reading (by offering explanations of meaning and expectation in music) as well as a model for its approach (by raising important questions about musical experience and seeking answers both through close examination of individual pieces of music and through interdisciplinary research focused on expectation and meaning). Thus, when Meyer offers an explanation of musical motion that seems to contradict the observable operation of musical forces in the same ways that many people misunderstand the laws of physics, it provides good evidence for the argument of this chapter.

In *Emotion and Meaning in Music,* Meyer said that "we expect continuation only so long as it appears significant and meaningful in the sense that it can be understood as motion toward a goal" (1956, 93). In a later book he repeats the idea that, "once established, a patterning tends to be continued until a point of relative tonal-rhythmic stability is reached" (1973, 130), and "once begun, a linear, conjunct motion implies continuation to a point of relative stability" (Meyer 1973, 131). This idea develops its own inertia; established in his early books, it is repeated in some of his later books as well.

According to the theory of musical forces, Meyer's statements mistakenly conflate two musical tendencies (the inertial tendency of a pattern to continue and the magnetic tendency of a motion toward a goal). They mistakenly suggest that musical inertia evaporates when a goal is attained. And, like Momigny's statement, they mistakenly imply that musical motion may be explained in terms of a single principle ("good continuation").

Plenty of musical passages seem to work in the way Meyer describes. Motion continues in the same direction until a point of repose is reached. But, according to the theory of musical forces, this is an incomplete and misleading explanation of our cognitive expectations for melody.

The theory of musical forces claims that musical inertia is analogous to physical inertia. As the park swing and pendulum examples of chapter 6 remind us, the inertial tendency of motion (to continue in the same fashion) will carry an object beyond a stable point to which it is drawn. Thus the theory of musical forces claims that if magnetism draws us *to* a goal, inertia will tend to carry us *beyond* that goal. This contradicts Meyer's assertion that "we expect continuation only so long as . . . it can be understood as motion toward a goal." A motion to a goal may give in to magnetism as it resolves to that goal, but it works against inertia by stopping on that goal.

ANALYSES

The first study described in chapter 10 provided examples of the phenomenon of inertia carrying motion beyond a goal in its elisions of three-, five-, and seven-note patterns. In each of those five- and seven-note patterns, two shorter patterns were combined so that inertia carried through the relatively stable point of elision (so as to follow the "pattern map" in Chart 6.1, p. 160). The following analyses find more examples of this phenomenon as well as musical analogues of some of the other physical phenomena described above.

"Twinkle, Twinkle, Little Star"

"Twinkle, Twinkle, Little Star" illustrates how inertia continues beyond points of stability in gestures that may be regarded as elided patterns shaped by musical forces. In this folk song we hear a number of three-

EXAMPLE 11.1. Analysis of "Twinkle, Twinkle, Little Star"
shows combinations of patterns.

note patterns. (Remember that, as noted in chapter 6, when I speak of a
three-note pattern following, or giving in to, a certain force, I mean that
the second note of the pattern resolves to the third by moving in the direction determined by that force.) In Example 11.1a, each of these patterns
is marked with a slur. Each pattern begins on a stable note (stemmed),
moves to an unstable note (unstemmed), and ends on a stable note (here
the stable pitches are the members of the tonic triad). Furthermore, these
three-note patterns are elided (the last note of one pattern is the first note
of the next). We can think of each of these patterns as giving in to the
musical force of gravity (the second note always goes *down* to the third).
The first and second patterns give in to magnetism (the second note
always resolves to the third – the *closest* stable pitch). The second and
third of these patterns may also be seen as giving in to inertia (in both,
the pattern continues in the *same* direction to its third note). But notice
that, in all these elisions, inertia continues beyond the stable notes that
begin and end each pattern – that is, in each elision, the motion continues
in the *same* direction from the end of the first pattern into the beginning
of the next pattern. When patterns are combined in this way, melodies
change direction only on unstable notes.

"My Country 'Tis of Thee" or "God Save the Queen/King"

Not all elided patterns are joined in this way. But the phenomenon is
common in graceful melodies. And it lends a quality of grace to even
the most common melodies. Consider "My Country 'Tis of Thee" (or
"God Save the Queen/King"). The melody and an analysis are given in
Example 11.2.

EXAMPLE 11.2. Analysis of "My Country 'Tis of Thee"
(or "God Save the Queen/King").

The overall path (the basic skeleton) of the melody (given in Example 11.2a) consists of two elided patterns, $\hat{1}$–$\hat{2}$–$\hat{3}$ and $\hat{3}$–$\hat{2}$–$\hat{1}$. Here the melody pauses on a stable pitch and changes direction there. (Alternatively, one could view the basic structure as an elision of three patterns – $\hat{1}$–$\hat{2}$–$\hat{3}$ in measures 1–3, $\hat{3}$–$\hat{4}$–$\hat{3}$ in measures 3–4, and $\hat{3}$–$\hat{2}$–$\hat{1}$ in measures 4–6 – in which case the patterns are joined as described in the pattern map given in Example 7.2. According to this alternate view, the melody does not pause, but it changes direction on the unstable pitch. Either way, it corresponds to what we said about graceful physical motions, which either change direction on a stable pitch where they pause or change direction on an unstable pitch without pausing.)

Notice that, in Example 11.2b, the third and fourth measures present two elided three-note patterns. The E–F–E of measures 3–4 gives in to gravity (F goes *down* to E) and magnetism (E is *closer* to F than G is). And the E–D–C of measure 4 gives in to gravity (D goes *down* to C) and inertia (D continues in the *same* direction to C). Furthermore, these two patterns are elided (the E of measure 4 is the end of the first pattern and the beginning of the second). And inertia continues through the elision (the E–F–E pattern ends by going down, and the E–D–C pattern starts by going down); the E shared by both patterns is approached and left in the same direction.

In both measure 2 and measure 5, the chord of the moment at level b is the dominant. In that context, B and D are stable pitches and C is

EXAMPLE 11.3. A turn figure.

unstable. The B–C–D pattern in measure 2 uses inertia to overcome gravity and magnetism. As the D of measure 2 moves to the E of measure 3 at level a, the inertia of the B–C–D pattern at level b reinforces that ascent. In other words, inertia carries through the locally stable D as the line moves up to E. The D–C–B pattern of measure 5 gives in to all three forces. As the D of measure 5 moves to the C of measure 6 at level a, the figuration at level b circles around the goal, creating the circling approach mentioned above.

A Chopin Impromptu

All of Chopin's Impromptus begin, or begin sections, with a turn figure. In most cases, that turn is on the fifth scale degree. Example 11.3 gives a schematic description of such a turn figure.

In this schematic, the fifth scale degree is embellished first with a diatonic upper neighbor and then with a half-step lower neighbor, creating the pattern $\hat{5}$–$\hat{6}$–$\hat{5}$–$\sharp\hat{4}$–$\hat{5}$. This five-note pattern may be viewed as two elided three-note patterns. Slurs show the three-note patterns. In the first of these patterns, $\hat{5}$–$\hat{6}$–$\hat{5}$, gravity pulls the diatonic upper neighbor back *down* to the note it elaborates. In the second of these patterns, $\hat{5}$–$\sharp\hat{4}$–$\hat{5}$, the half-step magnetism afforded by the chromatic lower neighbor seems needed to overcome inertia and gravity in order to pull the lower neighbor back up to the note it elaborates. Inertia continues through the point of elision; the descent at the end of the first pattern continues into the beginning of the second. At the end of the second pattern, inertia suggests continued upward motion. As noted in chapter 6, this may be one reason turn figures point upward. In all the Impromptus, these turns are followed by rising gestures, usually leaps. In other words, the turn figure is a gesture that points upward in the same way that analogous physical motions do – just as we jump up and then push down into a diving board before a dive or gather energy and crouch before a leap. Toch's (1948)

EXAMPLE 11.4. Analysis of Chopin's Impromptu in A♭ major,
op. 29, measures 1–5.

discussion of what he calls the "wind up" discusses this figure in similar gestural terms, and in the context of an explanation of melody that repeatedly invokes the metaphors of motion and forces.

The Impromptu in A♭ major, op. 29 (Example 11.4) begins with a notated triplet, $\hat{5}$–♯$\hat{4}$–$\hat{5}$. But since the first note of that triplet has a trill, the result is the turn $\hat{5}$–$\hat{6}$–$\hat{5}$–♯$\hat{4}$–$\hat{5}$. (In the analysis, small noteheads identify the notes that participate in patterns generated by this turn motive.) As Example 11.4b shows, the following three notes, C–B♭–A♭, make another three-note pattern that gives in to gravity and inertia. But, once again, inertia continues the motion beyond the stable pitch – to the following G. (Of course, the A♭ is *rhythmically* unstable, so the passage agrees with Meyer's description in the sense that motion continues until we reach a point of relative *rhythmic* stability.) The following F–F♭–E♭ echoes C–B♭–A♭, but it does so in a way that uses rhythmic stability to allow the pattern to close on its last note. Two initial statements of the opening measure are followed by a descending scale with interpolated embellishing leaps (another feature common to the Chopin Impromptus).

EXAMPLE 11.5. Analysis of "Bourrée" from Bach's English Suite in A minor, measures 1–6.

As Example 11.4a shows, the "tenor" and "bass" lines contained within the left-hand part also combine patterns so that inertia continues through points of relative repose. The bass line combines $\hat{1}$–$\hat{2}$–$\hat{3}$ with $\hat{3}$–$\hat{4}$–$\hat{5}$, with the elided pitch ($\hat{3}$) approached and left by ascent. The tenor line combines $\hat{3}$–$\hat{4}$–$\hat{5}$ with $\hat{5}$–$\hat{6}$–$\hat{5}$, with the elided pitch ($\hat{5}$) approached and left by ascent.

Bach's "Bourrée" from the English Suite in A minor

Example 11.5 gives the opening of the "Bourrée" from Bach's English Suite in A minor. The basic skeleton of this passage is the pattern $\hat{5}$–$\hat{4}$–$\hat{3}$ in minor (the stemmed "soprano" notes in Example 11.5a) – a pattern that gives in to gravity and inertia. Each note of this pattern, however, is elaborated with an upper neighbor (the unstemmed notes that are contained within the slurs in Example 11.5a). The result is that the pattern $\hat{5}$–$\hat{6}$–$\hat{5}$ pauses (while the melody leaps down to A) on a stable pitch before repeating, and then moves at a regular pace in such a way that the momentum created by that upper neighbor leads down to the note that begins the next pattern, and in such a way that the last elaboration produces an E–D–C that recalls the basic structure of the whole passage (a "confirmation"). Similar things may be said of the "tenor voice" in Example 11.5a, which moves in parallel tenths below the soprano.

Now consider how the melody itself (Example 11.5b and c) connects each of the basic notes shown in Example 11.5a. Every time that the basic melody (level a) steps from a lower to a higher note, the melody first decorates that lower note with its own lower neighbor; the result is that the inertia created by the lower neighbor is heard to carry through to the next (higher) note. Every time that the basic melody steps from a higher to a lower note, the melody first decorates that higher note with a passing motion to a third below; the result is that the melody circles around the next (lower) note. The elaborations added to the tenor in Example 11.5b also introduce inertia that carries through to the next pattern.

The use of a consistent set of elaborations gives a certain kind of logic to this passage. And the fact that those elaborations respect the tendency of inertia to continue motion in the same direction – even beyond a point of repose – gives a visceral sense of momentum to this passage. Thus its logic appears to be the logic of embodied knowledge about what makes physical gestures graceful.

Haydn Piano Sonata in D major (Hoboken XVI:19)

Example 11.6 shows two different passages from a Haydn Piano Sonata. Example 11.6b shows the opening measures of the Sonata. Example 11.6c shows the varied repetition of these measures after some intervening material. As Example 11.6a shows, the underlying structure of these passages is the same – a simpler melody that moves essentially in eighth notes. That simpler melody is composed entirely of the three-note patterns of our pattern map. And (with one exception) they are joined so that inertia carries through the elided pitch.

Haydn's sense of humor emerges in the way that those patterns are repeated. There is nothing odd in the repetition of measure 1 as measure 2 (see Example 11.6b). In fact, such a twofold statement of an opening idea is a common way to begin (and the ascent at the end of measure 1

EXAMPLE 11.6. Analysis of two passages from Haydn's Piano Sonata
in D major (Hoboken XVI:19).

leading into the ascent at the beginning of measure 2 adds to the smoothness of this repetition). But the fact that the melody does not stop at the
beginning of measure 3 does seem odd. Although the $\hat{3}-\hat{4}-\hat{5}$ pattern that
begins measure 3 seems "extra," it also arises as a very natural gesture:
because it continues the ascent of the $\hat{1}-\hat{2}-\hat{3}$ pattern that leads into measure 3, inertia carries through that downbeat. The silence after that pattern leaves it hanging "up in the air." The repetition of that pattern (with
different ornamentation) seems to mock the odd nature of the gesture.

When these three measures are repeated (Example 11.6c), the ornamentation is varied further. This time the triplets are introduced sooner.
And, starting halfway through the second bar, ascending half-step ap-
poggiaturas decorate each note of the $\hat{1}-\hat{2}-\hat{3}$ and $\hat{3}-\hat{4}-\hat{5}$ patterns. Beginning this new decoration halfway through the second bar (rather than on
the downbeat of the third measure) means that (just as the $\hat{1}-\hat{2}-\hat{3}$ pattern
leads into and through the downbeat of the third measure) inertia carries
this decoration across the bar line where the "extra" lick appears. Notice
also that the decoration chosen (the ascending half-step appoggiaturas)
joins those decorations into a longer (almost entirely) chromatic scale
whose inertia sweeps through the downbeat with even more momentum. In the second half of the third bar, the preservation of the prior trip-

let decoration in the repetition of this up-in-the-air gesture adds to the humor of its mocking repetition in a quintessentially Haydnesque way (so that it surprises us by being, at some level, what we had expected).

The wit and grace of this final example rely, at least in part, on our understanding of these patterns as forming "gestures" whose meaning depends on the fact that musical inertia (like physical inertia) may carry those gestures through the points of stability established by other forces.

CONCLUSION

From the vantage point of the theory of musical forces, these examples suggest that although Meyer's description of musical inertia (which he calls "good continuation") offers a correct *description* of what happens in many pieces, it is an incomplete (and, in fact, misleading) *explanation* of the operation of musical forces. Meyer's assertion that "we expect continuation only so long as . . . it can be understood as motion toward a goal" is contradicted by melodies in which musical inertia carries motion beyond the goals to which magnetism draws them, creating musical gestures that are analogous to the graceful physical gestures that circle about a goal, change direction at unstable points in continuous motions, or change direction at stable points on which they pause. Furthermore, those aspects of inertia that are not captured in Meyer's description help explain some important aspects of what makes the music of Bach, Haydn, Chopin, and others appealing to listeners.

The point, of course, is not to criticize Meyer and Momigny. Instead, the point is that misconceptions about the operation of musical forces (held by many, including these highly respected theorists) parallel popular misconceptions about the operation of physical forces – and that this parallel indirectly provides further evidence for the theory of musical forces.

12

Evidence from a Listener-Judgment Experiment

Chapter 8 noted that our thinking *about* music is shaped by musical forces. Chapter 9 made more credible the idea that thinking in other domains (such as visual perception as well as auditory perception) might draw on our embodied understanding of physical motion by importing forces analogous to gravity, magnetism, and inertia – and it noted brain structures recently discovered by neuroscience that might underlie such cross-domain mappings. Chapter 10 showed that the distribution of patterns within compositions and improvisations suggests that our thinking *in* music is also shaped by musical forces. And chapter 11 suggested that even mistaken theories about music provide evidence in support of the theory of musical forces. But this raises another question (which was hinted at in chapter 11). One interpretation of chapter 10 in light of chapter 11 is that the distribution of patterns within its analyses proves only that those analyses (rather than the compositions themselves) are shaped by the musical forces. What additional evidence can we find that listeners actually feel the impact of musical forces as they create or listen to music?

For such evidence, we can turn to psychological experiments. Earlier chapters have cited a number of experiments involving melodic expectation. Some of these experiments involve listener judgments of melodic continuations or completions. Chapter 12 focuses on one such judgment experiment, which asked listeners to make judgments about the experienced "strength" of presented pattern completions. The experiment reported in this chapter was originally published as a part of the third study discussed in chapter 10 (Larson and VanHandel 2005), which also involved the distribution of patterns in Schenker's *Five Graphic Music Analyses* ([1932] 1969).

We asked participants to rate the strength of each of the same sixteen patterns described in Table 10.4. Participants were presented with the two-note melodic "question" fragments (the notes x and y) given in the second column of Table 10.4 and both possible "answers" (the note z, the other answer being its z') given in the third column, and were asked to rate both patterns based on how well the second note (y) "led" to the third note (z). Participants were given a scale from 1 to 7 (7 being strongest or best) to rate the resultant three-note patterns.

We then used a multiple-regression analysis (described in chapter 10, in the section titled "A Study of Jazz Melody") to determine how well those ratings can be accounted for in terms of the factors described above (gravity, magnetism, inertia, and stability).

Ratings were collected from eighty-four participants recruited from the University of Oregon and Stanford University. Each participant was seated in front of a computer screen displaying a "Welcome" screen requesting participants to self-report aspects of their musical background, including years of musical training, current status as a musician, major instrument, and continent of origin.[1] All participants were at least moderately trained in music (M = 12.8 years, SD = 5) and most (seventy-two out of eighty-four) reported that they were currently either a student, a graduate student, or a university-affiliated teacher in music.[2]

Upon completion of the "Welcome" screen, participants were presented with a "Demonstration" screen, which introduced the experiment. The instructions indicated that participants would be presented with a tonal context, a melodic question (the notes x and y), and two possible answers for each melodic beginning (the note z, the other answer being its z'). The screen contained buttons for the participants to click in order to hear the tonal context, a sample melodic question, and sample melodic answers.

For this demonstration, the melodic question used was $\hat{5}$–$\hat{6}$–?, which is a fragment that does not meet the criteria of the fragments chosen for study in the experiment (it does not have two possible stepwise continuations where z and z' are both members of the tonic triad). The two patterns given were $\hat{5}$–$\hat{6}$–$\hat{5}$ and $\hat{5}$–$\hat{6}$–$\hat{8}$.

Participants were instructed to listen to both patterns and rate each on a scale from 1 to 7 (provided on a pull-down menu under each pattern), based on how strongly the participant felt that the second note (y) "led" to the third note (z). When the participant was satisfied with the ratings, he or she was instructed to click on a button at the bottom of the screen to complete the demonstration. The program was designed so that participants were not allowed to complete the demonstration until they had listened to the tonal context, each melodic question, and each answer – and until they had provided a rating for each three-note pattern.

Upon completion of the demonstration, the participants were given a set of eight three-note patterns, each presented in a single (major- or minor-key) context. There were four sets, each with a different tonal context (C Major, F$\sharp$ Major, C minor, and F$\sharp$ minor).

The tonal context, in the form of a perfect authentic cadence (I–IV–I$^6_4$–V–I, with $\hat{5}$–$\hat{6}$–$\hat{5}$–$\hat{7}$–$\hat{8}$ in the soprano), was provided via a button at the top of the screen. Participants were instructed and encouraged to click on the button often to keep the tonal context in mind as they progressed through each set. Four large buttons allowed participants to hear the four melodic questions (the notes x and y). Two smaller buttons under each larger button allowed them to hear the two possible stepwise answers (each answer being a possible note z, the other answer being its z') associated with that particular melodic question.

Participants were instructed to rate each three-note pattern on a scale of 1 to 7 (7 being highest, strongest, or best) based on how strongly they felt the second note (y) "led" to the third note (z). They were instructed to compare the eight patterns (given as a set on a single screen) against one another as a group before submitting their answers. They were also asked to use the widest scoring range possible. Participants had no time limit to complete the experiment and were asked to make careful, musically sensitive decisions about their answers.

When the participant was satisfied with the rankings within a set, he or she clicked on the button at the bottom of the screen to continue to the next set. The program would automatically verify that the participant had listened to the tonal context, each melodic fragment, and each continuation at least once, as well as verify that there was a response to all continuations. If so, the program automatically saved the results for that set and presented an intermediate screen informing participants that the next set would have a new tonal context; it also provided a reminder that they could hear the tonal context as often as they wished. At the end of the fourth set, a final screen thanked the participant and provided a button to save the results and quit the program.

The order of presentation for the four tonal contexts was chosen randomly, the four melodic "questions" were presented in random order within each set, and the two continuations associated with each fragment were randomized as to which would appear "first," or left-most, under each fragment. The ordering information was saved along with participant's responses.[3]

We first calculated the average of participant responses for each individual melodic fragment, taking key and mode into account, which resulted in thirty-two averages. The hypotheses being tested here do not make different predictions for the patterns in C vs. the patterns in F♯. The data support this idea; the correlation between the average ratings in C and those in F♯ is very high ($r = .971$, $N = 16$, $p < .001$). This suggests that the musical phenomena that we are studying are robust and that our experimental results are a good indicator of shared musical intuitions. Therefore we averaged the results for the patterns in both major keys and in both minor keys, resulting in sixteen averages: the eight possible patterns in major and the eight in minor.

The hypotheses being tested here, however, do make different predictions for the major- and minor-key patterns. Thus the major and minor results were not averaged together. The results are given in the rightmost column of Table 12.1.

The statistical technique of multiple regression allows us to assess the relative contributions of the musical forces. (None of the aspects of musical background, including years of musical training, current status as a musician, major instrument, or continent of origin, appeared relevant in explaining the data.) The following equation captures a hypothesis of the theory of musical forces:

$$F = w_G G + w_M M + w_I I$$

This equation (which resembles the algorithms of Bharucha, Larson, Lerdahl, and Margulis described above) asserts that the net force (F)

TABLE 12.1. AVERAGE RESPONSES FOR EACH CONTINUATION

MODE		C	F♯	AVERAGE RATINGS
minor	1 2 1	4.44	4.60	4.52
	1 2 3	5.29	5.29	5.29
	3 2 1	5.93	5.83	5.88
	3 2 3	4.36	4.12	4.24
	3 4 3	3.96	4.23	4.10
	3 4 5	5.08	4.92	5.00
	5 4 3	5.27	5.20	5.24
	5 4 5	4.26	4.24	4.25
major	1 2 1	4.49	4.55	4.52
	1 2 3	5.43	5.10	5.26
	3 2 1	5.74	5.63	5.68
	3 2 3	3.82	3.95	3.89
	3 4 3	4.20	4.51	4.36
	3 4 5	5.27	5.15	5.21
	5 4 3	5.51	5.58	5.55
	5 4 5	3.63	3.46	3.55

Note: Each response is rounded to two places.

acting on a given tone in a given pattern is a weighted sum of its gravity score (G), its magnetism score (M), and its inertia score (I), where the coefficients $(w_G, w_M,$ and $w_I,$ respectively) are weights that determine the relative contribution of each force. As noted in chapter 9, most statistical packages include multiple-regression software that will solve this equation by finding the values of $w_G, w_M,$ and w_I that produce the highest correlation (between the values for F and the average ratings given to each pattern completion) and then telling us that correlation. The results are reported in Table 12.2.

The results provide some support for the theory of musical forces. The extremely high correlation $(R = .951)$ means that variation in musical forces explains a great deal of the variation in the data. The probability that a correlation this high could have occurred by chance is very low $(p < .001)$. A closer look at the individual forces shows that gravity and inertia both make significant contributions to the model. The weights attached to these forces also suggest that inertia has a greater impact on

TABLE 12.2. SUMMARY OF MULTIPLE-REGRESSION ANALYSIS OF
EXPERIMENTAL DATA ACCORDING TO A MODEL OF MUSICAL FORCES

Summary of multiple-regression analysis	$R = .951$
	$N = 16$
	$p < .001$
Gravity	$w_G = .395$
	$\beta = .294$
	$p = .006$
Magnetism	$w_M = .102$
	$\beta = .066$
	$p = .476$
Inertia	$w_I = 1.210$
	$\beta = .902$
	$p < .001$

Note: Weights marked w are nonstandardized coefficients; weights marked β are standardized coefficients.

the ratings than gravity does. The results also suggest, however, that the contribution of magnetism is not statistically significant. Furthermore, additional statistical tests show that, of the other factors considered in chapter 10, only one (the stability of z according to Lerdahl's 1996 values, whose coding indicates only a preference for ending on the first scale degree) is significant. The remaining factors (the distance from y to z', the stability of z according to any other measure, the stability of z', and the stability of y) do not appear to be statistically significant. "Ending on $\hat{1}$" is also the only stability factor that is statistically significant; no values for the relative stabilities of other scale degrees helped explain variations in the data.

Including this factor (a preference for patterns that end on $\hat{1}$) in our model can improve its ability to account for the variations in the data. The results are given in Table 12.3.

Two interesting things can be seen in this table. First, it suggests that a model that includes this factor (a preference for patterns that end on $\hat{1}$) also gives a greater role to magnetism, which now appears statistically significant. Second, the inclusion of this factor means that gravity now appears not to be statistically significant. Of course, this reflects

TABLE 12.3. SUMMARY OF MULTIPLE-REGRESSION ANALYSIS FOR A MODEL
THAT INCLUDES A FACTOR FOR ENDING ON THE FIRST DEGREE OF THE SCALE

Summary of multiple-regression analysis	$R = .977$
	$N = 16$
	$p < .001$
Gravity	$w_G = .162$
	$\beta = .121$
	$p = .165$
Magnetism	$w_M = .257$
	$\beta = .166$
	$p = .038$
Inertia	$w_I = 1.210$
	$\beta = .902$
	$p < .001$
Ending on $\hat{1}$	$w = .466$
	$\beta = .301$
	$p = .005$

Note: Weights marked *w* are nonstandardized coefficients;
weights marked β are standardized coefficients.

TABLE 12.4. SUMMARY OF MULTIPLE-REGRESSION ANALYSIS FOR A MODEL
THAT INCLUDES A FACTOR FOR ENDING ON THE FIRST DEGREE OF THE SCALE
BUT NO FACTOR FOR MUSICAL GRAVITY

Summary of multiple-regression analysis	$R = .972$
	$N = 16$
	$p < .001$
Magnetism	$w_M = .298$
	$\beta = .192$
	$p = .020$
Inertia	$w_I = 1.210$
	$\beta = .902$
	$p < .001$
Ending on $\hat{1}$	$w = .588$
	$\beta = .379$
	$p < .001$

Note: Weights marked *w* are nonstandardized coefficients;
weights marked β are standardized coefficients.

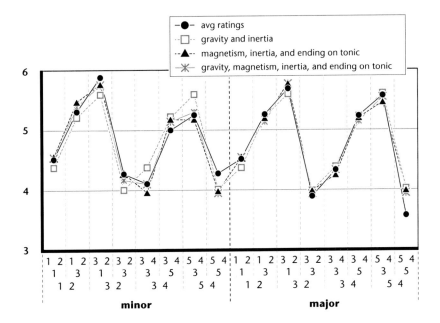

GRAPH 12.1. A graph comparing participants' average ratings of our patterns with the predictions of models based on gravity and inertia (cf. Table 12.2); gravity, magnetism, inertia, and ending on Î (cf. Table 12.3); and magnetism, inertia, and ending on Î (cf. Table 12.4).

the fact that these two factors (gravity and ending on Î) are correlated; because they are not independent variables we must be cautious in drawing conclusions about models that include both factors. Table 12.4 offers a model with only three factors: magnetism, inertia, and preference for ending on Î. In this model all factors are statistically significant. Graph 12.1 compares average participant ratings with the predictions produced by the values shown in Tables 12.3 and 12.4.

SUMMARY

The experiment reported in this chapter tested listener judgments of the strength of melodic pattern completions. The results provide some support for the hypotheses that all three forces contribute to listener judgments of the strength of pattern completions and that inertia is stronger than gravity or magnetism. The results also suggest that there may be a preference for patterns that end on the first scale degree. (The results, however – at least for the patterns investigated here – do not provide evidence to support the hypothesis that the stability profiles suggested by Krumhansl, Lerdahl, and Margulis account for any of the experimental results beyond their correlation with our model of musical forces. In fact, the multiple-regression analysis suggests that, beyond a preference for ending on the first scale degree, the stability of other ending notes has no statistical significance.)

The results thus add to the converging evidence that experienced listeners of tonal music not only think *about* music in terms of forces but actually think *in* music in ways that show musical forces interacting in the same kinds of quantifiable ways in which physical forces interact.

13

Evidence from Comparing Computer Models with Production-Experiment Results

The theory of melodic expectation presented in Chapter 5 claimed that experienced listeners of tonal music have expectations about how melodic beginnings will be completed, and also claimed that important aspects of those expectations are captured in the following summary statement:

> Experienced listeners of tonal music expect melodic completions in which the musical forces of gravity, magnetism, and inertia control operations on alphabets in hierarchies of elaboration whose stepwise displacements of auralized traces create simple closed shapes.

Chapter 13 describes two computer models that implement aspects of that theory, and shows that a comparison of the results of that model with the results of psychological experiments offers strong support for that theory.

A SINGLE-LEVEL COMPUTER MODEL

Some aspects of this theory have been implemented in what I shall call a "single-level" computer model.[1] The model is a simple one – every aspect of it is described in the pages below – no additional assumptions or mechanisms are "hidden" in the code. This model, when given a cue in a specified key, returns a rated list of predicted completions. For example, if we ask it to assume the key of C and give it the beginning G–A, it predicts that roughly half the participants will respond with G–A–G (giving in to gravity and magnetism), that roughly half will respond with G–A–B–C (giving in to inertia), and that none will respond with

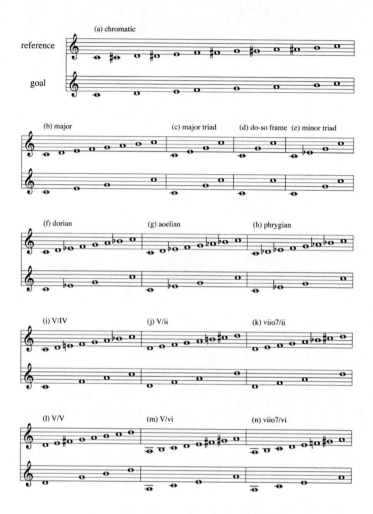

EXAMPLE 13.1. To make its predictions, the single-level model first chooses
a pair (or pairs) of reference and goal alphabets from the following list.

anything else. To calculate the ratings that it gives to each completion it
generates, it uses the algorithm given in chapter 4, with a factor added
for the stability of the final note.

To make its predictions, the single-level model first chooses a pair
(or pairs) of reference and goal alphabets from the list in Example 13.1.
To do so, it follows three simple rules: (1) diatonic cues may not use
chromatic alphabets; (2) reference alphabets must include the last pitch

of the cue; and (3) goal alphabets must not include the last pitch of the cue (an exception is noted below for unrated inertia predictions). Combinations other than those listed in Example 13.1 are possible, and the responses of some experimental participants suggest expectations that can be described in terms of other combinations, but this simple set is well defined and accounts well for the experimental results we shall examine.[2]

To illustrate the choice of reference and goal alphabets, consider the case of the melodic beginning G–A–?. According to the first rule, none of the chromatic reference alphabets (not choices a nor e–n, in Example 13.1) may be chosen as reference alphabets (because the cue contains no chromaticism); this leaves the combinations in Example 13.1b–d. According to the second rule, the triad and the frame (choices c and d) are eliminated (they do not contain A, the last note of the cue); together with the first rule, this leaves only the diatonic major scale shown in Example 13.1b. According to the third rule, all the combinations whose goal alphabets include A (choices a, i–k, and m–n in Example 13.1) are eliminated (because this would suggest that the goal is already reached and hence no notes need be added); this still allows the combination shown in Example 13.1b.

Once the reference and goal alphabets are chosen, the single-level model makes its predictions by moving within the reference alphabet until it arrives at a member of the goal alphabet. The direction of motion is determined by the musical forces.

Table 13.1 illustrates the resultant magnetism prediction for the beginning G–A–?. In Step 1, the reference and goal alphabets are chosen. In Step 2, the distances to the closest stable pitches, both up and down, are calculated (the "stable pitches" are simply the notes contained in the goal alphabet). For G–A–?, the closest stable pitches are G (two semitones from A) and C (three semitones from A). In Step 3, the computer chooses motion to G (because it is closer than C) and moves through the reference alphabet to that G. The result is that the computer has turned the cue G–A–? into the completion G–A–G.

Table 13.2 illustrates the resultant inertia prediction for the same beginning. In Step 1, the reference and goal alphabets are chosen. Because the last two notes of the cue are adjacent in the reference alphabet,

TABLE 13.1. A MAGNETISM PREDICTION FOR G–A–?

Step 1: The goal and reference alphabets are chosen.

reference alphabet (scale)   ———————>

C	D	E	F	G	A	B	C
C		E		G			C

goal alphabet (chord)

Step 2: The distances to the closest stable pitches are calculated (in half steps).

reference alphabet (scale)   <—2—— —3————————>

C	D	E	F	G	A	B	C
C		E		G			C

goal alphabet (chord)

Step 3: The prediction is for motion (through the reference alphabet) to the closest stable pitch (G).

reference alphabet (scale)   <———————

C	D	E	F	G	A	B	C
C		E		G			C

goal alphabet (chord)

Resultant prediction: G–A–G.

there is a pattern of motion (ascending through the reference alphabet) that can be continued. In Step 2, that pattern of motion is continued. G–A–? has now become G–A–B–?. Since the B is unstable (that is, it is not contained in the goal alphabet), we go on to Step 3, where the motion is continued further to C. Since the C is stable (that is, it is contained in the goal alphabet), the computer stops. The result is that the computer has turned the cue G–A–? into the completion G–A–B–C.

Because the goal alphabet is always a subset of the reference alphabet, the computer always knows when to stop. Although Narmour's implication-realization model does not clearly specify how long a continuation might go on, the computer model always does.

In the single-level model, inertia is only represented when the last two notes of the cue are adjacent in the reference alphabet (so that the

TABLE 13.2. A INERTIA PREDICTION FOR G–A–?

Step 1: The goal and reference alphabets are chosen.

reference alphabet (scale) ———→

C	D	E	F	G	A	B	C
C		E		G			C

goal alphabet (chord)

Step 2: Motion is continued in the same direction within the reference level, first to B (which is unstable).

reference alphabet (scale) ———→

C	D	E	F	G	A	B	C
C		E		G			C

goal alphabet (chord)

Step 3: Since B is also unstable, motion is again continued in the same direction within the reference alphabet, now to C (which is stable).

reference alphabet (scale) ———→

C	D	E	F	G	A	B	C
C		E		G			C

goal alphabet (chord)

Resultant prediction: G–A–B–C.

pattern is "motion by adjacency within the reference alphabet" and inertia can thus continue "in the same fashion").

The idea of traces is implemented in one feature of the program. In situations where the unstable second-to-last note of a cue leaps to a more stable pitch, the computer assumes that the leap has left the unstable note "hanging." It thus generates a continuation from that note rather than from the second note.

The contextual quality of melodic gravity is implemented in another feature of the program. If a melody descends only a half step below a stable base (imitating the physical motion that we make when we crouch) – so that we experience no natural lower position for gravity to take us to – the computer will not attempt to give in to gravity. A similar procedure prevents descending continuations where reference alphabets are uncertain or gapped.[3]

As reported elsewhere (Larson 1994), disabling these features weakens the performance of the computer model. Enabling them makes the program agree better with participant responses.

Some inertia predictions are not assigned ratings by the algorithm. For the beginning F–E–?, the single-level model uses the tonic triad as reference alphabet and the tonic-dominant frame as goal alphabet (as noted above, goal alphabets must not include the last pitch of the cue, and the goal alphabet must be the largest one contained in the reference alphabet). The result is the continuations F–E–G and F–E–C, which give in, respectively, to magnetism and gravity. It thus rates these two continuations accordingly (computing the differences in magnetic pulls from E to G above and E to C below). However – like physical inertia – musical inertia does not depend on stability. Thus, for the beginning F–E–?, if it is heard as a stepwise descent through the reference alphabet of the major scale, inertia predicts the continuation F–E–D–C. The single-level model will produce such inertia completions, but it is not clear what distances should be used in the algorithm for computing their magnetic pulls; thus the comparison of ratings for these continuations could seem arbitrary. In what follows, such inertia completions are suppressed whenever ratings are compared.

The single-level model can also make "recursive" predictions. For the melodic beginning, E–F–?, it predicts E–F–G and E–F–E. But it can then take one of these predictions, say E–F–E, and then reinterpret it as the new beginning E–F–E–?. It thus adds the predictions E–F–E–C, E–F–E–G, and E–F–E–D–C. Again, because more than one rating could be assigned, comparing ratings seems arbitrary. Such recursive predictions can also be suppressed when ratings are compared.

Two additional examples, shown in Table 13.3, illustrate the operation of the single-level model.

Consider the cue C–C$\sharp$–?. Because the cue ends with a C$\sharp$, the reference alphabet must include that note. (Of course, the same note may also be spelled D$\flat$ – the computer, like the human listener, may "hear" that note either way. Here I shall spell such notes according to music-theoretical conventions, that is, contextually.) This allows the

TABLE 13.3. TWO ADDITIONAL EXAMPLES ILLUSTRATING THE
SINGLE-LEVEL MODEL

CUE	REFERENCE AND GOAL COMBINATION*	GRAVITY	MAGNETISM	INERTIA
C–C♯–?	(a) chromatic	C–D♭–C	both C–D♭–C, and C–C♯–D or neither	C–C♯–D
	(h) phrygian	C–D♭–C	C–D♭–C	C–D♭–E♭
	(j) V/ii	n.a.	C–C♯–D	n.a.
	(k) viio7/ii	n.a.	C–C♯–D	n.a.
D–G–?	(b) major	D–G–C	both D–G–C and D–G–E, or neither	n.a.

* See Example 10.1.

reference and goal combinations given in Examples 13.1a, h, j, and k. For the combination in Example 13.1a, the gravity prediction is C–D♭–C (going down in the reference alphabet until we hit a member of the goal alphabet). For the combination in Example 13.1a, there are either two magnetism predictions or no magnetism predictions (the closest stable pitches, C and D, are equidistant from C♯). For the combinations in Examples 13.1a and h, the last two notes of the cue are adjacent in their alphabets, so they lead to inertia predictions (of C–C♯–D and C–D♭–E♭, respectively). The reference and goal combinations in Examples 13.1j and k do not allow an inertia prediction. For the combination in Example 13.1h, the gravity and the magnetism prediction are the same: C–D♭–C (because we can go to C by descending with gravity or by going to the closest stable pitch). For the combinations in Examples 13.1j and k, the magnetism predictions are C–C♯–D. For the reasons mentioned above, the combinations in Examples 13.1j and k do not produce gravity predictions (because these would take us below the "ground" of C).

Consider the cue D–G–?. As noted above, when the second-to-last note of the cue leaps to a more stable pitch, the single-level model computes the continuation from that note. The only available combination in Example 13.1 that includes D in its reference alphabet but not in its

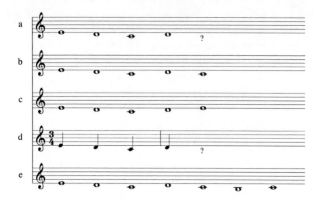

EXAMPLE 13.2. Completions generated by the single-level model for E–D–C–D–?.

goal alphabet is Example 13.1b. Because the cue is a single note, there is no inertia prediction. And because the closest stable pitches, E and C, are equidistant from D, there are either two magnetism predictions (D–G–C and D–G–E) or no magnetism predictions. The gravity prediction is D–G–C.

A MULTILEVEL COMPUTER MODEL

Further aspects of this theory have been implemented in what I shall call a "multilevel" computer model.[4] When given a melodic beginning and a Schenkerian analysis of that beginning, this second model returns a list of possible completions. Although the single-level model deals better with short beginnings than with longer ones, the multilevel model appears to respond effectively to melodic beginnings of any length. Again, the model is a simple one – every aspect of the model is described in the pages below – no additional assumptions or mechanisms are "hidden" in the code.

To make its predictions, the multilevel model takes the top (most basic) level of the analysis it has been given and calls on the single-level model to produce a completion at that level. It then fills in that "skeleton" by choosing notes (at levels closer to the "surface" of the melodic beginning) that give in to inertia.

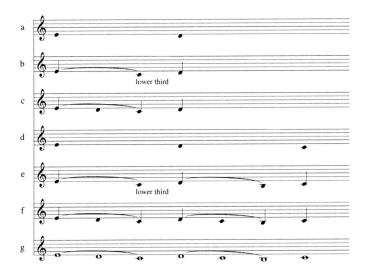

EXAMPLE 13.3. Completions generated by the multilevel model
for E–D–C–D–?.

Examples 13.2 and 13.3 illustrate the operation of the multilevel
model. Given the melodic beginning E–D–C–D in the key of C (Example 13.2a), the single-level model can give in to gravity by moving down
to C (Example 13.2b) or it can give in to inertia by continuing to move
stepwise up the C major scale to E (Example 13.2c). But if one hears
this melodic beginning in triple meter (as suggested by the notation
of Example 13.2d), then the continuation in Example 13.2e seems
natural.

This is the continuation that the multilevel model produces when
given the analysis shown in Examples 13.3a–c. Each level of such an
analysis shows how its structural notes (stemmed) are elaborated with
affixes (unstemmed notes connected by slurs to the note they embel-
lish) or with connectives (unstemmed notes contained within slurs between the notes they connect). Notes that are unstemmed on one level
do not appear on the next, more abstract level. Example 13.3c gives the
melodic beginning already given in Example 13.2a, but it also identifies
the D as a connective (a passing tone). Example 13.3b indicates that the
C elaborates the E (as a suffix lower third). Examples 13.3d–f show how

the model turns this analysis into a prediction. First, it adds a note to Example 13.3a that continues the pacing of that level – and (by calling on the single-level model) it chooses C (gravity and inertia both point to C). This C is shown at the end of Example 13.3d, and its presence there requires its appearance in the same location in Examples 13.3e and f. Second, it tries to give in to inertia by finding a suffix lower third for the D at the end of Example 13.3b to answer the C before it – and the only candidate is the B shown in Example 13.3e. Third, it tries to give in to inertia at the lower level, too, by finding a passing tone to answer the first D in Example 13.3c – and the only candidate is the second C shown in Example 13.3f. The result, Example 13.3g, is the one we already listed in Example 13.2e.

Further examples show that different analyses of the same beginning may lead to different completions. This reflects our intuition (and the results of some experiments, e.g., Kidd 1984; Larson 1997) that hearing a passage in a different key or different meter will lead us to expect a different completion.

Example 13.4a gives another melodic beginning. If given this beginning in the key of C, the single-level model produces the inertia and recursive predictions shown in Examples 13.4b and c. If represented in the key of F, it produces the prediction shown in Example 13.4d. If, however, the multilevel model is given the analysis shown in Example 13.4e and f (that is, if it is told that this beginning is in duple meter without a pickup note), then it produces the result given in Example 13.4g. This is because, at the top level, gravity (neither magnetism nor inertia apply here) leads the G to F, and because, at the next level, inertia answers the prefix step to G with a prefix step to F (of course, that prefix step could be G or E, but the model also avoids adding repeated notes to melodic beginnings that do not have repeated notes in them, so it chooses the E). If the multilevel model is given the analysis shown in Example 13.4h and i (same meter now but a different key), then it produces the results given in Example 13.4j–l. This is because the last note can be an upper C, giving in to inertia and magnetism, or a lower C, giving in to gravity, and because, when asked to find a step, it will seek a lower or an upper step (if the analysis specifies that the A is an *upper* step, then the

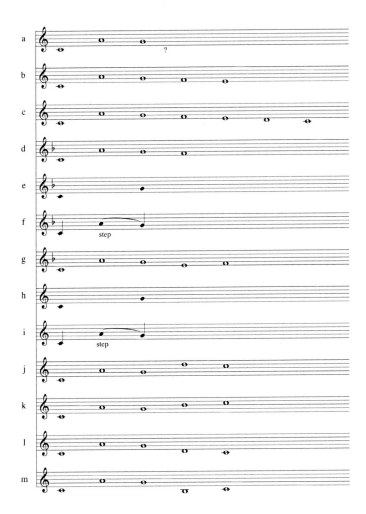

EXAMPLE 13.4. Computer responses to C–A–G–?.

multilevel model will produce only the completions shown in Example 13.4j and l).

The same melodic beginning was used in a recent experiment (Larson 1997a). Participants were given the melodic beginning C–A–G–? but were given no clues about meter or key. The responses they sang most often are given in Example 13.5. Notice that this list is almost identical to the list of computer-generated responses in Example 13.4.

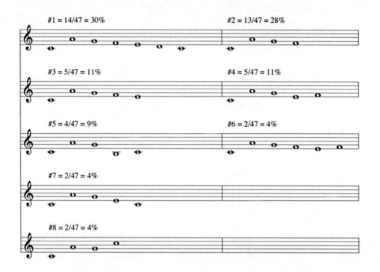

EXAMPLE 13.5. Subject responses to C–A–G–? (Larson 1997a).

EXPERIMENTAL EVIDENCE

The output of these computer programs also agrees with the results of a number of other experiments in ways which suggest that these programs may capture some important aspects of the expectations of experienced listeners of tonal music.

In what follows I compare the behavior of these computer models with the behavior of participants in experiments that involve responses to one-note cues (Povel 1996) and responses to two- and three-note cues (Lake 1987; Larson 1996b, 1997a).

Although the multilevel model is a more complete implementation of the theory, it introduces complexities that prohibit the kind of straightforward quantification that allows the single-level model to give weights to its completions. The following comparisons respect these differences between the models.

SINGLE-NOTE CUES WITH SINGLE-NOTE RESPONSES

Dirk-Jan Povel (1996) established a major-key context, gave a single-note cue, and then asked participants to produce one added note by finding

TABLE 13.4. THE "TONAL GROUP" IN POVEL'S (1996) EXPERIMENT, NONTONIC CUES, WITH C AS TONIC

to from	C	C♯/D♭	D	D♯/E♭	E	F	F♯/G♭	G	G♯/A♭	A	A♯/B♭	B
C♯/D♭	.69	.06	.07	0	0	0	0	0	0	.05	0	0
D	.48	0	0	0	.40	0	0	0	0	0	0	0
D♯/E♭	.51	0	0	0	.32	0	0	0	0	0	0	0
E	.81	0	0	0	0	0	0	.11	0	0	0	0
F	.15	0	0	0	.65	.09	0	0	0	0	0	0
F♯/G♭	.11	0	0	0	.07	0	0	.81	0	0	0	0
G	.76	0	0	0	.13	.05	0	0	0	0	0	0
G♯/A♭	.09	0	0	0	.07	0	0	.61	.05	.08	0	0
A	.28	0	.07	0	0	.07	0	.52	0	0	0	0
A♯/B♭	.24	0	0	0	0	0	0	.13	0	.39	0	.07
B	.95	0	0	0	0	0	0	0	0	0	0	0

the expected note on a synthesizer. Povel separated his participants into three categories: the "tonal group" (whose responses to nontonic cues are shown in Table 13.4); the "fourth group" (whose responses tended to lie a fourth or fifth from the cue, regardless of its tonal context); and the "random group" (whose responses showed no stable strategy).

In Table 13.4, the column on the left gives the cue, and the row at the top gives the response provided by Povel's participants. Each cell gives the proportion of participants in Povel's "tonal group" that responded with the continuation listed. Povel omits values below 5 percent (thus the sum of each row is 100%, minus the percentage of responses to any cues that were below 5%). This table also omits the tonic as cue (the computer responds to a single tonic with the computer's equivalent of "That sounds fine by itself, why should I add anything?"). The table does not distinguish between ascending and descending melodies.

Single-note cues tend to elicit single-note responses from the single-level model, too. Table 13.5 shows all twenty of the computer model's single-note responses to the eleven nontonic single-note cues. The computer model generates only three longer responses to these one-note cues (for one of the cues, the computer model generates one completion of more than one note; and for one other cue, it generates two completions of more than one note).

TABLE 13.5. THE SINGLE-LEVEL MODEL'S SINGLE-NOTE RESPONSES TO SINGLE-NOTE CUES

to from	C	C♯/D♭	D	D♯/E♭	E	F	F♯/G♭	G	G♯/A♭	A	A♯/B♭	B
C♯/D♭	1	0	1	0	0	0	0	0	0	0	0	0
D	1	0	0	0	1	0	0	0	0	0	0	0
D♯/E♭	1	0	1	0	1	0	0	0	0	0	0	0
E	1	0	0	0	0	0	0	1	0	0	0	0
F	0	0	0	0	1	0	0	0	0	0	0	0
F♯/G♭	0	0	0	0	0	1	0	1	0	0	0	0
G	1	0	0	0	0	0	0	0	0	0	0	0
G♯/A♭	0	0	0	0	0	0	0	1	0	1	0	0
A	0	0	0	0	0	0	0	1	0	0	0	0
A♯/B♭	1	0	0	0	0	0	0	0	0	1	0	1
B	1	0	0	0	0	0	0	0	0	0	0	0

TABLE 13.6. AGREEMENTS BETWEEN POVEL'S SUBJECTS' ONE-NOTE RESPONSES TO ALL ONE-NOTE CUES AND THE SINGLE-LEVEL MODEL'S ONE-NOTE PREDICTIONS FOR THE SAME CUES, WITH C AS TONIC

	Number of Those Responses Produced by the Single-Level Model	Number of Those Responses Not Produced by the Single-Level Model	Total
Number of unique responses produced by 5% or more of Povel's participants	**18**	15	33
Number of unique responses produced by fewer than 5% of Povel's participants	2	**86**	88
Total	20	101	**121**

Note: $df = 1$; $X^2 = 47.53$; $p < .0001$.

The striking agreement between the predictions of the single-level model and Povel's participant responses is summarized in Table 13.6. Out of 121 possible single-note responses, the single-level model produces only 20. All but 2 of these 20 single-note responses are included

TABLE 13.7. THE VALUES GENERATED BY LERDAHL'S (1998) ALGORITHM FOR "MELODIC ATTRACTION"

to from	C	C♯/D♭	D	D♯/E♭	E	F	F♯/G♭	G	G♯/A♭	A	A♯/B♭	B
C♯/D♭	4.00		2.00	0.25	0.33	0.13	0.04	0.08	0.04	0.13	0.11	0.50
D	0.50	0.50		0.50	0.38	0.11	0.03	0.06	0.01	0.04	0.03	0.11
D♯/E♭	0.44	0.25	2.00		3.00	0.50	0.11	0.19	0.04	0.06	0.04	0.13
E	0.08	0.04	0.17	0.33		0.67	0.08	0.11	0.02	0.03	0.01	0.03
F	0.08	0.03	0.11	0.13	1.50		0.50	0.38	0.06	0.06	0.02	0.03
F♯/G♭	0.11	0.04	0.13	0.11	0.75	2.00		3.00	0.25	0.22	0.06	0.08
G	0.05	0.01	0.03	0.02	0.11	0.17	0.33		0.33	0.17	0.04	0.04
G♯/A♭	0.25	0.04	0.06	0.04	0.19	0.22	0.25	3.00		2.00	0.25	0.22
A	0.22	0.03	0.04	0.01	0.06	0.06	0.06	0.38	0.50		0.50	0.25
A♯/B♭	1.00	0.11	0.13	0.04	0.08	0.08	0.06	0.33	0.25	2.00		2.00
B	2.00	0.13	0.11	0.03	0.06	0.03	0.02	0.09	0.06	0.25	0.50	

in Povel's "tonal group." Povel's "tonal group" includes only 15 responses not produced by the computer model, but many of those responses ended simply by adding a tonic (C) or by repeating the cue – and the remainder of those not produced by the computer model were among those sung by the smallest number of participants.

Lerdahl (1988) uses his algorithm to describe the attraction of any pitch to any other pitch (regardless of whether the pitches are adjacent in a relevant alphabet, and regardless of which pitch is more stable). Table 13.7 gives the values generated by Lerdahl's formula for "melodic attraction."

The values in Table 13.7 rely on Lerdahl's conjecture that "it may turn out to be more accurate just to take attractional values as correlating directly with degrees of expected continuation" (2001, 170). In other words, the values in Table 13.7 are calculated by multiplying the ratio of the stabilities of both notes by the inverse square of the semitone distance between them; opposing attractors are ignored. (Ignoring opposing attractors has an additional practical advantage here, namely, that it is not always clear for every cell in Table 13.7 which note should be considered the opposing attractor.) The diagonal is left blank because the algorithm does not produce values for the attraction of a note to itself.

TABLE 13.8. THE VALUES GENERATED BY MARGULIS'S (2003)
MODEL OF MELODIC EXPECTATION

to from	C	C♯/D♭	D	D♯/E♭	E	F	F♯/G♭	G	G♯/A♭	A	A♯/B♭	B
C	(144)	72	128	50	100	64	24	80	40	100	64	144
C♯/D♭	216	(48)	144	64	125	80	32	60	32	80	50	128
D	192	72	(96)	72	160	100	40	80	24	64	40	100
D♯/E♭	150	64	144	(48)	180	128	50	100	32	48	32	80
E	120	50	128	72	(120)	144	64	125	60	64	24	64
F	96	40	100	64	180	(96)	72	160	50	80	32	48
F♯/G♭	72	32	80	50	160	144	(48)	180	64	100	40	64
G	96	24	64	40	125	128	72	(120)	72	128	50	80
G♯/A♭	120	32	48	32	100	100	64	180	(48)	144	64	100
A	150	40	64	24	80	80	50	160	72	(96)	72	128
A♯/B♭	192	50	80	32	60	64	40	125	64	144	(48)	144
B	216	64	100	40	80	48	32	100	50	128	72	(96)

The remaining values correlate positively with those given in Table 13.9 ($R = .569, N = 121, p < .001$).

Margulis's model may also be used to describe the expectation produced by a single-note cue for any other pitch (regardless of whether the pitches are adjacent in a relevant alphabet and regardless of which pitch is more stable). Table 13.8 gives the values generated by Margulis's model of melodic expectation. The values in Table 13.8 were calculated by multiplying Margulis's proximity values (from Table 4.1) by her stability values (from Table 4.2). The values on the diagonal are in parentheses. These values, which represent the repetition of a pitch, incorporate an additional factor called "mobility," which reduces the value for the attraction of a pitch to itself by multiplying by $\frac{2}{3}$ the product of its proximity and stability values. If, as with Lerdahl's algorithm, cases involving the repetition of a pitch are not included, then the remaining values produce an even higher correlation with Povel's results than do those of Lerdahl ($R = .651, N = 121, p < .001$).

The multiple-regression analysis reported in Table 13.9 assesses the contributions of each of the factors in Lerdahl's 1996 algorithm. The three factors that go into Lerdahl's algorithm are the inverse stability of the cue,

TABLE 13.9. SUMMARY OF MULTIPLE REGRESSION ANALYSIS FOR FACTORS
IN LERDAHL'S (2001) MELODIC ATTRACTION ALGORITHM PREDICTING
DISTRIBUTION OF RESPONSES IN POVEL'S "TONAL GROUP"

	Using 1988 Values for Stability and Inverse Square for Distance	Using 1996 Values for Stability and Inverse Square for Distance	Using 1988 Values for Stability and Simple Inverse for Distance
Summary of multiple regression	$R = .732$ $p < .001$ $N = 121$	$R = .706$ $p < .001$ $N = 121$	$R = .730$ $p < .001$ $N = 121$
Stability of response	$w = .659$ $p < .001$	$w = .631$ $p < .001$	$w = .658$ $p < .001$
Inverse stability of cue	$w = -.052$ $p = .415$	$w = -.054$ $p = .416$	$w = -.052$ $p = .416$
Inverse square of distance between cue and response	$w = .311$ $p < .001$	$w = .312$ $p < .001$	$w = .308$ $p < .001$

Note: Weights given as w are standardized coefficients.

the stability of the response, and the distance between the cue and the response. Table 13.9 lists these factors in three different models. The first and third models use Lerdahl's 1988 values for stability. The second model uses his 1996 values. The first and second models use the inverse square of the semitones between the cue and the response for that distance (as in Larson 1993 and Lerdahl 1996). The third model substitutes the inverse (instead of the inverse square) of the distance (as in Bharucha 1996).

All three models show that two factors contribute significantly to account for these data: the stability of the response and the distance between cue and response. However, at least for Povel's data, the inverse stability of the cue does not help explain the result. Nor does the use of Lerdahl's 1996 values for stability improve the ability of the model to account for the data. Furthermore, substituting the simple inverse of the distance (as in Bharucha's algorithm), instead of the inverse square, does not give a better result.

The theory proposed here, however, goes beyond these algorithms for the interaction of musical forces. It also claims that melodic comple-

TABLE 13.10. SUMMARY OF MULTIPLE-REGRESSION ANALYSIS FOR
FACTORS IN LARSON'S (1993A) COMPUTER ALGORITHM PREDICTING
DISTRIBUTION OF RESPONSES IN POVEL'S "TONAL GROUP"

Summary of multiple regression	$R = .859$
	$p < .001$
	$N = 121$
Stability of response	$w = .327$
	$p < .001$
Gravity	$w = .322$
	$p < .001$
Magnetism	$w = .425$
	$p < .001$

Note: Weights given as w are standardized coefficients.

tions are created by operations on alphabets. Table 13.5 (above), which listed force-driven operations on alphabets, makes a large number of "correct rejections" (the eighty-six unique cue-and-response combinations for which Tables 13.4 and 13.5 both give the value 0). This helps to explain the strong correlation between the values given in Tables 13.4 and 13.5 ($R = .773$, $N = 121$, $p < .001$).

The multiple-regression analysis reported in Table 13.10 further assesses the contributions of individual factors. The factors listed include melodic gravity (scored 1 if the response is a gravity prediction, 0 if it is not), melodic magnetism (scored 1 if the response is a magnetism prediction, 0 if it is not), and the stability of the response (using Lerdahl's 1988, rather than his 1996, values for depth of pitch-space embedding).

All the factors in Table 13.10 – gravity, magnetism, and response-tone stability – contribute significantly to account for the data. I suspect, moreover, that Povel's "tonal group" could be further subdivided into a group whose answers correlated even more highly with the single-level computer model and a group whose responses could be described in terms of some other strategies (such as usually ending on the tonic, regardless of the cue).

It would be interesting to test Narmour's implication-realization model on these data, too, but Narmour's model requires an implicative interval (two notes) and Povel's cues are only one note. Thus Narmour's model cannot be tested on Povel's data.

To summarize, the single-level computer model comes close to predicting all and only the responses of Povel's participants. Furthermore, an algorithm that combines response-tone stability, gravity, and magnetism (inertia does not arise in these single-note cues) gives higher ratings to patterns that participants sing more often. At least with these data, substituting the algorithms of Bharucha, Lerdahl, or Margulis does not give a better result. That these data can be modeled well by an interaction of constantly acting but contextually determined musical forces lends support to the idea that we experience musical motions metaphorically in terms of our experience of physical motions.

TWO-NOTE CUES WITH RESPONSES OF VARIED LENGTH

In his dissertation study William Lake (1987) asked music students at the University of Michigan to sing melodic continuations of two-note cues. First he established a major-key context by playing a tonic major chord and scale for them. He then played a two-note cue. Finally, he asked the students to sing that two-note beginning, "adding another tone or tones of your own choosing" (31). Lake's cues include all two-note combinations in which the first tone is diatonic to the key. Excluding cues that end on the tonic gives us 70 cues (7 diatonic first notes times the 10 chromatic pitches that exclude the tonic and the first note equals 70 two-note cues). Perhaps because of the tone used for the cues (piano doubled in four octaves), some of the participants interpreted 5 of the cues as going up whereas the others interpreted them as going down. The result is a list of 75 unique melodic beginnings. Stating response frequency as a percentage of total responses to a given cue allows appropriate comparisons. Lake began with twenty-two participants. Two were unable to sing back the cues accurately in their responses, and so they were excluded. Lake (private communication) urged the elimination of a third participant whose responses appeared not to reflect the task. The method used here, in any case, eliminates most of the responses of this third participant because they rarely match more than one other

TABLE 13.11. PREDICTIONS OF THE SINGLE-LEVEL MODEL COMPARED
TO THE RESPONSES OF LAKE'S PARTICIPANTS

		Number of Responses	Number of Different Responses	Average Number of Times Sung
All	Participants' responses that exactly match more than one other response	1084	171	6.34
Hits	Responses produced by the single-level model (with unrated inertia predictions and recursive predictions suppressed)	789	98	8.05
	Additional responses produced as unrated inertia predictions or as recursive predictions	145	31	4.68
	Total hits of these types	934	129	7.24
Misses	Responses not produced by the single-level model	150	42	3.57
	Responses produced by the single-level model but not produced by Lake's participants	45	45	0
	Total misses	195	87	

Note: The table includes only those responses that exactly match
more than one other response.

response note for note. This leaves nineteen participants. And because
each participant responded twice to each cue, nineteen participants
produced 2,660 responses.

To explore the shared intuitions of these participants, we consider
only those responses that match note for note more than one other response to the same cue. The result is 1,084 responses from nineteen participants (41% of all the responses). These 1,084 responses include 171
unique responses, so each was sung an average of 6.34 times. This level
of note-for-note agreement between participants suggests that these data
are a highly reliable indication of shared musical intuitions about melodic expectations.

Table 13.11 summarizes the striking agreement between the predictions of the single-level computer model and these data. The computer
correctly predicts 129 out of these 171 unique responses (75%), account-

TABLE 13.12. EXACT MATCHES BETWEEN THE RESPONSES OF LAKE'S
PARTICIPANTS AND THOSE OF THE SINGLE-LEVEL MODEL FOR
ALL POSSIBLE FIVE-NOTE RESPONSES*

	Produced by the Single-Level Model	Adding Selected Recursive and Unrated Inertia Predictions	Not Produced by the Single-Level Model	Total
Sung by Lake's subjects	**98**	**129**	42	171
Not sung by Lake's subjects	45	45	205,584	205,629
Total	143	174	205,626	205,800

* Within the fifth above or octave below the final note of each beginning.

ing for 934 out of 1,084 total responses (86%). Moreover, the responses predicted by the computer are popular ones (they were sung an average of 7.24 times by these participants). The responses not predicted by the computer are less popular (they were sung an average of 3.57 times, and since we consider only those responses that match more than one other response, this is barely above the theoretical minimum of 3 times).

To further appreciate the level of agreement involved, it helps to describe "correct rejections." Some responses are produced neither by experimental participants nor by the single-level model. We may regard these as responses that the computer model correctly predicts no one will sing. They are, however, responses to which Lerdahl's, Narmour's, and Margulis's models give positive ratings. Lake's participants added one note (roughly three-fifths of the time), two notes (roughly one-fifth of the time), or three notes (roughly one-fifth of the time). And their responses usually (but not always) stay within a fifth of the last note of their beginning. For these 75 cues, there are 205,800 unique responses that meet these criteria.[5] These results are summarized in Table 13.12.

A closer look at some of the "misses" shown in Table 13.11 further suggests that the theory proposed here also accounts for several of those responses as well. For example, some of the responses may be regarded as inertia predictions within alphabets not included as reference alphabets in the single-level model: for the descending cue C–A–?, the response C–A–F would be the inertia prediction if it included the subdominant chord as a reference alphabet; for the ascending cue D–F$\sharp$–?, the response D–F$\sharp$–A would be the inertia prediction if it included V/V as a reference alphabet.

Other responses show the need for hierarchical descriptions of elaboration structure – and the multilevel model predicts their completion well. Consider the cues E–C$\sharp$–? and C–A$\flat$–? and the respective "misses" E–C$\sharp$–D–B–C and C–A$\flat$–G–B–C. If the cue E–C$\sharp$–? is given to the single-level model, one result is E–C$\sharp$–D. If that C$\sharp$ is then represented as a suffix lower third, then the multilevel model will produce the continuation E–C$\sharp$–D–B–C. If the cue C–A$\flat$– ? is given to the single-level model, the result is C–A$\flat$–G. If that A$\flat$ is then represented as a prefix half step, then the multilevel model will produce the continuation C–A$\flat$–G–B–C.

AN ARTIFICIAL-INTELLIGENCE APPRAISAL

Within the field of artificial intelligence, it is often suggested that the best test of a computer model is to enter it in a kind of contest where it competes against human participants. The "Turing Test" (which is supposed to test machine "intelligence") and computer chess tournaments (which are supposed to assess machine skill at chess) may be the best-known examples of such contests. In the Turing Test, a human judge at one terminal sends questions to both a human at another terminal and to a computer. Responses from both appear on the judge's screen. The object is for the human judge to determine which responses come from the computer program and which come from another human. If the human judge cannot make that determination, then the computer is deemed intelligent. No computer has passed the Turing Test yet. The computer chess program "Deep Blue," however, recently beat top-rated Garry Kasparov in a chess tournament.

By analogy, we ask what would happen if the single-level computer model were one of the participants in Lake's experiment – and we regard that experiment as a contest. As with the Turing Test, we regard the computer as more successful the more often it agrees with the human participants. Thus each participant (the computer program included) gets a score based on how often its responses agree – note for note – with

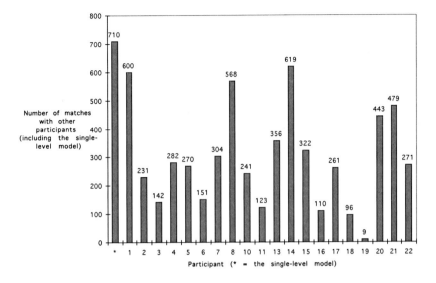

GRAPH 13.1. The single-level model can produce a set of responses that exactly matches the entire responses of Lake's (1987) participants as often as do the responses of any one of those participants.

those of other participants. The winner is the participant that gets the highest score.

To do this, we allow the rating that the single-level computer model assigns to each prediction to determine the frequency with which it produces that response. We then let it produce two responses to each cue (as did Lake's participants). Finally, we ask how often it agrees note for note with Lake's other participants. The answer is that the single-level model can produce a set of responses that creates as many as 710 note-for-note matches with Lake's participants. When it does, the average number of such note-for-note matches for each of Lake's participants is 294 and the highest is 619 (see Graph 13.1). In other words, the computer model can match the experimental participants note for note as often as any one of the participants does. (In order to choose among responses with probabilities that depend on ratings, the single-level model must call on a random number generator. The result is that each time the program is run, different choices may be made. In this sense, its behavior resembles that of the experimental participants, who sometimes give different responses to the same cues. I have run this "contest" many times, and, although the computer scored differently on different runs, it always came in first or second place.)

To summarize, the single-level computer model predicts most of the responses of Lake's participants and predicts few responses not produced by those participants. Furthermore, an algorithm that combines gravity, magnetism, inertia, and stability gives higher ratings to patterns that participants sing more often. That this model can exactly match the responses of participants in Lake's study as often as do those of any of the participants in that study gives strong support to the idea that we experience musical motions metaphorically in terms of our experience of physical motions.

USING LAKE'S (1987) DATA TO COMPARE NARMOUR'S IMPLICATION-REALIZATION MODEL WITH THE THEORY OF MUSICAL FORCES

In a recent article Krumhansl (1995) compared the predictions of the bottom-up component of Narmour's (1990) implication-realization model to the judgments given to selected melodic continuations by her experimental participants. Her approach allows us to compare Narmour's model, as well as the theory proposed here, to the results of Lake's experiment.

To test Narmour's model, Krumhansl identified and quantified the five principles listed in Table 13.13. According to the implication-realization model, the two-note beginnings (the notes x and y) used in Lake's experiment form the "implicative interval." When followed by a third note (z, the first response tone), the second and third notes form the "realized interval." According to the quantification that Krumhansl devised, every realized interval earns five scores, one for each of the principles listed in Table 13.13. (The scores for registral direction, intervallic difference, and registral return are "all or nothing" scores: if the realized interval follows the principle, it earns a score of 1; otherwise, it earns a 0. The scores for proximity and closure earn "graded" scores: the score for proximity varies from 0 to 6; the score for closure can be 0, 1, or 2.)

TABLE 13.13. FIVE PRINCIPLES OF MELODIC EXPECTANCY UNDERLYING THE
BOTTOM-UP COMPONENT OF THE IMPLICATION-REALIZATION MODEL
(FROM KRUMHANSL 1995)

Registral Direction
Small implicative intervals imply realized intervals in the same direction.
Large implicative inervals imply realized intervals in a different direction.

Intervallic Difference
Small implicative intervals imply realized intervals that are similarly sized.*
Large implicative intervals imply realized intervals that are smaller in size.**

Registral Return
The interval formed by the first tone of the implicative interval and the second tone
of the realized interval is no greater than a major second.

Proximity
Independent of the size and direction of the implicative interval, implied realized
intervals are no larger than a perfect fourth.

Closure
Closure is strongest when (1) the implicative interval is large and the realized interval is smaller,** and (2) registral direction of implicative and realized intervals are
different.

---

*Within a minor third if registral direction of implicative and realized intervals is the
same; within a major second if registral direction is different.
**Smaller by more than a minor third if registral direction is the same; smaller by more
than a major second if registral direction is different.

To Narmour's five principles, Krumhansl added two, which she
called "unison" and "tonality." If the realized interval is a unison, it scores
a 1 for that principle; otherwise, it earns a 0 (regardless of the implicative
interval). For her experiment on tonal melodies (using excerpts from
British folk songs), the tonality score is the position of the second tone
of the realized interval (z, the first added note) in her tonal hierarchy
(and thus varies from 1 to 7). Thus Krumhansl's "tonality" is equivalent
to what is called "stability" in this book.

Krumhansl then used the technique of multiple regression to assess
how well the judgments made by her participants could be explained
as a weighted sum of these seven scores. The results for her experiment
on tonal melodies (using excerpts from British folk songs) are given in
Table 13.14.

TABLE 13.14. KRUMHANSL'S (1995) TEST OF THE IMPLICATION-REALIZATION MODEL

	British Folk Songs (Krumhansl 1995)
Summary of multiple regression	$R = .846$
	$p < .0001$
	$N = 120$
Registral direction	$W_{RD} = .17$
	$p < .005$
Intervallic difference	$W_{ID} = .17$
	$p < .1$
Registral return	$W_{RR} = .31$
	$p < .0001$
Proximity	$W_{PR} = .50$
	$p < .0001$
Closure	$W_{CL} = .21$
	$p < .005$
Unison	$W_{UN} = -.06$
	n.s.
Tonality	$W_{TN} = .17$
	$p < .005$

Note: W values are standardized coefficients.

The coefficients given each of these factors tell us that proximity has the greatest predictive value for these data. Proximity – an element of magnetism – is also important in the theory of musical forces.

In order to compare the implication-realization model to the theory of musical forces, we apply Krumhansl's approach to Lake's data, comparing the contributions of factors derived from Narmour's theory and from the theory of musical forces. To be consistent with her approach, we consider all of Lake's data, but we limit our attention to the first response tone (the note z). For each cue (notes x and y, the "implicative interval"), we list all possible responses within an octave above and below the last note of the cue (y). There are 1,800 such possible responses (75 cues times 24 responses – 12 above and 12 below). For each resultant three-note pattern, we list the number of Lake's continuations that begin with those three notes. We calculate the same scores for Narmour's bottom-up factors that Krumhansl did (except that we again use levels of pitch-space embedding to represent stability). Then we calculate analogous scores for the musical forces. (For a given three-note pattern, if there is a gravity prediction for that cue that includes that first response tone it scores a 1; otherwise, it scores a 0. If there is a magnetism prediction for that cue that includes that first response tone it scores a 1; otherwise, it scores a 0. Here the magnetism factor is "all or nothing"; proximity, included in the magnetism scores above, is listed here as the same separate factor coded by Krumhansl. If there is an inertia prediction for that cue that includes that first response tone, it scores a 2; if that cue does not generate an inertia prediction, it scores a 1; and if that cue does generate an inertia prediction but not one that includes that first response tone, it scores a 0.) The results of this statistical analysis are given in Table 13.15.

For these data the analysis fails to support four of Narmour's five factors (they are either statistically insignificant or negatively affect the performance of the model). Only Narmour's proximity and the added factor of stability – both of which are also relevant in the theory of musical forces – contribute significantly to explaining Lake's data. (The cues in Lake's data feature mostly intervals smaller than a tritone. Had he included a greater number of larger cues, it is possible that more of Narmour's factors may have contributed positively to explaining the data.)

All factors in the theory of musical forces, however, contribute significantly to explaining Lake's data. This gives additional support to the idea that we experience musical motions metaphorically in terms of our experience of physical motion.

Furthermore, although the stability of the goal pitch does turn out to be a significant factor, the analysis of these data also fails to support the other hypotheses suggested by a comparison of my computer's algorithms with more recent algorithms by Bharucha, Lerdahl, and Margulis: the stabilities of the other pitches are statistically insignificant, and gravity has significant predictive power (regardless of whether stability is included in the model).

The comparison also underscores important differences between my computer models of musical forces and the bottom-up component

TABLE 13.15. MULTIPLE-REGRESSION ANALYSIS RESULTS FOR
LAKE (1987), COMPARING THE IMPLICATION-REALIZATION
MODEL TO THE THEORY OF MUSICAL FORCES

	Narmour's Five Bottom-Up Factors Plus Stability	Musical Forces Plus Stability, with Proximity Encoded Separately
Summary of multiple regression	$R = .614$ $p < .0001$ $N = 1800$	$R = .773$ $p < .0001$ $N = 1800$
Registral direction	$w_{RD} = -.082$ $p = .0065$	
Intervallic difference	$w_{ID} = .049$ $p = .1151$	
Registral return	$w_{RR} = -.076$ $p = .0107$	
Proximity	$w_{PR} = .545$ $p < .0001$	$w_{PR} = .280$ $p < .0001$
Closure	$w_{CL} = .034$ $p = .1466$	
Stability of first response tone (Lerdahl 1988)	$w_S = .314$ $p < .0001$	$w_S = .174$ $p < .0001$
Gravity		$w_G = .088$ $p < .0001$
Magnetism		$w_M = .432$ $p < .0001$
Inertia		$w_I = .187$ $p < .0001$
Stability of last tone of cue		$w = .009$ $p = .543$

of Narmour's implication-realization model. In order to compare these models, we must restrict our attention to just the first response tones. At least for Lake's data, my single-level computer model does a better job of predicting those first response tones than does the bottom-up component of Narmour's implication-realization model. But far more important, as noted above, my model can predict completions that match the *entire* completions produced by experimental participants *note for note* as often as any one of those participants does. The operational modeling of tonal relationships in terms of reference and goal alphabets and musical forces allows the computer models to predict listener expectations in a way which suggests that these models may capture important aspects of the underlying cognitive processes.

MORE STUDIES WITH RESPONSES OF VARIED LENGTH

Two partial replications of Lake's study (Larson 1996b, 1997a) suggest that the responses of more experienced musicians may not only match those of other participants more often that do those of less experienced musicians, but they may also more often match those of my computer models. In both experiments, musicians recruited from those attending national meetings of the Society for Music Theory were given melodic beginnings in notation, asked to assume the context of C major, and then asked to write the responses that they thought would appear most often on the pages of other participants.

Table 13.16a compares the responses of participants in the first of these experiments (Larson 1996) with those of Lake's participants and with those of my single-level and multilevel computer models. Table 13.16b makes the same comparison for the second of these experiments (Larson 1997a).

Four of these cues in Table 13.16a were the same as cues used in Lake's study (the fifth was an inversion of one of Lake's cues). Because Lake's nineteen participants responded twice to each cue, and because Larson's thirty-eight participants responded once to each cue, both groups supplied 38 responses to each cue, or 152 responses for these four cues. Out of their 152 responses, 92 (61%) of Larson's appear in Table 13.16a. Out of their 152 responses, 60 (39%) of Lake's appear in Table 13.16b. The number of cases (these 304 responses represent 14 unique responses to four different cues) is small enough to limit the conclusions that can be drawn, and the tasks differ (one difference is that the undergraduates sang responses to *heard* sounds whereas the professional theorists wrote responses to *imagined* sounds; another difference is that the professional theorists were offered a reward for matching one another's responses

TABLE 13.16a. COMPARISON OF THE RESPONSES OF LARSON'S (1996B) EXPERIMENTAL PARTICIPANTS WITH THOSE OF LAKE (1987), AND WITH THE SINGLE-LEVEL AND MULTILEVEL MODELS

RESPONSE		PRODUCED BY EXPERIMENTAL PARTICIPANTS (LARSON 1996B)		PRODUCED BY EXPERIMENTAL PARTICIPANTS (LAKE 1987)		RATING ASSIGNED BY THE SINGLE-LEVEL MODEL		PRODUCED BY THE MULTI-LEVEL MODEL
Integers	Letter Names	Number of Responses	Portion of Responses to That Cue	Number of Responses	Portion of Responses to That Cue	Numerical Ratings	Portion of Ratings for That Cue	
949	AEA	4	.24	0	0			
945	AEF	5	.30	0	0			√
94520	AEFDC	5	.30	0	0			√
947	AEG	3	.18	5	1	20.85	1.00	√
087	CA♭G	14	.70	*	*	26.06	.58	√
089	CG♯A	0	0	*	*	18.59	.42	√
0871112	CA♭GBC	3	.15	*	*			√
0875320	CA♭GFE♭DC	3	.15	*	*	i, r		√
212	DC♯D	13	.68	9	0.50	18.59	.43	√
210	DD♭C	6	.32	9	0.50	25.00	.57	√
420	EDC	27	.90	16	0.72	23.13	1.00	√
420-10	EDCBC	3	.10	6	0.27	r		√
7912	GAC	0	0	4	0.20			
79740	GAGEC	0	0	3	0.15			√
7911	GAB	3	.12	0	0			
791112	GABC	13	.5	9	0.45	20.15	.49	√
797	GAG	7	.27	4	0.20	20.85	.51	√
7975420	GAGFEDC	3	.12	0	0	r		√

Note: i = unrated inertia prediction; r = recursive prediction; * = not a cue used in Lake's study.

RESPONSE		PRODUCED BY EXPERIMENTAL PARTICIPANTS (LARSON 1996B)		PRODUCED BY EXPERIMENTAL PARTICIPANTS (LAKE 1987)		RATING ASSIGNED BY THE SINGLE-LEVEL MODEL		PRODUCED BY THE MULTI-LEVEL MODEL
Integers	Letter Names	Number of Responses	Portion of Responses to That Cue	Number of Responses	Portion of Responses to That Cue	Numerical Ratings	Portion of Ratings for That Cue	
Two-Note Cues								
2 5 4	D F E	11	.30	9	0.24	21.88	1.00	√
2 5 4 0	D F E C	7	.19	5	0.13	r		√
2 5 4 2 0	D F E D C	15	.41	5	0.13	r		√
2 5 4 7 5 2 0	D F E G F D C	4	.11	0	0			√
5 2 – 1 0	F D B C	0	0	4	0.11			√
5 2 0	F D C	10	.23	5	0.13	23.13	1.00	√
5 2 4	F D E	6	.14	4	0.11			√
5 2 4 0	F D E C	12	.27	0	0			√
5 2 4 0 2 – 1 0	F D E C D B C	5	.11	0	0			
5 2 4 2 0	F D E D C	8	.18	0	0			
5 2 4 5 4 2 0	F D E F E D C	3	.07	0	0			
Three-Note Cues								
7 4 5 2	G E F D	3	.07	*	*			
7 4 5 2 0	G E F D C	19	.42	*	*			√
7 4 5 2 4 2 0	G E F D E D C	5	.11	*	*			
7 4 5 4	G E F E	4	.09	*	*	21.88	.63	√

TABLE 13.16b. (cont.) COMPARISON OF THE RESPONSES OF LARSON'S (1997A) EXPERIMENTAL PARTICIPANTS WITH THOSE OF LAKE (1987), AND WITH THE SINGLE-LEVEL AND MULTILEVEL MODELS

RESPONSE		PRODUCED BY EXPERIMENTAL PARTICIPANTS (LARSON 1996B)		PRODUCED BY EXPERIMENTAL PARTICIPANTS (LAKE 1987)		RATING ASSIGNED BY THE SINGLE-LEVEL MODEL		PRODUCED BY THE MULTI-LEVEL MODEL
Integers	Letter Names	Number of Responses	Portion of Responses to That Cue	Number of Responses	Portion of Responses to That Cue	Numerical Ratings	Portion of Ratings for That Cue	
Three-Note Cues								
745420	GEFEDC	6	.13	*	*	r		√
7457	GEFG	3	.07	*	*	13.13	.38	√
74570	GEFGC	6	.13	*	*	r		√
75420	GFEDC	44	.92	*	*	i,r		√
7545420	GFEFEDC	4	.08	*	*			√
0975420	CAGFEDC	14	.32	*	*	i		√
09754	CAGFE	14	.32	*	*	i		√
0974520	CAGEFDC	5	.11	*	*			√
09740	CAGEC	4	.09	*	*			√
0971112	CAGBC	4	.09	*	*			√
09712	CAGC	3	.07	*	*	21.12	.48	√

Note: i = unrated inertia prediction; r = recursive prediction; * = not a cue used in Lake's study.

and the undergraduates were not). Nevertheless, the results are striking enough (61% vs. 39%) to raise the question of whether the higher level of agreement might result from greater musical training. Furthermore, Larson's participants come closer to the predictions of the single-level computer model. Once again, those predictions not listed for that model include many that would be produced as unrated inertia predictions, as recursive predictions, or by the multilevel model (if their hierarchical elaboration structures were represented).

Table 13.16b shows that the sixty-one participants in the second experiment (Larson 1997a) produced 219 responses, forming 26 unique responses, to these five cues, meaning that each unique response was sung an average of 8.42 times. Once again, these participants agreed more often with themselves and more often with the computer models than did Lake's participants.

The high levels of agreement between participants in these different studies argue that we are measuring robust musical behaviors. They also raise the question of whether the differences between these participants may be the result of differences in musical training. And, finally, they confirm the value of these data for testing the model presented here.

Once again, the computer programs come close to predicting all and only the responses of participants in various different experiments. Where ratings may be assigned to predictions, moreover, the computer model gives higher ratings to patterns that participants sing more often.

CONCLUSIONS

Chapter 5 argued that "experienced listeners of tonal music expect completions in which the musical forces of gravity, magnetism, and inertia control operations on alphabets in hierarchies of elaboration whose stepwise displacements of auralized traces create simple closed shapes." That chapter also gave a list of instructions that suggests how this may happen. The two computer programs described here implement aspects of that instruction set.

The completions generated by the single-level model match, note for note, the entire completions produced by participants in several psycho-

logical studies as often as do the completions of any one of those participants. Furthermore, the ratings it gives to its completions correlate with
the popularity of those responses; higher ratings are given to responses
that participants sing more often. Those ratings are assigned by the computer's algorithm for the interaction of musical forces. Although the best
results are achieved by adding to that original algorithm a separate factor
for the stability of the response tone, none of the studies reported here
supports any of the other hypotheses suggested by the differences between my original algorithm and the more recent algorithms proposed
by Bharucha, Lerdahl, and Margulis.

The multilevel model takes a melodic beginning, together with
a description of its hierarchical elaboration structure (a Schenkerian
analysis), and returns a completion that reflects all the levels of that
structure. The success of the multilevel model suggests the importance
of hierarchical structure in melodic expectation and illustrates how different interpretations of the same melodic beginning may lead to different expectations for its completion.

These data and computer models also allow us to compare the
explanatory power of the theory of musical forces with that of Narmour's implication-realization model. For Povel's data, the theory of
musical forces can give a good account of the experimental participant
responses; Narmour's model, which is based on implicative intervals
instead of musical forces, requires at least a two-note beginning and
thus cannot be used to account for Povel's data. For Lake's data, all
factors in the theory of musical forces contribute significantly to explaining the experimental participant responses; however, analysis
of Lake's data fails to support four of Narmour's five factors (they are
either statistically insignificant or negatively affect the performance
of the model) – the only factors of Narmour's models that contribute
significantly to explaining Lake's data (proximity and the added factor
of stability) are ones common to the theory of musical forces and the
implication-realization model. Of course, we might find different results
with different data sets.

The striking agreement between computer- and participant-gener-
ated responses in these data sets suggests, however, that the theory of

musical forces captures some important aspects of melodic expectation. Furthermore, that these data can be modeled well by the interaction of constantly acting but contextually determined musical forces lends support to the idea that we experience musical motions metaphorically in terms of our experience of physical motions.

PART 3

Conclusion

14

Summary and Prospects

This final chapter of the book summarizes its findings and suggests directions for further research.

The book begins by asking two questions: "Why do we talk about music as if it actually moved?" and "Why does music actually move us?" Our sense that common-practice tonal music actually does move (that it accelerates or decelerates, that it ascends or descends, that it goes by steps or leaps) is so strong that it is necessary to remind ourselves that this visceral, immediate sense of motion is a metaphor. Nevertheless, that metaphor is experienced so deeply by members of our musical culture that we not only *think about music* as if it were shaped by musical analogs of physical gravity, magnetism, and inertia, but we also actually *think in music* in terms of "melodic gravity" (the tendency of notes heard as above a stable platform to descend), "melodic magnetism" (the tendency of an unstable note to move to the closest stable pitch, a tendency that grows stronger as the goal gets closer), and "musical inertia" (the tendency of motion to continue in the pattern perceived) – as well as "metric magnetism" (the pull of a note on a metrically unstable attack point to a subsequent and more metrically stable attack point, a pull that grows stronger as the attracting attack point grows closer) and "rhythmic gravity" (that quality we attribute to a rhythm, when we map its flow onto a physical gesture, that reflects the impact physical gravity has on that physical gesture).

Part 1 shows that these musical forces can be rigorously defined. And it hypothesizes that we experience musical motion as if it were shaped by the constant interaction of all three forces – in ways that are logically consistent with our experience of physical motion, mathematically quantifiable, central to melodic expectation, part of our experience of rhythm and meter, and intimately tied to our experience of music and its expressive meaning.

Part 2 demonstrates that evidence from a variety of sources supports these hypotheses. Millennia of writings describe music in terms of motion. Centuries of treatises implicitly or explicitly describe musical events in terms of one or more musical forces. Experiments on visual perception show that "representational gravity" (analogous to musical gravity), the "landmark attraction effect" (analogous to musical magnetism), and "representational momentum" (analogous to musical inertia) shape visual experience in consistent and quantifiable ways, giving further support to the idea that these forces arise through the cross-domain mappings described in part 1. Recent findings in neuroscience describe underlying brain mechanisms that would support such cross-domain mappings. Studies of the distribution of patterns within composed and improvised music suggest that their frequency can be well accounted for by the degree to which they satisfy a combination of musical forces. Parallels between "naïve physics" and what appear to be misunderstandings concerning musical forces (by highly respected music theorists) show that analogies between our understanding of physical and musical forces run even deeper. And the results of other experiments – testing participant judgments of the strength of musical completions or comparing their own melodic completions, note for note, with those created by computer models based on the theories of this book – can be accounted for with remarkable consistency and completeness by simple weighted combinations of interacting musical forces. Together, this converging evidence provides growing support for the claims of the theory of musical forces.

LIMITS ON CLAIMS POINT TO DIRECTIONS
FOR FURTHER RESEARCH

At the same time it is useful to recall what this book does *not* claim. As I mentioned in chapter 1,

> I do not claim that the account given here completely explains the roles of musical forces in our experience of music. I do not claim that musical forces

completely explain musical experience. I do not claim that music always gives in
to musical forces. I do not claim that musical forces have the same universality or
"natural" status that physical forces do. I do not claim that gravity, magnetism,
and inertia are the only forces that shape melodic expectations. I do not claim
that musical forces and musical motion are the only metaphors that inform
music discourse and musical experience. And I do not claim that the theory of
pattern, analogy, and metaphor offered in this book gives a complete account of
human meaning-making.

In addition to clarifying the goals of this book, these qualifications also
point to interesting future directions for study.

A PARTIAL ACCOUNT

Let us consider my first qualification: I do not claim that the account
given here completely explains the roles of musical forces in our experience of music. Instead, I hope to have offered an invitation to others to
expand, qualify, and improve the theory. In my own future work, I hope
to explore in greater depth how Schenkerian analysis – informed and
aided by this theory of musical forces – can reveal interesting aspects
of individual compositions and improvisations. The work that I have
already done in that area suggests that such analysis has the potential to
tell us important things: about the attribution of intention, inevitability,
and agency; about the nature and importance of improvisation; about
musical and social roles; about the psychology of repetition (including
the "hidden repetitions" discussed by Schenker and his followers); about
the role of narrative processes and the stories we tell ourselves in creating musical meaning; and about visceral musical qualities such as swing,
surprise, and humor. As suggested in chapter 1, the idea of musical forces
may be regarded as part of a larger theory of expressive meaning in music that sees musical meaning as (at least in part) an emergent property
of the musical forces described in this book. I hope many thinkers will
contribute to advancing that larger theory.

I hope, too, that others will find further ways to test and possibly refine
the theory. Perhaps the approach described in Gibbs (1994) for priming
studies could be used to test whether certain metaphorical entailments
shape descriptions of musical experience. Work by Margulis and others

suggests that studies of melodic expectation exploring response times in judgment tasks may be fruitful for further expanding our understanding of musical forces. The theory claims that evenly paced patterns tend to change direction on the unstable pitches; when changes in direction occur in stable pitches, however, those stable pitches tend to be rhythmically lengthened. This, and other claims of the theory, could be more thoroughly tested in a variety of ways. Thoughtful experimental designers might find ways to test the experience of musical forces in chromatic patterns excluded from the experiment reported in chapter 12 (perhaps accompanying the patterns with appropriate harmonies could facilitate such an experiment). Experiments on intonation and expressive timing may provide further illumination. Studies by Janina Fyk (1995) suggest that intonation choices in string playing may reflect melodic magnetism. Johanna Devaney is developing software and approaches that may help us investigate intonation in vocal performance, and includes questions about musical forces in her inquiries. Robert Hatten notes that Bruno Repp's experiments on expressive timing "offer evidence that the vectoral fields provided by meter and tonality have entrained Western musicians with habitual expressive responses to their forces" (2004, 119). Later in this chapter I offer a list of questions that could guide ethnomusicological and other cultural studies. Eric Nichols (of the Center for Research on Concepts and Cognition at Indiana University) is exploring ways to expand the computer models described in chapter 13. I hope that creative researchers will find various ways to experimentally test these ideas.

PEDAGOGICAL IMPLICATIONS AS A FURTHER TEST

Another way to test the value of a theory of music is to ask how it helps us improve our teaching of music to musicians. I have already explored the application of these ideas to aural skills and counterpoint (Larson 1992, 1993e, 1994a; Hurwitz and Larson 1994). William Pelto (1994) has discussed their application to the teaching of part writing. It seems to me that other applications of the theory of musical forces might not only improve music pedagogy but might also provide additional ways to assess the theory.

OTHER ASPECTS OF MUSICAL EXPERIENCE

My second qualification, that musical forces do not completely explain musical experience, steers us toward many other factors that influence our experience of music. For example, I take delight in certain chord colors or their successions, and I doubt that the theory presented here could ever fully explain that. Certain pieces of music appeal to me because of the circumstances under which I learned them, and such associations do not necessarily have anything to do with musical forces. Nevertheless, exploring other factors that contribute to musical meaning also seems a promising avenue for research, as well as an important way to understand the context and limits of musical forces.

FORCES AND INTENTION

I do not claim that music always gives in to musical forces. During an early presentation of this theory to the Society for Music Theory (Larson 1992), I described how, in hearing three-note patterns (like those described in chapter 6), listeners might hear the motion from the second note to the third as giving in to one or more of the musical forces. One music theorist asked, "What force leads the first note to the second note?" I explained that the claim was not that all musical motions give in to some musical force; instead, one could hear patterns that begin with a descent as giving in to gravity but that (at least for ascending patterns) the motion from a stable to an unstable pitch cannot be heard as giving in to a musical force. I then suggested that my claim – that experienced listeners give meaning to tonal music by hearing it as purposeful action within a dynamic field of musical forces – implies that listeners impute intention to musical motions that go against the forces acting on them, hearing those motions as evidence of an intentional agent. I later learned that analogous claims had been made about visual perception (see studies cited in Lerdahl 2001). Hatten's theory of musical gesture, by recognizing musical forces "as environmental," explicitly notes the relationship between those forces and "a perceived or implied *source* of gestural energy" (2004, 115–116).

Furthermore, one of the delights of listening to music is that it often does something different from what we expect. The theory presented here argues that experienced listeners of tonal music expect it to give in to musical forces. But the same listeners expect to be fooled by music that goes against their expectations.[1]

PHYSICAL FORCES VS. MUSICAL FORCES

I do not claim that musical forces have the same universality or "natural" status that physical forces do, nor do I claim that these metaphors shape the music of all cultures or shape musical experience in the same way in every culture. Nevertheless, metaphors of musical motion and musical forces do seem to crop up in a variety of musical cultures.

If, for example, a musical culture conceptualizes its pitches as "thick and thin" or as "big and little" instead of as "low and high," then we might expect members of that culture to have melodic expectations that differ from the expectations of Western listeners who feel a kind of melodic gravity pulling down on "high" notes.

The argument posed in chapter 3 (that we acquire our basic embodied understanding of physical motion in four different ways and that these basic experiences of physical motion give rise to the principal ways in which we conceptualize musical motion) suggests that the tendency to conceptualize music in terms of motion may be common to musical cultures around the globe. And, in fact, it appears that the tendency to conceptualize music in terms of physical motion *is* a worldwide phenomenon. Phatak Prabhakar (e-mail 2004) reports that "Indian musical communication (between musicians on the dais during the course of a musical performance, amongst critics and members of the audience listening to a performance, and beyond that, in written commentaries on the theory and practice of classical music) abound with references to physical motion." According to Kathy McKinley (2002) and Sam-Ang Sam (1988), performers of Cambodian traditional instrumental music each simultaneously plays his or her own version of the same basic melody. They come together at certain points but otherwise freely explore their own variations on that melody. Cambodian musicians usually de-

scribe those variations as "roads" (*pliw* in Khmer), and they describe
their ensemble playing as "following your own road" or "making your
own road."

The idea of musical forces also appears in different cultures. For
example, I have heard Indian musician Ravikiran describe the "magnetic attractions" he feels in different ragas. My own transcription and
analysis of performances by Ravi Shankar suggest that his shaping of
individual melodic lines reflects the influence of musical forces. Leonard
Meyer notes that, "in the music of China, non-structural tones take the
name of the structural tone to which they move together with the word
pièn, meaning 'on the way to' or 'becoming'" (1956, 56).Chapters 1 and 2
suggest that just as a culture is shaped by its metaphors, so, too, does a
culture shape its metaphors. Thus we should expect to find that different
cultures understand musical motion in different ways. Perhaps rather
than asking, "Are there musical universals?" we should ask, "To what extent are the ideas described in this book shared by different cultures, and
what differences do the differences make?" The theory of musical forces
suggests a framework for exploring these differences. Instead of asking,
"Are there musical universals?" the following list of questions (Larson
1997b) asks, "To what extent are the ideas described in this book shared
by different cultures, and what differences do the differences make?"

1. In what musical cultures are sounds *heard as* meanings?
2. In what musical cultures does the shaping of musical time map
   onto the shaping of nonmusical time?
3. Does the shaping of musical time in different cultures *reflect*
   cultural values, ideas, and practices concerning the shaping of
   nonmusical time? If so, how?
4. Does the use of musical repetition in different cultures *reflect*
   cultural values, ideas, and practices concerning other types of
   repetition? If so, how?
5. In what musical cultures are sounds heard as *embodied*
   meanings?
6. In what musical cultures are *musical motions* experienced as a
   mapping of physical *gestures*?

7. Does *musical motion* in different cultures reflect cultural values, ideas, and practices concerning dance and other physical *gestures*? If so, how?

8. In what musical cultures is *musical space* mapped onto *physical space*?

9. What relationships exist between the use of *visual space* and *musical space* in different cultures?

10. If such relationships exist, do they reflect cultural values, ideas, and practices? If so, how?

11. In what musical cultures does the mapping of physical space on musical space involve a mapping of *physical high and low* onto *musical high and low*?

12. In what languages is descent in pitch associated with reduction in tension?

13. In what musical cultures is descent in pitch associated with reduction in tension (*musical gravity*)?

14. What relationships exist between *musical contour* and *speech* in different cultures, and how do these reflect cultural values, ideas, and practices?

15. In what musical cultures do musical *states* map onto *goals*?

16. Does the pursuit of *musical goals* in different cultures reflect cultural values, ideas, and practices concerning the pursuit of *other life goals*? If so, how?

17. In what musical cultures do specific *pitches* map onto *goals*?

18. In what musical cultures is arrival at a pitch goal associated with reduced tension (*melodic magnetism*)?

19. In what musical cultures is reduced distance from a pitch goal associated with heightened tension (*melodic magnetism*)?

20. What advantages and disadvantages are offered by viewing the music of any given culture in terms of the definitions offered here, including (for example) the definition of *meter* as the expectation that a pattern of physical motion that reflects the movement quality and fluctuations in rhythmic stability of the patterns heard in a passage of music will, upon repetition, continue to reflect the qualities of the following passage?

21. In what cultures is arrival at a metrically stable moment associated with reduced tension (*metric magnetism*)?
22. In what cultures is reduced distance from a metrically stable moment associated with heightened tension (*metric magnetism*)?
23. In what musical cultures do patterns of pitches and patterns of durations show a tendency to continue in the same fashion (*musical inertia*)?
24. How does the use of *musical inertia* in different cultures reflect cultural values, ideas, and practices concerning *repetition* in other life pursuits?
25. In what musical cultures do *operations* of sameness, similarity, and successorship on *alphabets* of pitches efficiently generate common or basic *patterns* of pitches?
26. What roles are played by collection-adjacency and collection-nonadjacency in different musical cultures?
27. Do these ways of structuring tones reflect cultural values, ideas, and practices concerning the structuring of *other life relationships*? If so, how?
28. In what musical cultures do physical *steps and leaps* map onto some type of collection-adjacency and collection-nonadjacency (*trace displacement*)?
29. In what musical cultures does the *critical band* correlate with a distinction between intervals that function as *steps vs. leaps*?
30. In what musical cultures are *step collections* important constructive elements?
31. In what musical cultures with steps of different sizes do departures from closed proper *step collections* occur most often (if at all) at stable boundary pitches?
32. In what musical cultures are repeated "time lines" (such as African bell patterns) built of successive short and long durations such that successive short durations tend to be avoided – and in these cultures, do exceptions (successive short durations) occur most often (if at all) at stable boundary pitches?

33. In what musical cultures does *elaboration* create *hierarchies of dependence* among pitches (*tonal stability*)?

34. Does the experience of *musical forces* in different musical cultures reflect cultural values, ideas, and practices concerning *image schemata* of source, path, and goal? If so, how?

OTHER FORCES

Although I do not claim that inertia and the melodic and rhythmic forms of gravity and magnetism are the only forces that shape musical expectations, these forces do seem to capture much of the variability of direction we experience – it is difficult to imagine ways of describing the direction of motion besides up/down (gravity), toward/away (magnetism), and same/different (inertia). And the "other" forces discovered by physicists (like the strong and weak nuclear forces), since they are not experienced with our bodies, seem unlikely to contribute to our embodied musical understanding. And yet I have been working with the idea of musical forces for more than twenty years and keep running into new ideas. For example, I had never thought about "musical friction" before William Rothstein's (2005) recent and elegant essay on a Chopin Prélude discussed tempo rubato in terms of motions such as slipping off a log or traveling through viscous fluids and Robert Hatten (2004, 116) suggested its addition to the other forces I describe. The notion of musical friction finds a nice analogy in studies of "apparent friction" in visual perception (Hubbard 1995a, 1998b).

OTHER METAPHORS

Another qualification to my theory is that musical forces and musical motion are not the only metaphors that inform music discourse and musical experience. Other important metaphors include Music As Language Or Story, Music As Game Or Play, Music As Sex Or Reproduction, Music As Architecture Or Other Physical Structure, Music As Emotion, and Music As Food Or Nutrition. Musicians have written about each of these metaphorical topics at great length.

The point I wish to make here is that one promising avenue for further research now is the idea of how such metaphors interact. Recent work in linguistics explores "force metaphors" in language. The metaphors of motion and forces are central to games, play, and other metaphors.

MEANING

I do not claim, furthermore, that the theory of pattern, analogy, and metaphor described in this book provides a complete account of human meaning-making. The creation of meaning is a complicated and fascinating topic, and musical meaning is just one part of that topic.

Some of the implications of this book for further work in human meaning-making do include, however, the recognition that embodiment is essential to meaning, the acknowledgment that meaning is not purely verbal, the acceptance of the central role of emotive experience in what we call reason, the unavoidability of metaphor in conceptual thinking, and the possibility that music study might be one of the best ways to understand that it is the fusion of our minds, bodies, and souls that allows us to make sense of what is important to us.[2] However, although the evidence for the theory of musical forces presented in this book seems to support the larger theory of expressive meaning sketched in chapter 1, it might also be worthwhile to examine other "larger theories" of meaning that might incorporate the idea of musical forces.

BLISS, MUSIC, AND MOTION

The central claim of this book is that we not only talk about music in terms of physical motion, but we also experience it in terms of musical forces analogous to physical gravity, magnetism, and inertia. One assertion in chapter 6 is that analogies between patterns of pitch, patterns of duration, and patterns of physical motion afford embodied opportunities to map them onto one another. Of course, this is what good dancing does. Because the point is one of blissful visceral experience (and in part because I have referred to the motions we make when tossing and juggling balls), I also suggest that the theory of musical forces may be able to illuminate the arts of dance and juggling – and might help explain some of the pleasure we experience in their coordination with music.[3]

SUMMARY

This book has described a theory of musical forces – that we not only *think about music* as if it were shaped by musical analogs of physical gravity, magnetism, and inertia, but we also actually *think in music* in terms of analogous musical forces – and it has presented converging evidence that appears consistent with that theory. The point of this final chapter has been to suggest that the qualifications offered in chapter 1 not only limit its claims but also point to potentially useful avenues for further research in music analysis, experimental psychology, the pedagogy of musicianship, phenomenology, cognitive linguistics, ethnomusicology, and computer science.

GLOSSARY

Accent. A quality of a note or time point that draws our attention. There are, for example, *Agogic accents* and *Metric accents*.

Affix. A note of *Elaboration* added before (*Prefix*) or after (*Suffix*) the note it elaborates.

Agent. To hear music as purposeful action means to *Hear* it as the intent of an animate agent. See *Hear . . . as . . .*

Agogic accent. An *Accent* that accrues to a note because it is relatively longer than surrounding notes.

Algorithm. A "recipe" that is specific enough for a computer to follow. The computer models in chapter 13 use an algorithm (Larson 1993) that gives ratings to melodic completions that are a weighted combination of several factors (the *Musical Forces* and *Stability*). Subsequent similar algorithms have been proposed by Bharucha (1996), Lerdahl (1996, 2001), and Margulis (2003).

Alphabet. Deutsch and Feroe (1981) define an alphabet as a basic collection of pitches (such as the chromatic scale, the major scale, or specific chords) in terms of which listeners understand passages of music, and which may be economically described as complete, theoretically well-defined pitch collections.

Analogy. Any *Mapping* that calls attention to similarities between two different things. Analogies include mappings within a single domain and *Cross-domain mappings*. In this book I reserve the term *Metaphor* for cross-domain mappings. Thus, as this book uses the terms, all metaphors are analogies but not all analogies are metaphors.

Anchoring, melodic. Bharucha's (1984a) term for the tendency of unstable pitches to resolve by step, and thus related to what I call *Melodic magnetism*. See also *Tonal force vector* and *Yearning vector*.

Apparent motion. An "optical illusion" that results from seeing a succession of still images as a moving object. To "see . . . as . . ." that may be compared with "to *Hear . . . as . . .*" See also *Phi phenomenon*.

Appoggiatura. An *Unstable* note of elaboration that occurs on a more metrically stable location than its *Resolution*. Typically leapt up to and resolved down by step.

As Times Go By. See *Moving Times metaphor*.

Association. Whenever two notes are *Heard* as related, an association is created. *Prolongation* is a kind of association. Notes may be heard as associated because of their similarity in any dimension (pitch, register, duration, timbre, etc.) or participation in a *Pattern*.

Atomism or Atomistic fallacy. The assumptions that scientific inquiry should make no assumptions and that any explanation of music perception must be based solely on principles applied in *Bottom-up* fashion to note-to-note relationships, ignoring possible relationships between nonadjacent notes; the view that we can only understand "wholes" by building them up from "parts."

Attraction. Brower's (1997–98, 2000) and Lerdahl's (1996) term for *Musical magnetism*.

Auditory scene analysis. Albert Bregman's (1990) term for the process by which our minds sort out sonic "objects" by grouping sounds into streams and attributing them to sources.

Auralize. To think in sounds – what happens when we hear music in our heads – especially when the music is not actually sounding (we also auralize when we listen attentively, especially when we anticipate what will happen next).

Background. See *Ursatz*.

Bottom-up. A process that leads from specific details or facts to generalizations or theories; induction. Bottom-up mental processes take parts and create wholes. Compare *Top-down*.

Chord scale. In jazz, a collection of pitches that can be associated melodically with a given chord. Chord scales tend to be *Step collections*.

Closed step collection. A *Proper step collection* in which every adjacent pair of notes is a step apart.

Complete leap collection. A *Proper leap collection* to which no other notes can be added and still create a *Proper leap collection*. Proper complete leap collections can be further distinguished on the basis of whether they contain a perfect fifth (those that do, the major and minor triads, play a central role in tonal music).

Complete step collection. A *Proper step collection* to which no other notes can be added and still create a *Proper step collection*.

Completion. The theory of musical forces distinguishes between melodic continuation (which answers the question "What note comes next?") and melodic completion (which answers the question "How will this melody end?"). The theory claims that *Experienced listeners* of *Tonal music* have expectations not only about how melodic beginnings will continue but also about how they will be complete.

Compound melody. A melody (one note at a time) that gives the impression that it is based on multiple underlying voice-leading strands. Such underlying strands tend to move by a *Step* and be separated by a *Leap*.

Confirmation. A *Hidden repetition* in which two versions of a single melodic idea, on two different levels of musical structure, are completed at the same time. I also call the shorter, more foreground idea itself the "confirmation."

Connective. A note of *Elaboration* added between the notes it connects.

Consonance. See *Stability*.

Continuation. See *Completion*.

Converging evidence. The more evidence we have that is consistent with a given hypothesis, and the larger the number and wider the variety of sources from which it comes, the greater the support it provides for that hypothesis.

Correct rejection. When comparing models to experimental data, correct predictions ("hits" as opposed to "misses") can include the correct prediction of events that do not take place.

Correlation. A mathematical relationship between two strings of numbers, stated as a number between +1 and −1 (the R value). An R of +1 means that the first set of numbers changes in the same way as the second set – that is, corresponding numbers go up or down in proportionate amounts. An *R* of 0 means that there is no relationship between the two sets of numbers. An *R* of −1 means that they change in opposite directions.

Critical band. For a given pitch, the range of frequencies that arouse the same part of the basilar membrane as that pitch. In common-practice tonal music, within much of the register used for melody, the critical band lies between a minor third and major second (thus separating *Steps* and *Leaps*).

Cross-domain mapping. See *Metaphor*.

Declarative knowledge. Knowledge that can be verbalized. *Thinking* about *music* is declarative knowledge.

Diachronic. A relationship through time. An *Event hierarchy* is diachronic. See Synchronic.

Diatonic. Belonging to mode. For a piece in C major, this would mean the white keys of the piano. For a piece in F♯ minor, this would mean the notes indicated by the key signature of F♯ minor.

Diatonic collection. A collection of pitches that is transpositionally equivalent to the white notes on a piano.

Diatonic collection position. A "location" within the diatonic collection, determined by distance from other members of the collection. The pitch F♯ is in the same diatonic collection position in E Dorian as it is in A Mixolydian.

Direction. A single factor in Margulis's (2003) model of melodic expectation that combines two aspects of Narmour's (1990, 1992) implication-realization model. For small intervals, Margulis's "direction," like Narmour's "process," is equivalent to what I call *Musical inertia*; for larger intervals, Margulis's "direction" produces something like Narmour's "reversal."

Displacement. See *Trace*.

Displacement dissonance. The term Krebs (1987, 1999) uses for a type of *Metric dissonance* in which a *Pattern* of durations is shifted from (earlier or later than) its normative or expected location. To speak of such displacement is to make a metaphor that spatializes time. See also Grouping dissonance.

Dissonance. See *Stability* and *Metric dissonance*.

Elaboration. A process through which a basic sound is transformed into a more complex one. The following transformations can create elaboration: (1) the addition of an *Affix* or *Connective*, (2) the registral shifting of a note, (3) the temporal shifting of a note, (4) the *Elision* or overlap of shared pitches, (5) the suppression of an implied tone.

Elision, elided. Two *Patterns* are said to be elided when the end of the first pattern does "double duty" and also serves as the beginning of the second pattern.

Embellishment. See *Elaboration*.

Embodied, Embodiment. The degree to which our knowledge or experience is embodied is the degree to which that knowledge or experience is connected with our bodily experience of the world. The cognitive theory of metaphor (Lakoff and Johnson 1980, 1999) claims that all concepts are metaphorical, that all metaphors are physically grounded, and therefore that all concepts are (to some degree) embodied.

Emergent property. A global phenomenon that results from the interactions of more local phenomena – in which it appears that the whole is unexpectedly greater than the sum of its parts. Two classic examples of emergent properties are the flocking behavior of birds and the chemical properties of molecules. To say that a thing has an "emergent property" is not so much an observation about a property literally possessed by that thing as it is an observation about how our minds work. If our minds understood immediately – that is, if we could feel in our bodies, without having to think it out – how the (poisonous) individual properties of sodium and chorine combine to create the (life-sustaining) emergent properties of salt, then we would not regard the latter properties as emergent.

Entailment. According to Lakoff and Johnson 1980, 1999), in a *Metaphor* (such as Understanding Is Seeing), a *Source domain* (in this case, vision) may include relationships (such as the fact that obstacles can occlude our view or that illumination can enhance it) that are imported into the *Target domain* (in this case, understanding). When such relationships are imported, they are called entailments.

Event hierarchy. Jamsched Bharucha's (1984b) term for a temporally ordered *Hierarchy*, such as a Schenkerian analysis.

Experienced listeners. Listeners of tonal music who have internalized the regularities of a musical style to a degree that allows them to experience the expectations generated by that music.

Expressive meaning. That quality listeners experience in music that allows it to suggest (for example) feelings, actions, or motion. This quality may not translate well into words nor relate clearly to the emotions felt by the creators (the composers, performers, and improvisers) of the music, but it seems to be one reason that we derive so much pleasure from listening to music. I use this term in the same way that Robert Hatten (1994, 2004) does and in the same way that Rudolf Arnheim (1974) uses the term "expression."

Fernhören. *Structural hearing* on a *Global* level.

Force. See *Musical forces.*

Foreground. The "surface" level of a musical structure (or the levels closest to the surface; usage varies from author to author). See also *Ursatz* and *Middleground.*

Frame. See *Tonality Frame.*

Fugue paradigm. William Renwick's (1991) term for certain more basic pitch patterns *Elaborated* by fugue subjects.

Fundamental structure. See *Ursatz.*

Gesture. Robert Hatten defines musical gesture as meaningful and expressive "significant energetic shaping through time" (2004, see esp. 93–132). Hatten's theory of gesture draws on the theory of musical forces (2004, see esp. 115–117) in order to describe what he calls the "virtual environmental forces" that contribute to the shape and meaning of musical gestures.

Goal alphabet (also called **Goal collection** or **Goal level**). A subset of more *Stable* pitches within a *Reference alphabet* that can serve as a goal of melodic motion within that *Reference alphabet.*

Good continuation. Leonard B. Meyer's (1956, 1973) term (borrowed from Gestalt psychology) for the tendency of motion to continue in the same direction or fashion, and thus related to what I call *Musical inertia.* In Gestalt psychology, good continuation is a law of perceptual organization that says we tend to see individual elements as part of a *Pattern* when they appear to trace a predictable (straight, smooth, or regular) path.

Gravity. See *Melodic gravity* and *Rhythmic gravity.*

Group, grouping. A mentally created unit of percepts. According to the Gestalt psychologists, we tend to group things according to principles of perceptual organization such as proximity, similarity, good continuation, common fate, and so on.

Grouping dissonance. The term Krebs (1987, 1999) uses for a type of *Rhythmic* *dissonance* in which a *Pattern* of durations groups time points in a way that differs from the grouping experienced by the underlying meter. See also *Displacement dissonance*.

Hallelujah figure. A family of musical figures that feature an alternation between 5̂ to 6̂ in major, preceded or followed by a leap to or from 1̂ (as in the "Hallelujah Chorus" from the *Messiah*).

Hear ... as ... Our minds create musical meanings when they *Hear* sounds *as* meanings.

Hidden repetition. Heinrich Schenker's term for what happens when a musical idea occurs on two different levels of musical structure (Burkhart 1978) or its function changes so that it is not clearly heard as a repetition (*Linkage technique*). See also *Confirmation*.

Hierarchy. An organization of relationships in levels. Bharucha (1984b) distinguishes between *Event hierarchies* (which this book also calls *Diachronic*) and *Tonal hierarchies* (which this book also calls *Synchronic*).

I/We. See **We/I**.

Icon. In *Semiotics*, a sign whose *Meaning* we recognize because of a static similarity between aspects of the icon and what it signifies. An icon *looks* like (or sounds like, etc.) what it represents.

Implication-realization model. Narmour's (1990, 1992) theory of melodic expectation, which combines bottom-up factors (described in connection with Example 13.19) and top-down factors (such as the influence of intra-opus style and the influence of extra-opus style).

Index. In *Semiotics* a sign whose *Meaning* we recognize because of a dynamic likeness between the behaviors of the index and of what it signifies or because it points to what it represents. An index *acts* like what it represents (or directs our attention to what it represents).

Inertia. See *Musical inertia*.

Inter-onset interval (IOI). The time between the beginnings of two successive events.

Internal representation. The way in which a *Pattern* is stored in a mind.

Inverse square (or **cube**) *law*. When an effect, such as physical gravity or illumination, varies "inversely" with respect to the square (or cube) of the distance between the source of the effect and the location at which it is felt. For example, according to the inverse square law, an object twice as far from a point source of light receives a quarter of the illumination, and an object three times as far receives a ninth of the effect.

Key. The most *Stable* pitch on which a melody can end. For a piece in C major, the key is C and the mode is major.

Knüpftechnik. See *Linkage technique*.

Lamento bass. A bass line that descends chromatically from tonic to dominant in minor, usually repeated and typically in a slow triple meter. The lamento bass has a long history of association with texts expressing sadness and death (Williams 1997).

Landmark-attraction effect. A metaphorical *Visual force* that seems to pull visual targets toward more massive visual landmarks, distorting our memory of the target's location in the direction of the landmark.

Leading tone. The seventh degree of the scale when it is a half step below the tonic. Compare *Subtonic*.

Leap. An interval larger than a *Step* – a minor third or larger. In a melodic leap, the second note tends to support the Trace of the first, leaving two traces in musical memory.

Leap collection. A group of notes in which no two notes are a step apart. See also *Proper leap collection* and *Complete leap collection*.

Level of explanation. A set of assumptions about what is assumed and what is to be explained. If the level of explanation (say, for the action of a drug) is chemical (and thus relies on the action of molecules) it typically assumes lower levels of explanation (that is, it might not attempt to explain how the action of molecules it describes relies on the action of subatomic particles).

Linkage technique. A *Hidden repetition* in which a pattern of pitches is repeated, but the repetition is disguised by the changed function of the pitches, as might happen when the last few notes of a phrase are repeated as the first few notes of a subsequent phrase.

Magnetism. See *Melodic magnetism* and *Rhythmic magnetism*.

Meaning. Something that our minds create when they group things into patterned relations.

Melodic continuation and **Melodic completion.** See *Completion*.

Melodic forces. See *Melodic gravity, Melodic magnetism,* and Musical inertia.

Melodic gravity. One of the *Musical forces*. The tendency of notes above a reference platform to descend.

Melodic inertia. See *Musical inertia*.

Melodic magnetism. One of the *Musical forces*. The tendency of unstable notes to move to the closest stable pitch, a tendency that grows stronger as the goal pitch becomes closer. Bharucha (1996) calls magnetism *"Tonal force vector."* Brower (1997–98, 2000), Lerdahl (1996), and Margulis (2003) call magnetism *"Attraction."*

Meme. Ideas that Richard Dawkins (1976) describes as analogous to genes. Like genes, memes live in a particular environment: our thoughts and our culture. Like genes, their survival depends on how well they fit in their environment.

Metaphor. That conceptual process described by George Lakoff and Mark Johnson (1999) in which we understand one (typically less familiar or more abstract) thing (from a *Target domain*) in terms of some other kind of (usually more familiar or more concrete) thing (the *Source domain*). Metaphors are thus *Cross-domain mappings*. All metaphors are analogies; not all analogies are metaphors.

Meter. The expectation that a pattern of physical motion (think of conducting or dancing) that reflects the movement quality and fluctuations in rhythmic stability of the patterns heard in a passage of music will, upon repetition, continue to reflect the qualities of the following passage (which is thus experienced as "in the same meter").

Metric accent. An Accent that accrues to a note because it has greater *Metric stability* than surrounding notes.

Metric dissonance. A relationship between two patterns of duration. When two durational patterns are simply nested so that one is a subset of the other (for example, with eighth notes and quarter notes in a given meter), the patterns are said to be "metrically consonant." When they do not coincide in this way (for example, in syncopated patterns or with the pattern combination called "two against three"), the patterns are said to be "metrically dissonant." Harald Krebs (1987, 1999) speaks of two kinds of metric dissonance: *Displacement dissonance* and *Grouping dissonance*. To speak of "metric dissonances" is to make an *Analogy* with tonal dissonance.

Metric gravity. See *Rhythmic gravity*.

Metric magnetism. The pull of a note on a metrically unstable attack point to a subsequent and more metrically stable attack point, a pull that grows stronger as the attracting attack point grows closer. We may also experience notes as pulling away from prior attack points.

Metric stability. See *Stability, metric*.

Middleground. A level of musical structure more elaborate than the background (see *Ursatz*) and less elaborate than the *Foreground*.

Mirror neurons. A special group of neurons that are activated both when a certain action is performed – and when one observes someone else perform the same action – apparently important in the experience of empathy. Mirror neurons may thus be part of the underlying brain mechanisms by which we understand music as motion and music as emotion.

Mode. A collection of notes (and, typically, a set of assumptions of how melodies will move within that collection). For a piece in C major, the key is C and the mode is major. See also *Chord scale*.

Moving Music metaphor and **Moving Times metaphor.** A spatial schema in which an observer is facing in a fixed direction ("*facing the future*"), is situated at "the present" (the "*here and now*"), and times or musical events are conceptualized as objects moving toward and then past the stationary observer. Also called *As Times Go By.*

Moving Observer metaphor. A spatial schema in which the observer moves across a landscape and times are points or regions on that landscape. Also called *Time's Landscape.*

Multilevel computer model. A computer model of melodic expectation (Larson 1999a, 2004). When given a melodic beginning and a Schenkerian analysis of that beginning, this model returns a list of possible completions. To make its predictions, the multilevel model takes the top (most basic) level of the analysis it has been given and calls on the single-level model to produce a completion at that level. It then fills in that "skeleton" by choosing notes (at levels closer to the "surface" of the melodic beginning) that give in to inertia. (This model

was called *Voyager* in some of my prior publications).

Multiple regression. A technique of statistical analysis used with models that attempt to explain how some observed phenomenon (the dependent variable) varies with respect to a combination of factors (the independent variables). Regression determines what weighting of those factors produces the highest correlation between the predictions of the model and the observed phenomenon.

Music As Moving Force metaphor. The metaphorical force is the music itself, moving the hearer from one metaphorical location (state) to another (different state).

Musical forces. Metaphorical tendencies we attribute to music. Although we may be consciously unaware of these attributions, they contribute to the meanings given to the music by our minds. See *Melodic gravity, Melodic magnetism, Metric magnetism, Musical inertia*, and *Rhythmic gravity.*

Musical gravity. See *Melodic gravity* and *Rhythmic gravity.*

Musical inertia. One of the *Musical forces.* The tendency of musical motion to continue in the pattern perceived. Musical inertia can apply both to patterns of pitches and to patterns of duration. Leonard B. Meyer (1956, 1973) calls the same tendency *Good continuation.*

Musical Landscape metaphor. A spatial schema in which the observer moves across a landscape and times are points or regions on that landscape.

Musical magnetism. See *Melodic magnetism* and *Rhythmic magnetism.*

Naïve physics. A layperson's understanding of physics (also called "folk physics"), especially when it contradicts the current understanding of physicists. Naïve physics usually accords fairly well with the apparent behavior of physical objects but often assumes greater underlying simplicity or regularity (or perhaps just a different logic) than physicists attribute to the same phenomena. For example, naïve physics long held that the sun rotates around the earth. Many people now believe the *Single-mechanism explanation/fallacy* that only one force acts upon a physical object at a time ("inertia carried it upward, *and then* gravity started pulling it down") when, in fact, the trajectory of a physical object is shaped by the interaction of more than one force.

Natural. A potentially confusing term that is avoided in this book. The musical forces are not "natural" or "*Universal*" the way physical forces are. Although people tend to assume that "natural" means better (and it does, in some contexts), this assumption can be misleading in music theory. Is natural the opposite of artificial? Is art better when it is natural? Then why does "art" have the same root as "artificial"?

Neutralization. Arnold Schoenberg's ([1911] 1978) term for that phenomenon when chromatic pitches (notes not in the diatonic *Reference collection*, such as F♯ in C major) resolve to a note a step away (such as F♯ resolving to G) before being replaced with their diatonic counterparts (in this case, F replacing F♯, so that F♯ is neutralized).

Next Generation. See *Single-level computer model.*

Observer perspective. In the *Musical Landscape metaphor*, the perspective of a distant standpoint from which we can observe the path through a musical landscape that defines a particular work.

Operation. Deutsch and Feroe (1981) define an operation as a simple way of moving within an *Alphabet*, such as repetition, or motion to the next higher or lower member. This book and the computer implementations it describes limits itself to operations that transform a single note by adding one note (an *Affix*) before it (a *Prefix*) or after it (a *Suffix*) or that transform a pair of notes by adding all the *Alphabet* notes between (*Connective*). Each transformation results in a motion that stays (repeats the same member of the *Alphabet*), goes up (moves to the next higher member of the *Alphabet*), or goes down (moves to the next lower member of the *Alphabet*).

Ornamentation. See *Elaboration.*

P value. The probability that a reported result (such as a *Correlation*) at least this significant would occur by chance. By convention, *p* values below .05 are considered statistically significant.

Participant perspective. In the *Musical Landscape metaphor*, the perspective in which you, the listener, are moving over the musical landscape. As listener, you are metaphorically *in* the piece, that is, you are traveling over the *Path* that defines a particular musical piece, and you are actually hearing it.

Path. One *Entailment* of the *Metaphor* Musical Succession is Physical Motion is that we tend to hear melodies as moving along or tracing out paths that are like physical paths (that, for example, have beginnings and endings, can be blocked, may involve detours, etc.).

Pattern. We tend to use the word "pattern" to describe at least three sorts of things – and they all seem related to repetition. First, we may use the word "pattern" to describe a design or shape (such as a dress pattern used in sewing) that could serve as a model. Such a pattern is something we can imagine repeating. Second, we speak of a pattern when a single thing (such as a cross or a mandala) has some kind of internal symmetry or logic. Such a pattern may be said to contain repetition (of a shape or of a rule) within it. Third, we speak of a pattern (such as the rhythm of an engine or a pattern of behavior) when we notice something being repeated. Since this last sort of pattern may consist of things that would themselves be called patterns, we can also have higher-level patterns of patterns. Some of the patterns studied in this book are three-note pitch patterns that start and end on *Stable* pitches and move by *Step*.

Phi phenomenon. The *Apparent motion* that results from seeing separate blinking lights as a single moving object.

Pitch space. One *Entailment* of the *Metaphor* Musical Succession Is Physical Motion is the tendency to hear melodies as moving within a space (in which, for example, pitches of higher frequency may be heard as occupying higher locations within that space).

Polymeter. A *Metric dissonance* in which a pattern of durations suggests a meter that differs from the notated or underlying meter.

Prefix. A note of *Elaboration* added before the note it elaborates.

Probability. See *p value*.

Probe-tone profile. In the experiments of Carol Krumhansl and colleagues (e.g., 1990), the set of averaged participant ratings given to each note of the scale, when subjects were asked to judge how well a given scale degree "fit" with the harmonic context established just prior to hearing that degree.

Procedural knowledge. Knowledge of a thing that is demonstrated by doing that thing (rather than talking about it). *Thinking* in *music* is procedural knowledge.

Process. Eugene Narmour's (1990, 1992) "implication-realization model" predicts that listeners expect intervals smaller than a tritone to be followed by intervals that are similar in size

and direction. For intervals smaller than a tritone, Narmour's "process" and *Musical inertia* describe the same tendency.

Prolongation. A type of *Association*. We speak of an abstract note (or simpler passage) being prolonged when it can be *Heard* as being *Elaborated* by *Transformation(s)* that turn it into a more complex passage.

Proper leap collection. A *Leap collection* in which no two notes – nor any of their octave equivalents – are a step apart.

Proper step collection. A *Step collection* in which, when its pitches are arranged in ascending pitch order, no two notes – nor any of their octave equivalents – that are not adjacent in the list (except the first and last) are a step apart.

***R* value.** See *Correlation*.

Recursive predictions. The computer models of melodic expectation (the *Single-level model* and the *Multilevel model*, described in chapter 13) can create longer predictions by taking a melodic beginning as input, creating a continuation, and then using that continuation as a new melodic beginning to create an even longer prediction.

Reference alphabet (also called **Reference collection** or **Reference level**). An *Alphabet* in terms of which a passage of music is *Heard as* moving. A scale passage in C major may be described as motion through the reference alphabet of the C major scale.

Representational gravity. A metaphorical *Visual force* that seems to pull down on images, distorting our memory of their location downward.

Representational momentum. A metaphorical *Visual force* that seems to carry moving images in the same direction that they were moving, distorting our memory of their location in that same direction.

Resolution. The motion of an unstable note to a more *Stable* pitch that *Displaces* the *Trace* of that unstable note.

Retrospection of anticipation Browne's (1982) term for the experience of a listener who assumes, after hearing a given musical completion, that the specific completion that actually occurred was the one they had expected.

Rhythm. Part of the meaning we attribute to music when we hear a musical succession in terms of physical motion – that quality of motion we experience in it, a quality that is only partly dependent on its timing. *Grouping* and *Meter* are thus both part of rhythm.

Rhythmic forces. See *Musical inertia*, *Metric magnetism* and *Rhythmic gravity*.

Rhythmic gravity. That quality we attribute to a rhythm, when we map its flow onto a physical *Gesture*, that reflects the impact physical gravity has on that physical *Gesture*.

Rhythmic inertia. See *Musical inertia*.

Rhythmic magnetism. See *Metric magnetism*.

Rhythmic stability. See *Stability, metric*.

Semiotics. The study of how *Meanings* (such as facts, relationships, or feelings) become associated with *Signs*. Many semioticians, such as Ferdinand de Saussure ([1916] 1966), begin with the assumption that signs bear only a conventional (that is, purely arbitrary) relation to their meanings. Semiotician Charles Sanders Peirce ([1931] 1960), has suggested, however, a more nuanced view of signs, which distinguishes between *Icon, Index*, and *Symbol*.

Sentence. A durational pattern and theme type (Caplin 1998), typically 2 + 2 + 4 measures or similar proportions, that presents a basic idea (2 measures), repeats that idea (2 measures), and then balances that idea with a longer continuation (4 measures).

Signs. In *Semiotics* a sign is something with which we associate a meaning or referent (and may thus include, for example, pictures, sounds, or gestures). Three kinds of signs are *Icon, Index*, and *Symbol*.

Single-level computer model. A computer model of melodic expectation (Larson 1993, 2004). This model, when given a cue in a specified key, returns a rated list of predicted completions. To make its predictions, the single-level model first chooses a pair (or pairs) of reference and goal alphabets from the list in Example 13.1. Once the reference and goal alphabets are chosen, the single-level model makes its predictions by moving within the *reference alphabet* until it arrives at a member of the *goal alphabet*. The direction of motion is determined by the *musical forces*. To calculate the ratings that it gives to each completion it generates, it uses the algorithm given in chapter 4, with a factor added for the stability of the final note. (This model was called *Next Generation* in some of my prior publications).

Single-mechanism explanation (or **Single-mechanism fallacy**). The notion that an event is best explained as the result of the operation of a single force or mechanism; the assumption (sometimes false) that a given effect must have only one cause.

Skeleton, melodic. A simpler (usually stepwise) line that is *Elaborated* by a melody.

Source domain. In a *Metaphor*, the more familiar domain (from which we draw information and inferences to help us understand the *Target domain*). In the metaphor Love Is A Journey, relationship is the target domain and motion is the source domain.

Stability, metric. A comparative quality that we attribute to a point in time, and thus to a note happening at that time. We hear a note as metrically unstable to the degree that we *Auralize* a more stable time point to which it could move – and that we experience a desire to hear that motion. To say that a time point is more metrically stable is to say that it belongs to deeper levels of meter (where, for example, in $\frac{4}{4}$, the quarter-note level is deeper than the eighth-note level but not as deep as the half-note level).

Stability, tonal. A comparative quality that we attribute to a note. We hear a note as tonally unstable to the degree that it leads us to *Auralize* another (more stable) pitch and a path that will take the melody to that pitch (displacing the *Trace* of that unstable note) – and that we experience a desire to hear that motion. To say that a pitch is more tonally stable is to say that it belongs to deeper levels of pitch structure in a Schenkerian analysis.

Standardized coefficients. When the *Weights* attached to various factors in a *Multiple regression* model are stated as standardized coefficients (*b* values), larger weights indicate that the factor has a greater impact on the outcome.

States Are Locations metaphor. A *Metaphor* in which states (such as drunkenness or boiling) are understood as locations, so that we can be "in a stupor" or water can be "brought to a boil."

Step. An interval smaller than a minor third – a half step or whole step. In a melodic step, the second note tends to displace the trace of the first, leaving one trace in musical memory.

Step collection. A group of notes that can be arranged in ascending pitch order to satisfy the following two conditions: (1) every adjacent pair of notes is a step (that is, a half step or a whole step) apart; and (2) no nonadjacent pair of notes is a step apart (that is, the collection contains no consecutive semitones). See also *Closed step collection*, *Complete step collection*, and *Proper step collection*.

Step inertia. Paul von Hippel's (2002) term for the tendency for steps (whole steps and half steps) to continue in the same direction.

Stream, streaming. Albert Bregman's (1990) term for the perceptual association of a succession of events as a single event (so that a string of notes might be *Heard as* a melody).

Strict use of analytic notation. A restricted form of Schenkerian analytic notation (Larson 1996c). In *Strict use*, symbols are limited to noteheads, stem, and slurs – and all and only the stemmed notes on a given graphic level appear on the next, more remote level (where some of them may be unstemmed).

Structural hearing. Salzer's (1952) term for the act of *hearing* a passage of music *as* containing a prolongation.

Subtonic. The seventh degree of the scale when it is a whole step below the tonic. Compare *Leading tone*.

Suffix. A note of *Elaboration* added after the note it elaborates.

Suspension figure. A musical figure of three parts, consisting of a (tonally stable) "preparation," a (usually tonally unstable) "suspension," and a (tonally stable) resolution. The suspension figure is always a syncopated figure in which the preparation occurs on a (metrically unstable) upbeat and is tied into the following (metrically stable) downbeat, and the resolution happens on the following (metrically unstable) upbeat. Suspensions always resolve by step, usually downward. In a "rearticulated suspension figure," the preparation is not tied (that is, the suspension has the same pitch as the preparation but its own attack).

Symbol. In *Semiotics*, a sign whose meaning is purely conventional and therefore presumably completely arbitrary (but as Hatten [1994] notes, symbols are nevertheless typically "motivated").

Synchronic. A nontemporal or systematic relationship. A *Tonal hierarchy* is synchronic. See *Diachronic*.

Target domain. The less familiar or more abstract domain that a *Metaphor* seeks to illuminate (in comparison with the *Source domain*). In the metaphor Love Is A Journey, relationship is the target domain and motion is the source domain.

Thinking about music; thinking in music. Thinking in music means *Auralizing* pitches and duration; thinking about music is done in words, gestures, or anything other than pitches and durations.

Time's Landscape. See *Moving Observer metaphor*.

Tonal force vector. Bharucha's (1996) term for *Melodic magnetism*. See also *Yearning vector* and *Anchoring*.

Tonal hierarchy. Bharucha's (1984b) term for a *Synchronic* (not temporally ordered) *Hierarchy*, such as one of Krumhansl's *Probe-tone profiles*.

Tonal music, tonality. A way of relating tones one to another so that melodies form tonic-triad frames and harmonies progress toward perfect authentic cadences.

Tonality frame. Thomson's (2004, 441ff.) term for an interval drawn from the tonic triad (especially the root and fifth) that is elaborated by a melody (especially by its opening) and against which we interpret the motion of that melody.

Top-down. A process that leads from generalizations or theories to specific details or facts; deduction. Top-down mental processes take wholes and create parts. Compare *Bottom-up*.

Trace. The internal representation of a note that is still melodically active. In a melodic *Step*, the second note tends to displace the trace of the first, leaving one trace in musical memory; in a melodic *Leap*, the second note tends to support the trace of the first, leaving two traces in musical memory.

Turing test. A test of machine "intelligence" in which a human judge at one terminal sends questions to both a human at another terminal and to a computer. Responses from both appear on the judge's screen. The object is for the human judge to determine which responses come from the computer program and which come from another human. If the human judge cannot make that determination, then the computer is deemed intelligent.

Turn or **Turn figure.** A figure that transforms a single note into a short melodic *Gesture*, usually beginning on that note, moving up a *Step*, returning to that note, moving down a step, and then returning to that note. $\hat{5}$–$\hat{6}$–$\hat{5}$–$\sharp\hat{4}$–$\hat{5}$ is a turn figure that *Elaborates* $\hat{5}$. Such turns are typically followed by an ascending leap.

Universal. Principles of music theory typically apply to a limited repertoire. When such principles appear to apply to *all* musical cultures, they are called "universals."

Unstable. See Stability.

Ursatz. Schenker's term for the most remote level of musical structure. Also called *Background* or *Fundamental structure*, it is the simplest pattern of pitches underlying a piece of tonal music, and its upper voice is always a descending stepwise pattern that ends on the tonic, harmonized with an authentic cadence. The upper voice of the *Ursatz* is always $\hat{8}-\hat{7}-\hat{6}-\hat{5}-\hat{4}-\hat{3}-\hat{2}-\hat{1}$, $\hat{5}-\hat{4}-\hat{3}-\hat{2}-\hat{1}$, or $\hat{3}-\hat{2}-\hat{1}$.

Visual forces. Metaphorical tendencies attributed to images. Although we may be consciously unaware of these attributions, they contribute to the meanings given to the images by our minds. See *Representational gravity, Represen-tational momentum*, and *Landmark-attraction effect*.

Voyager. See Multilevel computer model.

Yearning vector. Bharucha's (1996) term for the sum of all forces acting on a given note in a given context. He describes this net force as an expectation, and explains it in terms of attention and the *Anchoring* of dissonances. See also *Tonal force vector*.

NOTES

1. INTRODUCTION

1. For a review, see Rothfarb 2002.

2. My prior publications (spanning almost two decades) used the terms "musical gravity" and "musical magnetism" to describe melodic tendencies. Introducing the terms "rhythmic gravity" and "metrical magnetism" suggests the use of (the more specific) "melodic gravity" as an alternative to my previous term "musical gravity" (and "melodic magnetism" as an alternative to "musical magnetism"). This book continues to apply "musical inertia" both to patterns of pitches and to patterns of durations.

3. Hallgjerd Asknes (2002) presents a theory of musical meaning that is (as she notes) consistent with the idea of musical forces, and I believe that the theory of expressive meaning sketched in the following pages is consistent with her excellent writings. Robert Hatten (2000, 2004) also presents a compelling theory of musical meaning. Although it may not contradict the theory described here, it differs substantially from it (the differences seem to flow more from the differences in *what* we seek to explain than from differences in *how* we think meaning arises in music). Nevertheless, Hatten's theory grants an important role to what he calls "virtual environmental forces," and he grounds his explanation of these forces in the theory of musical forces described in this book.

4. In fact, this is precisely what one of the two (anonymous) professional referees engaged by my publisher wrote in response to the previous paragraphs.

5. This example is from Port's Web page (http://www.cs.indiana.edu/~port/teach/103/sign.symbol.html), which offers a clear discussion of the differences between the terms "icon," "index," and "symbol."

6. According to Roland Barthes (1968, 50–51), "The association of sound and representation is the outcome of a collective training (for instance the learning of the French tongue); this association – which is the signification – is by no means arbitrary ... in the same way, Lévi-Strauss specified that the linguistic sign is arbitrary *a priori* but non-arbitrary *a posteriori*" (quoted in Clarke 2005, 40).

7. In fact, there is a sense in which even pitch is not literally in the sound itself. The process by which our musical minds select out one bunch of frequencies (to the exclusion of others) and then synthesize those disparate frequencies (which may even be "inharmonic") into our perception of a single percept is a complicated one (Terhardt 1974). The important point here is that throughout

this book, wherever I speak of "musical forces," the reader should understand that I am speaking not of tendencies literally present in the music as stimulus but of tendencies attributed by the minds of experienced listeners (who experience the music *as if* it were literally subject to such forces).

8. To describe knowledge as "embodied understanding" is to say that it is physically grounded. This does not require that the knowledge be gained only in a direct, hands-on fashion. Seeing motion at a distance is not direct bodily experience, but it contributes to embodied understanding and becomes physically grounded as soon as we understand that motion by relating it to motions of, and motions made by, our bodies. Hatten (2004, 131) notes that "embodiment, then, is understood as broader than that which is literally manifested through a body. We do not have to perform to understand and experience the embodiment of a gesture – we embody gesture imaginatively as participating listeners."

2. THINKING *ABOUT* MUSIC AND THINKING *IN* MUSIC

1. Tobias Matthay (1913) and Daniel W. Martin (1952) seem to have coined the term "auralize" independently.

2. In his *Meta-Variations* ([1968–69] 1995), Benjamin Boretz begins with – and returns repeatedly to – this same distinction (between thinking in music vs. thinking about music). The title of chapter 2 of Hallgjerd Aksnes's (2002) dissertation – "Being-In and Writing-About Music" – makes this same distinction, and the chapter itself not only illuminates both aspects of musical experience but also notes ways in which they can inform each other.

3. For more on analogies in music, see Kielian-Gilbert 1990.

4. For important writings on metaphor by a variety of other authors, see Ortony 1979.

5. For a more detailed account of the history of metaphor theory and its attendant views of thought and language, see Lakoff and Turner 1989. For a more detailed comparison of traditional theories with the theory of conceptual metaphor, see Lakoff and Johnson 1999.

6. See, for example, Bonds 1991; Coker 1972; Ferguson 1960; Guck 1981, 1991; and Hatten 1994, esp. chapter 7.

7. See, for example, Aksnes 1997, 2002; Bauer 2004; Brower 1997–98, 2000; Echard 1999; Fatone 2010; Feld 1981; McClary 1991; Mead 1997–98; O'Donnell 1999; Saslaw 1996, 1997–98, 2000; Saslaw and Walsh 1996; and Zbikowski 1997, 1997–98, 1998, 2002.

8. See, for example, Cusick 1994; Graybill 1990; McClary 1991; Mead 1999; and Pierce 1989.

9. For an example of its application to law, see Bjerre 2005.

10. Although some aspects of Schenker's theories (such as the degree to which the deepest-level structures shape musical experience) have proven controversial, the fundamental notions of his theories guide current music-theoretical thought to such an extent that most modern music theory concerning tonal music – including most of what presents itself as an alternative to Schenkerian thought – may fairly be described as resting upon his insights. I believe that most readers will find that the discussion in this chapter will acquaint them with enough of Schenker's ideas to follow the arguments I make in this book. Because those arguments primarily concern levels of structure close to the surface of the music, they do not engage the more controversial aspects of Schenker's theories.

11. In this book, where the symbol ˆ appears above a number, it means that number understood as a scale degree.

3. SOMETHING IN THE
WAY SHE MOVES

1. This chapter was originally published as Johnson and Larson 2003; it is
also a chapter in Johnson 2007.

2. An extensive treatment of metaphors for events and causes is given in
chapter 11 of Lakoff and Johnson (1999),
and Arnie Cox (1999b, 2006) has discussed musical instances of the States Are
Locations metaphor.

3. On purpose and agency in music,
see, for example, Clarke 2005; Cone
1974; Hatten 2004; and Maus (1988) 1997.
Davies (1994, 151) writes that "as Cavell
notes (1977), what is needed is an explanation of why we describe artworks in
terms usually confined to the description
of sentient creatures."

4. Note also that, in describing
something as "truly perceptual *rather
than* metaphorical, symbolic, or analogical" [emphasis added], Clarke seems
to assume that it can only be one of
these things. As noted in chapter 2,
"single-mechanism explanations" can be
misleading.

5. Walter Everett (1999) reached a
related conclusion about "Something."
Although speaking of a different section
of the song, Everett suggested that "the
structural core of the song's melody, a
fully supported $\hat{3}\,\hat{2}\,\hat{1}$ descent heard only in
the guitar solo, is best expressed in a musi-
cal fantasy. A poetic text here would only
get in the way" (251).

4. MELODIC FORCES

1. Huron's Figure 5.2 (2006, 76) summarizes the results for Vos and Troost
(1989).

2. In his later book Lerdahl conjec-
tures that "it may turn out to be more
accurate just to take attractional values
as correlating directly with degrees of
expected continuation." Nevertheless, he
retains the addition of opposing vectors to

quantify what he calls "the power of implicative denial" (2001, 170).

3. Given that physical magnetism is
not the only source domain we have for
experiencing attractions to a goal, the
physics fact that the strength of attraction to a magnetic dipole varies with the
inverse *cube* of the distance (rather than
the inverse *square* used in the algorithms
discussed above) may seem irrelevant.
The point here is to show that introspec-
tion about the phenomenon of physical
magnetism can lead to testable hypotheses
concerning musical magnetism. (Current
evidence, discussed in part 2, is consistent
with the notion that melodic magnetism
varies inversely with distance, but does not
appear capable of distinguishing between
inverse-square and inverse-cube effects.)

4. The addition of such contextual
qualifications makes Margulis's model
more complex than those of Bharucha and
Lerdahl, but it still allows one to calculate
stability values. The addition of such contextual qualification also brings her model
closer in line with the assertion (Larson
1997c) that relevant stability values are
better represented in a diachronic "event
hierarchy," such as a Schenkerian analysis
(e.g., Schenker (1935) 1979) or a similar
prolongational reduction (e.g., Westergaard 1975; or Lerdahl and Jackendoff
1985) rather than by a synchronic "tonal
hierarchy" (e.g., Krumhansl 1990; or Lerdahl 1988).

5. A THEORY OF MELODIC
EXPECTATION

1. In fact, by itself, the bottom-up
component of Narmour's model leads
to two contradictory conclusions: first,
that the larger an implicative interval,
the *stronger* its implications; and, second,
that the larger an interval, the greater the
number of implied continuations (that is,
possible "reversals"), thus the *less specific*
our expectations. Since, in experience,

stronger implications are *more* specific, this also suggests that, if Narmour's model is to capture important aspects of melodic expectation, then the top-down component must be included. Elizabeth Margulis (2003) notes as an advantage that, in her model of melodic expectation, the strength of an expectation tends to correlate with the specificity of that expectation.

2. The fact that the major scale has a common name helps make its status as an alphabet clear, but, in addition to being all the notes available with a given key signature, it might be described as the collection of pitch classes generated by going as far as possible around the circle of fifths without creating adjacent half steps (by "adjacent half steps," I mean something like E–F–F$\sharp$, which would require notation with a "chromatic semitone"). And the fact that the major triad has a common name helps makes its status as an alphabet clear, but, in addition to being all and only the scale degrees in the chord that ends most tonal pieces, it might be described as the collection of pitch classes generated by going as far as possible up the overtone series without creating steps. I mention these multiple derivations here not only to foreshadow the next topic in this chapter (steps and leaps) but also to underscore a recurring theme of this book – that the continued survival of complex mental/experiential phenomena (what Dawkins [1976] calls "memes") in our musical culture is usually best thought of in terms of more than one mechanism or explanation.

3. For transcriptions and analyses of Parker's entire performance, see Larson 1996a; Owens 1974; Russell 1959; and Woideck 1996.

4. For a transcription and analysis of other passages from this performance, see Larson 1997–98b.

5. The basic harmonies are G7 (measures 17 and 18), Cmin7 (measures 19 and 20), and A♭7 (measures 21 and 22). The tonic chord, B♭maj7, follows in measure 23.

6. G7 has altered ninths and an altered thirteenth; Cmin7 has a ninth and eleventh (as well as a passing thirteenth); and A♭7 has a ninth, a raised eleventh, and a thirteenth.

7. Although different jazz musicians might give these chord-scales different names, we can call them, respectively, "G altered-dominant" (if we assume D♭, as played in the Center part) or "G minor-dominant" (if we assume D, as played in the melody), "C Dorian," and "A♭ Lydian-dominant."

8. As of this writing, the only computer models that successfully implement the theory simply list candidate alphabets and provide a simple set of rules for choosing appropriate alphabets in generating completions. Those computer models are described in chapter 13.

9. For a transcription of Evans's entire performance, see Evans n.d.

10. Strict use of analytic notation (Larson 1996c) limits the analysis to stems, noteheads, and slurs. Rules governing the use of stems and slurs, such as prohibitions on changing direction under a single slur in anything but a three-note returning-note figure (like a complete-neighbor figure) or prohibitions on combining steps and leaps under a single slur, make the meaning of every elaboration clear. Furthermore, strict use requires that all notes and only those notes that are stemmed on a given level must appear (as a stemmed or unstemmed note) on the next more remote level. The meaning of any exceptions should be self-evident. This clarifies the assertions of the analysis and requires that every note must be accounted for. The result is that each note of elaboration appears as an unstemmed notehead in a

slurred figure at one and only one level of structure. This will have additional advantages, as we shall see below.

11. All proper step collections that are closed and complete satisfy the condition of "maximal evenness" as described in recent publications on scale theory (e.g., Balzano 1980, 1982; Clough and Douthett 1991; Clough and Myerson 1985; Cohn 1996; and Gamer 1967). They also satisfy the "nonadjacent half-step hypothesis" tested by Jeff Pressing (1978), which is also called the "semitone constraint" by Dmitri Tymoczko (1997). Jay Rahn's (1991) discussion of "ambiguities" and "differences" in seven-tone collections is also relevant here. Pressing finds that many chord-scales important in jazz practice satisfy his hypothesis. Tymoczko's work offers his constraint as an important connection between jazz and impressionism. Recent work by Keith Waters (2005) builds on these ideas to illuminate the musical language of Herbie Hancock.

12. Huron (2006, 110) also argues that listeners generate multiple conflicting predictions about what will happen next, using different internal representations.

13. Schenker's *Counterpoint* ([1910] 1987, 188–189) describes how our experience of a passage might include rapid-fire retroactive reinterpretations of the functions of single pitches (his example is a passage from Schubert's "Der Kreuzzug").

14. For an illuminating view of the place of repetition in music, see Zuckerkandl 1956, 212ff.

15. Although such analyses are often called "reductive" (implying that they are constructed in a bottom-up fashion), the theory of musical forces follows the work of Douglas Hofstadter and colleagues in arguing that mental representations of the types that create such expectations combine bottom-up and top-down processing

(see, e.g., Meredith 1986; and Hofstadter et al. 1995).

16. Marvin Minsky's 1986 *Society of Mind* offers an insightful view of multiple mental mechanisms.

17. Van Egmond and Butler (1997) extend this work on diatonic-collection subsets by considering subsets of melodic-minor and harmonic-minor collections and their possible relationship to key determination.

18. Theoretically further levels are needed for a complete specification. As a practical matter, however, we know that D–F–A specifies Dorian. But this is because of the special status of the perfect fifth within leap collections. We know, in other words, that D–F–A may be thought of as containing the more basic level D–A, which contains the more basic level D.

19. These computer algorithms were first proposed by Krumhansl and Schmuckler (see Krumhansl 1990) but have been subsequently refined by others (Huron and Parncutt 1993; Temperley 1999; Toiviainen and Krumhansl 2003).

6. RHYTHM, METER, AND MUSICAL FORCES

1. Although the discussion that follows describes musical gestures in terms of pitch and duration patterns, Hatten also points out that "gestures may be comprised of any of the elements of music, although they are not reducible to them; they are perceptually *synthetic* gestalts with *emergent* meaning, not simply 'rhythmic shapes'" (2004, 94).

2. The D in measure 3 could also be called a rearticulated suspension. On metric stability, see Westergaard 1975 and Berry 1976.

3. Lerdahl (2001, 285–297) makes this same analogy. He notes that attack points closer to a metrically stable moment are felt to be pulled toward that moment with

something analogous to melodic magnetism (which he calls "attraction"); he goes on to discuss "metrical attractions."

4. On the relationships between the rules for and the effects of sixteenth-century sacred polyphony, see also the work of Dalia Cohen 1971.

5. Christopher Hasty (1997, 108–115) offers an interesting and extensive discussion of these two rhythms.

6. Notice, however, that the opening of the Boccherini Quintet suggests that its first note is $\hat{8}$ and not $\hat{1}$ – in a way that not incidentally respects Schenker's notion of the "obligatory register" (the register in which ultimate melodic closure must occur).

7. See Krebs 1987, 1999, and Kaminsky 1989. Greer 1998 discusses Charles Seeger's expansions of dissonance to other domains.

8. The following discussion owes much to conversations with Anne Danielsen.

9. For an exceptionally thorough and insightful discussion, see Danielsen 2006.

10. In fact, although the comparison here is between African rhythm and west European pitch, it is worth remembering that Simha Arom (2004) has produced a substantial body of work studying temperament and tuning in African music. For an overview and listing of further research, see Fernando 2007.

11. Theoretically, further levels are needed for a complete specification. As a practical matter, however, we know that D–F–A specifies Dorian. But this is because of the special status of the perfect fifth within leap collections; that is, we know that D–F–A may be thought of as containing the more basic level D–A, which contains the more basic level D.

12. Asymmetrical subsets (akin to those shown in Example 6.13a) may be important patterns in African music involving such time lines (see, esp., Agawu 2006), but they do not articulate the ref-

erential meter made clearly evident by the feet of the dancers.

13. By the way, although the diatonic collection is asymmetrical, it is not necessarily *heard as* asymmetrical. Most tonal listeners – if asked to sing a note, then up a step, then up a step, and then up a step – will sing up a whole step, up a whole step, and then up a *half* step.

14. I am, however, somewhat skeptical of a third point of view: that it is simultaneously heard in three and four. It may be that, like the famous "rabbit-duck," the bell pattern can and is heard sometimes in three and sometimes in four (that is my experience). It may be that some listeners quickly move from one to the other interpretation (that is also my experience). And it may even be that the bell pattern can be heard as "threeness against an underlying four" or "fourness against an underlying three" (and, as long as one of the meters is privileged as "the underlying one," I think that this is also my experience). But I simply am unable to imagine what it would mean to say that it is experienced as being in both at the same time – just as I am skeptical that one can see both a rabbit and a duck at the same time. (Nevertheless, I am also skeptical of my own skepticism – that I cannot imagine such an experience of simultaneous contradictory meters may simply be a shortcoming on my part, and one that is not shared by African musicians.)

15. See sources cited in chapter 5, note 11.

16. Notice also that in chapter 14 I present a list of questions concerning how the ideas of this book may be applied to music of other world cultures. One type of question involves explaining exceptions to the generalizations offered here. Because the boundaries created by stable pitches seem like the most likely place for us to find exceptions to the avoidance of consecutive semitones

(because the boundaries reduce the possibility of confusion, one of the reasons for avoiding consecutive semitones), the analogy being discussed here may lead us to add another question to that list: "In what musical cultures are repeated 'time lines' (such as African bell patterns) built of successive short and long durations such that successive short durations tend to be avoided – and in these cultures, do successive short durations occur most often (if at all) at stable boundary pitches?" The approach taken in this chapter suggests that we explore both the physical ease associated with performing the patterns (at the specific tempos in which they are used) and the frequency with which exceptions occur at boundaries (created by more metrically stable beats).

7. ANALYSES

1. An aside here not only adds to our understanding of this passage but also illustrates a point made by William Pelto (1994) – that the theory of musical forces can give us a clearer and more accurate formulation of the principles that guide rules of voice-leading and doubling than traditional theory does. Traditional theory might say that our expectation for chordal sevenths to resolve down by step leads us to expect $\hat{4}$ (on "Dic" and "up"), as seventh of V, to resolve down to $\hat{4}$. Here this explanation seems sensible, but this expectation is not true of all chordal sevenths. For example, the soprano line $\hat{3}$–$\hat{4}$–$\hat{5}$, when harmonized in parallel tenths by the bass $\hat{1}$–$\hat{2}$–$\hat{3}$ often results in $\hat{4}$ harmonized by V, a chordal seventh that resolves upward (giving in to inertia). Although the theory of musical forces does not deny a general expectation that chord sevenths in many situations will resolve downward, it regards that tendency as an emergent property of the musical forces operating in specific contexts.

2. Larson 2009 makes this point and cites additional studies.

3. In Schenkerian theory a "hidden repetition" is the appearance of a single musical pattern on more than one structural level of a piece of music. A "confirmation" is a hidden repetition in which two different versions of a hidden repetition are completed at the same time.

4. For a complete score and another analysis of this piece, see Lindsay 1995.

5. For Parker, see Larson 1996a.

6. The ideas that transcriptions are in some sense analyses and that analyses are in some sense transcriptions are further explored in Larson 2009, 2.

7. This example is also rendered in "strict use of analytic notation"; see Larson 1996c and chapter 5, the section titled "The Stepwise Displacement of Auralized Traces." For a more complete analysis of the same piece, see Larson 2002.

8. CONVERGING EVIDENCE

1. In preparing this chapter I had the benefit of reading an early draft of "Energetics" (Rothfarb 2002), which led me to additional sources not referred to in the final version of Rothfarb's article. Hatten also discusses the school of energetics in his theory of musical gesture (see, esp., 2004, 113ff.).

2. An early draft of Rothfarb's article "Energetics" (2002) notes that "the extraordinary ethical power of music was thought to derive from its inherent motion – motion being the recognized foundation of existence." Gafurius was well aware of this intellectual legacy, which he documented in *Theorica musice* ([1492] 1993). Rothfarb (Unpublished ms., n.d.) discusses nineteenth-century empathist theories on music.

3. As noted in chapter 5, Rudolf Arnheim (1966, 1974) shows nicely how this anthropomorphizing relies on our propensity to attribute dynamic tendencies to

the objects of our perceptions, and argues (1986) that musical forces allow us to do the same with music.

9. EVIDENCE FROM EXPERIMENTS IN VISUAL PERCEPTION AND NEUROSCIENCE

1. For an excellent overview of Freyd's "representational momentum," see Thornton and Hubbard 2002.

2. See also Freyd's website, http://dynamic.uoregon.edu/~jjf/rm-rect/, which offers a real-time display of the phenomenon.

3. Current research, indicating that mirror-neuron systems also play a central role in human emotion and empathy, seems to provide evidence consistent with the larger theory of expressive meaning described in chapter 1.

4. The literature on representational momentum tends to describe the effect as an "error." Although this term seems accurate in some ways, it is also possible to regard the effect as an advantageous "ability" afforded by natural selection to the benefit of those who experience it.

10. EVIDENCE FROM COMPOSITIONS AND IMPROVISATIONS

1. The articles are Beach 1984, 1987; Berry 1980; Burkhart 1978, 1990; Cadwallader 1983, 1984, 1988, 1990; Cadwallader and Pastille 1992; Carpenter 1983; Everett 1990; Forte 1983; Jonas 1982; Kamien 1983; Lester 1979; Neumeyer 1982; Oster 1983; Rothgeb 1980, 1983, 1990; Schachter 1983a, 1983b; Schmalfeldt 1985; and Wen, 1990.

2. The journals and book collections include (in alphabetical order) *Aspects of Schenkerian Theory, Intégral, Journal of Music Theory, Music Analysis, Music Perception, Music Theory Spectrum, Schenker Studies, Theory and Practice,* and *Trends in Schenkerian Research.*

3. My thanks to an (anonymous) reviewer of this book whose question about

this movement led me to these hidden repetitions.

4. An additional problem may arise in assigning stability values to some patterns that include chromatic pitches; compare Figures 4.23 and 4.24 in Lerdahl 2001.

12. EVIDENCE FROM A LISTENER-JUDGMENT EXPERIMENT

1. The experiment was administered by a computer program written using MAX, an object-oriented, music-programming language (MAX was initially distributed by Opcode Systems; it is now being supported by Cycling '74). The experiment was designed as a stand-alone application to be run on a Macintosh PowerPC computer using the standard piano sound from the MIDI-controllable OMS/Quick-Time instruments as a sound source. All velocities were controlled via MIDI at 80 on a scale of 0 to 127; each note was 450 ms long with a 150 ms break between pitches. Readers may download the experiment software at a website maintained by Leigh VanHandel, http://www.ccrma.stanford .edu/~leigh/research.html.

2. One participant self-reported compromised hearing but reported no difficulties in completing the experiment.

3. It might have been better from the standpoint of experimental design to use a counterbalanced order. Fortunately, however, the use of random ordering achieved a similar result here; it meant that subjects heard roughly even numbers of each ordering.

13. EVIDENCE FROM COMPARING COMPUTER MODELS WITH PRODUCTION-EXPERIMENT RESULTS

1. Elsewhere I have called this model "Next Generation" (see Larson 2004, 470).

2. One simplification is that for every reference alphabet in Example 13.1, there is only one goal alphabet, and that example includes no other proper subset of that ref-

erence alphabet that has more notes than that goal alphabet.

3. The result obeys Schoenberg's (1978) dictum about "neutralization" (which could be restated here as a tendency of altered step collections to use trace displacement to return to unaltered step collections).

4. Elsewhere I have called this model "Voyager" (see Larson 2004, 476).

5. Even if we were to limit ourselves to diatonic responses within a fifth above and below the last note of a beginning (limits that Lake's participants did not adhere to), we would still have 38,400 unique responses.

14. SUMMARY AND PROSPECTS

1. In other words, we have levels of expectation. In a particular context, for example, inertia may lead to the expectation that a pattern will repeat. At the same time, and in the same context, we may have a higher-level stylistic expectation that there will not be "too much" pattern repetition. The expectations described by the theory of musical forces are lower-level expectations.

2. Mark Johnson (2007) makes these points eloquently, persuasively, and in much greater depth in his book *The Meaning of the Body: Aesthetics of Human Understanding*. Chapter 3 of the book you are now reading was coauthored by Johnson, and that chapter also appears with the title "Music and the Flow of Meaning" in Johnson's book cited above.

3. For a wonderful example of such coordination, see Chris Bliss juggling with the music that ends the Beatles album *Abbey Road* (available at http://www.youtube.com).

BIBLIOGRAPHY

Aarden, Brett. 2003. "Dynamic Melodic Expectancy." Ph.D. dissertation, Ohio State University.

Agawu, Kofi. 2006. "Structural Analysis or Cultural Analysis? Competing Perspectives on the 'Standard Pattern' of West African Rhythm." *Journal of the American Musicological Society* 59 (1): 1–46.

Akioshi, Toshiko. 1976. "I Ain't Gonna Ask No More." *Tales of a Courtesan (Oirantan)*.

Aksnes, Hallgjerd. 1997. "A Cognitive Approach to Musical Analysis: Metaphorical Projection in Music." *Proceedings of the Third Triennial ESCOM Conference in Uppsala, Sweden* (Uppsala University), 551–556.

———. 2002. "Perspectives of Musical Meaning: A Study Based on Selected Works by Geirr Tveitt." Ph.D. thesis, University of Oslo.

Alperson, Philip. 1980. "'Musical Time' and Music as an 'Art of Time.'" *Journal of Aesthetics and Art Criticism* 38 (4): 407–417.

Amuedo, John W. 1996. "Computational Description of Extended Tonality." Master's thesis, University of Southern California, Los Angeles.

Arnheim, Rudolf. 1966. *Toward a Psychology of Art: Collected Essays.* Berkeley: University of California Press.

———. 1974. *Art and Visual Perception: A Psychology of the Creative Eye.* The New Version. Berkeley: University of California Press.

———. 1986. Perceptual Dynamics in Musical Expression. In Rudolf Arnheim, *New Essays on the Psychology of Art.* Berkeley: University of California Press.

Arom, Simha. 2004. *African Polyphony and Polyrhythm: Musical Structure and Methodology.* Translated by Martin Thom, Barbara Tuckett, and Raymond Boyd. Cambridge: Cambridge University Press.

Augustinus, Aurelius. (391) 1962. *Musik.* Translated by Carl Johann Perl. Paderborn: Ferdinand Schöningh.

Bach, C. P. E. (1753) 1949. *Essay on the True Art of Playing Keyboard Instruments.* Translated and edited by William Mitchell. New York: Norton.

Baker, James. 1983. "Schenkerian Analysis and Post-Tonal Music." In *Aspects of Schenkerian Theory,* edited by David Beach, 153–186. New Haven: Yale University Press.

Balzano, Gerald J. 1980. "The Group-Theoretic Description of 12-fold and Microtonal Pitch Systems." *Computer Music Journal* 4:66–84.

———. 1982. "The Pitch Set as a Level of Description for Studying Musical Pitch Perception." In *Music, Mind, and Brain,*

edited by M. Clynes, 231–351. New
York: Plenum.

Barthes, Roland. 1968. *Elements of Semiology*. Translated by A. Lavers and C.
Smith. New York: Hill and Wang.

Bauer, Amy. 2004."'Tone-Color, Movement, Changing Harmonic Planes':
Cognition, Constraints and Conceptual Blends in Modernist Music." In *The
Pleasure of Modernist Music: Listening,
Meaning, Intention, Ideology,* edited by
Arved Ashby, 121–152. Eastman Studies
in Music. Rochester, NY: University of
Rochester Press.

Beach, David. 1984. "Motive and Structure in the *Andante* Movement of
Mozart's Piano Sonata K. 545." *Music
Analysis* 3 (3): 227–241.

———. 1987. "Motive and Structure in
Beethoven's Piano Sonata Op. 110. Part I:
The First Movement." *Intégral* 1:1–29.

Becker, Judith. 1981. "Hindu-Buddhist
Time in Javanese Gamelan Music." In
The Study of Time IV, edited by J. F. Fraser, 161–172. New York: Springer-Verlag.

Benjamin, William. 1981. "Schenker's Theory and the Future of Music." *Journal of
Music Theory* 25 (1): 155–173.

———. 1984. "Models of Underlying
Tonal Structure: How Can They Be
Abstract and How Should They Be Abstract?" *Music Theory Spectrum* 4:28–50.

Berry, Wallace. 1976. *Structural Functions
in Music.* Englewood Cliffs, NJ: Prentice Hall.

———. 1980. "On Structural Levels in
Music." *Music Theory Spectrum* 2:19–45.

Bharucha, Jamshed J. 1984a. "Anchoring
Effects in Music: The Resolution of Dissonance." *Cognitive Psychology* 16 (4):
485–518.

———. 1984b. "Event Hierarchies, Tonal
Hierarchies, and Assimilation." *Journal of Experimental Psychology* 113 (3):
421–425.

———. 1996. "Melodic Anchoring." *Music
Perception* 13 (3): 383–400.

Bjerre, Carl S. 2005. "Mental Capacity as
Metaphor." *International Journal for the
Semiotics of Law* 18:101–140.

Blum, David. 1977. *Casals and the Art of
Interpretation.* Berkeley: University of
California Press.

Bonds, Mark Evans. 1991. *Wordless Rhetoric: Musical Form and the Metaphor of
Oration.* Cambridge, MA: Harvard
University Press.

Boomsliter, P. C., and W. Creel. 1979.
"Prestimulus Perceptual Activity in
Perception of Tone in Musical Sequences." *Journal of the Acoustical Society of America* 65 (1): S123.

Boretz, Benjamin A. (1968–69) 1995.
Meta-Variations: Studies in the Foundations of Musical Thought. Red Hook,
NY: Open Space.

———. 1989. "The Logic of What?" *Journal of Music Theory* 33 (1): 107–116.

Bregman, Albert S. 1990. *Auditory Scene
Analysis: The Perceptual Organization
of Sound.* Cambridge, MA: MIT Press.

Brower, Candace. 1993. "Memory and the
Perception of Rhythm." *Music Theory
Spectrum* 15 (1): 19–35.

———. 1997–98. "Pathway, Blockage, and
Containment." In *Density 21.5. Theory
and Practice* 22–23:35–54.

———. 2000. "A Cognitive Theory of Musical Meaning." *Journal of Music Theory*
44 (2): 323–379.

Brown, Helen. 1988. "The Interplay of Set
Content and Temporal Context in a
Functional Theory of Tonality Perception." *Music Perception* 5:219–250.

Brown, Helen, and David Butler. 1981.
"Diatonic Trichords as Minimal Cue
Cells." *In Theory Only* 5 (6–7): 39–55.

Brown, Helen, David Butler, and Mari
Riess Jones. 1994. "Musical and Temporal Influences on Key Discovery." *Music
Perception* 11 (4): 371–407.

Browne, Richmond. 1981. "Tonal Implications of the Diatonic Set." *In Theory
Only* 5 (6–7): 3–21.

———. 1982. "The Tonal Art of Gerry Mulligan." Paper presented at the University of Michigan, Ann Arbor.

———. 1985. "The Dialectic of Good Continuation in Tonal Music." *Music Analysis* 4:5–13.

Bryant, D. J., and I. Subbiah. 1994. "Subjective Landmarks in Perception and Memory for Spatial Location." *Canadian Journal of Experimental Psychology* 48:119–139.

Burkhart, Charles. 1978. "Schenker's 'Motivic Parallelisms.'" *Journal of Music Theory* 22:145–175.

———. 1990. "Departures from the Norm in Two Schumann Songs." In *Schenker Studies*, edited by Hedi Siegel, 4–14. Cambridge: Cambridge University Press.

Butler, David. 1989. "Describing the Perception of Tonality in Music: A Proposal for a Theory of Intervallic Rivalry." *Music Perception* 6:219–241.

———. 1998. "Tonal Bootstrapping: Re-Thinking the Intervallic Rivalry Model." In *Music, Mind, and Science,* edited by Suk Won Yi, 7–12. Seoul: Seoul National University Press.

Cadwallader, Allen. 1983. "Motivic Unity and Integration of Structural Levels in Brahms's Intermezzo Op. 119, No. 1." *Theory and Practice* 8 (2): 5–24.

———. 1984. "Schenker's Unpublished Graphic Analysis of Brahms's Intermezzo Op. 117, No. 2: Tonal Structure and Concealed Motivic Repetition." *Music Theory Spectrum* 6:1–13.

———. 1988. "Foreground Motivic Ambiguity: Its Clarification at Middleground Levels in Selected Late Piano Pieces of Johannes Brahms." *Music Analysis* 7 (1): 59–91.

———. 1990. "Form and Tonal Process: The Design of Different Structural Levels." In *Trends in Schenkerian Research,* edited by Allen Cadwallader, 1–21. New York: Schirmer Books.

Cadwallader, Allen, and William Pastille. 1992. "Schenker's High-Level Motives." *Journal of Music Theory* 36 (1): 119–148.

Caplin, William Earl. 1998. *Classical Form: A Theory of Formal Functions for the Instrumental Music of Haydn, Mozart, and Beethoven.* New York: Oxford University Press.

Carlsen, James C. 1981. "Some Factors Which Influence Melodic Expectancy." *Psychomusicology* 1:12–29.

Carlsen, James C., and Pierre L. Divenyi, and Jack A. Taylor. 1970. "A Preliminary Study of Melodic Expectancy in Melodic Configurations." *Council for Research in Music Education Bulletin* 22:4–12.

Carpenter, Patricia. 1983. "*Grundgestalt* as Tonal Function." *Music Theory Spectrum* 5:15–38.

Cavanaugh, Joanne P. 1998. "Arithmetic of the Soul." *Johns Hopkins Magazine* (February).

Cavell, Stanley. 1977. *Must We Mean What We Say?: A Book of Essays.* Cambridge: Cambridge University Press.

Cazden, Norman. 1980. "The Definition of Consonance and Dissonance." *International Review of the Aesthetics and Sociology of Music* 11 (2): 123–168.

Chomsky, Noam. 1957. *Syntactic Structures.* The Hague: Mouton.

Christensen, Thomas. 1993. *Rameau and Musical Thought in the Enlightenment.* Cambridge: Cambridge University Press.

Clark, William. 1982. "Heinrich Schenker on the Nature of the Seventh Chord." *Journal of Music Theory* 26 (2): 221–257.

Clarke, Eric. 2005. *Ways of Listening: An Ecological Approach to the Perception of Musical Meaning.* New York: Oxford University Press.

Clough, John, and Jack Douthett. 1991. "Maximally Even Sets." *Journal of Music Theory* 35 (1): 93–173.

Clough, John, and Gerald Myerson. 1985. "Variety and Multiplicity in Diatonic

Systems." *Journal of Music Theory* 29:249–270.

Clynes, Manfred. 1995. "Microstructural Musical Linguistics: Composer's Pulses are Liked Best by the Best Musicians." *Cognition – International Journal of Cognitive Science* 55:269–310.

Cohen, Dalia. 1971. "Palestrina Counterpoint – A Musical Expression of Unexcited Speech." *Journal of Music Theory* 15:84–111.

Cohn, Richard. 1996. "Maximally Smooth Cycles, Hexatonic Systems, and the Analysis of Late-Romantic Triadic Progressions." *Music Analysis* 15 (1): 9–40.

Cohn, Richard and Douglas Dempster. 1992. "Hierarchical Unity, Plural Unities: Toward a Reconciliation." In *Disciplining Music: Musicology and Its Canons,* edited by Katherine Bergeron and Philip Bohlman, 156–181. Chicago: University of Chicago Press.

Coker, Jerry. 1964. *Improvising Jazz.* Englewood Cliffs: NJ: Prentice Hall.

Coker, Wilson. 1972. *Music and Meaning.* New York: Free Press.

Cone, Edward T. 1974. *The Composer's Voice.* Berkeley: University of California Press.

Cooke, Deryck. 1959. *The Language of Music.* New York: Oxford University Press.

Coppola, Francis Ford, dir. 1986. *Peggy Sue Got Married.* Warner Bros.

Cox, Arnie. 1997. "Metaphors in Musical Discourse." Paper presented at the West Coast Conference on Music Theory and Analysis, Santa Barbara, CA.

———. 1999a. "Imagined Meaning in Immediate and Reflective Musical Experience." *Music Perception* 16 (4): 467–473.

———. 1999b. "The Metaphoric Logic of Musical Motion and Space." Ph.D. dissertation, University of Oregon.

———. 2006. "Hearing, Feeling, Grasping Gestures." In *Music and Gesture,* edited by Elaine King and Anthony

Gritten, 45–60. Hampshire, England: Ashgate.

Cuddy, L. L., and C. A. Lunney. 1995. "Expectancies Generated by Melodic Intervals: Perceptual Judgments of Melodic Continuity." *Perception & Psychophysics* 57:451–462.

Cumming, Naomi 2000. *The Sonic Self: Musical Subjectivity and Signification.* Bloomington: Indiana University Press.

Cusick, Susanne G. 1994. "Feminist Theory, Music Theory, and the Mind/Body Problem." *Perspectives of New Music* 32 (1): 8–27.

Danielsen, Anne 2006. *Presence and Pleasure: The Funk Grooves of James Brown and Parliament.* Middletown, CT: Wesleyan University Press.

Davies, Stephen. 1994. *Musical Meaning and Expression.* Ithaca, NY: Cornell University Press.

Dawkins, Richard. 1976. *The Selfish Gene.* New York: Oxford University Press.

Dembski, Stephen. 1988. "Steps and Skips from Order and Content: Aspects of a Generalized Step-Class System." Paper presented at the National Meeting of the Society for Music Theory, Baltimore, MD.

Densmore, F. 1926. *Pawnee Music.* Bulletin 93 of the Smithsonian Institution, Bureau of American Ethnology. Washington, DC: Government Printing Office.

Deutsch, Diana. 1978. "Delayed Pitch Comparisons and the Principle of Pitch Proximity." *Perception & Psychophysics* 23:227–230.

Deutsch, Diana, and John Feroe. 1981. The Internal Representation of Pitch Sequences in Tonal Music. *Psychological Review* 88 (6): 503–522.

Dewey, John. (1934) 1979. *Art as Experience.* New York: Putnam.

Dibben, Nicola. 1994. "The Cognitive Reality of Hierarchic Structure in Tonal and Atonal Music." *Music Perception* 12 (1): 1–25.

Dogantan, Mine. 2002. *Mathis Lussy: A Pioneer in Studies of Expressive Performance.* New York: Peter Lang.

Dowling, W. J. 1967. "Rhythmic Fission and the Perceptual Organization of Tone Sequences." Ph.D. dissertation, Harvard University.

Echard, William. 1999. "An Analysis of Neil Young's 'Powderfinger' Based on Mark Johnson's Image Schemata." *Popular Music* 18 (1): 133–144.

Eitan, Zohar. 1997. "Registral Direction and Melodic Implication." Paper presented at the Sixteenth Congress of the International Musicological Society, London.

Ellis, C. J. 1969. "Structure and Significance in Aboriginal Song." *Mankind, Australia* 7 (5): 3–14.

Evans, Bill. n.d. "Who Can I Turn To?" Unattributed transcription of a performance from *Bill Evans at Town Hall.* TRO Ludlow Music.

Everett, Walter. 1990. "Grief in *Winterreise:* A Schenkerian Perspective." *Music Analysis* 9 (2): 157–175.

————. 1999. *The Beatles as Musicians.* New York: Oxford University Press.

Fatone, Gina. 2010."'You'll Break Your Heart Trying to Play It Like You Sing It': Intermodal Imagery and the Transmission of Scottish Classical Bagpiping." *Ethnomusicology* 54:3 (fall): 395–424.

Feld, Steven. 1981."'Flow Like a Waterfall': The Metaphors of Kaluli Musical Theory." *Yearbook For Traditional Music* 13:22–47.

————. 1988. "Aesthetics as Iconicity of Style, or 'Lift-up-over-sounding': Getting into the Kaluli Groove." *Yearbook for Traditional Music* 20:74–113.

Ferguson, Donald. 1960. *Music as Metaphor: The Elements of Expression.* Minneapolis: University of Minnesota Press.

Fernando, Nathalie. 2007. "Study of African Scales: A New Experimental Approach for Cognitive Aspects."

TRANS – Transcultural Music Review 11, article 3.

Fétis, François-Joseph. (1844) 1994. *Esquisse de l'histoire de l'harmonie: An English-Language Translation of the François-Joseph Fétis History of Harmony.* Translated and edited by Mary I. Arlin. Stuyvesant, NY: Pendragon.

Finke, Ronald A., and Jennifer J. Freyd. 1985. "Transformations of Visual Memory Induced by Implied Motions of Pattern Elements." *Journal of Experimental Psychology: Learning, Memory, and Cognition* 11:780–794.

————. 1989. "Mental Extrapolation and Cognitive Penetrability: Reply to Ranney, and Some Other Matters and Proposals for Evaluative Criteria." *Journal of Experimental Psychology: General* 118:403–408.

Finke, Ronald A., Jennifer J. Freyd, and G. C. W. Shyi. 1986. "Implied Velocity and Acceleration Induce Transformations of Visual Memory." *Journal of Experimental Psychology: General* 115:175–188.

Folio, Cynthia. 1995. "An Analysis of Polyrhythm in Selected Improvised Jazz Solos." In *Concert Music, Rock, and Jazz since 1945,* edited by Elizabeth West Marvin and Richard Hermann, 103–134. Rochester, NY: University of Rochester Press.

Forte, Allen. 1983. "Motive and Rhythmic Contour in the Alto Rhapsody." *Journal of Music Theory* 27 (2): 255–271.

Freyd, Jennifer J. 1983. "The Mental Representation of Movement When Static Stimuli Are Viewed." *Perception & Psychophysics* 33:575–581.

————. 1993. "Five Hunches about Perceptual Processes and Dynamic Representations." In *Attention and Performance XIV: Synergies in Experimental Psychology, Artificial Intelligence, and Cognitive Neuroscience – A Silver Jubilee,* edited by D. Meyer and S. Kornblum, 99–119. Cambridge, MA: MIT Press.

Freyd, Jennifer J., and Ronald A. Finke. 1984. "Representational Momentum." *Journal of Experimental Psychology: Learning, Memory, and Cognition* 10:126–132.

———. 1985. "A Velocity Effect for Representational Momentum." *Bulletin of the Psychonomic Society* 23:443–446.

Freyd, Jennifer J., and J. Q. Johnson. 1987. "Probing the Time Course of Representational Momentum." *Journal of Experimental Psychology: Learning, Memory, and Cognition* 13:259–268.

Freyd, Jennifer J., Michael H. Kelly, and Michael L. DeKay. 1990. "Representational Momentum in Memory for Pitch." *Journal of Experimental Psychology: Learning, Memory, and Cognition* 16:1107–1117.

Freyd, Jennifer J., Teresa M. Pantzer, and Jeannette L. Cheng. 1988. "Representing Statics as Forces in Equilibrium." *Journal of Experimental Psychology: General* 117:395–407.

Fyk, Janina. 1995. *Melodic Intonation, Psychoacoustics, and the Violin*. Zielona Góra, Poland: Organon.

Gaffurio, Franchino (1492) 1993. *The Theory of Music*. Translated by Walter K. Kreyzig. Edited by Claude V. Palisca. New Haven: Yale University Press.

Gamer, Carlton. 1967. "Some Combinatorial Resources of Equal-Tempered Systems." *Journal of Music Theory* 11:32–59.

Gardner, Howard. 1983. *Frames of Mind: The Theory of Multiple Intelligences*. New York: Basic Books.

Gibbs, Raymond. 1994. *The Poetics of Mind: Figurative Thought, Language, and Understanding*. Cambridge: Cambridge University Press.

Gjerdingen, Robert O. (1994) 1999. "Apparent Motion in Music?" in *Musical Networks: Parallel Distributed Perception and Performance*, edited by N. Griffith and P. Todd, 141–173. Cambridge, MA: MIT Press.

———. 1996. "Courtly Behaviors." *Music Perception* 13 (3): 365–382.

———. 2007. *Music in the Galant Style*. New York: Oxford University Press.

Gonda, Janos. 1971–72. "Problems of Tonality and Function in Modern Jazz Improvisation." *Jazzforschung/Jazz Research* 3 (4): 194–205.

Graybill, Roger. 1990. "Towards a Pedagogy of Gestural Rhythm." *Journal of Music Theory Pedagogy* 4 (1): 1–50.

Greer, Taylor A. 1998. *A Question of Balance: Charles Seeger's Philosophy of Music*. Berkeley: University of California Press.

Guck, Marion A. 1981. "Metaphors in Musical Discourse: The Contribution of Imagery to Analysis." Ph.D. dissertation, University of Michigan.

———. 1989. "Beethoven as Dramatist." *College Music Symposium* 29:8–18.

———. 1991. "Two Types of Metaphoric Transfer." In *Metaphor: A Musical Dimension*, edited by Jamie C. Kassler, 1–12. Sydney: Currency.

Gur, Golan. 2008. "Body, Forces, and Paths: Metaphor and Embodiment in Jean-Phillipe Rameau's Conceptualization of Tonal Space." *Music Theory Online* 14 (1). Available at http://www.mtosmt.org/issues/mto.08.14.gur.html.

Gushee, Lawrence. 1981. "Lester Young's 'Shoeshine Boy.'" In *Report of the Twelfth Congress (Berkeley, 1977) of the International Musicological Society*, edited by Daniel Heartz and Bonnie Wade, 151–169. Kassel: Barenreiter.

Halm, August. (1900) 1905. *Harmonielehre*. Leipzig: Göschen'sche Verlagshandlung.

Halpern, A. R., and M. H. Kelly. 1993. "Memory Biases in Left versus Right Implied Motion." *Journal of Experimental Psychology: Learning, Memory, and Cognition* 19:471–484.

Hanslick, Eduard. (1891) 1986. *On the Musically Beautiful*. Translated by Geoffrey Payzant. Indianapolis: Hackett.

Harrison, Sir George. 1969. "Something." *Abbey Road*. EMI: CD P7464462, Apple.

Hasty, Christopher F. 1997. *Meter as Rhythm*. New York: Oxford University Press.

Hatten, Robert S. 1985. "The Place of Intertextuality in Music Studies." *American Journal of Semiotics* 3 (4): 69–82.

———. 1994. *Musical Meaning in Beethoven: Markedness, Correlation, and Interpretation*. Bloomington: Indiana University Press.

———. 2004. *Interpreting Musical Gestures, Topics, and Tropes: Mozart, Beethoven, and Schubert*. Bloomington: Indiana University Press.

Hindemith, Paul. 1945. *The Craft of Musical Composition*. Book 1, *Theory*. Translated by Arthur Mendel. New York: Associated Music Publishers.

Hofstadter, Douglas R. 1979. *Gödel, Escher, Bach: An Eternal Golden Braid*. New York: Basic Books.

———. 1985. *Metamagical Themas: Questing for the Essence of Mind and Pattern*. New York: Basic Books.

———. 1987. "Fluid Analogies and Human Creativity." CRCC Technical Report #16. Bloomington, IN: Center for Research on Concepts and Cognition, Indiana University.

Hofstadter, Douglas R., and the Fluid Analogies Research Group. 1995. *Fluid Concepts and Creative Analogies: Computer Models of the Fundamental Mechanisms of Thought*. New York: Basic Books.

Hubbard, Timothy L. 1990. "Cognitive Representation of Linear Motion: Possible Direction and Gravity Effects in Judged Displacement." *Memory and Cognition* 18:299–309.

———. 1994. "Judged Displacement: A Modular Process?" *American Journal of Psychology* 107:359–373.

———. 1995a. "Cognitive Representation of Linear Motion: Evidence for Representational Friction and Gravity Analogues." *Journal of Experimental Psychology: Learning, Memory, and Cognition* 21:241–254.

———. 1995b. "Environmental Invariants in the Representation of Motion: Implied Dynamics and Representational Momentum, Gravity, Friction, and Centripetal Force." *Psychonomic Bulletin and Review* 2:322–338.

———. 1997. "Target Size and Displacement along the Axis of Implied Gravitational Attraction: Effects of Implied Weight and Representational Gravity." *Journal of Experimental Psychology: Learning, Memory, and Cognition* 23:1484–1493.

———. 1998. "Some Effects of Representational Friction, Target Size, and Memory Averaging on Memory for Vertically Moving Targets." *Canadian Journal of Experimental Psychology* 52:44–49.

———. 2001. "The Effect of Height in the Picture Plane on the Forward Displacement of Ascending and Descending Targets." *Canadian Journal of Experimental Psychology* 55:325–330.

Hubbard, Timothy L., and J. J. Bharucha. 1988. "Judged Displacement in Apparent Vertical and Horizontal Motion." *Perception & Psychophysics* 44:211–221.

Hubbard, Timothy L., and Susan E. Ruppel. 2000. "Spatial Memory Averaging, the Landmark Attraction Effect, and Representational Gravity." *Psychological Research/Psychologische Forschung* 64:41–55.

Huron, David 2006. *Sweet Anticipation: Music and the Psychology of Expectation*. Cambridge, MA: MIT Press.

Huron, David, and Richard Parncutt. 1993. "An Improved Model of Tonality Perception Incorporating Pitch Salience and Echoic Memory." *Psychomusicology* 12:154–171.

Hurwitz, Robert, and Steve Larson. 1994. "Step Collections in Aural Theory."

Presentation to a special panel, "Applying a Theory of Expressive Meaning in the Written-and Aural-Theory Classrooms," national meeting of the College Music Society, Savannah, GA.

Janata, Petr, Jeffrey L. Birk, John D. Van Horn, Marc Leman, Barbara Tillmann, and Jamshed J. Bharucha. 2002. "The Cortical Topography of Tonal Structures Underlying Western Music." *Science* 298:2167–2170.

Johnson, Mark. 1987. *The Body in the Mind: The Bodily Basis of Meaning, Imagination, and Reason.* Chicago: University of Chicago Press.

———. 2007. *The Meaning of the Body: Aesthetics of Human Understanding.* Chicago: University of Chicago Press.

Johnson, Mark, and Steve Larson. 2003. "Something in the Way She Moves." *Metaphor and Symbol* 18 (2): 63–84.

Johnston, Heather M., and Mari Riess Jones. 2004. "The Effects of Pitch Structure on Auditory Representational Momentum." Presentation to the Eighth International Conference on Music Perception and Cognition, Evanston, IL.

Jonas, Oswald. 1982. *Introduction to the Theory of Heinrich Schenker.* Translated and edited by John Rothgeb. New York: Longman.

Jones, Mari Riess. 1981. "Music as a Stimulus for Psychological Motion: Part I. Some Determinants of Expectancies." *Psychomusicology* 1:34–51.

———. 1982. "Music as a Stimulus for Psychological Motion: Part II. An Expectancy Model." *Psychomusicology* 2:1–13.

Jungbluth, A. 1983. "Harmonische Analyse (Bill Evans: Very Early: Chromatik als übergeordnetes Regulativ)." *Musik und Bildung* 15:29–32.

Kamien, Roger. 1983. "Aspects of Motivic Elaboration in the Opening Movement of Haydn's Piano Sonata in C♯ minor."

In *Aspects of Schenkerian Theory,* edited by David Beach, 77–93. New Haven: Yale University Press.

Kaminsky, Peter. 1989. "Aspects of Harmony, Rhythm, and Form in Schumann's *Papillons, Carnaval,* and *Davidsbündlertänze.*" Ph.D. dissertation, University of Rochester.

Karl, Gregory. 1997. "Structuralism and Musical Plot." *Music Theory Spectrum* 19 (1): 13–34.

Karpinski, Gary S. 2000. *Aural Skills Acquisition: The Development of Listening, Reading, and Performing Skills in College-Level Musicians.* New York: Oxford University Press.

Kassler, Jamie C., ed. 1991. *Metaphor: A Musical Dimension.* Sydney: Currency.

Keil, Charles, and Steven Feld. 1994. *Music Grooves: Essays and Dialogues.* Chicago: University of Chicago Press.

Keiler, Allan. 1983–84. "On Some Properties of Schenker's Pitch Derivations." *Music Perception* 1 (2): 200–228.

Kelly, M. H., and Jennifer J. Freyd. 1987. "Explorations of Representational Momentum." *Cognitive Psychology* 19:369–401.

Kidd, Gary Richard. 1984. "The Perception of Tonal Relationships in Music." Ph.D. dissertation, Ohio State University.

Kielian-Gilbert, Marianne. 1990. "Interpreting Musical Analogy: From Rhetorical Device to Musical Process." *Music Perception* 8 (1): 63–94.

Kivy, Peter. 1989. *Sound Sentiment: An Essay on the Musical Emotions.* Philadelphia: Temple University Press.

Koch, Heinrich Christoph (1787) 1969. *Versuch einer Anleitung zur Composition.* Hildesheim: Olms.

Komar, Arthur J. 1971. *Theory of Suspensions: A Study of Metrical and Pitch Relations in Tonal Music.* Princeton, NJ: Princeton University Press.

———. 1988. "Pedagogically Speaking: The Pedagogy of Tonal Hierarchy." *In Theory Only* 10 (5): 23–28.

———. 1992. *Linear-Derived Harmony.* Cincinnati: Ovenbird.

Krebs, Harald. 1987. "Some Extensions of the Concepts of Metrical Consonance and Dissonance." *Journal of Music Theory* 31 (1): 99–120.

———. 1999. *Fantasy Pieces: Metrical Dissonance in the Music of Robert Schumann.* New York: Oxford University Press.

Krumhansl, Carol L. 1990. *Cognitive Foundations of Musical Pitch.* New York: Oxford University Press.

———. 1995. "Music Psychology and Music Theory: Problems and Prospects." *Music Theory Spectrum* 17 (1): 53–80.

Krumhansl, Carol L., and E. J. Kessler. 1982. "Tracing the Dynamic Changes in Perceived Tonal Organization in a Spatial Representation of Musical Keys." *Psychological Review* 89:334–368.

Kurth, Ernst. (1917) 1946. *Grundlagen des linearen Kontrapunkts, Bachs melodische Polyphonie.* Bern: Krompholz.

Lake, William. 1987. "Melodic Perception and Cognition: The Influence of Tonality." Ph.D. dissertation, University of Michigan.

Lakoff, George, and Mark Johnson. 1980. *Metaphors We Live By.* Chicago: University of Chicago Press.

———. 1999. *Philosophy in the Flesh: The Embodied Mind and Its Challenge to Western Thought.* Chicago: University of Chicago Press.

Lakoff, George, and Mark Turner. 1989. *More Than Cool Reason: A Field Guide to Poetic Metaphor.* Chicago: University of Chicago Press.

Larson, Steve. 1981. "Some Aspects of the Album *Out of the Woods* by the Chamber Ensemble 'Oregon.'" Master's thesis, University of Oregon.

———. 1987a. "A Tonal Model of an 'Atonal' Piece: Schoenberg's Opus 15, Number 2." *Perspectives of New Music* 25:418–433.

———. 1987b. "Questions about the *Ursatz*: A Response to Neumeyer." *In Theory Only* 10 (4): 11–31.

———. 1992. "Scale-Degree Function." Presentation to the SMT Special Session on Cognition Research and Its Application to Aural-Skills Pedagogy, National Meeting of the Society for Music Theory, Kansas City. Available (from the Center for Research on Concepts and Cognition, 510 North Fess, Bloomington, IN 47408) as "Scale-Degree Function: Cognition Research and Its Application to the Teaching of Aural Skills," CRCC Technical Report #67.

———. 1993a. "Computer Models of Melodic Implication and Key Determination in Tonal Music." Presentation to the Society for Music Perception and Cognition, Philadelphia. Available (from Center for Research on Concepts and Cognition, 510 North Fess, Bloomington, IN 47408) as CRCC Technical Report #77.

———. 1993b. "Dave McKenna's Performance of 'Have You Met Miss Jones?'" *American Music* 11 (3): 283–315.

———. 1993c. "Modeling Melodic Expectation: Using Three 'Musical Forces' to Predict Melodic Continuations." In *Proceedings of the Fifteenth Annual Conference of the Cognitive Science Society,* 629–634. Hillsdale, NJ: Erlbaum.

———. 1993d. "On Rudolf Arnheim's Contributions to Music Theory." *Journal of Aesthetic Education* 27 (4): 97–104.

———. 1993e. "Scale-Degree Function: A Theory of Expressive Meaning and Its Application to Aural-Skills Pedagogy." *Journal of Music Theory Pedagogy* 7:69–84.

———. 1994a. "Another Look at Schenker's *Counterpoint*." *Indiana Theory Review* 15 (1): 35–52.

———. 1994b. "Musical Forces, Step Collections, Tonal Pitch Space, and Melodic Expectation." In *Proceedings of the Third International Conference on Music Perception and Cognition*, Liège, Belgium, 227–229. Available (from the Center for Research on Concepts and Cognition, 510 North Fess, Bloomington, IN 47408) as CRCC Technical Report #111.

———. 1996a. "The Art of Charlie Parker's Rhetoric." *Annual Review of Jazz Studies* 8:141–166.

———. 1996b. "Expert Expectations: Professional Theorists' Continuations Compared with a Computer Model of Musical Forces." *Current Research in Music Cognition and Aural Training* [poster]. National Meeting of the Society for Music Theory, Baton Rouge.

———. 1996c. "'Strict Use' of Analytic Notation." *Journal of Music Theory Pedagogy* 10:31–71.

———. 1997a. "Continuations as Completions: Studying Melodic Expectation in the Creative Microdomain *Seek Well*." In *Music, Gestalt, and Computing: Studies in Cognitive and Systematic Musicology*, edited by Marc Leman, 321–334. Berlin: Springer-Verlag.

———. 1997b. "Great Expectations: The Interdisciplinary Promise of a Theory of Expressive Meaning in Music." In a study session titled "Implications for Mainstream Musicology of Recent Research in Music Cognition," at the meeting of the International Musicological Society, London.

———. 1997c. "The Problem of Prolongation in *Tonal* Music: Terminology, Perception, and Expressive Meaning." *Journal of Music Theory* 41 (1): 101–136.

———. 1997–98a. "Musical Forces and Melodic Patterns." *Theory and Practice* 22–23:55–71.

———. 1997–98b. "Triple Play: Bill Evans' Three-Piano Performance of Victor Young's 'Stella by Starlight.'" In "An Analysis Symposium: Alternate Takes – Stella by Starlight." *Annual Review of Jazz Studies* 9:45–56. Response to Forte's Questions, 105–107.

———. 1998. "Schenkerian Analysis of Modern Jazz: Questions about Method." *Music Theory Spectrum* 20 (2): 209–241.

———. 1999a. "Musical Imagery and Melodic Expectation." Paper presented at the Conference on Musical Imagery, Oslo, Norway.

———. 1999b. "Swing and Motive in Three Performances by Oscar Peterson." In "'Analysis Forum' on Cole Porter's 'Night and Day.'" *Journal of Music Theory* 43 (2): 283–313.

———. 2001. "What Makes a Good Bridge?" *Tijdschrift voor Musiektheorie/ Dutch Journal of Music Theory* 8 (1): 1–15.

———. 2002. "Musical Forces, Melodic Expectation, and Jazz Melody." *Music Perception* 19 (3): 351–385.

———. 2003. "Recapitulation Recomposition in the Sonata-Form First Movements of Haydn's String Quartets: Style Change and Compositional Technique." *Music Analysis* 22:1–2, 139–177.

———. 2004. "'Musical Forces' and Melodic Expectations: Comparing Computer Models with Human Subjects." *Music Perception* 21 (4): 457–498.

———. 2006a. "Musical Gesture and Musical Forces: Evidence from Music-Theoretical Misunderstandings." In *Music and Gesture*, edited by Anthony Gritten and Elaine King, 61–74. Hampshire, England: Ashgate.

———. 2006b. "Rhythmic Displacement in the Music of Bill Evans." *Structure and Meaning in Tonal Music: A Festschrift for Carl Schachter*, edited by David Gagné and Poundie Burstein, 103–122. Hillsdale, NY: Pendragon.

———. 2009. *Analyzing Jazz – A Schenkerian Perspective.* Hillsdale, NY: Pendragon.

———. Unpublished ms. n.d. "Species Counterpoint: A Study of Musical Expression."

Larson, Steve, and Mark Johnson. 2002–2003. "Architectural Metaphors in Music Discourse and Music Experience." *Yearbook of Comparative and General Literature* 50:141–154.

Larson, Steve, and Leigh Van Handel. 2005. "Measuring Musical Forces." *Music Perception* 23 (2): 119–136.

Le Guin, Elisabeth. 2006. *Boccherini's Body: An Essay in Carnal Musicology.* Berkeley: University of California Press.

Lerdahl, Fred. 1988. "Tonal Pitch Space." *Music Perception* 5 (3): 315–350.

———. 1989. "Atonal Prolongational Structure." *Contemporary Music Review* 4:65–87.

———. 1996. "Calculating Tonal Tension." *Music Perception* 13 (3): 319–363.

———. 2001. *Tonal Pitch Space.* New York: Oxford University Press.

Lerdahl, Fred, and Ray Jackendoff. 1983. *A Generative Theory of Tonal Music.* Cambridge, MA: MIT Press.

Lester, Joel. 1979. "Articulation of Tonal Structures as a Criterion for Analytic Choices." *Music Theory Spectrum* 1:67–79.

Levinson, Jerrold. 1997. *Music in the Moment.* Ithaca, NY: Cornell University Press.

Levitin, Daniel J. 2009. "The Neural Correlates of Temporal Structure in Music." *Music and Medicine* 1:9–13.

Lewin, David. 1983. "An Interesting Global Rule for Species Counterpoint." *In Theory Only* 6 (8): 19–44.

———. 1986. "Music Theory, Phenomenology, and Modes of Perception." *Music Perception* 3 (4): 327–392.

Lindsay, Julie Anne. 1995. "Analytical Approaches to Jazz Polyphony, with Special Reference to the Use of Pitch-Class Theory in the Works of Toshiko Akiyoshi and Phil Woods." Master's thesis, La Trobe University, Australia.

Lomax, Alan. (1968) 2000. *Folk Song Style and Culture.* New Brunswick, NJ: Transaction.

London, Justin. 2004. *Hearing in Time: Psychological Aspects of Musical Meter.* New York: Oxford University Press.

Lorteije, Jeannette A. M., J. Leon Kenemans, Tjeerd Jellema, Rob H. J. van der Lebbe, Frederiek de Heer, and Richard J. A. van Wezel. 2006. "Delayed Response to Animate Implied Motion in Human Motion Processing Areas." *Journal of Cognitive Neuroscience* 18 (2): 158–168.

Margolis, Howard. 1987. *Patterns, Thinking, and Cognition: A Theory of Judgment.* Chicago: University of Chicago Press.

Margulis, Elizabeth Hellmuth. 2003. "Melodic Expectation: A Discussion and Model." Ph.D. dissertation, Columbia University.

Margulis, Elizabeth Hellmuth, and W. H. Levine. 2004. "Melodic Expectation: A Priming Study." In *Proceedings of the Eighth International Conference on Music Perception and Cognition,* 364–366.

Martin, Daniel W. 1952. "Do You Auralize?" *Journal of the Acoustical Society of America* 24:416.

Martin, Henry. 1988. "Jazz Harmony: A Syntactic Background." *Annual Review of Jazz Studies* 4:9–30.

———. 1996. *Charlie Parker and Thematic Improvisation.* Lanham, MD: Scarecrow.

Marvin, Elizabeth, and Alexander Brinkman. 1999. "The Effect of Modulation and Formal Manipulation on Perception of Tonic Closure by Expert Listeners." *Music Perception* 16 (4): 389–408.

Matthay, Tobias. 1913. *Musical Interpretation.* Boston: Stanhope.

Maus, Fred Everett. (1988) 1997. "Music as Drama." In *Music and Meaning,* edited by Jenefer Robinson, 105–130. Ithaca, NY: Cornell University Press.

Mazo, Margarita. 1994. "Lament Made Visible: A Study of Paramusical Elements in Russian Lament." In *Themes and Variations: Writings on Music in Honor of Rulan Chao Pian,* edited by Bell Yung, 161–211. Hong Kong: Chinese University Press.

McClary, Susan. 1991. *Feminine Endings: Music, Gender, and Sexuality.* Minneapolis: University of Minnesota Press.

McCloskey, M. and D. Kohl. 1983. "Naïve Physics: The Curvilinear Impetus Principle and Its Role in Interactions with Moving Objects." *Journal of Experimental Psychology: Learning, Memory, and Cognition* 9:146–156.

McCloskey, M., A. Caramazza, and B. Green. 1980. "Curvilinear Motion in the Absence of External Forces; Naïve Beliefs about the Motions of Objects." *Science* 210:1139–1141.

McKinley, Kathy. 2002. "Ritual, Performativity, and Music: Cambodian Wedding Music in Phnom Penh." Ph.D. Dissertation, Brown University.

Mead, Andrew. 1997–98. "Shedding Scales: Understanding Intervals in Different Musical Contexts." *Theory and Practice* 22–23:73–94.

———. 1999. "Physiological Metaphors and Musical Understanding." *Journal of Music Theory* 43 (1): 1–19.

Meredith, Marsha. 1986. "Seek-Whence: A Model of Pattern Perception." Ph.D. dissertation, Indiana University.

Merriam, A. P., S. Whinery, and B. G. Fred. 1956. "Songs of a Rada Community in Trinidad." *Anthropos* 51:157–174.

Meyer-Baer, Kathi. (1930) 1975. *Bedeutung und Wesen der Musik.* 2nd ed. Baden-Baden: Valentin Koerner.

Meyer, Leonard B. 1956. *Emotion and Meaning in Music.* Chicago: University of Chicago Press.

———. 1967. *Music, the Arts, and Ideas: Patterns and Predictions in Twentieth-Century Culture.* Chicago: University of Chicago Press.

———. 1973. *Explaining Music.* Berkeley: University of California Press.

Minsky, Marvin Lee. 1986. *The Society of Mind.* New York: Simon and Schuster.

Miranda, Eduardo Reck, and Katie Overy. 2009. "The Neuroscience of Music." *Contemporary Music Review* (special issue) 28:3.

Mitchell, William J., and Felix Salzer, eds. 1967. "A Glossary of the Elements of Graphic Analysis." *The Music Forum* 1:260–268.

Momigny, Jérôme-Joseph. 1806. *Cours complet d'harmonie et de composition, d'après une théorie neuve et générale de la musique.* Paris: Bailleul.

Monsaingeon, Bruno. 1980. *Glenn Gould Plays Bach: A Film by Bruno Monsaingeon.* Available in *The Glenn Gould Collection* "XV. An Art of the Fugue," SHV 48426.

Monson, Ingrid. 1996. *Saying Something: Jazz Improvisation and Interaction.* Chicago: University of Chicago Press.

Mooney, Kevin. 1988. "Forum: Theoretic Problems in Komar's Conception of Tonal Hierarchy." *In Theory Only* 10 (7): 31–35.

Morgan, Robert. 1976. "Dissonant Prolongation: Theoretical and Compositional Precedents." *Journal of Music Theory* 20:49–91.

———. 1980. "Musical Time/Musical Space." *Critical Inquiry* 6 (3): 527–538.

Mukherji, S., and C. Krumhansl. Unpublished ms. N.d. "Cross-Cultural Perception of Melodic Structure in Indian Classical Music."

Munger, M. P., J. L. Solberg, K. K. Horrocks, and A. S. Preston. 1999. "Representational Momentum for Rotations in Depth: Effects of Shading and Axis." *Journal of Experimental Psychol-*

ogy: Learning, Memory, and Cognition 25:157–171.

Nagai, M., and A. Yagi. 2001. "The Pointedness Effect on Representational Momentum." Memory and Cognition, 29:91–99.

Narmour, Eugene. 1977. Beyond Schenkerism: The Need for Alternatives in Music Analysis. Chicago: University of Chicago Press.

———. 1990. The Analysis and Cognition of Basic Melodic Structures: The Implication-Realization Model. Chicago: University of Chicago Press.

———. 1992. The Analysis and Cognition of Melodic Complexity: The Implication-Realization Model. Chicago: University of Chicago Press.

———. 1996. "Analyzing Form and Measuring Perceptual Content in Mozart's Sonata K282: A New Theory of Parametric Analogues." Music Perception 13:265–318.

Neumeyer, David. 1982. "Organic Structure and the Song Cycle: Another Look at Schumann's Dichterliebe." Music Theory Spectrum 4:92–105.

———. 1987. "The Urlinie from $\hat{8}$ as a Middleground Phenomenon." In Theory Only 9 (5–6): 3–25.

O'Donnell, Shaugn. 1999. "Space, Motion, and Other Musical Metaphors." In Perspectives on the Grateful Dead: Critical Writings, edited by Robert Weiner, 127–135. Westport, CT: Greenwood.

Ortmann O. R. 1926. On The Melodic Relativity of Tones. Psychological Monographs 35/1. Princeton, NJ: Psychological Review.

Ortony, Andrew, ed. 1979. Metaphor and Thought. Cambridge: Cambridge University Press.

Oster, Ernst. 1983. "The Fantasie-Impromptu: A Tribute to Beethoven." In Aspects of Schenkerian Theory, edited by David Beach, 189–207. New Haven: Yale University Press.

Owens, Thomas. 1974. "Charlie Parker: Techniques of Improvisation." Ph.D. dissertation, University of California at Los Angeles.

Palisca, Claude V., and Natasha Spender. 1980. "Consonance." The New Grove Dictionary of Music and Musicians, edited by Stanley Sadie, 4:668–671. London: Macmillan.

Parker, Charlie. 1946. "Solo on Gershwin's 'Oh, Lady Be Good.'" Recorded at a jazz performance at The Philharmonic, Los Angeles, January 28. Appears in the most recent edition of the Smithsonian Collection of Classic Jazz, which lists supporting personnel as Arnold Ross (piano), Billy Hadnott (bass), and Lee Young (drums).

———. 1947. "Confirmation." Recorded in Carnegie Hall, New York, September 29, with Dizzy Gillespie (trumpet), John Lewis (piano), Al McKibbon (bass), and Joe Harris (drums).

———. 1953. "Confirmation." 1953. Verve, July 30, with Al Haig (piano), Percy Heath (bass), and Max Roach (drums).

Pederson, Eric, E. Danziger, S. Levinson, S. Kita, G. Senft, and D. Wilkins. 1998. "Semantic Typology and Spatial Conceptualization." Language 74 (3): 557–589.

Peirce, Charles Sanders. (1931) 1960. Collected Papers of Charles Sanders Peirce. Cambridge, MA: Harvard University Press.

Pelto, William. 1994. "An Alternative to Rule Memorization for Written Theory." Presentation to a special panel, "Applying a Theory of Expressive Meaning in the Written-and Aural-Theory Classrooms," national meeting of the College Music Society, Savannah, GA.

Peretz, Isabelle, and Robert J. Zatorre. 2005. "Brain Organization for Music Processing." Annual Review of Psychology 56:89–114.

Pierce, Alexandra. 1989. *Spanning: Essays on Music Theory, Performance, and Movement.* New York: Plenum.

Port, Robert 2000. "Icon, Index, and Symbol." Available at http://www.cs.indiana.edu/~port/teach/103/sign.symbol.html (accessed October 15, 2009).

Povel, Dirk-Jan. 1996. "Exploring the Fundamental Harmonic Forces in the Tonal System." *Psychological Research* 58:274–283.

Pressing, Jeff. 1978. "Towards an Understanding of Scales in Jazz." *Jazzforschung/Jazz Research* 9:25–35.

———. 1983. "Cognitive Isomorphisms between Pitch and Rhythm in World Musics: West Africa, the Balkans, and Western Tonality." *Studies in Music* (Australia), 38–61.

Rahn, Jay. 1979. "Logic, Set Theory, Music Theory." *College Music Symposium* 19 (1): 114–127.

———. 1991. "Coordination of Interval Sizes in Seven-Tone Collections." *Journal of Music Theory* 35:1–32.

———. 2010. "Maximizing Similarity in Pitch and Time Cycles." Bellairs Music and Mathematics Workshop, Holetown, Barbados.

Rameau, Jean Philippe (1722) 1971. *Treatise on Harmony.* Translated by Philip Gossett. New York: Dover.

———. (1737) 1974. *Harmonic Generation.* Translated by D. Hayes. Ann Arbor, MI: UMI Research Press.

Ranney, M. 1989. "Internally Represented Forces May Be Cognitively Penetrable: Comment on Freyd, Pantzer, and Cheng (1988)." *Journal of Experimental Psychology: General* 118:399–402.

Reed, C. L., and N. G. Vinson. 1996. "Conceptual Effects on Representational Momentum." *Journal of Experimental Psychology: Human Perception and Performance* 22:839–850.

Renwick, William. 1991. "Structural Patterns in Fugue Subjects and Fugal Expositions." *Music Theory Spectrum* 13 (2): 197–218.

Rizzolatti, Giacomo, and L. Craighero. 2004. "The Mirror-Neuron System." *Annual Review of Neuroscience* 27:169–192.

Rizzolatti, Giacomo, L. Fadiga, L. Fogassi, and V. Gallese. 1996. "Premotor Cortex and the Recognition of Motor Actions." *Cognition and Brain Research* 3:131–41.

Robinson, Jenefer, ed. 1997. *Music and Meaning.* Ithaca, NY: Cornell University Press.

Roth, Hermann. 1926. *Elemente der Stimmführung [Der strenge Satz].* Stuttgart: Carl Grüniger.

Rothfarb, Lee. 2002. "Energetics." In *The Cambridge History of Western Music Theory,* edited by Thomas Christensen, 927–955. Cambridge: Cambridge University Press.

———. Unpublished ms. n.d. "Nineteenth-Century Fortunes of Musical Formalism."

Rothgeb, John. 1980. "Chopin's C minor Nocturne, Op. 48, No. 1, First Part: Voice Leading and Motivic Content." *Theory and Practice* 5 (2): 26–31.

———. 1983. "Thematic Content: A Schenkerian View." In *Aspects of Schenkerian Theory,* edited by David Beach, 39–60. New Haven: Yale University Press.

———. 1990. "Schenkerian Theory and Manuscript Studies: Modes of Interaction." In *Schenker Studies,* edited by Hedi Siegel, 4–14. Cambridge: Cambridge University Press.

Rothstein, William. 1991. "On Implied Tones." *Music Analysis* 10 (3): 289–328.

———. 2005. "Like Falling off a Log: Rubato in Chopin's Prelude in A-flat Major (op. 28, no. 17)." *Music Theory Online* 11:1. Available at http://www.societymusictheory.org/mto/issues/mto.05.11.1/mto.05.11.1.rothstein_frames.html.

Russell, George Allan. 1959. *The Lydian-Chromatic Concept of Tonal Organization for Improvisation, for All Instruments*. New York: Concept.

Sachs, Curt. 1962. *The Wellsprings of Music.* The Hague: Martinus Nijhoff.

Salzer, Felix. (1952) 1962. *Structural Hearing: Tonal Coherence in Music.* New York: Dover.

Sam, Sam-Ang. 1988. "The Pin Peat Ensemble: Its History, Music and Context." Ph. D. Dissertation, Wesleyan University.

Saslaw, Janna K. 1996. "Forces, Containers, and Paths: The Role of Body-Derived Image Schemas in the Conceptualization of Music." *Journal of Music Theory* 40 (2): 217–243.

————. 1997–98. "Life Forces: Conceptual Structures in Schenker's *Free Composition* and Schoenberg's *The Musical Idea.*" *Theory and Practice* 22–23:17–33.

————. 2000. "Intention and Image Schema in the Perception of Early Works by Ornette Coleman." Presentation to the West Coast Conference of Music Theory and Analysis, Eugene, OR.

Saslaw, Janna K., and James P. Walsh. 1996. "Musical Invariance as a Cognitive Structure: 'Multiple Meaning' in the Early Nineteenth Century." In *Music Theory in the Age of Romanticism*, edited by Ian Bent, 211–232. Cambridge: Cambridge University Press.

Saussure, Ferdinand de (1916) 1966. *Course in General Linguistics.* Translated by Wade Baskin. Edited by Charles Bally and Albert Sechehaye. New York: McGraw-Hill.

Schachter, Carl. 1983a. "Motive and Text in Four Schubert Songs." In *Aspects of Schenkerian Theory,* edited by David Beach, 61–76. New Haven: Yale University Press.

————. 1983b. "The First Movement of Brahms's Second Symphony: The Opening Theme and Its Consequences." *Music Analysis* 2:55–68.

————. 1995. "The Triad as Place and Action." *Music Theory Spectrum* 17 (2): 149–169.

Schellenberg, E. Glenn. 1996. "Expectancy in Melody: Tests of the Implication-Realization Model." *Cognition* 58:75–125.

————. 1997. "Simplifying the Implication-Realization Model of Melodic Expectancy." *Music Perception* 14:295–318.

Schenker, Heinrich. (1906) 1954. *Harmony.* Translated by Elisabeth Mann Borgese. Edited and annotated by Oswald Jonas. Chicago: University of Chicago Press.

————. (1910) 1987. *New Musical Theories and Fantasies.* Vol. 3, *Counterpoint: A Translation of "Kontrapunkt" by Heinrich Schenker.* Bk. 1. Translated by John Rothgeb and Juergen Thym. Edited by John Rothgeb. New York: Schirmer.

————. (1921–24) 1990. *Der Tonwille.* Issues 1–10. Hildesheim: Olms.

————. (1923) 1987. "Ph. Em. Bach: *Kurze und leichte Klavierstücke mit veränderten Reprisen* (1766), Nr. 1, Allegro." In *Der Tonwille: Flugblätter zum Zeugnis unwandelbarer Gesetze der Tonkunst einer neuen Jugend dargebracht von Heinrich Schenker,* 4:10–11. Vienna: Tonwille-Flugblätterverlag. Translated [1987] by Steve Larson in *In Theory Only* 10 (4): 5–10.

————. 1925. "Fortsetzung der Urlinie-Betrachtung." In *Das Meisterwerk in der Musik Jahrbuch I,* 185–205. Munich: Drei Masken. Reprinted in facsimile, Hildesheim: Olms. Translated as "Resumption of Urlinie Considerations," in Sylvan Kalib, "Thirteen Essays from the Three Yearbooks *Das Meisterwerk in der Musik* by Heinrich Schenker: An Annotated Translation" (Ph.D. dissertation, Northwestern University, 1973), 130–155.

————. 1925. "Weg mit dem Phrasierungsbogen." In *Das Meisterwerk in der Musik Jahrbuch I,* 41–60. Munich:

Drei Masken. Reprinted in facsimile, Hildesheim: Olms. Translated as "Let's Do Away with the Phrasing Slur," in Sylvan Kalib, "Thirteen Essays from the Three Yearbooks *Das Meisterwerk in der Musik* by Heinrich Schenker: An Annotated Translation" (Ph.D. dissertation, Northwestern University, 1973), 52–83.

———. (1926) 1970. "The Sarabande of J. S. Bach's Suite No. 3 for Unaccompanied Violoncello [BWV 1009]." In *The Music Forum*, edited by William J. Mitchell and Felix Salzer, 2:274–282. New York: Columbia University Press.

———. (1932) 1969. *Five Graphic Music Analyses*. Edited by Felix Salzer. New York: Dover.

———. (1935) 1979. *New Musical Theories and Fantasies (Der freie Satz)*. Vol. 3, *Free Composition*. Translated and edited by Ernst Oster. New York: Longman.

Schmalfeldt, Janet. 1985. "On the Relation of Analysis to Performance: Beethoven's Bagatelles Op. 126, Nos. 2 and 5." *Journal of Music Theory* 29 (1): 1–31.

Schmuckler, Mark A. 1990a. "Expectation in Music: Investigation of Melodic and Harmonic Processes." *Music Perception* 7:109–149.

———. 1990b. "The Performance of Global Expectations." *Psychomusicology* 9:122–147.

Schoenberg, Arnold. (1911) 1978. *Theory of Harmony*. Translated by Roy E. Carter. Berkeley: University of California Press.

———. (1954) 1969. *Structural Functions of Harmony*. Rev. ed. Edited by Leonard Stein. New York: Norton.

———. 1975. *Style and Idea*. New York: St. Martin's.

Scruton, Roger. 1997. *The Aesthetics of Music*. Oxford: Clarendon.

Senior, C., J. Barnes, V. Giampietro, A. Simmons, E. T. Bullmore, M. Brammer, and A. S. David. 2002. "Representational Momentum and the Brain: An Investigation into the Functional Necessity of V5/MT." *Visual Cognition* 9:81–92.

Shanon, B. 1976. "Aristotelianism, Newtonianism, and the Physics of the Layman." *Perception* 5:241–243.

Shepard, Roger N. 1981. "Psychophysical Complementarity." In *Perceptual Organization*, edited by M. Kubovy and J. R. Pomerantz, 279–341. Hillsdale, NJ: Erlbaum.

———. 1984. "Ecological Constraints on Internal Representation: Resonant Kinematics of Perceiving, Imagining, Thinking, and Dreaming." *Psychological Review* 91:417–447.

Shepard, Roger N., and L. A. Cooper. 1982. "Mental Images and Their Transformations." Cambridge, MA: MIT Press.

Shepard, Roger N., and J. Metzler. 1971. "Mental Rotations of Three-Dimensional Objects." *Science* 171:701–703.

Simon, Herbert A., and Richard K. Sumner. 1968. "Pattern in Music." In *Formal Representation of Human Judgment*, edited by Benjamin Kleinmuntz, 219–250. New York: Wiley.

Spitzer, Michael 2004. *Metaphor and Musical Thought*. Chicago: University of Chicago Press.

Strunk, Steven. 1979. "The Harmony of Early Bop: A Layered Approach." *Journal of Jazz Studies* 6:4–53.

———. 1985. "Bebop Melodic Lines: Tonal Characteristics." *Annual Review of Jazz Studies* 3:97–120.

———. 1996. "Linear Intervallic Patterns in Jazz Repertory." *Annual Review of Jazz Studies* 8:63–115.

———. 1998. "Melodic Structure in Bill Evans' 1959 'Autumn Leaves.'" John Donald Robb Composers' Symposium. Albuquerque, NM.

Tekman, Hasan Gurkan, and Jamshed J. Bharucha. 1992. "Time Course of Chord Priming." *Perception and Psychophysics* 51:33–39.

Temperley, David. 1999. "What's Key for Key? The Krumhansl-Schmuckler Key-Finding Algorithm Reconsidered." *Music Perception* 17 (1): 65–100.

———. 2001. *The Cognition of Basic Musical Structures.* Cambridge, MA: MIT Press.

———. 2003. "Review of *Tonal Pitch Space*, by Fred Lerdahl." *Musicæ Scientiæ* 7:141–155.

Tenney, James. 1988. *A History of "Consonance" and "Dissonance."* New York: Excelsior Music.

Terhardt, Ernst. 1974. "Pitch, Consonance, and Harmony." *Journal of the Acoustical Society of America* 55:1061–1069.

Thompson, William Forde, Lola L. Cuddy, and Cheryl Plaus. 1997. "Expectancies Generated by Melodic Intervals: Evaluation of Principles of Melodic Implication in a Melody-Completion Task." *Perception & Psychophysics* 59:1069–1076.

Thomson, William. 2004. "From Sounds to Music: The Contextualizations of Pitch." *Music Perception* 21:3 (spring): 431–456.

Thornton, Ian M., and Timothy L. Hubbard. 2002. *Representational Momentum: New Findings, New Directions. Visual Cognition* (special issue). New York: Psychology Press.

Thurmond, James Morgan. 1982. *Note Grouping: A Method for Achieving Expression and Style in Musical Performance.* Camp Hill, PA: JMT Publications.

Toch, Ernst. 1948. *The Shaping Forces in Music: An Inquiry into the Nature of Harmony, Melody, Counterpoint, and Form.* New York: Criterion.

Todd, Neil P. McAngus. 1999. "Motion in Music: A Neurobiological Perspective." *Music Perception* 17 (1): 115–126.

Toiviainen, Petri, and Carol L. Krumhansl. 2003. "Measuring and Modeling Real-Time Responses to Music: The Dynamics of Tonality Induction." *Perception* 2 (6): 741–766.

Turner, Mark. 1991. *Reading Minds: The Study of English in the Age of Cognitive Science.* Princeton, NJ: Princeton University Press.

Tymoczko, Dmitri. 1997. "The Consecutive-Semitone Constraint on Scalar Structure: A Link between Impressionism and Jazz." *Intégral* 11:135–179.

Unyk, A. M., and James C. Carlsen. 1987. "The Influence of Expectancy on Melodic Perception." *Psychomusicology* 7:3–23.

Van Egmond, Rene, and David Butler. 1997. "Diatonic Connotations of Pitch-Class Sets." *Music Perception* 15:1–29.

Vega, Diego 2003. "A Perceptual Experiment on Harmonic Tension and Melodic Attraction in Lerdahl's *Tonal Pitch Space*." *Musicae Scientiae* 7 (1): 35–55.

Verfaillie, K., and G. d'Ydewalle. 1991. "Representational Momentum and Event Course Anticipation in the Perception of Implied Periodic Motions." *Journal of Experimental Psychology: Learning, Memory, and Cognition* 17:302–313.

Vivier, Albert-Joseph. (1862) 1890. *Traité complet d'harmonie théorique, pratique, vocale et instrumentale.* 5th ed. Bruxelles: M. J. Lumay.

von Hippel, Paul 2000a. "Redefining Pitch Proximity: Tessitura and Mobility as Constraints on Melodic Intervals." *Music Perception* 17 (3): 315–327.

———. 2000b. "Questioning a Melodic Archetype: Do Listeners Use Gap-Fill to Classify Melodies?" *Music Perception* 18 (2): 139–153.

———. 2002. "Melodic Expectation Rules as Learned Heuristics." In *Proceedings of the Seventh International Conference on Music Perception and Cognition.* Adelaide: Causal Productions.

von Hippel, Paul, and David Huron. 2000. "Why Do Skips Precede Reversals? The Effect of Tessitura on Melodic Structure." *Music Perception* 18 (1): 59–85.

Vos, Piet G., and Jim M. Troost. 1989. "Ascending and Descending Melodic Intervals: Statistical Findings and Their Perceptual Relevance." *Music Perception* 6 (4): 383–396.

Waters, Keith. 1996. "Blurring the Barline: Metric Displacement in the Piano Solos of Herbie Hancock." *Annual Review of Jazz Studies* 8:19–37.

———. 2005. "Scales, Modes, Functional Harmony, and Nonfunctional Harmony in the Compositions of Herbie Hancock." *Journal of Music Theory* 49 (2): 333–357.

Wen, Eric. 1990. "Enharmonic Transformation in the First Movement of Mozart's Piano Concerto in C minor, K. 491." In *Schenker Studies,* edited by Hedi Siegel, 4–14. Cambridge: Cambridge University Press.

Westergaard, Peter. 1975. *An Introduction to Tonal Theory.* New York: Norton.

Wikipedia 2007. "Rhythm." http://en.wikipedia.org/wiki/Rhythm.

Williams, Peter. 1997. *The Chromatic Fourth during Four Centuries of Music.* Oxford: Clarendon.

Woideck, Carl. 1996. *Charlie Parker: His Music and Life.* Ann Arbor: University of Michigan Press.

Yeston, Maury. 1976. *The Stratification of Musical Rhythm.* New Haven: Yale University Press.

Zbikowski, Lawrence. 1997. "Conceptual Models and Cross-Domain Mapping: New Perspectives on Theories of Music and Hierarchy." *Journal of Music Theory* 41 (2): 11–43.

———. 1997–98. *"Des Herzraums Abschied:* Mark Johnson's Theory of Embodied Knowledge and Music Theory." *Theory and Practice* 22–23:1–16.

———. 1998. "Metaphor and Music Theory: Reflections from Cognitive Science." *Music Theory Online* 4 (1). Available online at http://www.mtosmt.org/issues/mto.98.4.1.zbikowski_frames.html.

———. 2002. *Conceptualizing Music: Cognitive Structure, Theory, and Analysis.* New York: Oxford University Press.

Zuckerkandl, Victor. 1956. *Sound and Symbol: Music and the External World.* Princeton, NJ: Princeton University Press.

———. 1959. *The Sense of Music.* Princeton, NJ: Princeton University Press.

INDEX

MUSICAL MEANING & INTERPRETATION

Robert S. Hatten, editor

STEVE LARSON is Robert M. Trotter Professor of Music at the University of Oregon and a member of its Institute of Cognitive and Decision Sciences. He also served as visiting faculty researcher at Indiana University's Center for Research on Concepts and Cognition and at the University of Oslo's Institutt for Musikkvitenskap research group on "Music, Motion, and Emotion." His publications include more than three dozen articles and book chapters, as well as the 2009 book *Analyzing Jazz – A Schenkerian Approach.*